SECOND EDITION

Thresholds

to Adult Living

HAZEL THOMPSON CRAIG

College home economics
department head for 20
years; author; homemaker

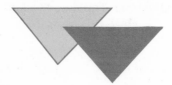

CHAS. A. BENNETT CO., INC.
Peoria, Illinois 61614

Acknowledgments

The author wishes to express special appreciation to Pauline Fish and Grace Orr, teachers at Mt. Lebanon High School, Pennsylvania, who reviewed the original manuscript. The manuscript was also checked by a number of other people who are authorities in such areas as home management, vocational guidance, foods, textiles, investments, and real estate.

Appreciation is also expressed to the many other persons and organizations— including magazine editors, food, furniture, textile, and equipment manufacturers, insurance companies, and advertising agencies—who have contributed a wealth of educational materials and illustrations.

To everyone else who helped in any way with producing THRESHOLDS TO ADULT LIVING, the author extends a very grateful "thank you."

HAZEL THOMPSON CRAIG

CONTENTS

Introduction

The world today is changing in more ways and at a faster pace than ever before. Many of the changes are supposed to solve our problems and make our lives easier. Indeed, many of them do.

However, it often seems that as one problem is solved, a new one takes its place. For instance, labor-saving equipment in homes, factories, and offices has brought opportunities for leisure that would have been unheard of when your grandparents were young. But many people do not know how to use free time constructively. They become idle and bored.

To take another example, modern concepts in living have made traditional skills obsolete. Many working wives rarely have time to make elaborate preparations for a meal. They must rely on convenience foods. For them, shopping intelligently among the thousands of items in a supermarket is even more important than skill in cooking.

The point of all this is clear: Young people today must cope with a world that is growing increasingly complex. To find their proper role they must learn to distinguish those changes which bring real improvement from those which are merely fads. They must put aside whatever is truly outmoded, but not reject that which is of lasting value. This re-quires the development of sound values and the adoption of realistic goals.

Young people, on the threshold of adult living, are faced with decisions and responsibilities that require mature and independent thought. They must be prepared to take marriage and parenthood seriously; to assume leadership in the community and beyond; to live harmoniously not only with their families and co-workers but also with people of other backgrounds and cultures.

Every high school student—boy or girl—whether bound for work, college, or marriage, will benefit from a course in adult living. Eventually over ninety per cent of young people will marry, and far too few will be adequately prepared for homemaking responsibilities. Most students have no opportunity to take courses in marriage and family living, food and nutrition, housing and home furnishings, or financial management beyond high school level.

Although the age at which young people marry has risen somewhat in recent years, and families are becoming smaller, there are more and more outside pressures that interfere with family life—war tension, increasing delinquency and crime, inflation, and competition in education and business, to name a few. As our society becomes more mobile, the home must provide greater security and *greater independence for all family members*. This book is planned to help students to:

- Establish short-term and long-range goals.
- Strive to improve personality and personal appearance.
- Emphasize and appreciate the good qualities of family and friends, while being tolerant of their shortcomings.
- Understand basic nutrition and meal planning principles.
- Enrich life by learning how to use leisure time constructively—helping in community and church activities, appreciating the arts, sports, and other wholesome entertainment.
- Realize the need for manners and concern for the welfare of others.
- Choose and care for clothing wisely.
- Prepare for a rewarding family life by a better understanding of family relationships.
- Understand the place that religion and good citizenship should hold in a well-balanced life.
- Appreciate the importance of good home management.
- Make wise decisions in the choice of a home and in savings and investments for future security.

The Teacher's Guide will facilitate lesson planning. Suggestions are given for outside speakers, correlation of activities with other subjects, selection of visual aids, supplementary educational material, special exhibits, field trips, evaluation tests, and class surveys for opinion polls.

Chapter 1

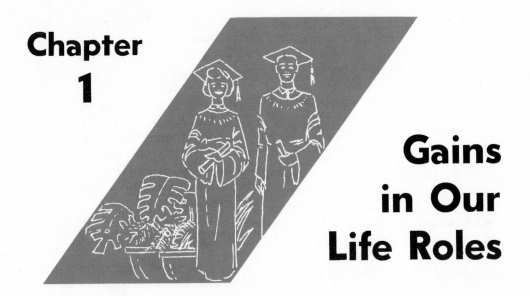

Gains in Our Life Roles

Among the most important decisions of your life are the ones you make *as you approach adulthood*. A young man often chooses his career then. The education or training needed to prepare him for that career is another important matter which must be decided then, and so is the choice of a way to meet his military obligation. A young woman often is considering the *role* of marriage, or further education, or business, or a combination of these. These decisions need to be made wisely. They will influence your entire future.

This chapter will help you to think about the attitudes and values you have developed, and to decide whether they are the ones that will lead you to future happiness and success. There are important goals and worthwhile reasons for living. When you have realized this, and have formed your own wholesome ideas about finding satisfaction in life, you will have taken a long step toward becoming a responsible, mature person.

The importance of establishing goals for living is pointed up in a book for naval personnel, *The Navy Blue Book*. The book stresses the need for integrating moral principles with military training, for having a purpose in life, and for setting a good example in positions of leadership.

Adult living means learning to understand yourself; endeavoring to live in harmony with others; discovering how to be a good mother or father; accepting responsibilities of citizenship; leading a life of devotion and service to your country. It means a great deal more—it means the contributions you can make to your entire world.

One of the most important things you must learn as an adult is to think independently. Thinking independently does not mean being stubborn, and insisting that you are right whether you know all the "angles" or

9

not. It means being open minded enough to use the advice, opinions, and experiences of others to determine what is right for you. Everything in the adult living course is directed toward this goal.

GROUP STATUS VERSUS PERSONAL CHOICE

We hear much about "status" which is gained by belonging to the "right group" and doing the "right things." Older persons may feel that they must join a free-spending crowd; you may be attracted to companions who get attention by breaking adult rules.

Recently the editors of an international service club magazine asked a large number of prominent men what they would do if they were sixteen again. One of the most challenging answers was that of Angelo Patri, family counselor and syndicated writer:

"If I were sixteen again . . . . I would strive with might and main to build a sturdy character that knew the difference between right and wrong, and be steered by it. I would know the necessity for cultivating my spiritual life, and adopt a personal creed to support it. I would search for all that is beautiful in the world of people and in Nature and treasure it reverently . . . . One thing above all others I hope I would do, and that is exercise my right to differ from the pattern laid down by 'They' . . . . that invisible force at work in the world. I would battle to think for myself.

"Sixteen cannot know this, but he can make his way toward it if he will . . . . If youth but would, if age but could."

10

Many people find it easier to follow the crowd even when they disapprove of what the crowd does. We all realize the importance of companionship; we do not like to be left out. However, we enjoy a group more if we think and act for ourselves.

Being different just to win attention or sympathy is one thing; upholding an ideal is another. The person whose behavior is crudely "different" or whose actions consist only of "bids" for attention is simply advertising his shortcomings. Crimes and other social failures often may be traced to this mistake. If upholding sound principles and convictions sets you apart from a certain crowd and costs you a few dubious friends, remember that your choice is to lower your code of behavior in order to keep these friends, or uphold your standards and

People nearing adulthood must often make decisions that will affect their entire lives.

BEST STUDENT   **BEAUTY QUEEN**   **BEST ATHLETE**   **MOST VERSATILE**   **MOST POPULAR**

If you are ever singled out for special recognition, learn to take the honor graciously.

make friends who will give your life new meaning.

In our world where pressures are so great, it takes strength of character to establish a personal code of behavior. Therefore every step you take in your adult living course is based on character improvement; translated, this means getting the most out of life —by planning.

When you are faced with an important decision, look beyond the present. Ask yourself not simply, "What do I gain right now?" but also, "Will this decision hurt my future? How will it affect the kind of character I am trying to develop?" We cannot all agree on exactly the same moral, religious, and social behavior, but we can maintain a high standard or code.

The first step is analyzing the meaning of success.

ANALYZING SUCCESS

In your school yearbook, you can pick out friends who are considered the best looking, friendliest, best athletes, most courteous, most versatile— and most likely to succeed.

It will be interesting to make a study of personalities from the same yearbook fifteen or twenty years

from now to see how many actually achieved unusual success. If your father or mother has retained an old high school yearbook, you might check through with them. The results will be interesting.

Each of us has his own opinion of what represents success in any field of life. What qualities must a person have to succeed in business, marriage, or teaching? When is a doctor, a scientist, or an entertainer successful? If a top TV star suddenly finds his program off the air, can he be successful in other entertainment fields? Is a person successful if he amasses a fortune, yet fails in his home life? *Who is the more successful*—a doctor who saves lives or a teacher or pastor who inspires lives? Success, as you see, is difficult to measure.

Can we always measure success by the evidence that shows? Is any person successful if he is not at peace with himself? Men like Hitler and Napoleon became powerful military leaders, but caused great misery to their fellow man. Others have amassed fortunes but never enjoyed what they had. Can we call these persons successful?

Mohandas K. Gandhi, also known by the title the people of India gave

11

him, "Mahatma" (Great Soul), may be considered one of the most successful men of all times, yet he displayed none of the ordinary symbols of success. When he died his earthly possessions consisted of a pair of spectacles, a pair of sandals, a few simple garments, a book, and a spinning wheel.

On the other hand, many people have been fortunate enough to combine outward symbols of success with inner satisfactions—Andrew Carnegie, the Guggenheims, Russell Sage, Irving Berlin, Eleanor Roosevelt — you can think of some in your own community.

If anyone has ever enjoyed all the usual signs of success, William Larimer Mellon is one such person. Aside from owning a summer lodge in Can-

Dr. William Larimer Mellon put aside a life which most of us would call successful. He found greater satisfaction helping people in the jungles of Haiti.

ada, a houseboat in Florida, and being heir to a remarkable fortune, Larry Mellon was a success in banking, advertising, operating a ranch, and in the diplomatic service. But none of these outward accomplishments was inwardly satisfying. He remembered his mother's answer to a question he had asked as a little boy. "What is the greatest thing on earth to be?"

"A medical missionary" was the reply. Finally, at thirty-seven Mellon re-entered college as an undergraduate student, against the advice of professors. He graduated with a degree in medicine and at forty-seven established the Albert Schweitzer Hospital in the jungles of Haiti.

Despite their handicaps, you can think of Negroes who have risen in all roles of life. Forgetting the violence that accompanies change, try listing names of Negroes in your city and nationally who have made places for themselves in all kinds of ways. All you have to do is study other lives to make your own opportunities look better!

As you look about you, among your

A growing number of Negro politicians are proving that voters care more about public service than about skin color. Edward Brooke, shown here, was elected U.S. Senator from Massachusetts in 1966. A year later in Cleveland, Ohio, Carl B. Stokes became the first Negro mayor of a major American city. Both men drew support from many white voters.

classmates, teachers, coaches, and community leaders, how do you judge success? In school, is it the best student, the best athlete, the most popular teacher? In your neighborhood, is it the man with the biggest house, the finest car, the woman with the most expensive clothes, or is it the person who does the most for his family, his community, or for the people with whom he works?

Success depends on skill in living with others as well as in a career. Many stories and plays are based on the failure of a person to achieve personal success in his relation to others even though he may achieve success financially or as a political or social leader.

You may wish to take time for discussion of TV plays that have this theme. You have heard of actors and other famous persons who have committed suicide at the height of their careers. Why? It is worth discussion.

FINDING SUCCESS

It is debatable how much your personal success depends upon a high IQ or good looks. Beauty queens are no longer chosen for beauty alone. Psychologists say that a person of only average looks is more likely to make a good marriage partner than one who is exceptionally attractive. The person who relies too heavily on beauty tends to become self-centered.

People who are quite ordinary in regard to appearance and intelligence have become successful in many fields. Your IQ is not as important as what you do with the brain power you have. Even in research, brain power without drive and determination is not enough.

Although there is no set rule for success in life, a close relationship between a person's work and his self-concept usually brings success. If a person's job lets him accomplish what he thinks is important in life, his chances for success are best. Frequently careers are imposed upon people through family tradition or pressure—a banker's son may be expected to be a banker or a doctor's son a doctor. If the son's self-concept, interests, abilities and aptitudes coincide with the occupation chosen for him, he probably will succeed. If not, he may find his job and his life unpleasant.

Success affects people in different ways. Some people, especially those in the entertainment field, *thrive on publicity*. If film, stage, and screen stars were not constantly publicized, their popularity would not last.

Many persons *bear their fame gracefully*. Charles Lindbergh, the first aviator to make a solo flight across the Atlantic, and John Glenn, the first American to orbit the earth, have viewed their great achievements with humility and used their experience to bring about greater progress in their respective fields.

Many successful persons become indifferent to fame. A good example is Dr. Jonas Salk, who developed polio vaccine in 1955. "Fame is transitory, a time waster," he said. "I'd rather stay in my laboratory and work."

Success usually comes *through hard work*. Only rarely do we get a "big role" *accidentally*. We can't depend on the star dancer in a musical comedy breaking a leg, although it happened to Shirley MacLaine. As an understudy, she stepped into the role and soon won the attention of Hollywood producers.

Another odd case involved Eugene O'Neill's long play *Strange Interlude*. Banned from Boston, it opened in the suburbs. The play began at six, with intermission at eight. The nearest snack bar was run by a man named Howard Johnson. Almost overnight, business soared; thus began the rapid growth of Howard Johnson restaurants and motels.

Generally, to find true success: (1) Take advantage of opportunity. (2) Refuse to admit defeat. (3) Try to overcome handicaps. (4) Broaden your contacts. (5) Show enthusiasm for what you do.

Take Advantage of Opportunity This is not as much a matter of getting the breaks as making the breaks. In the following case studies, the breaks did not come to the individual; he helped to make his own.

CASE STUDY: A car was bogged down on a muddy country road. A boy familiar with farm machinery, and also interested in finding a job, offered to help pull the car out with his father's tractor. The owner of the car happened to be on his way to town to locate a building from which to distribute farm equipment. Shortly afterward, the boy was offered a job and eventually became part owner of the store.

CASE STUDY: An older couple from Oklahoma, touring the campus of one of our large southern universities, asked a student where to find a particular building. The student replied, "I'm not busy right now; suppose I take you over. You might be interested in some of our other buildings." The visitor was so impressed with this courtesy that he handed the student his card and said, "You have given us a very good impression of your university. We like to hire people like you. If you should ever want to locate in Oklahoma, get in touch with me."

Perhaps you can think of schoolmates who seem to get all the breaks. Think about it. They are ready when opportunity knocks, aren't they?

Refuse to Admit Defeat If you are going to give up every time something goes wrong, you are not giving yourself even a slight chance of success. Being able to profit by your disappointments will take self-discipline and determination, but many people have turned defeat into success.

CASE STUDY: John Paul Jones, brilliant American admiral of the Revolutionary War, seemingly had no chance to win the battle between his ship, *Bon Homme Richard*, and the British vessel, *Serapis*. The American ship had scarcely half the fire power of her opponent, and seemed for hours on the verge of sinking. But when the British commander asked him to surrender, Jones bravely answered, "I have not yet begun to fight." Courage, determination, and ability paid off as Jones finally forced his opponent to surrender, winning one of history's most famous encounters.

CASE STUDY: Few people have been as determined as Abraham Lincoln in refusing to admit defeat. To begin with, he had an awkward figure and homely face. He was defeated for the State Legislature; a store he bought on credit failed; Ann Rutledge, his

14

H. Armstrong Roberts

The statue of Abraham Lincoln in the Lincoln Memorial, Washington, D. C., is a symbol of character. Ability to benefit from disappointments, to apologize and forgive, and to give others due credit, all help to build character.

first sweetheart, died unexpectedly while they were engaged, and Mary Owens, to whom he later proposed, turned him down; three of his four children died before reaching maturity; he failed to be nominated for Congress and when finally elected he became so unpopular that he did not run again. It was only after a succession of disappointments and continued determination that he was elected to the highest office in the country.

Try to Overcome Handicaps Some people accept a handicap as an excuse; others accept it as a challenge. Which would you do? Here is how some people changed a handicap to a challenge and did the seemingly impossible.

15

- Charles Steinmetz, with a spinal deformity in youth, came to America as an immigrant and became the "wizard of General Electric," discoverer of alternating current.
- Dr. Edward L. Trudeau, at the beginning of a brilliant medical career, developed tuberculosis and was sent to the mountains near Saranac Lake, New York, to die. He did not die, but lived to build the most famous hospital for tuberculosis patients in the world.
- John Milton, after becoming blind, wrote "Paradise Lost."
- Ludwig van Beethoven composed many of his musical masterpieces after he became deaf.
- While suffering paralysis, Louis Pasteur isolated bacteria and developed the process of pasteurization, and George Frederick Handel composed some of his best music.

Broaden Contacts The more "leads" you pursue and the more contacts you make, the better opportunities you will have for success.

Enthusiasm is necessary for a happy, satisfying life; it should be channeled in the right direction.

American Machine and Foundry Company

CASE STUDIES: Tom put in an application for summer work at a filling station where he had worked before and felt sure of getting a job. He did not notice that the filling station had changed management until a few days before he expected to report to work. By this time school was out and jobs were scarce, so Tom failed to get work.

During spring vacation Phil made a list of jobs that are plentiful in the summer. He contacted a soft beverage bottling firm, landscape gardner, surveying firm, and contractor. Out of four contacts he was offered three jobs. Phil decided upon the job with the contractor who was building homes in a new development. Not only did Phil get a job but it steered him into a career as an architectural engineer.

When you expand your interests, contacts, and friends, you never know what connection may open the door to a greater opportunity. When you limit your sights, you limit your opportunities.

Show Enthusiasm Enthusiasm can be contagious. When plans for a dance are going wrong and someone shows enthusiasm about starting anew, or when a team is losing a game and the spectators continue enthusiastic support, the entire course of events can be changed. Samuel Goldwyn, one of the greatest forces behind the growth of the film industry, has said that "enthusiasm for work and life is the most precious ingredient in any recipe for successful living. . . it is available to everyone within himself." Moreover, enthusiasm makes life interesting.

16

OVERCOMING FEARS

There are times when we all have fears. As a child you may have been afraid of the dark or of lightning. Now you may be afraid of speaking before people, of appearing for a personal interview, of asking for a date, or of losing in athletic competition.

Great actors, basketball players, and public speakers are often nervous and afraid as they face the public. Many great military men have been tense and even fearful before an attack.

To prepare us for times of fear, our glands release adrenalin, a stimulating substance which helps us to face emergencies. Sometimes fear may save us from danger, such as a fire or oncoming car. To be afraid does not necessarily reflect cowardice.

We need *action* to release built up fears. That is why it is often wise to do the thing you fear. When a tight rope walker, a ski champion, or a paratrooper suffers a minor injury while performing, he is often urged to return to his specialty as soon as possible to avoid building up fear.

Dale Carnegie built his world-wide course in self-improvement on Ralph Waldo Emerson's quotation "Do the thing you fear and the death of fear is certain," and wrote one of the most widely read books of all time, *How to Win Friends and Influence People.*

As a young YMCA teacher back in 1912, Dale Carnegie finished his first evening lecture too soon. He stumbled on the idea of asking his students to discuss the things that made them afraid. This idea formed the basis of the Carnegie courses which have helped thousands of executives and salesmen to control their fear of meeting people and speaking before groups. Many corporations now give potential executives special training to help them acquire greater self-confidence.

Can you cite incidents when you have been afraid to try a new venture? When you feared an experience, then tried it, has it usually been as bad as you expected? Discuss.

HONESTY

Many prominent men today say that the greatest danger to our country is not from outside nuclear attacks, but from inside moral decay—dishonest practices in business, government, and personal relationships.

The sharp rise in shoplifting can be offered as evidence of this moral decay. Between 1958 and 1968 teen-age shoplifting rose from a few thousand cases a week to about 100,000. One supermarket chain took over 150,000 persons into custody in just one year. Our nation's stores lose an estimated four million dollars worth of goods to shoplifters *each day.*

It is interesting to learn that teen-age girls are the most frequent offenders. They are not all from economically deprived families, nor are they all kleptomaniacs. At a time when young people have more money than ever, why do so many shoplift?

True, self-service stores are more and more common. Displays are increasingly attractive, and counters have been removed from many stores to encourage impulse buying. All these changes have made shoplifting easier. Do you think these are the only reasons for the rise in shoplifting or are moral standards in our society falling?

Thomas Macaulay, English historian and statesman, once wrote, "The measure of a man's real character is what he would do if he knew he would never be found out." If anyone ever had an opportunity to be dishonest and never be found out it was a Spaniard whose true story is summarized here.

CASE STUDY: A young man was in the railroad station in Madrid, bidding goodbye to a friend. It was the day before the annual drawing of a national Spanish lottery in which the first prize was about $400,000.

"I am about to buy myself a lottery ticket," he told his departing friend.

"Please buy one for me," said the friend, as his train pulled out. Returning from his trip the traveler was greeted by his friend, "Your ticket won first prize!" "But, how did you know which was which?" asked the friend. "Simplest thing in the world," replied the honest man. "I marked your name on one envelope and mine on the other."

What would you have done had you been the purchaser?

Many high schools and colleges over the country have adopted the *honor system*. It has been especially successful at the University of Virginia where emphasis on honor is one of the traditions handed down by Thomas Jefferson. Before a student registers, the honor code is explained,

The statue of Thomas Jefferson in front of the rotunda at the University of Virginia symbolizes the university's famed honor system—"its most priceless heritage and beloved tradition."

Ralph Thompson

18

and the student signs a card indicating that he understands and wants to live by it. The three violations of the code are cheating, lying about serious matters, and stealing. If a student is even suspected of violating the code he is warned. If the offense is suspected again, he is tried before a student court and, if found guilty, quietly dismissed.

The origin of the Honor Code, adopted in 1842, goes back to Thomas Jefferson's personal code for life. In 1785, Jefferson gave the following advice to his nephew, Peter Carr, about to enter college—"I can assure you that the possession of (knowledge)—next to an honest heart—is what will, above all things, render you dear to your friends and give you fame . . . Give up money, give up fame, give up science, give up the earth itself and all it contains, rather than do an immoral act . . . an honest heart is the first blessing, a knowing head, the second."

Students at the University of Virginia may leave classes for refreshments or a walk during an examination. They may leave books and belongings anywhere on the campus without fear of losing them. Any merchant in town will cash a student's check without question.

Is it clear to you why the University of Virginia, the U.S. military academies, and other similar great institutions are proud of their honor systems—and bitterly resent those who dishonor it?

Once in a while we are tempted to be dishonest, especially if we think no one will ever find out. Occasional mild deceptions are only human, but can we live our best with a feeling

that we are second-rate? After repeated dishonesty, we lose character. We live a cheap, ugly existence, even though we seem successful to others. Remember the quotation from Shakespeare's *Hamlet*. "To thine own self be true, and it must follow, as the night the day, thou canst not then be false to any man."

Honesty is as much a part of success as is the ability to judge an opportunity for advancement.

On the following test of honesty, how do you rate? Do not check what you know is the desired answer, but what you think you would do under the circumstances.

ARE YOU AS HONEST AS YOU THINK?*

1. If you had a summer job in an office where you had access to papers, pencils, erasers, and paper clips, and needed these items for school, would you:

   A. *Take home a supply?*
   B. *Buy them at the store?*

2. If your paper came back with a B and you discovered that your teacher had made a mistake and you should have had a C grade, would you:

   A. *Keep quiet about it?*
   B. *Call the teacher's attention to the error?*

3. If you and a friend were assigned to work on a class report together and you did not have time to do your share before turning in the report, would you:

   A. *Sign your name to it anyway?*
   B. *Ask to have more time to do your share?*

---

*Adapted from "So You Think You're Honest," by David R. Lindsay. (*This Week* magazine, June 3, 1956.)

4. If you were driving your friends to a movie and you sighted a parking area which another car in front of you was already preparing to back into, would you:

    A. *Pretend you did not know he wanted to back in, and try to drive into it?*

    B. *Drive on, hoping to find another place?*

5. If at the grocery store, the cashier gave back more change than was due, would you:

    A. *Keep it and say nothing?*

    B. *Explain the error?*

6. If you forgot to pay your bus fare and the driver were none the wiser, would you:

    A. *Settle down and forget it?*

    B. *Go back and pay your fare?*

7. If you picked up a dollar bill on a school walk, would you:

    A. *Slip it into your wallet?*

    B. *Take it to the principal's office?*

8. If you were buying a $20 watch and the sales person forgot to add the luxury tax, would you:

    A. *Be smug and forget it?*

    B. *Call her attention to the error?*

9. If you were given $15 to spend for refreshments for a class party and you got some items wholesale, making the cost $13.50, would you:

    A. *Keep the change?*

    B. *Turn in the change and your itemized account?*

10. If the highway speed limit were 55 miles an hour but the road were clear and you liked the feeling of power, would you:

    A. *Speed your car up to 65 or 70?*

    B. *Stay within the speed limit?*

Add up all the A scores.

0 - 3 You are extremely honest.

4 - 7 You are an average citizen, generally honest.

8 - 10 You are really fooling no one but yourself.

YOUR STAND ON DRINKING

Whether to drink or not, and how far to go, are decisions you must make for yourself. The following discussion will help you to take an adult stand.

Dr. Marvin A. Block, an international authority on drinking, has made this frank statement: "Drinking is no sign of manliness and certainly not of womanliness . . . . Excessive drinking marks a feeling of inferiority, and the more this fact is denied, the more accurate is the diagnosis."

A generation ago drinking was no serious problem among high school people. A number of factors are believed to be causing an increase in teen-age drinking. Our *affluent society* has provided young people with larger allowances to spend for alcoholic beverages and cars to drive to places where alcoholic drinks can be obtained. Respect for adult authority has grown weaker. Tension over many matters, from schoolwork to possible atomic war, is also blamed. Advertising makes drinking seem glamorous, a symbol of social status and the "good life."

The best defense against the drinking problem rests within the home. Parents who reasonably control their children's activities seldom have a child with a drinking problem. An example of over-indulgent parents received national publicity not long ago when a 17-year-old girl was killed after a wild drinking party in a small

Where do you stand?

wine, fewer Europeans, by percentage, become serious alcoholics; however, more have organic diseases traced to alcohol.

Chemical tests (accepted by the American Medical Association, American Bar Association, and National Safety Council) can determine when drinking impairs physical reactions. A driver with .15 per cent or more alcohol in his blood is considered intoxicated. (In some places, laws penalize drivers who have even a lower percentage.) People differ in their ability to oxidize or "burn up" alcohol in the body. Many people can oxidize one ounce of whiskey or one bottle of beer within an hour, so that it will hardly register in a chemical test. A person who has had two drinks has no business driving until his system has oxidized the alcohol.

The social drinker is one who means to use alcoholic drinks only to provide temporary relaxation. However, such a drinker takes risks. Business and pleasure do not always mix.

CASE STUDY: Tom Perkins, a popular newscaster in a large Eastern city, began stepping up his intake of alcohol before reporting to the studio. On two occasions an assistant tactfully took over the program to save face for the studio. The evening after the broadcaster's three-year contract was renewed, he became so mixed up in reporting that his contract was torn up after the broadcast.

The economic angle of drinking is another consideration. If you begin to serve alcoholic beverages you may find they can cost as much as food.

The person who decides to drink, risks 1 chance in 15 of becoming an alcoholic (1 in 10 according to some

New England town. It was not just the fact that teen-agers were getting drunk and driving recklessly, or even that a girl was killed, that made the headlines. It was rather that the judge invoked a seldom-used law and arrested 13 parents who served alcoholic drinks to persons under age. Parents in other areas have since been charged similarly.

If you have grown up in a home where cocktails are served as a matter of course, yet drinking is moderate, you may seldom question the custom from a moral standpoint. On the other hand, if you have been reared in a very strict home you might consider drinking any kind of alcoholic beverage dangerous and immoral, yet exciting.

In Germany and Belgium, beer is a family beverage. This is true of wine in France and Italy. Such beverages are served in place of water, and not primarily as a stimulant. In spite of this general acceptance of beer and authorities). Perhaps the meaning of the word *alcoholic* is not clear. An alcoholic is a person who cannot control his drinking. He or she will obtain alcohol at any cost or sacrifice. It is said that a person can become an alcoholic on nothing stronger than beer.

Three-fourths of problem drinkers or alcoholics are between the ages of 35 and 55. It takes many years for a person to become a compulsive drinker. He becomes an alcoholic when social drinking develops into long, compulsive bouts of drinking alone. According to some authorities, an alcoholic affects the lives of seven to ten people in one way or another. A problem drinker endangers his job, his family's happiness, and his status in the community.

Alcoholism is considered a disease. An alcoholic needs medical treatment plus understanding from family and friends. He or she cannot be cured by preaching or criticizing. Once "cured", an alcoholic cannot go back to social drinking. He may feel ill at ease with "the old crowd" but he has to realize that he must exert strong discipline or face another attack. It is much easier for you to refuse a drink now than it is for a "cured" alcoholic, despite all the misery he knows it will bring him. This is worth serious consideration.

A young New England architect felt better when not drinking, so for a number of years he would say "Make mine ginger ale." He was "needled" by his business associates till he eventually concluded, "It's easier just to sit holding a cocktail glass and appear to be sociable." Do you agree?

WHY PEOPLE DRINK

· Some people drink because they like the taste of light alcoholic beverages in the same way they like the taste of certain foods. Controlled social drinking may be the answer to the drinking question for many persons.

· Many people drink to win social approval—because it is easier to go along with the crowd than risk being set apart. Yet we like to feel that people seek us out for what we are and not for what we drink.

· Others drink because they want to escape from conditions they cannot face—fear, anxiety, mistakes, failures, disappointments. Of course, the condition still exists after the effects of alcohol have worn off.

· A person may use alcohol as a kind of security—for instance, the "grown-up child" who has been overprotected, who cannot measure up to what he feels is expected of him, or who has been reared in an unhappy family. He finds temporary security in drinking, even though it is false.

· Shy people may drink to feel less awkward or inferior in a group. Of course, they do not become less awkward or less shy, but less aware of their problem.

· Certain people drink because they think they can be the life of the party —even at the risk of losing self-respect. Alcohol does tend to lessen the impact of reality and ease strain, but not because it is a stimulant. Although the first few sips may be stimulating, once alcohol enters the blood stream, it has an anesthetizing effect.

· Some think drinking gives the feeling of confidence. Too often such people begin to depend upon alcohol as a "crutch" for their shortcomings. As time goes on, they need it more and more to "boost" their confidence. This type often becomes alcoholic.

It is pathetic enough for a man to let his drinking habits control him, but it is worse to see a *woman problem drinker* headed for skid row. Here are the facts about women alcoholics:
• The number of women alcoholics has doubled in the last 20 years.
• Many are in their late teens and early twenties. A large number comes from what we refer to as "respectable homes."
• Women often pay a high price for the alcoholic kind of popularity: unwed motherhood, divorce, crime.
• Women are less inclined to admit their condition than men until they are beyond help. Therefore women alcoholics degenerate faster than men. Children whose mothers are alcoholic usually develop a serious sense of insecurity.

No one's *goals* may be gained effectively in an alcoholic state. Alcoholism is the *fourth* most prevalent disease in the country, surpassed only by heart disease, cancer, and mental illness. A person is in danger of becoming an alcoholic when he or she keeps taking "just one more;" begins to drink alone; craves "straight" rather than mixed drinks; loses appetite; or drinks to forget problems.

After you are of legal age, drinking in moderation or not at all is a personal matter. But when drinking becomes excessive, it goes beyond individual responsibility. It may threaten the happiness, welfare, reputation, even the very life of the drinker, his family, or the unsuspecting victim of a drunken driver. When it is most urgent for the drinker to break his habit, he is then least able to help himself. When this point has been reached, it is too late for easy solutions, sometimes too late for any solution at all. The only time to solve the problem is before it becomes a problem.

Laws that say you must not drink until you reach a certain age are not meant to hinder you, but to help.

YOUR PART IN TRAFFIC SAFETY

Statistics indicate that 36 per cent of all Americans who die between ages 15 and 24 are killed in automobile accidents. One factor that accounts for this shocking accident rate is the high proportion of young people constantly on the go. The majority of teen-agers, especially those who have taken driver training seriously, have good records. Nevertheless, there are so many reckless drivers under 24 that insurance companies impose higher than average rates for this age group, penalizing good young drivers as well as bad ones.

Drivers under 24 account for 5,700,000 mishaps a year, and figures released from the National Safety Council indicate that each accident costs an average of $700.

Driver education, long considered unnecessary and too expensive, has now become a federally supported part of the high school curriculum. Most insurance companies give a 10 to 15 per cent discount to students who have taken accredited driving courses—about four out of ten qualify. Many authorities believe that driver education *combined with education in the use of alcohol* should be mandatory.

Some accidents are caused by ignoring precautions.

As an adult your gains and goals depend a great deal on personal safety through the years. Before you take hold of the wheel next time, pause to consider the following:

· Fasten your seat belt, even on short trips. Most fatal accidents happen within 20 miles of home.

· Obey the posted speed limit. It is for your protection. At 60 MPH a car will move at least 66 feet before the driver's foot acts on the brain's message to step on the brake, and another 300 feet before stopping. Also, keeping within speed limits can save you money. Electronic devices help police to catch speeders.

· When you see a stop sign, STOP completely. Many accidents are caused at busy intersections by persons who ease past a stop sign.

· Stay on your side of the road in a *No Passing* zone.

· Avoid jockeying in and out of traf-fic. The time you save is not worth the risk you take.

· Dim your lights at night for approaching cars to avoid blinding the other driver.

· In slowing down, pump your brakes to flash tail lights as a warning signal.

· Give the impatient driver the right of way.

· Stay a safe distance back of the vehicle ahead of you, especially a truck. Accidents in which a car runs under a truck bed are often fatal. "Tailgating" also results in many chain-reaction accidents which can cause whiplash injury.

· Never drive if you have been drinking intoxicating beverages. Let a non-drinker take the wheel.

· Guard against "highway hypnosis" by making frequent stops, singing, turning on the radio. Go easy on "stay awake pills."

· Use your rear vision mirror and signal before pulling into traffic.

· Keep your windshield and lights clean.

· If you have car trouble, pull off the road. Avoid parking just over a hill. Once off the road, signal with a white handkerchief in daytime, a flashlight at night. Stand away from the car to avoid being pinned against it by another car.

· If involved in an accident, do not try to lift injured persons. Notify police. Show your driver's license but sign nothing until the police arrive. Obtain names and addresses of witnesses. Check the other driver's license and insurance protection. *Notify your own insurance company within 24 hours.*

· Never hitchhike or pick up hitch-hikers. Your life may be endangered.

CARS AND SCHOLARSHIP

There is scarcely a young adult who does not want to own a car. If you want a car, and have the means to get one, consider your long-range goals and how owning a car will affect them. A car is fine for dating, driving to games, and taking trips on weekends, but it costs money, takes time away from studying, and is one major source of friction between young people and their parents.

There are many *ifs* in car ownership. For instance, owning a car may cause you no serious problems *if* your family provides it (along with the necessities of life) or *if* you can earn enough to buy and maintain the car without neglecting schoolwork, but only *if* you are mature enough to say *NO* to friends who might try to persuade you to use the car when you should be doing something else.

Nationwide surveys consistently show that almost no straight "A" students own cars but that 80 per cent of the "D" students do and that students who begin using a car more than a day or two a week begin to show a noticeable drop in grades. Only the most mature students are likely to keep their marks high while using a car frequently. During the week such students often use a car only as needed on a job or to save time. One survey indicated that students with cars missed twice as many days of school as those without cars. Another survey showed that car users tended to choose non-academic courses. Still another survey by an insurance company revealed that the accident rate among high school age drivers was twice that for adult drivers.

CASE STUDY: Jim Bucknell wanted to buy a car, but in order to do so he had to double his income. After frequent visits to used car lots he found a good, six-year-old model. He gave up football, and got a job working after school and on Saturday at a gas station. He figured he could pay for the car in about five months.

Expenses on the car kept him broke the rest of the year. His grades fell. He missed the prestige of football, and fellowship of other players on the team. He was too busy to join in social affairs. Do you think owning a car made up for the things Jim missed?

MORAL STANDARDS

You cannot make a gain in life, or reach a goal, without certain standards. You must set and maintain standards of business conduct, of educational goals, and of moral values. Morals affect all standards, as a matter of fact. The way you treat others, at all times, is probably the strongest moral responsibility you have. This is especially true in close, personal relationships. We hear much about freedom between the sexes, but we do not have to know much about history to realize that it is the wrong standard for any lasting social culture.

Loose moral habits preceded the fall of nearly all great civilizations. The internationally known historian, Arnold Toynbee, has pointed out that nineteen of twenty-one notable civilizations crumbled from immoral practices within, not from foreign conquerors.

His study of history stresses the need for emphasis on spiritual and moral laws.

25

A few years ago Russia passed laws permitting so-called "free morals," and encouraged citizens to practice immorality. The experiment failed. Russia became weaker, not stronger, as the importance of family unity was ignored. As a result, the government reversed its ideas, began issuing statements praising chastity, and made divorces hard to obtain.

Of course, we have never lost sight of the great moral principles in this country. Our nation was founded on strong ethical codes which uphold us to this day. You must examine carefully your own attitudes on the subject, and be able to take a firm stand on your beliefs. The high price in permanent damage to one's character, reputation, and health is too great for a few "kicks." Although sexual compatibility is one ingredient of a successful marriage, few marriage counselors consider it the most important. People who seem to be successful, despite lives strewn with divorces and dishonest moral relationships, must

Love can be shown in many ways—planning and working toward future goals, enjoying similar interests, sharing joys and disappointments.

Heirloom Sterling

either injure others or themselves along the way. You can think of cases which demonstrate this. When the marriage code is defied, at least one partner must be hurt and humiliated. The other may appear to go on as before, yet sometimes we see through his armor, as he grows older and all standards lose meaning for him. Even good looks, fame, and fortune become empty. In extreme cases, such a person finds the way out in suicide. Love does not mean "freedom." It means just the opposite. It means the *bond* that holds persons together. You should realize that love includes much more than temporary fascination, which is easy to find—and easy to lose. It includes planning together, whether for a party or to finance a home; standing by each other in times of disappointment and sorrow, and making sacrifices for the good of the other.

In a symposium "Must We Change Our Sex Standards?" published in the *Reader's Digest,* many nationally known educators, writers, sociologists, and clergymen expressed their viewpoints on our sex attitudes. Here are a few excerpts to ponder over:

"The hope of civilization lies in your obedience to the moral laws rather than surrender to animal instincts." As humans, we have the ability to think things out—to base our actions on understanding. It is natural that one dog will take a bone from another. We humans covet things, too. But we have the intelligence to realize that the rights of others will be violated if we just grab whatever we want.

"Moral values are the product of will and intelligence, which enable us to submit ourselves to discipline."

26

Do you want to *gain* happiness and fulfillment in love? Then set a high *goal* for yourself.

RELIGION IN DAILY LIVING

The great men of our country have shown us how they valued religion. When delegates to the Constitutional Congress could not agree on drawing up our Constitution, Benjamin Franklin called for daily prayer. You may be familiar with the Jefferson Bible— Thomas Jefferson's own compilation of the teachings of Jesus, in parallel columns in four languages. Lincoln knew the power of prayer and the need for faith. He referred frequently to the Bible as "the greatest book ever written," and its teachings formed the basis for many of his discussions. Dwight D. Eisenhower opened both inaugural addresses with prayer. Herman Wouk, author of *The Caine Mutiny* and other fine novels, returned to his Jewish faith, and prayer, when material things failed.

These men found that it is impossible to separate spiritual values from everyday living.

Whatever our faith, most of us feel a sense of religion. Sometimes high school and college students drift away from church, but most of them come back when they have families of their own. C. G. Jung, the famous psychiatrist, after studying human minds and emotions for over fifty years said, "Among all my patients in the second half of life, every one of them fell ill because he had lost what the living religions of every age have given their followers, and none of them has been really healed who did not regain his religious outlook."

Even though we may be sure our religion is the best, we should make an effort to understand and appreciate the way others worship. If you would like to know something about the major religions of the world, you may enjoy reading the beautifully illustrated book published by *Life* magazine, "The World's Great Religions," or "Religions in America" edited by Leo Rosten and published originally in *Look* magazine.

Whether we attend church because it is a family tradition, because it is what our friends do, or because we want to meditate and worship, most of us find that religion offers us a great deal. Going to church and practicing religion in our daily lives helps to give life more meaning. It can be a key to successful homes and careers.

Besides its spiritual benefits, religion can bring personal pleasure and satisfaction.

H. Armstrong Roberts

27

CAREERS WITHOUT COLLEGE

With a high school diploma you have made one of your greatest gains toward playing adult roles. Your next step may be in one of many directions. Automation has done away with certain types of work, but other jobs have been created. The job seeker today can choose from more than 6,000 types of jobs which did not even exist in 1950.

Many of the new jobs do not require a college degree, but most good jobs do call for some formal or on-the-job training beyond high school. For instance, after training, a skilled chef, steelworker, real estate or insurance salesman, or department store buyer may earn more than many college professors. Aware of the need for a special skill, about 8 of every 10 high school graduates plan to continue their education in one of the areas discussed on the following pages.

On-the-Job Training This may mean training within a large business, or it may mean apprenticeship training. Federal apprenticeship training is available in many major industries. There are 90 *basic* trade classifications, some of which are airplane mechanic, barber, electrician, lithographer, printer, tailor, upholsterer, and tile setter. A minimum of 144 hours of instruction each year is normally considered necessary. Federal apprenticeship programs do not apply to retailing, marketing, managerial, clerical, professional, or agricultural occupations, but you can get on-the-job training in food stores, department and specialized stores, factories, with telephone companies and businesses, in banks and insurance companies.

Courses in Military Service Many courses are available in military service. Some young men become interested enough in military life to make it a career. Others secure a basic education in fields that lead to good jobs upon release from the service. For instance, Russell Williams, capable of doing college work, became dissatisfied with school and enlisted in the Air Force at mid-semester. Tests indicated that he had an aptitude for languages. During the first year of his military service he was enrolled at Yale to study Russian. At the end of his term of service, he entered college again to pursue a career in the diplomatic service.

Nurses Training in Hospitals Large hospitals have their own training programs for nurses. Some hospitals have a cooperative plan with colleges by which

The rush for higher education. By 1970 the number of college students will be nearly double what it was in 1960. A still higher enrollment is forecast for 1975.

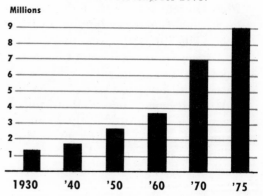

Millions

28

On-the-job Training: Skills may be learned on the job in industry.

Job Training in Military Services: Training opportunities for women, as well as for men, are available. Here a Women's Army Corps member operates radar equipment.

a girl may become a nurse and earn a degree.

Vocational, Business, and Technical Schools There are vocational, business, and technical schools as well as trade schools for specialized training in every large city. These courses are usually geared to the business and industrial needs in the area. For instance, Pittsburgh, an industrial and medical center, has business schools

which provide *training for engineering and medical secretaries.* Courses are given in basic physics and chemistry for engineering secretaries, and in biology and chemistry for medical secretaries.

Most large cities have schools that offer training in office practices, practical nursing, modeling, commercial art, drafting, mechanics, and electron-

On-the-job Training: Retailing is another field that offers opportunities for training while you work.

Nurses Training in Hospitals: Almost all hospitals have openings for students who desire a career in nursing.

29

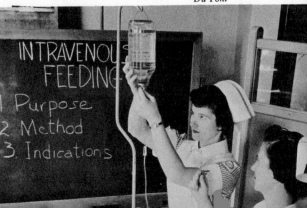

The Federal Apprenticeship Program: Nearly 200,000 persons are trained in 90 basic trades every year.

Technical and Vocational Schools: The demand for skilled technicians increases in industry.

Business Schools: There is always a demand for secretaries, typists, business machine operators, filing clerks, and others.

ics. There are schools in many localities where you can study photography, music, theater arts, real estate, television techniques, foreign languages, public speaking, aeronautics and flying, skilled building trades, or airline hostessing.

Correspondence and T.V. Courses Through correspondence, you can take courses in writing, art, interior decorating, drafting, tailoring, accounting, business practices, and scores of other subjects. But be cautious. Don't let the success stories of some correspondence schools influence you. Any school can find isolated success cases to advertise. Before you sign up for a correspondence course, unless it is with a nationally recognized university or school, read the contract carefully. Find out about its reputation from the Better Business Bureau. Study *all the small print* and know what you are signing, or you may be making monthly payments long after you have lost interest in the course. Studies show that only about 6 per cent of those who enroll in private correspondence schools complete their training.

Perhaps you are familiar with courses for credit over television stations. If you want to find out more about them, write to the Educational Television and Radio Center, 2715 Packard Avenue, Ann Arbor, Michigan.

COLLEGE EDUCATION

Those of you who expect to go to college may have been making plans for the past three years or more. You should know what subjects are required, and have a general idea of the kind of college you would like to attend. A college education may be both desirable and possible for many of you. You have a choice of a *liberal arts* college for men or women, or both; a *university*—state or private; a *teachers college;* or a specialized college.

If you are planning to enter the professions—law, medicine, the ministry, education, or highly specialized scientific fields, a college education is a "must." Even though a young woman may not plan to work, she will find college education worthwhile, and if her husband has been to college, she probably will find similar education an asset in her marriage.

Fine Arts Academies: People with special talents may want a career in music, art, drama, or other specialized fields.

The Pittsburgh Playhouse.

According to one study, a college graduate's chances of holding top ranking positions—executive, managerial, professional—are 84 in 100 against a non-college man's chances of 16 in 100. The salary of a college graduate usually increases with his age, leveling off at age 50, whereas an average non-college graduate's salary levels off and tends to decrease at age 40.

During the middle to late 1950's the rush to college began, spurred by the rising birth rate, competitive instincts, generally increasing family income, and greater emphasis on the need for a college education. Colleges began to expand, but the rate of expansion has not kept pace with the rate of student demand for higher education, even though private tuitions have soared.

"Associate"-degree colleges, called junior or community colleges, are helping to ease the situation. Since 1964 their growth has been amazing. By 1970 it is estimated there will be 1,000 junior colleges, with two million students. Many are located in large population areas so students can attend while living at home.

The junior college provides terminal courses for many vocations—

Teachers' Colleges: The demand for teachers increases. There are state or municipally supported teachers' colleges within close reach of every community.

National Dairy Council

Better Living, Du Pont

Technological Colleges: Careers in engineering and science are available to graduates.

that is, training that leads to a job, without need of further schooling. Liberal arts or general courses are also taught for those who may want to transfer to a regular degree-granting institution.

Junior colleges have been thought of as chiefly for students of limited means or ability, but they are also attracting good students and those who could afford private schools. Some students prefer the junior college because classes are usually smaller and there is often more chance for personal contact with instructors. Gifted students are encouraged to pursue honors courses, and those who need remedial work can take such courses in basic subjects.

For many persons the junior college serves as a bridge between high school and a large degree-giving college or university. Between 75 and 80 per cent of students who transfer to regular degree-giving colleges remain to graduate.

Obviously the "associate" college is not suited to everyone's needs, but anyone seeking education beyond high school should become aware of the opportunities these institutions offer.

32

Getting into College

Educational levels keep rising. Not too long ago the great majority of people had only a high school education or less. Then college attendance rose, and a high school diploma meant less. Now the same is happening to the bachelor's degree. A master's degree is needed to get ahead in many fields, and a Ph.D. is required to reach the top in research and teaching, among other areas.

By the end of your junior year in high school, or the beginning of your senior year, you should have selected three colleges, but not ones that are equally difficult to enter. You may apply to one college that has a standard a little above what your high school grades have been, to another with somewhat lower academic and extra-curricular requirements, and a

University of Pittsburgh

Liberal Arts Colleges: Liberal arts colleges offer general background for many careers.

Specialized Colleges: Home economics provides training for a career or homemaking.

Drexel Institute of Technology

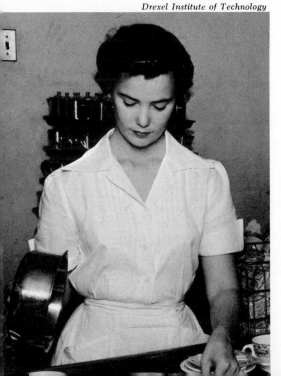

third college where you are fairly sure of being accepted.

Competition is keen for entry to "prestige" schools, but there are many small private colleges, mainly in the South and Midwest, which often have vacancies. Openings especially occur in the spring, due to cancellations from students who have been accepted at two or more colleges. There are agencies that keep track of such vacancies. Some are:

American College Admissions Center
12th and Walnut Sts.
Philadelphia, Pa. 19107

College Admission Center of ACAC
610 Church St.
Evanston, Ill. 60201

College Admissions and
Assistance Center
41 East 65th St.
New York, N.Y. 10021

33

If you plan to practice law, medicine, dentistry, or architecture in a particular state, you may want to attend a college in that state. Perhaps you will want to choose a college that offers reserve officer training so you can serve your military obligation as an officer. You may be interested in forestry, fisheries, or mining engineering, which may make it necessary to find a college far from home. A school that is excellent in training engineers may be just average in the English or biology department, so do not be too hasty in your investigation.

You will find that you get out of college only as much as you put into it. You can go to a school with the finest faculty and facilities, but unless you work at educating yourself, you will learn very little. On the other hand, if you attend a small school which does not have a national reputation, you are still certain to find many excellent teachers, and plenty of opportunity for learning, if you do *your* part.

Staying in College Of every 5 students entering college, only 2 graduate from the college they entered. The freshman year is the time when most of the drop-outs occur. The rate at which students leave is much lower among the highly ranked private schools than at institutions where entrance requirements are less strict.

Most students who drop out of college do so because they are not capable of doing college work; some drop out to marry; others quit because they are unhappy, and still others because they cannot afford to stay. A look at each of these reasons may help you.

Capability Of course, if a person is truly incapable of college work, he will do best to admit it, and not waste his or his parents' money. But don't sell yourself short. Thousands of people are graduated from colleges each year, and most of them are just ordinary people, not geniuses. Good study habits and willingness to work have brought college success to many people who did not have exceptional ability. Remember, in college you can specialize in a field of your choice. By choosing your courses wisely, in a field which interests you, it is possible to increase greatly your chances of staying in college.

Marriage College students often have money problems even when they are single. Marriage imposes further burdens on the pocketbook, and frequently ends the college hopes of bright students. This is unfortunate because it means that money already spent on college has been partially wasted, and because it hampers the financial future of the young couple. In many drop-outs, if the couple waited just one more year to marry, the husband could finish college and get a job with a good future.

Marriage does not always mean the end of college, though. If the couple has thought out the situation well—particularly if the husband is nearing graduation and the wife is able to work—marriage and college education can succeed together. Marriage always requires the most mature kind of thinking, and this is even more necessary when the possible loss of a college education is involved.

34

There is no easy way to choose a college where you will be **Happiness** happy with the atmosphere as well as with the educational facilities. It is not wise to let social or athletic programs determine your choice entirely, but these points should not be ignored, either. Some people cannot be happy without a schedule of major social events and "big games" which a large college often provides. Others are better satisfied with the simpler, usually friendlier atmosphere of a small college. Again, some people like a home town school; others do better away. The main thing is to analyze maturely what you want in a college, and to choose one that will suit all your needs —educational, financial, and personal.

There are several ways to curtail college costs. One is to **Money** secure a *scholarship*. Most scholarships are related to need as well as ability. However, thousands of scholarships go unused every year because no one knows about them. If you think you may be scholarship material, talk with your guidance counselor and consult the references at the end of the chapter. If you want an education but are not eligible for a scholarship, you can secure a loan through a college loan fund, through one of the education plans at a local bank, or through the National Defense Education Act of 1958. Under the federal program you may borrow $1,000 a year if you are a full-time student or up to a total of $5,000 for four years. You have 10 years to pay it back. Interest at 3 per cent begins after you have your degree. If you teach in public elementary or secondary schools, 50 per cent of the loan may be canceled. Many colleges participate in this program. You may learn more about the program by writing to the U. S. Government Printing Office, Washington 25, D. C., for a leaflet—*The National Defense Student Loan Program* — published by the U. S. Department of Health, Education, and Welfare, and the Office of Education.

A college education may be financed through a tuition plan, available through national organizations as well as at many local banks. The loan usually includes a term insurance policy which guarantees that the student can finish his education even if the person paying for it should die.

College employment offices also help students to find jobs, on campus or in the community, which help meet college costs.

If you would like to attend college away from home, but are afraid it will be too expensive, investigate costs at state supported schools. Sometimes the cost of tuition alone at a private school is very little less than board, room, and tuition at a state school, particularly a state teachers college. When comparing the costs of a home town college with the costs of going away, many people forget to include their food bill at home. You may be able to eat almost as inexpensively in a college dining hall as you can at home.

Round-up for College The following schedule has proved helpful in making college plans.

SEPTEMBER: Review your plans. Examine the college catalogues in your library. List your academic, professional, or vocational interests, and colleges most likely to satisfy them.

OCTOBER: If you have not already visited college campuses, do so very early. Talk with admissions officers who visit your school. Talk with students currently enrolled in colleges that interest you, and graduates of those colleges.

NOVEMBER: If you have not taken entrance examinations, make application for taking them in January. At many schools, this is the last examination date for scholarship applicants. Be sure your scholarship application is on file.

DECEMBER: Be on the alert for special scholarship examinations. Naval ROTC Scholarship examinations come in December. Apply to several colleges early in the month, if you have not already done so. Be sure to ask permission from the persons you name as references.

JANUARY: Study all month for midterms. These are the last grades your college will see. Some colleges require achievement tests in algebra, English, science, or language. You can still apply for these tests in March or May in some cases.

FEBRUARY: Re-check the College Handbook to see if you want to apply to other colleges. A few colleges do not consider applications after January 15, but others accept applications until April or even later.

MARCH: Be on the lookout for the letter that tells the outcome of your application. Some colleges are as late as May sending notices.

APRIL: Give thought to finding a vocational school or a job if colleges turn you down.

YOUR WORLD OF WORK

The *Dictionary of Occupational Titles,* published by the U.S. Department of Labor, lists over 22,000 different occupations. Some of the occupations in greatest demand are: *professional*—translators, clinical psychologists, librarians, veterinarians, statisticians, soil scientists, production planners, and meteorologists; *clerical*—clerk typists, stenographers, secretaries, and general office clerks; *craft*—instrument repairmen, sheet-metal workers, millwrights, electronics mechanics, draftsmen, bakers, welders; *technical*—X-ray technicians, computer programmers, physical therapists, dental technicians; *service*—airline hostesses, police patrolmen, practical nurses, hospital ward attendants, dental hygienists. School counselors and your state employment office have more information.

Analyzing a Job The perfect job does not exist. Every job has its advantages and disadvantages. If you can weigh the good and bad points of jobs that interest you, you should be able to make a wise choice. For instance, Judy Landis wanted to be either a teacher or a nurse—she especially wanted to be in some field of service. She talked with teachers and nurses; she investigated how much money it would cost her to prepare for each field. Most of all, she tried to judge which job would suit her personality better, and which she could do more successfully. Judy kept notes of what she liked and disliked about each job. She finally decided on nursing. This is how she rated nursing:

36

A CAREER IN NURSING

Advantages

Rewarding experience
Opportunity to help humanity
Job has status or prestige
Good preparation for marriage
Opportunity for employment when
 family obligations lighten
Liked hospital work in Y-teens
Jobs always available
Training not too costly
Salaries attractive

Disadvantages

Work confining
Work requires stamina
Not pleasant to watch people suffer
Not always easy to be cheerful

When you think about a future job *you must be realistic* and not let superficial factors affect your choice. For instance, jobs in movies, on television, on the stage, or in the world of fashion sound *glamorous,* but only a few people ever make a really good living in these fields. Being an archaeologist, missionary, or F.B.I. man may sound adventurous but it takes superior physical endurance and infinite patience to become a success. A job in an office may appear to have greater *social prestige* than a job in a factory, but it may not be as satisfying, or even pay as well, sometimes. The social barriers between kinds of jobs are not what they used to be. Some of you may be trying hard to *follow in your parents' footsteps* when you might be better off doing something else.

You will spend the greater part of a day on the job, so *you must be happy in your work.* Your relationships with your employer and fellow workers must be pleasant. You should see some future in your job, so you will have an incentive to work. You will want benefits such as sick leave, paid holidays, an adjustable schedule, retirement pay, reasonable salary increases, and promotion opportunities.

Value of Guidance Counseling

So many new types of jobs and training programs are available today that the young person cannot possibly know about them all. This is why guidance counseling is so important. The counselor keeps constantly informed about many promising openings; also he can give tests which help people find the type of work that suits them best. These tests are based not only on a person's intelligence but also on such equally important factors as drive, creativeness, ability to work with others, and skill in using one's hands.

CASE STUDY: Ginny Bristol had to work hard to get through high school. Her birthday in December made her younger than most others in her class. The school counselor advised that she work for a year before going to college. She wanted to "stay with her friends," so she enrolled in a fashionable girls' college with extremely high standards. She lasted only one semester! Wouldn't it have been better if she had waited just a year?

CASE STUDY: Upon entering college Kevin Lannert was given an aptitude test, but he ignored the results. He knew what he wanted to be—a newspaper reporter. Kevin's grades were good, until he began taking journalism courses. In a course which involved on-the-job training at a local newspaper he almost flunked. Puzzled and upset, Kevin talked with a counselor who checked the aptitude test and solved Kevin's problem.

A formal, scholarly boy, Kevin lacked the outgoing personality a newsman needs to make contacts. Also, he was a perfectionist who rewrote his material several times. This made it hard for him to meet deadlines. These and other traits had shown up on the test two years before, indicating that Kevin was not meant for newspaper work. Kevin changed majors and did much better.

Contrast Kevin's story with that of H. J. Heinz who began by selling vegetables from his family garden and went on to found the huge company which now bears his name, a leader in the foods industry. This was a century ago, before aptitude tests and counseling. Almost by instinct Heinz knew which career to choose. However, most people are like Kevin—they do *not* know.

Big businesses no longer depend on trial and error when selecting people to fill important positions. Over 70 per cent of the country's large corporations use psychological tests to screen job applicants and candidates for promotion. Many people in high school and college, who are uncertain about their own interests, arrange for psychological tests. Almost every large city has a center for psychological services.

At one such service center, Stanford University, Dr. Edward K. Strong Jr. kept a record of personality traits as they related to certain jobs. Using Dr. Strong's findings, other psychologists have continued studies, and have paired personality traits and jobs under seven categories. In four out of five instances, they claim there has been a direct relationship between personality and success in related jobs. Here are their job categories. Perhaps you can use this information to guide some of your decisions.

BIOLOGICAL SCIENCE: (Doctor, dentist, biologist, biochemist) Introspective, analytical, patient. Like precise, creative work with hands. Concerned with objective data. Not too sympathetic with people.

PHYSICAL SCIENCE: (Engineer, mathematician, chemist, physicist) Much the same as above, plus an interest in working with symbols and formulas.

SUB-PROFESSIONAL TECHNICAL: (Mechanic, artisan, farmer, policeman) Introverts interested in things rather than people. Often highly self-sufficient. Limited creativity.

SOCIAL WELFARE: (Clergyman, teacher, social worker, nurse, institutional worker) Idealistic extroverts. Strong interest in people and community affairs.

BUSINESS DETAIL: (Office worker, accountant, banker, purchasing agent, production foreman) Introspective, perfectionists on small details. Often take refuge from people in impersonal matters. Limited creativity. Artisans with paper and pencil.

BUSINESS CONTACT: (Salesman, merchandiser, owner of small business) Strong interest in people, but not necessarily extroverts. Like to influence others.

PERSUASIVE ARTS: (Lawyer, writer, advertising, public relations) Introspective, not particularly sympathetic with people, though they desire to influence others, the lawyer within an established framework, the writer in a world of his own making.

Applying for a Job Whether you are looking for a summer, part-time, or career job, take time to plan. Before you apply, take stock of your own qualifications, interests, experience, and education. It will help to list these things on a data sheet similar to that in the text.

As a rule your first contact with a potential employer will be by letter. Learn as much as you can about the firm before you compose a letter. Make your letter brief, neat, and interesting. You may have to write a letter several times before you are satisfied with it. Your English teacher or vocational counselor will be willing to help. Remember that your letter will be competing with many others. If it makes a good impression, an employer will want to find out more about you. Your personal interview is as important as your letter. Your appearance, poise, and response to questions, your manners, and many other things will give a potential employer a good idea of your qualifications.

Here are points to observe when preparing for a personal interview.

• Do not arrange an interview at a time when many distractions will be on your mind.

• Dress well. Neatness and good taste are essential. Get a good night's sleep before the interview so that you will feel alert.

• Brief yourself. Make a note of the name and address of the interviewer and any facts you know about the firm.

• Be on time or even early. If you find that you will be late, phone and tell briefly why you will be late and what time you will arrive.

• Be at ease. When you enter the office, tell a receptionist or secretary that you have an appointment at a certain time, giving the name of the interviewer. If you are kept waiting more than half an hour, courteously ask someone in the office how long the interviewer will be busy.

• When you are called for your interview, step up and extend your hand if the interviewer offers his or hers. Do not sit down until you are asked to be seated. Sit up straight and gracefully. Listen until you are called upon, then speak in a natural voice. Do not interrupt.

• Do not brag about yourself but at the same time do not be too shy. You may be asked why you are applying for the particular job. Be ready with a good answer.

• If you are asked about salary, you may reply, "That is certainly important, but inasmuch as this is my first job, it is hardly up to me to say." If you have had a previous job, you may mention your salary, and perhaps state that you would like to earn a little more.

• When the interview ends, extend your hand and express your appreciation.

• A day or two after your interview, follow up with a letter thanking the interviewer and expressing the hope that you will hear from him soon. Be sure your letter is neat and correct.

Practice makes perfect. It is a good idea to apply for one or two jobs in which you are only slightly interested so that when you apply for the job you really want, you will be more at ease.

110 Main Street
Edgemont, Pennsylvania
February 18, 1968

Mr. Clarence Davis, Editor
The Morning Monitor
100 Broad Street
Edgemont, Pennsylvania

Dear Mr. Davis:

    I should like to apply for a position on the staff of your newspaper for the summer months. On June 4th I shall be graduated from Edgemont High School. After college, I hope to make journalism my career.

    My favorite subjects have been English and journalism. I have served on the editorial staffs of the school newspaper and yearbook. This year I have been asked to report high school activities to your Teens Topics column.

    If you have an opening on your staff, I shall appreciate having you consider my application. I am enclosing a data sheet and photograph. Should it be advisable to come for a personal interview, I can come any day after school or on Saturday.

        Sincerely,

        Sue James

SAMPLE LETTER

Sue James
110 Main Street
Edgemont, Pa.

SAMPLE DATA SHEET

PERSONAL: Date of birth: November 21, 1951
             Height: 5'5"   Weight: 120 pounds
             Hair: Brown

EDUCATION: Edgemont High School, Edgemont, Pa.   1968
             Academic Course, B+ average
             Editor, yearbook
             Activity editor "News and Views"
             Member Glee Club
             President, Dramatic Club
             Secretary, Westminster Fellowship

SPECIAL   American Field Scholarship between Junior and
RECOGNITION: Senior years in high school (France)
             Second place in county—wide essay contest

HOBBIES   Writing
             Square dancing
             Piano
             Swimming
             Tennis
             Designing clothes
             Collecting old and unusual dolls

EXPERIENCE: Supervised deaf children at play after school
             three afternoons a week
             Worked as volunteer in hospital gift shop and
             snack bar one summer

REFERENCES: Mr. Milton Green, Principal, Edgemont High
             School
             Dr. Raymond Miller, minister, Presbyterian
             Church, Edgemont, Pa.

Staying on a Job Competition is keen for good jobs and for promotions after you have a job. Some people drift from one job to another, while others stay on the same job indefinitely. It is wise to be aware of other jobs and to make an effort to secure better work if it is available. However, it is not advisable to change jobs without a good reason. If you have a job you like, and want to hold it, observe the following suggestions:

· Get to work promptly and regularly.
· Keep up your interest in your work, and do not loaf on the job.
· When you see extra work to be done, do it. Avoid being a clock watcher.
· Continue to "grow" on your job through study, reading, and observing the way things operate.
· Broaden your contacts through professional organizations, clubs, community activities, and church work. These contacts may lead to better jobs.
· Make an effort to get along with your employer and fellow workers.
· Keep up your personal appearance. Good grooming pays!
· Get enough rest and recreation. Eat well balanced meals so that you can work with vitality.

Summer Employment The most easily available summer jobs are related to businesses that are busiest during warm weather. Here is a partial list from which to choose.

Resorts
Day camps
Swimming pools
City parks
National parks
Farms
Food processing plants
Ice cream distributors
Soft drink distributors
Photo finishers
Construction firms
Libraries
Department stores
Mills
Restaurants (especially drive-ins)
Lumber yards
Motels
Travel agencies
Landscape gardeners and nursery operators
Roofers
Breweries
Surveying firms
Service stations
Drive-in movies
Parking lots
Playgrounds

The best job is not always the one that pays the most money. Every year about half a million young people give their time to volunteer work, without pay. Their chief reward is in knowing they have helped others, but there are other benefits. A girl who plans to become a nurse can learn much by working in a hospital. There are opportunities in research laboratories for future scientists. Young people interested in sociology are needed to help with housing surveys and to work with the aged, the blind, and the underprivileged. Playground recreation programs often need volunteers, and so do tutoring programs which are often set up to help students in deprived areas.

Many people have found enjoyable and profitable careers as a result of experience they first gained in volunteer work. Also, college scholarships

42

are often available for people preparing for careers in social work, recreation, and similar occupations. To have worked effectively as a volunteer in these fields is a great advantage toward getting such a scholarship.

ACTIVITIES

1. Conduct a class survey, using questions on the following: the importance of belonging to a group; ideas on success; feelings about honesty; attitudes toward drinking, driving, sex, and religion.

2. Discuss the Angelo Patri quotation compared with your own code for living.

3. List some groups in your school that give status to members. What do you think about college fraternities and sororities?

4. Name some people in public life whom you consider successful. Why do you rate them so? Name some people you know personally who are successful, and tell why they are. What things hinder success? What are some dangers of success?

5. Name some people you know about who used the five keys to success—who took advantage of opportunity, refused to admit defeat, overcame handicaps, broadened contacts, and showed drive and enthusiasm.

6. Discuss some of your own fears and how you overcame them.

7. How do you evaluate honesty? Discuss its value in daily living. If you cheat on a test, or take credit for something you did not do, is anyone hurt? Discuss the honor system as practiced in some schools.

8. Discuss dishonest business practices such as false "bargain sales" and misrepresented guarantees.

9. From the discussion on drinking, make your own observations and discuss your stand. List the things you *gain* and *lose* by drinking. What is moderation in drinking? What do you think of women drinking? Women alcoholics?

10. Discuss both sides of these statements about entertaining at home:
• It costs too much to serve alcoholic beverages.
• If alcoholic drinks are served, soft drinks should be provided also.
• A big party cannot be a success without some kind of alcoholic beverage.
• A host should urge guests to drink.
• If you disapprove of drinking, you should avoid a crowd that drinks a lot.

11. Find out about the operations of Alcoholics Anonymous.

12. **Bulletin Board:** Post stories of traffic accidents from a newspaper; discuss how the accidents might have been avoided.

13. How do you *honestly* feel about obeying traffic laws? Discuss the value of driver training. How much does a driver's permit cost in your state?

14. Discuss state and local punishments for traffic violations, theft, vandalism, sex offenses.

15. Did the architect (page 22) act weakly? What would you have done?

16. How has religious training helped you? How do you expect to handle religious training in your own home?

17. **Bulletin Board:** Assemble copies of the following: Rudyard Kipling's "If"; "The Optimist Creed" from the Optimist International service club; "The Prayer of St. Francis of Assisi"; other quotations concerning character building.

18. List three occupations that interest you. Study these occupations; talk with people in them. In one column list

as many advantages of each occupation, and in another as many disadvantages as you can.

19. Discuss several careers that might be described by each of the following terms—*glamour, adventure, white collar, blue collar, unskilled labor.*

20. List summer jobs in your area that might be good background for careers that interest you.

Correlation

JOURNALISM: Summarize the class survey on attitudes (page 43); publish the results in the school paper.

ENGLISH; HISTORY; SOCIOLOGY: Write a 1,000 word composition on your outlook on life. After it has been corrected, seal it in an envelope. At the end of this course, read Chapter I again, and write another paper on your outlook. Compare your compositions.

Write a brief biography of one of the following, discussing how they attained success in spite of handicaps: Helen Keller, Charles Steinmetz, Edward Trudeau, John Milton, Ludwig van Beethoven, Louis Pasteur, or George Frederick Handel. Read aloud the best biography for each person.

Write a 400-500 word composition on "My Favorite Summer Job," "How I Supplement My Allowance," or "What I'd Look for in a Future Job."

Compose a letter and data sheet for a real or make-believe job. After they have been criticized, type final copies of them. Keep one copy for future reference.

GUIDANCE: Discuss education and jobs with your guidance counselor.

Home Experiences

Ask your parents to read the chapter with you and discuss the quiz on honesty, attitudes toward drinking, driving, success, religious beliefs, education, and jobs.

Select a wholesome quotation that expresses your feelings about life, and post it where you can see it every day. Good sources would be the Bible, or "Words to Live By," written by William Ichabod Nichols. You may want to find several quotations, and post a different one from time to time.

Chapter 2

How Personality Affects Our Roles

It has been said that we have three personalities—the one we think we have, the one others think we have, and the one we strive to achieve. Let's take the case of Jerry Haines and see if this can be true.

CASE STUDY: Jerry, good looking and ambitious, always seemed to fall short of his goal. It caused a personality problem.

By hard work and determination he won a place on the football team but lost it halfway through the season. Later a friend succeeded in being admitted to a college that turned down Jerry's application. Another friend got an excellent summer job that Jerry thought he should have had. Finally, Jerry lost his steady—or thought he did. Possibly she really never went steady with him. With each disappointment, Jerry became more critical and sullen. Each time he blamed someone else for his failure.

Jerry's personality problem could be traced to his choice of objectives, and impossible goals set up by his parents.

Unconsciously, his parents had been comparing Jerry with his more talented sister and more athletic brother. Because Jerry was the oldest, and best looking, his parents thought he should excel in everything. So when Jerry fell short in athletics and scholarship, he tried to gain recognition in another way, by wearing flashy clothes and boasting about how much he was liked by coaches, girls, and others.

The kind of personality Jerry thought would please his parents was too good to be real, but this was the personality he tried to believe he had. The impression others had of him was that of a good looking fellow, highly nervous, too fond of himself, and somewhat a failure.

Jerry finally developed the kind of personality he was striving for when he attended a small college away from home. His good looks, natural ability, and fine home background began to show up more as pressures were lifted. Not being pressed to excel, he relaxed and became not only a good student but also a good athlete and one of the most valuable members of his fraternity.

TYPES OF PERSONALITIES

Introvert and Extrovert Many attempts have been made to classify personalities. Most of you are familiar with the terms *introvert* and *extrovert,* first used by Carl G. Jung, a world renowned Swiss psychologist. The *extrovert* likes people and activity, adjusts readily to social situations and is not easily discouraged or offended. The *introvert* prefers to work with ideas or things, feels uneasy in social situations, and may be sensitive to criticism.

However, it is difficult to draw a line and say, "These people are extroverts and those are introverts." There are actually few people at either extreme. We *tend* to be one or the other, but the majority of people are *ambiverts*—fluctuating between timidity and self-assurance according to circumstances. It is to one's advantage to be adaptable.

Another way of classifying personalities is by masculine and feminine traits. Anthropologist Margaret Mead believes that no one is completely masculine or feminine, but that everyone has tendencies of both kinds.

Ideal Types In clothing classes you may have used such terms as *gamine, dramatic, ingenue,* and *romantic.* These are ideal types—oversimplified for easy description. Such terms are useful when applied to fashions, but personalities are too complex to be described so simply. A model may be able to wear ingenue fashions quite well, yet be a most sophisticated person. (Ingenue, as you may know, means naive and childlike, just the opposite of sophisticated.)

At various times a person may seem to have traits of several ideal personality types; seldom if ever is a person found whose behavior consistently fits one of these types. Therefore it is best not to describe persons in terms of ideal types. As psychologist G. W. Allport has said, such terms were "invented in the armchair and not in the laboratory."

CLUES TO PERSONALITY

A stranger, seeing you in a crowd would notice your dress and grooming first of all, perhaps your mannerisms next. Upon meeting you, the way you spoke would be another clue to your personality. After closer acquaintance, your hobbies and interests also might be clues to your personality.

Appearance A plainly dressed person might give one impression, a gaudily dressed person another, and a person in high fashion clothes still another. Of course, you will want to make the most of your appearance. When you wear becoming, appropriate clothes, are well groomed, and watch your posture, you will make a good first impression. *First impressions are important.*

Mannerisms Little mannerisms of which we are often completely unconscious can give others the wrong impression. Yet few of us like to be reminded of our faults.

46

Expressions such as, "You know," "I mean," "In other words," or "See," when repeated frequently, can become very annoying.

CASE STUDY: Ann Jarvey and Don Allen had been going steady for a long time, but Ann over-used an expression "That's neat!" which came to annoy Don. Everything was *neat*—a test mark, a party, a new blouse. On the class trip to Washington, D. C., our national documents were neat—so were the paintings in the National Art Gallery, the statue of Lincoln in the Lincoln Memorial, and the boat ride to Mount Vernon.

Each time Ann used neat, Don made note of a substitute adjective. Finally, when she met Don in the hotel lobby for dinner, Ann said, "Gee, you look neat!" Don reached into his pocket and handed Ann the card with this note, "How about retiring *neat?* Here are twenty good adjectives to substitute; take your choice." Ann had a sense of humor but pretended to look puzzled, "Can't find the right one," she said. "I'll add one. Let me have your pencil." She wrote, "Gee, you look SWELL tonight!" and passed the slip back to Don. But Ann stopped saying neat.

Have you ever stopped to think about some of the things that detract from a person's personality? Here are a few:

Showing off
Talking all the time
Interrupting conversation
Picking your teeth
Biting your nails
Chewing gum
Flattering everyone
Scratching your head

Delta Air Lines

A pleasant smile and a sincere interest in others are signs of a good personality.

Talking baby talk
Moving your hands nervously
Slurping soup
Twisting your ear or hair
Slouching in your seat

If you have any of these or other habits that might annoy people, you will want to be aware of them and try to correct them.

CASE STUDY: Caroline Day was extremely nervous about any new situation. She always sought to control her nervousness by chewing gum. When she was a bridesmaid in a wedding she nearly ruined her part by chewing gum as she walked down the aisle. Someone was able to attract her attention before she walked very far. Poor Caroline had to swallow the gum.

Voice and Personality Few of us stop to think of the effect our voices have upon others, or what they reveal about the way we feel. For instance, it is claimed by psychologists that the progress of a mentally ill patient can be traced by listening to tape recordings. If he is depressed, his voice will be soft, slow, and low. If he is angry, his voice will be high, fast, and loud. If he is tense and anxious, he will hesitate and repeat. Consider the effect one's voice has upon others in the following remarks:

"You know very well who was in line for that job. I guess his voice was against him. When you meet the public you must have a pleasing voice."

"It looks as if Dr. Clyde isn't going to last long as a preacher. Before his sermon is over, I get the fidgets. That preacher tone of his!"

"Isn't it a shame that Evelyn stutters. She is so attractive but stuttering has done something to her personality."

The first fellow had a nasal voice of which he was not aware until he signed up for a course in public speaking. Speech therapy eventually corrected his voice defect, and he was promoted later.

Dr. Clyde's voice affectation came from trying to sound impressive. Unfortunately, no one dared tell him he should use a natural tone.

Evelyn needed a long time to correct her speech difficulty, but with help she learned to speak with scarcely any trace of stuttering.

It is said that only five persons in every hundred have naturally pleasing voices. Study the common voice defects in relation to your own voice.

If possible, make tape recordings. Note your shortcomings and try to overcome them.

SLURRING: The Bell Telephone Company lists this as the number one defect. For instance, "J'eat yet?" or, "Whyncha c'mover?" Can you translate? If people ask you to repeat often, you are probably slurring your words. Slurring is usually the result of carelessness. To correct this defect, read aloud before a mirror; practice listening to and imitating good radio or TV voices.

VOICE WEAKNESS: If, while you are talking, people begin to interrupt, your voice may be uncertain, shy, and weak. A weak voice is the result of poor breath control and sometimes timidity. Practice singing; read aloud.

NASAL VOICE: This is one of the most common voice defects, but one that is not difficult to correct.

HIGH PITCH: You know of people whose voices carry above all others. You wish sometimes they would lower their voices just a little. It may take time to learn to pitch one's voice lower, but it can be done.

FLAT MONOTONE: Some people speak with little inflection. Showing genuine interest in conversation will help overcome a monotonous quality.

Hobbies and Interests Psychologists have attempted to tie in hobbies and interests with certain personalities. Their findings indicate that people who like gardening and outdoor life are often well balanced mentally, and feel secure and contented most of the time; people who like working with tools are usually well adjusted; those with musical and artistic hobbies tend to

48

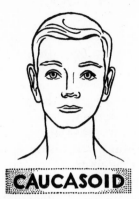

Our racial heredity stems from three great races: Mongoloid, representing 43 per cent of the world's population; Caucasoid, 33 per cent; Negroid, 24 per cent. Although each race has its own physical characteristics, no race is biologically superior.

be sensitive and high strung; and those who enjoy collections are likely to have good minds. Do you agree with these findings?

UNDERSTANDING OUR PERSONALITIES

To understand how personality develops we should know something about heredity and environment as well as causes for our actions and reactions. Let's take the case of two brothers, Roger and Chris Soderman.

CASE STUDY: At seventeen, Roger is six feet tall and weighs nearly two hundred pounds. He has dark brown hair and blue eyes. He has a high IQ but his marks are only a little above average. A leader, he has held class offices every year. He gets along well with people. He is kind, and seems concerned about the welfare of others.

Chris, a year younger, is five feet eight inches tall and weighs one hundred and forty pounds. He has blonde hair, blue eyes, and a high IQ. He gets very high marks. He plays basketball and tennis. He is not interested in school offices but prefers to spend his spare time reading. Although he is sympathetic towards others who have problems, he is not deeply concerned.

How can we explain the differences as well as similarities in the two brothers? We can attempt to explain their physical appearance and mental ability by *heredity* and their attitudes by *environment*. Heredity is both racial and ancestral. We are all descended from three great races—Caucasoid, Negroid, and Mongoloid. Each race has its own distinguishing characteristics. When people of two different races marry, certain physical traits will become dominant and others recessive.

Roger and Chris inherited their racial and family traits. Being descended from the Caucasoid race, they have the basic skin coloring and general features of that race. From their parents, grandparents and great grandparents, they inherited ancestral characteristics. Their maternal grandfather was very tall, but their paternal grandfather was short. Their mother has blonde hair; their father's is dark brown. Their parents and grandparents had above average intelligence, as indicated by the positions they held

49

in business. This background would account for the boys' stature, coloring, and general intelligence.

The Influence of Heredity In the case of Roger and Chris heredity and environment were about equally important. In some instances heredity may be more important than environment and the opposite may also be true.

Which do you think is likely to produce a healthy plant—good seed planted in poor soil or poor seed planted in good soil? Often people with poor heredity also have poor environment and those with good heredity, good environment. For instance the Bach, Darwin, and Wedgwood families had both good heredity and good environment. The Bachs produced musicians for two hundred years. The Darwins and Wedgwoods produced leaders in science, the fine arts, and other fields as well.

Much research is now being done on the problem of birth defects. It is claimed that no more than 20 per cent of birth defects can be traced to heredity. Abnormality in a child may be caused by a *chemical* defect when a bad gene or genes unite, or by a *chromosome* defect which may produce a mongoloid child. Birth defects can be prevented to some extent, especially if the physician can diagnose the problem early enough in pregnancy.

An expectant mother's health problems can cause birth defects. For example, an abnormal baby may be born if the mother contracts *German measles* during the first twelve weeks of pregnancy. (A vaccine for this disease is in the experimental stage.) In the early 1960's a drug called *thalid-omide* was given to many women during pregnancy. A number of defective children were born in Europe and America, apparently because of this drug. Not all mothers reacted in the same way to the drug, but the danger was great enough to have the drug withdrawn from the market.

There are enough real causes behind abnormal births without adding imaginary ones. Years ago many people used to trace birthmarks, hare lips, and similar defects to some experience the mother had during pregnancy. There is no scientific basis for such beliefs.

There is, however, some truth in the saying that the oldest child in the family has the best chances for success. Environment may be a factor, because the first child is likely to receive a great deal of care and attention from both parents, at least until a second child arrives. However, if you are not the oldest child in the family, don't let it worry you. Benjamin Franklin was the fifteenth of seventeen children.

A number of studies have revealed that children born to a mother who is between 21 and 26 have somewhat better than average chances of being superior physically and mentally. Environment again may be a factor because some older parents may not be able to give their children quite as much attention as younger parents can. On the other hand, many superior persons have been born to mothers in their thirties and even in their late forties.

To determine the influence of heredity and environment, several sets of twins were separated as young orphans and reared under different home conditions, then brought together at maturity. They were found to have retained their outward resemblances, but their personalities were different. Those reared in isolated areas with little education became withdrawn, whereas those who had the benefit of a more socially active home and better education appeared more alert and interested in life. These differences seemed to go deep.

Some of the things we inherit are bone structure; coloring of skin, hair,

Gregor Mendel's discoveries in crossing peas laid the basis for genetics or the prediction of inherited traits.

MENDEL'S PEAS

R = dominant red genes

W = recessive white genes

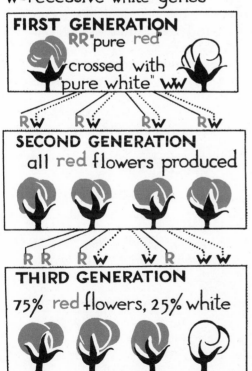

and eyes; and native intelligence. We may inherit a *susceptibility* to a number of diseases, including diabetes, rheumatic fever, tuberculosis, anemia, cancer, certain heart diseases, allergies, and forms of deafness and blindness. If the same condition has been present in the families of two people who marry, the chances of passing on the condition increase.

Occasionally a handicapped or ugly child is born to healthy, fine-looking parents, or a beautiful child to homely parents. *Chance* is a big factor in determining the traits of the new individual. Normal parents are not likely to have some hidden defect which will show up in their children.

For normal parents, there is one chance in sixteen that a child will be born with some defect. In marriages between close relatives, the chances

Heredity and environment are two strong influences on personality.

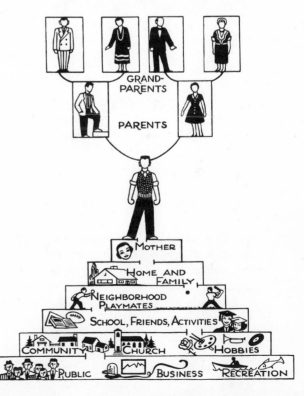

51

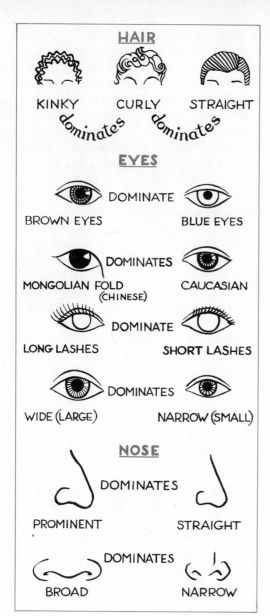

HAIR

KINKY | CURLY | STRAIGHT

dominates   *dominates*

EYES

BROWN EYES — DOMINATE — BLUE EYES

MONGOLIAN FOLD (CHINESE) — DOMINATES — CAUCASIAN

LONG LASHES — DOMINATE — SHORT LASHES

WIDE (LARGE) — DOMINATES — NARROW (SMALL)

NOSE

PROMINENT — DOMINATES — STRAIGHT

BROAD — DOMINATES — NARROW

Some genes are dominant and other recessive in passing traits from one generation to another.

increase because each may carry a "recessive gene" for a certain abnormality and increase the danger of union.

Multiple births tend to be hereditary. In the United States, twins oc-cur once in every 90 births; triplets once in every 8,000 births; and quadruplets once in every 700,000 births. The birth of the Dionne quintuplets in 1934 was a most rare incident in that all were of the same sex and all lived beyond infancy. The Fischer quintuplets, born in 1963, were not all of the same sex.

Nature, in passing on characteristics, seems to follow a pattern. About a century ago an Austrian monk, Gregor Mendel, became interested in the heredity of flowering peas. In his small monastery garden he conducted experiments that later proved to be as applicable to humans as to plants.

His concern arose over the fact that only red flowers resulted when seeds from red peas were mated with seeds from white peas. But when he carried his experiments through to the third generation, he found one white flower and three red flowers among the family of four. We refer to the genes producing the red peas as *dominant* and the genes producing the white peas as *recessive*. Recessive traits may be temporarily hidden.

The laws of Mendel briefly are:

Inherited characteristics are carried by genes, which are unchanged from generation to generation.

Genes are found in pairs in each individual. When the pairs are unlike, one gene dominates the other.

At conception, only one gene of each pair unites with its counterpart to produce the offspring's characteristics.

Although physical and mental traits may not be forecast accurately, scientists have found out many things concerning heredity:

- All humans potentially may mate and produce offspring.
- The children of two relatively tall people will likely be taller than the average but not always as tall as either parent. The children of two short people will tend to be short but not necessarily as short as their parents. If one parent is tall and the other short, the children will incline toward the shorter parent.
- More males than females tend to be bald. However, it is thought that the tendency toward baldness is often passed down through the female line.
- More men than women are color blind—four per cent against less than one half of one per cent.
- Certain genes are dominant when they unite to determine physical traits. The illustration shows what happens.

Gerber Baby Foods

Learning to get along with brothers and sisters is one of the first steps in personality development.

The Influence of Environment Since the time you were born, your environment has influenced your personality. Home, family, school, church, and community have had a direct or indirect influence upon your actions and attitudes. People you know, the job you will get, and the contacts you will make, can alter your personality. Personality is not static.

Family relationships influence personality. Children need love, security, companionship, approval, and praise as much as they need food, clothing, and shelter. When these needs are not met, they feel neglected and rejected. As a result they may resent anything people do for them, try by any means possible to demand attention, or perhaps withdraw completely from everyone.

- If parents go to the opposite extreme—become overprotective or overindulgent, a child also suffers. It is difficult for parents of an only child or parents who have lost one of two children not to feel anxious and concerned. But when parents fail to "wean a child away" as he develops, they deny him opportunities to mature normally.
- Authoritative or overstrict parents often make too high demands of their children, who feel set apart from their friends.
- Parents who overdo the father-son or mother-daughter relationship make it difficult for children to adjust normally to their peers.
- When parents fail to grant them the usual freedoms, children become submissive—or defiant.
- When parents fluctuate between

53

stern discipline and laxity, children grow up frustrated.

Yet the situation is not as difficult as it sounds! Why not approach it from the positive side—the meaning of good parenthood? Every child needs to be loved for what he is, and accepted despite faults over which he has no control.

• It is not a child's fault if he is not as attractive physically as other children, or as bright or capable. Many unattractive children who have loving families develop attractive personalities. When groups have been asked to list traits they like or do not like about a person, these traits more often represent unlikable things he *does* rather than what he *is*. Thus you might say you don't like a certain "little pipsqueak." Actually you don't care about his size; you dislike his show-off manner.

• The good parent knows that a child needs discipline as well as freedom. He needs the security proper discipline provides and the independence certain freedoms provide. Remember your own younger days!

• Praise, approval, and thoughtful little acts are as necessary in family relationships as in school or at work. Could you enjoy school if you never received a kind word for your work? Praising a person when he does well often helps more than scolding him when he does poorly.

• Rivalry within a family often affects personality. When a new baby arrives or another child is singled out for attention, even a well-adjusted brother can become jealous. The wise parent lets older children help, and discusses the baby with them, rather than shutting them out.

• Parents lose their children's respect if they threaten punishment for doing wrong, but never enforce these threats. Parents who support each other along this line seem to rear excellent children. If your parents are happy, interested in others, able to meet emergencies, and have a sense of humor, you will be likely to "borrow" those traits. If they are tense, irritable, easily upset, interested only in themselves, you may imitate them, whether you want to or not.

• Parents have deep influence on children's religious, political, and racial attitudes. They must think wisely in these fields, and set up high standards.

The varied experiences of scouting help to develop independence and co-operation, two ingredients of a good adult personality.

Giving a child responsibility may take time and direction, but the child gains in initiative and independence.

54

• Children who have been overprotected or too sternly disciplined at home may have trouble adjusting in school. The neglected child also may suffer. If a child has heard his mother say frequently, "I'll be glad when you are in school so I can have some time to myself," he is likely to develop bad attitudes toward both home and school. This leads to the question of outside influences.

School and other outside influences affect personality. School makes new demands, hence six is often a trying age. Regular daily competition occurs for the first time. Each child reacts differently to competition, whether he succeeds or fails.

Being left out of a group, or being given undue recognition, can harm personality unless a person is a good judge of values. If a child learns to communicate easily with others, takes his share of responsibility, and acquires normal social skills as he grows up, he will have less trouble adjusting.

Community life—or lack of it—also affects personality. Junior Achievement groups, amateur theaters, fund drives, fellowship organizations, church groups, political campaigns, and other community activity can be very beneficial. We can't "live in a shell," or our personality will suffer. You will be smart to take an interest in worthwhile activities.

The transition from school to work (or to military service) can create personality problems. Living at home and holding a summer job is far different from having to depend upon a job for support (or living under military regimentation). How you adjust to the demands and competition for promotion in service or on a job, how well you learn to get along with others whose backgrounds and values may differ from yours, will mean much to you.

If you can be happy and successful at work, it will show in your personality. Look for the following "assists" from any prospective position:
• Praise and recognition, as well as a satisfactory salary, good hours, and special benefits.
• The privilege of voicing your grievances to an understanding employer. Avoid an employer who is stern and demanding. When your boss keeps you informed about your progress, listens to questions, and responds well to constructive criticism, the job environment will help make you a better person.
• Appreciation of the importance of your job from friends and family. If they belittle or criticize your work, you will become dissatisfied and irritable.

Being thoughtful of older people—parents, grandparents, older friends, teachers—is another sign of a mature personality.

Hallmark Cards

Personalities are less likely to clash when each individual has a clear understanding of his responsibilities.

• A challenge to become absorbed in your work. When you are interested only in watching the clock, a career becomes just a bore, and your indifference can harm your personality.

• Opportunity and ability to achieve what is expected of you. When you accept unsuitable work that places you under an unreasonable strain, your disposition will be affected. Some work requires mathematical ability or good space perception; some requires motor skills—quick reactions, coordination, and manipulation; other work demands high resistance to fatigue, good eyesight, or steady nerves; still

Ability to communicate with others in the classroom or on the job, as well as on social occasions, is a major step toward personality development.

other calls for mental finesse and exceptional social skills. If you have the skills and interests that your job requires, you will be happy. "Square pegs in round holes" do not work out very well, to say the least.

However, the fact that a person has a certain ability does not always mean that he will be successful in that field. For instance, a person may get high marks in mathematics and science courses, but not be interested in engineering; or he may excel in public speaking and debate, but make a much better journalist than lawyer. A good handshaker with a friendly smile may find public service rather than selling to be his field. *Interest* must accompany *aptitude,* or a person will not be well adjusted.

• Congenial co-workers. One dominating person who is out of harmony with others can cause personality clashes.

• A clear understanding of your responsibilities through written and verbal instructions, and a reasonable idea of what you may expect in a few years, if you make satisfactory progress on the job. When you do not know where you stand, or where you are going, you are likely to become indifferent. In military as well as civilian work, seek "sub" goals which lead to future gains.

This brief discussion of relationships in your daily environment is meant not only to help you understand your personality better, but to strive to improve it. Investigate further on your own. It is a vital subject.

Aside from hereditary and environmental influences, personality is affected by the way we react to circumstances.

The Influence of Defense Mechanisms —besides its other functions—warns us of danger or steers us from things we should not do. Emotional "triggers" cause us to protect ourselves from harm or displeasure in different ways. Psychologists call these reactions "defense mechanisms," and have given them names. You have all had experience in the following situations at some time. When you *habitually* use any defense mechanism, your personality may suffer.

The marvelous network of our nervous system

FLIGHT: When we run from problems we fear or cannot solve, the flight defense is at work. Flight can be physical or mental. We may simply quit a class. Or, instead of paying attention we may "take flight" by daydreaming. Of course, daydreaming may sometimes be a sign of creativeness. When Edison, Einstein, and a few other brilliant thinkers appeared to be daydreaming, they were creating. We may need to daydream sometimes, but when we resort to it as a release from responsibility, we lessen our achievement ability. People lose respect for us.

FIGHT: Some people, instead of running away from a troublesome incident or an opponent, "fight the air." They become needlessly cross and abusive about something they have to do. For instance, when you leave for school in the morning, your mother

The flight reaction may show up early. Which children are listening to the little story teller? Which ones are taking flight into their own fantasies?

Brashear Association, Pittsburgh

57

may remind you to do some unpleasant task. If you bang the door, throw your books down, or shout around "to let off steam," you are using the fight defense.

If you have a reputation for either "flight" or "fight" in the face of routine problems, you give people a bad opinion of your personality. Actually, you degrade yourself. To face a problem coolly and solve it is better in every way. Concentrating on your task with full power will give true release to emotions.

SUBLIMATION: This means directing your excess energy from a primitive aim into more desirable channels—sports, writing, social service, helping at home, in school, at church, or in the community.

COMPENSATION: Perhaps you have heard someone remark, "It is his way' of compensating." When a social or physical handicap prevents a person from accomplishing certain goals, he may attempt to overcome this obstacle by trying to excel in other ways. This is a normal defense reaction. For instance, when a boy is just average in school work, he may go all out for

athletics, or when a girl lacks leadership ability, she may make more than average effort in music or scholarship. Of course, this is not true of all athletes, musicians, or scholars!

Compensation may be good or bad. For instance, a person who is not handsome may develop an unusually friendly or kind personality. This is good. Frequently, such people in later years become more popular than their more attractive classmates who may have depended too greatly upon looks. Compensation is bad when a poorly adjusted person compensates for lack of attention by turning to scandalous living or crime. A lonely or insecure person may resort to overeating and heavy drinking to make up for a lack of pleasant companionship.

NEGATIVISM: Some people always respond in the negative, out of habit or because they are afraid of responsibility. Some people may not say "No," but will go out of their way to avoid doing what is expected of them. A child told not to step in the mud may deliberately do so. As a person grows older, he may not be quite that childish, but he may decline all invi-

People with well adjusted personalities enjoy fellow workers and are likely to be successful in their work.

Delta Air Lines

58

Children imitate their elders. Little boys may try to smoke and little girls like to play mother. Adults set a behavior pattern for children.

tations, expecting to be coaxed. This response may arise from real timidity, making it difficult to change. Such people, unless they realize their problem, may go through life unco-operative, listless, stubborn, or rebellious. To correct negativism, examine your own responses to suggestions from others. After that, you can break the habit, if you are over-negative.

IDENTIFICATION: We have talked about the need for belonging. Whether we belong to a crowd or not we like to be identified with people our own age, to dress and act like them. Hero worship is another form of identification which shows up in adolescence. Early in life, children seek identification by acting the roles of their mother or father. When we seek to be identified with the right group, this is a good defense mechanism; but when the group has poor standards, identification will harm you.

INTROJECTION: Not only do we like to dress like others; sometimes we even try to make our religious beliefs and moral attitudes similar to those of our friends, or of some fashionable group. Our friends, however, may have unrealistically high standards, impossible to achieve; society may seem to encourage things that we feel are wrong. In changing our moral viewpoint, the questions to ask are: "Does this change satisfy *my* needs? Or am I changing in an attempt to please someone else? Will it really work?"

PROJECTION: When we try to blame other people or circumstances for our own mistakes, we are using projection. This is certainly true of Jerry Haines, page 45. Usually a person criticizes in others the qualities he unconsciously dislikes about himself.

IDEALIZATION: High ideals are desirable, but they must be based on reality, or they will not be obtainable. For instance, a girl may seek the counterpart of her father in a mate (or a boy the counterpart of his mother). Seldom do these people find an ideal husband or wife. The ideal is based on an image of someone else. An example of this is found in the case study under *Toward a Successful Marriage,* page 209.

DISPLACEMENT: When a person feels unwanted or loses a loved one, he may transfer affection to a dog or cat. After a broken engagement, the injured party often seeks another partner quickly, and even may marry just to fill an emotional need—to prove that he is still desirable. In moderate degree, this defense mechanism is good. We would become very melancholy if we could not substitute friends or activities to fill a void in our lives. But be sure you are not just feeling sorry for yourself on some trivial excuse. Many people do. And never make an important decision when strong jealousy or injured feelings can prevent you from thinking clearly.

RATIONALIZATION: When we do a thing that is not quite right, or neglect our obligations, we often try to justify our actions. We make excuses for our failures, and pretend that the things we should have done were not very important anyway. This is the "sour grapes" reaction. For instance, you want very much to have the lead in the class play; when someone else gets it, you say, "I didn't want it anyway, especially with exams coming up right afterward." Or you get a bad report card and say, "Well, other things are more important than grades."

It is much more mature to analyze a disappointment and try to avoid having a similar thing happen again than to continue to fail through planless thinking. You might kid yourself, but no one else.

Changes in Personality Personality may change when a person does not have the inner strength to face and overcome obstacles or disappointments. Crucial periods for personality change are during adolescence, upon leaving home for school or a job, upon marriage or the birth of a child, during late middle age (especially for women), after retirement, and upon the death of a loved one.

Drugs can also cause personality to change. Even relatively mild drugs, such as the so-called "pep pills," can have this effect. These pills, more properly called *amphetamines* or *barbiturates*, do have a proper use. When used correctly they can help a person to stay alert, and a doctor can prescribe them as an aid in psychiatric treatment. However, when used improperly they are a danger to health and can cause a person to act irrationally and violently.

The dangers of more powerful drugs are truly frightening. For instance, research shows that using LSD may cause a person's children to be born with severe abnormalities. Does anyone have the right to take such a chance?

At one famous university several students tried LSD. When four of them had to be sent to mental hospitals, the rest quickly stopped. Though sad, this story offers hope that people are learning the dangers of powerful drugs.

The Drug Abuse Control Act, which became law in 1966, is a step toward solving this problem. Do you think, though, that the real answer will come from laws? Or will it come from responsible people, young and old, realizing that drugs must be used properly?

Complexes and Personality Many of us develop complexes about certain things. At one extreme is the *inferiority* complex and at the other the *superiority* complex.

Many of us imagine we have an inferiority complex. Under certain conditions, anyone can feel inferior. A psychologist, who feels at ease with a group of educators, may feel out of place or inferior at a gathering of engineers, or a business tycoon may

PERSONALITY ANALYSIS

Do not write in this book.

	Satisfied	Should Improve	Have Improved
Appearance			
Weight (_____)			
Posture and poise			
Grooming			
Facial expression			
Clothes (neatness, attractiveness)			
Behavior			
Disposition			
Interest in others			
Courtesy toward family and friends			
Approach to personal problems			
Appreciation of the rights of others			
Dependability			
Enthusiasm			
Initiative			
Emotions			
Ability to control fear			
Ability to control anger			
Capability for expressing love			
Capability for showing gratitude			
Conversation			
Tone of voice			
Ability to listen			
Ability to contribute to conversation			
Interests			
Knowledge of sports			
Knowledge of current events			
Reading background			
Hobbies			
Skill in games			
Attitudes			
Toward family			
Toward classmates			
Toward teachers and other adults			
Regarding sex			
Regarding the spending of money			
Regarding religion			
Regarding work and study			
Habits			
Promptness to classes and meals			
Orderliness in school work and at home			
Regularity in eating			
Regularity in sleeping			
Obligations in regard to borrowing and returning favors			
Other personal habits			

feel inferior among a group of symphonic musicians. These feelings are temporary and do not indicate an abnormal personality.

Sometimes there are real causes for an inferiority complex, such as a physical handicap, poverty, or repeated failures. In such cases, professional help might be needed. Most of the time inferiority feelings are imaginary, and more pronounced in people who think mainly about themselves. Feelings of inferiority may be controlled by keeping busy, doing things for others, observing attractive traits in people, and trying to acquire those traits. However, a person who is naturally quiet would be unhappy if he tried to be a show-off, and a person who is full of enthusiasm would feel miserable trying to be retiring.

A show-off may give the impression of having a superiority complex, but usually he is inwardly insecure. By putting on a bold front, he thinks he conveys an impression of importance. Other people may actually become aloof or conceited because of constant praise. Success can "go to a person's head" and give him a superiority complex. You may know someone who firmly believes he is great. Lord Chesterfield, in *Letters to His Son,* wrote, "Never seem wiser . . . than the people you are with." It is good advice to remember.

Some men, in positions of leadership, must act overconfident, even conceited, but a good leader will not exploit his ego at the expense of others.

By knowing that all of your traits are explainable, you can understand yourself better and work toward improving your personality.

After discussing the meaning of terms that may be new to you, check yourself on the Personality Analysis Chart (page 61), now and at the end of the course. If you place MY before each term, you will be able to answer more effectively.

Words and Phrases to Know

attitude	heredity
compensation	identification
complex	inferiority complex
defense mechanism	introjection
dominant (gene)	introvert
ego	negativism
environment	personality
extrovert	projection
genes	rationalize
genetics	recessive (gene)

ACTIVITIES

1. Bring to class an interesting picture of yourself as a child—not a baby picture. Number them and pass them around the room, or mount them on the bulletin board. Give a prize from the homemaking food center to the person who guesses the most pictures correctly.

2. Cite cases (no names) you know about that remind you of Jerry Haines (page 45).

3. List several TV personalities. Tell why you like or dislike them. How do you decide whether you like famous people whom you know only by reputation or by seeing them in films and on TV? Discuss the difficulty of judging people you know personally by comparing them with celebrities.

4. Elect a class member to tell briefly the story of *Dr. Jekyll and Mr. Hyde*

by Robert Louis Stevenson. Discuss this split personality.

5. List two or three of your favorite hobbies. Do they seem to fit in with the remarks about hobbies and personality?

6. Act out situations in school, on the street, at home, and at a friend's home that show socially immature personalities. Discuss a better approach to each situation.

7. What mannerisms do you consider most annoying? How would you suggest telling others of their faults?

8. List and comment on television personalities who have good voices, and others who have characteristic accents. List some whose voices irritate you, and discuss them in regard to voice defects mentioned in this chapter.

9. Make a diagram of your own "family tree" back to your grandparents, indicating height, bone structure, hair, eye and skin coloring.

10. Using the "family trees," discuss hereditary features as applied to individuals in class.

11. Discuss inherited traits that cannot be changed by environment.

12. From personal observation, mention instances of inherited susceptibility to a disease; of other definite family traits being transmitted.

13. Discuss situations that might give a person an *inferiority* complex—a *superiority* complex. Discuss how each may be overcome.

14. Think of cases in which parents have been neglectful, too authoritative, or over-protective. How were children affected?

15. Discuss some adjustments you have had to make to school, social life, or a job.

16. List defense mechanisms on the chalkboard, and discuss each according to your own experience. Observe members of your own class in relation to their use of defense mechanisms.

Correlation

ENGLISH: To improve your skill in conversation, invite an English teacher to discuss common errors in the use of grammar.

Select a famous person who has influenced history and write a sketch of his life in about 600 words. Indicate how inheritance and circumstances may have influenced that person's traits.

Write a three or four page composition on how you think heredity and environment have affected your personality. If you believe you have shortcomings, how can you overcome them?

SOCIOLOGY: Discuss the chart showing how people from various parts of the world have sprung from three races: Caucasoid, Negroid, Mongoloid.

Invite your sociology teacher to discuss customs of other nations and how these customs might have originated.

SPEECH: Arrange with the speech teacher to spend a class period discussing exercises or remedies for voice defects.

Home Experiences

Ask your mother and father to tell you something about character traits of your grandparents and great grandparents.

Observe behavior of your family members and try to recognize some of the emotional reactions discussed in class.

Chapter 3

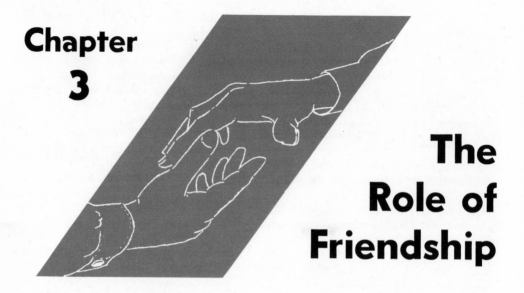

The Role of Friendship

An 11-year-old boy, who had recently moved to a new community, was asked by his grandmother how he liked school. Looking a little puzzled he replied, "The first day, I didn't have any friends. Last week I had lots of friends. Now I've got friends and enemies."

This little boy was wise beyond his years.

Volumes have been written on how to make people like us, and much of the advice has a sound basis; still the phenomenon remains—we have definite likes and dislikes, we are liked and disliked, and we do not always know why. Often, people who are well liked by some, may, with those same traits, repel others.

I do not like thee Dr. Fell.
The reason why I cannot tell,
But this I know and know full well,
I do not like thee, Dr. Fell.

A student wrote the above verse on a wall at Oxford University many years ago.

How often have you come from your first class under a new teacher with such a feeling? Have you changed your mind after becoming better acquainted?

When new students come to your school do you make an effort to know them before you form opinions? We can find likable qualities in nearly everyone if we look for them. Friendship is a kind of pleasant feeling which envelops persons and makes them accept each other with their shortcomings as well as their good points, without trying to make them over. Do you have friends you like very much *in spite of their faults?*

FRIENDLINESS BEGINS WITH THE FAMILY

Families who enjoy entertaining their friends, and their children's friends, have more fun than others. Art Linkletter feels we should seize every chance to entertain. When we postpone entertaining until we "move into a larger home," "get the house-cleaning done," "have enough silver and china," or "more time," we never accomplish our ends.

People who grow up in a friendly family, and in a neighborhood of friendly families, should find it easy to make friends. Yet, some people from small, friendly towns often keep to themselves at first when they leave home to work in a big city, attend a large college, or enter military service. Friendliness is more important than ever in these situations. Some people can feel more lonely in a crowd than in a mountain retreat! When one person has the initiative to "break the ice" in strange surroundings, he usually finds that others have felt just as timid and lonely as he. They are as shy about approaching him as he is about them.

Although it is well to be friendly in a large group, you should not be in too great a rush about forming close friendships. Some people "wear well." Others do not. You can be discriminating about forming friendships without being snobbish to people who are not your close friends.

Families active in PTA, community groups, scouts, and church work, usually like people and enjoy having guests in their homes. When family members share work as well as fun, disappointment as well as pleasure among themselves, they rarely have trouble getting along with others. Children tend to reflect their parents' pleasure in enjoying friends, so they in turn make an effort to take part in activities. This leads to learning how to work harmoniously with others, which is as much of an accomplishment as being a good musician or athlete.

PARTICIPATE IN ACTIVITIES

Interests and Hobbies Expanding your interests will broaden your circle of friends, give you more self-confidence, contribute to good mental and physical health, and enrich your life. If you do not develop worthwhile interests while you are young, you probably will not do so later. You soon may become satisfied to spend too much spare time

Sometimes we find out how to make friends too late!

Point Park College, Pittsburgh

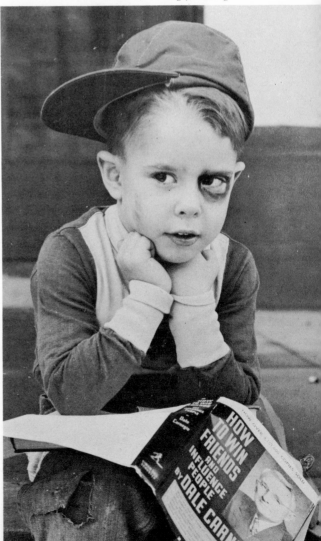

65

watching TV and movies. You may limit your reading to the daily paper and a few magazines—or less. Every homemaker should have at least one outside activity to provide relief from daily routine.

Some of your present activities may carry over into later life—others may not. After studying the following list, select activities that you think you will enjoy now and later.

OUTDOOR RECREATION. The season, and region in which you live, will determine your choice of outdoor activities, but people of all ages enjoy the following: swimming, golf, tennis, water or snow skiing, bicycling, camping, boating, roller skating or ice skating, croquet, shuffleboard, fishing, hunting, and hiking.

INDOOR RECREATION. Although you may think you don't like bridge and other card or table games, you will find that it helps socially to know something about playing cards—especially bridge. In some high schools, students learn to play bridge and chess during the noon hour. In addition, singing, instrumental music, dancing, and bowling are popular recreations.

READING: Now is a good time to start building your personal library.

Mobile Homes Manufacturing Association
Friendliness begins with the family.

Mention to friends and relatives that you would like to receive books as birthday, Christmas, and graduation gifts. Your school or community librarian will help you to compile a list of books that you will want to have for permanent reference.

When you are interested in reading, it is much easier to become a good conversationalist.

OTHER CULTURAL INTERESTS: In many communities, civic art centers, the YM and YWCA, YM and YWHA offer courses in painting, ceramics, photography, drama, sewing, bridge, languages, and other subjects. If you go to a new city to work, you will find such classes stimulating and you will meet worthwhile people interested in things that interest you. Fund raising for church, school or community offers wonderful opportunity to make lasting friends as well as a contribution where it is needed.

Sharing cultural interests in college leads frequently to stimulating discussions and lifelong friendships.

A SMILE IS LIKE A RAY OF LIGHT

A smile may not only win friends, but in many instances it may win a career. A person with a friendly smile is certainly more pleasant than someone who always wears a scowl like a

People who enjoy wholesome recreation usually find it easy to make friends.

Eastman Kodak Company

cold fish. Look at yourself in the mirror and try a real smile. Now try a sneer, a gloomy look, and a frown. Notice that your expression actually seems to light up when you "turn on the smile" again.

There is a story about a businessman who was always too tense to smile. A friend persuaded him to enroll in one of the famous Dale Carnegie courses. One of his assignments was to take a good look at himself in the mirror before coming downstairs to breakfast and then smile—and use that smile throughout one day.

The first morning he *smiled* at his wife and said, "Good morning, dear." His wife's answering smile was a little puzzled, because she wasn't prepared for such a change—but she smiled back.

He *smiled* and said, "Thank you," to the ticket man in the parking lot.

He *smiled* as he greeted the man operating the elevator.

He *smiled* at the employees in his office.

He discovered that everyone smiled back. By the time he started working, he felt more relaxed and refreshed than he had for months.

Akin to a smile is a sense of humor. If you have seen pictures of Mohandas Gandhi, you know what a tiny, withered person he was. One day an Indian authoress visited Gandhi to secure his autograph on a picture of him she thought was especially good. To her bewilderment, Gandhi burst out laughing. He hastened to explain, "It's an excellent picture. It's just that I sometimes forget what an ugly little man I am."

If you have a ready smile and a good sense of humor, cherish them.

Do not lose them by becoming too busy or too tense.

SHOW GENUINE INTEREST IN PEOPLE

If you can leave a person feeling better than he did before you came along, you may have made a friend. When someone performs an act of courtesy, say "Thank you." When a friend achieves recognition, forget jealousy or envy; compliment him. If someone makes a special effort to help you, comes to see you when you are sick, or sympathizes when you are in trouble, remember to do the same for others, as well as for him.

CASE STUDY: Allen McDaniels was an unusually popular senior class president. Friends said it was because of his knack for working with people. For example, when the time came to make plans for the senior prom, he was not content just to read a list of names for committee chairmen. After discussing plans and making a

A warm, friendly smile is an asset in any social situation, not only when the camera is on you.

Eastman Kodak Company

At school, on a job, or in a social situation, pay attention to what others are saying and doing. This is polite, and it will help you make friends.

few good-natured remarks to other officers and friends, he began to appoint chairmen by saying something friendly about each. No one could possibly have turned him down or accepted the appointment half-heartedly. All class members felt as though they had a part in the selections. How did Allen do it?

After calling the meeting to order and reviewing previous plans for the prom, he began: "We all know what a good sense of design Jean Frankel has, from her choice of clothes and her good reputation in the art department. How about Jean for decorations chairman?" Everybody applauded. He used flattery, yet based his choices on *ability* rather than *personal feelings*.

"With his mechanical brain computer and unchallenged grades in mathematics, wouldn't Ted Rieseling make a perfect business manager?"

"How many of you remember the big party we had at Evelyn's open house last year? What about those hamburgers! Can anyone think of

someone better than Evelyn Lowry for chairman of refreshments?"

"Even his family tells me that Jack Bruerton is a hi-fi wizard. I think we could use that kind of talent on our sound and lighting system. What do you say?"

Afterward, during the prom, Allen saw to it that all his workers were given credit.

Sometimes praise can be too commonplace, as for the person who knows he excels in some special field. A friend who is often praised for musical ability may appreciate a kind word about his personality or taste in clothes more than a repetition of the compliments he has heard so often.

CASE STUDY: Dennis Parr, an accomplished pianist and outstanding student, was used to being complimented for his musical and mental abilities. He knew he was an outstanding pianist and the best student in his class; he often felt something of an oddity because of it. One afternoon, after an assembly, Sharon Hartley, who was attractive but rather shy, greeted Dennis in a different way. "Isn't that a new suit, Dennis? Gee, I like it. You looked so good while you were playing." A few days later, Dennis invited her to the junior prom.

Has it ever occurred to you how good it makes your mother feel to tell her "how young" or "how pretty" she looks—"how sweet" or "how smart" you think she is, or "what a marvelous meal that was"? Your dad can appreciate warm, sincere words of praise too, after a tiring day at work.

Perhaps if you praise others when they honestly deserve it, you will be praised more in turn. Grove Patterson, editor of the *Toledo Blade*, once

68

wrote, "Friendship is a plant that has to be cultivated; it must be watered and tended if it is to produce sweet, wholesome fruit." We respond in direct relation to the way we are treated. This philosophy goes back two thousand years to the best of all advice for making and keeping friends —the Golden Rule.

Acts of Kindness Often we mean to do small acts of kindness, but it's easy to postpone them until finally we feel awkward even trying. People respond to kind, spontaneous attentions that really take little effort. A card with a simple, personal message sent to someone who is ill; a phone call to a friend you haven't had much chance to see because of summer vacation or a busy schedule; a note to someone who has gone out of his way to entertain you or help with a problem—such little acts can do wonders for you and the other person. Teachers who receive notes from graduating students whom they have helped, cherish the thought

for years, and other students who follow you benefit from your kindness.

You remember the Bible story of the Good Samaritan. Kindness to *strangers* is just as important as treating your *friends* and *family* in a considerate way. The rewards of being kind to others often outweigh the apparent sacrifices.

CASE STUDY: A vacationing elderly couple—let's call them the Burts—had an automobile accident just outside the home of a young couple, the Edwins, in a very small, isolated, far western town. The Edwins were about to leave on their own vacation trip. The driver of the car causing the accident had not stopped after side-swiping the Burt's car.

The Burts were dazed and shocked —and alone, 2,500 miles from their eastern home. The Edwins called the local doctor. He found nothing radically wrong, but the older couple had no place to stay while awaiting car repairs. The young people delayed their vacation long enough to care for their new friends, help them recover

Lasting friendships often begin in high school and college. Taking part in school activities increases your social opportunities.

Edgewood High School (Zundel)

In many schools students make an effort to include new students on committees or the publications staff.

Edgewood High School (Zundel)

from their shock, and send them off in good spirits. Although the Edwins had to cut their vacation short three days, they did not mention it, and expected no reward. Their only gain was two new friends, who could never return the kindness except with small Christmas remembrances and personal correspondence which they maintained the rest of their lives. The Edwins always felt this was enough. They seemed to gain a friend every time the story was told in the community.

Do you honestly try to put yourself in the other fellow's place? Are you usually on the *giving* or *receiving* end? Think this over carefully.

CASE STUDY: Bill Jefferson was chairman of the Tryout Party for the "Hi Politics" club.* He wanted to invite a girl and a boy who, because of shyness, had not gained popularity with the crowd. In chats during games and at "rec" hall Bill had found them

*The author does not recommend any specific organization. However, prestige groups of this nature can be as beneficial to members as athletic groups, which are recognized with much emphasis in many schools. Prestige opportunities are extremely important to the non-athlete.

to possess talents needed for work on school elections, which was the basis of the club. They were interested in joining. He could not understand why they did not mix easily.

Bill weighed his desire to invite the two young people against the fact that many of his friends thought they might be boring, and decided that it was his job to ask them — why shouldn't he! Their fine home training and promising ability seemed likely to make them fit into the spirit of the club better than some of their more aggressive classmates. The invitation might be just what they would need to give them more self-confidence. So Bill invited them. He was criticized at first. Later that year, the girl proved to be a valuable and popular member of the club. The boy did not fit in quite as well, but he benefited and Bill never regretted his act.

If a new student comes to school, do you try to make him feel welcome? In some communities, teenagers have set up a Junior Newcomers' Club or a Host and Hostess Committee to take new students to all of their classes the first day and introduce them to their teachers. The teachers, in turn, help them to become acquainted with classmates. New students may like to be asked to help with school projects. What are you doing in your own school and community to make strangers feel welcome?

If you should be the stranger yourself, you will make a better impression if you do not "push." Be a good listener, show appreciation, and if someone has extended an unusual courtesy, recall the incident later and return the kindness.

KNOW WHEN TO USE NAMES

People respond to the sound of their own names. A good politician or public official makes it his business to know names. James Farley is credited with the first nomination of President Franklin D. Roosevelt because he could recall so many convention delegates by name.

When you go down the school hall, notice how much better you feel if someone says "Hi, Sally," or "Hi, Tom," than just "Hi, how you doin'?" However, some people may use a person's name in conversation so much that it becomes annoying.

There has been a trend in recent years toward greater informality between employer and employee. Some employers feel that there is a closer bond of friendship when first names are used. Nevertheless, if there is doubt, it is safer to use the prefix Miss, Mr., or Mrs., than to risk being disrespectful. If you should teach or work in an office, you will find it wiser to be more formal with a superior on the job, even though you may know the person well enough to use his first name on social occasions.

REALIZE THE VALUE OF GRATITUDE

Some people go through life expecting everything and never trying to return a kindness. Others may be generous in giving, but lack graciousness in receiving praise or kindness. Courtesy begins at home. When graciousness becomes a habit at home, it is easier to be gracious in situations away from home. When those closest to us fail to recognize our good deeds, we often feel hurt and unappreciated. Why does it seem more difficult sometimes to thank or praise a member of the family than someone outside the home?

A secretary, an auto mechanic, a typesetter, or a teacher who receives sincere praise—and feels he is a center of true interest—will work harder to please a superior. A smile and "thank you" as you pay a bill, leave an elevator, or receive extra help from a teacher makes the day a little more pleasant for both. You will feel better if you respond with a word of appreciation next time a member of your family does something nice for you. Try it.

CASE STUDY: Millie Arnold, a poor, almost helpless woman suffering from exhaustion, arthritis, and a feeling of neglect, was brought back to health after several months in the hospital. Her story of gratitude is heart warming. Dr. Spear, a young psychiatrist, had become personally interested in the woman's problems, and had restored her to health. For a year after Millie's health was restored she worried about how to repay Dr. Spear but could think of no way. Finally, she remembered how much the young doctor had admired some bittersweet

71

Participation in sports leads to contacts with other people who have similar interests.

her sisters had brought from their family farm. She had a hospital attendant place the bundle, wrapped in newspaper, on Dr. Spear's desk.

At the end of a tiring day, the young doctor was feeling very low. Before going home he checked in at his office and found the bundle tied with twine; inside, a slip of paper lay on top of freshly cut bittersweet and moist moss; "For what you did for me." The bittersweet, and the crude handwriting gave a clue to the sender. Perhaps you think this meant nothing to the doctor. Well, he still talks about it. Dr. Spear had his wife place the bittersweet in their living room to remind them of how much richer their lives were because of interest in others.

CONVERSATION TIPS

One of the biggest problems of young people as well as others is that of communication. People may be too quiet, too talkative, or too anxious to make an impression.

For instance, Sue may ask, "How can I learn 'small talk'? Some kids just babble along forever while I stand tongue-tied!"

Jim, on the other hand, may say, "Cathy never shuts up—I'm always worn out listening to her."

There is a real art in knowing when to talk and when to listen. People will go to a lot of trouble to develop the right conversation. Consider how Dave, Melissa, and Bob prepare for a social evening.

Dave, anxious to be the center of conversation, buys new joke books, tries out the jokes on his younger brothers, and comes prepared to "wow" the crowd with his wit.

Melissa, a little unsure of herself in a group, makes a habit of gathering facts about sports events (for the boys) and personal lives of TV stars (for the girls), so she can have facts to add to the conversation.

Bob reads current popular magazines, looks at TV occasionally, plays tennis, collects coins, belongs to several clubs, but never seems to worry much about keeping up a conversation. He has many interests and knows the interests of his friends so that keeping up a conversation takes almost no effort.

It is a good idea to be posted on the latest jokes and current social news, but often when conversation is too carefully planned, it lacks warmth and liveliness. Dave and Melissa must be "on edge" all evening awaiting the right moment "to shine," whereas Bob is relaxed, sharing ideas and experiences.

We do not make friends because we use the latest slang, talk incessantly, tell a joke well, or act like a walking encyclopedia. We make friends by being interested in people and showing enthusiasm about life's activities.

Jargon, jive talk, or slang may sound good, but it can be difficult to drop. When you find yourself unable to speak properly in applying for a job, you may wish you had never learned anything but correct English. Slang phrases may become a social handicap rather than an asset.

Here are a few conversation tips:

* Learn to listen; be sincere about it. Ask questions, and give the other person a chance to talk.
* Let people express their opinions without interrupting or correcting them.
* Avoid petty arguments. No one ever wins, and often you may wish later to take back much of what you have said.
* Be willing to admit that you could have been wrong. You can make more friends if you give them credit for being right than by being haughty or stubborn.
* Use words correctly. When you aren't sure of a word's meaning, look it up.
* Do not be a fraud. If a person wants to tell you something, don't act as if you already know it all. Even if you do know something about it, let the other fellow tell you what he knows. It isn't important to impress him with how smart you are. After listening for a while, you will have your opportunity to comment, and your friend will be pleased to learn that you share his interest.
* Be smart, but don't outsmart yourself. Avoid pitfalls such as the one in the following anecdote, which humorist H. Allen Smith tells on himself. In trying to make conversation with the person sitting near him at a large banquet, Smith once said, "Now tell me about your fascinating job." The stranger, looking a little quizzical, replied, "I'm an undertaker."

Do you agree with author Frank V. Morley's remark: "Friendship is something you can't buy and can't command, but you can lose"? We cannot neglect or ignore people and keep them as friends. We are all happier when we know there are others who care about us.

THE DANGER OF GOSSIP

Gossip can become a vicious habit and a business handicap. Dr. Gordon W. Allport of Harvard University, who has studied many aspects of gossiping, states that the habitual gossip is a victim of "uncertainty or anxiety."

Bowling is fun and offers friendship opportunities.

With such a person, gossip fills an emotional need, but the wrong way. In emphasizing the faults of others, he is often trying to make up for his own shortcomings by bringing another down to his level. People who are bored, jealous, envious, or insecure often gossip. Busy people are less likely to gossip. We all like to share some choice bit of news—it is human nature. Often during a political campaign one party will try to bring out a scandal about some candidate in the other party. This is referred to as a "smear campaign." Scandalous propaganda is gossip on a big scale.

Before we start a questionable rumor, we might save embarrassment by asking ourselves the following questions:

Is it *true*—do we have all the facts?

Is it *kind?*

Is it *necessary?*

CASE STUDY: Alice Foster came home from the junior prom long after dawn and limped up the walk to her home. A neighbor who happened to be looking out her window noticed that Alice's dress was soiled and crumpled and her hair disarranged. By noon Alice's reputation was fading. The jealous neighbor, whose daughter was not invited to the prom, started a gossip chain that was exaggerated with each telling. It turned out that Alice and her date had been involved in an accident, yet many people, through malicious gossip, were convinced that Alice had been delinquent. The neighbor's gossip resumed again in the summer when Alice and her mother went out of town for a month. She was certain that her suspicions were true and Alice "needed a doctor's care." The neighbor's remarks were neither true, kind, nor necessary. They did no one any good.

You remember the Bible story and Jesus' classic rebuke to those who wished to have the adulteress judged. "Let him who is without sin among you be the first to cast a stone." It is well for all of us to remember this advice because few of us are beyond criticism. No one can risk having a gossip for a friend.

OTHER TRAITS THAT MAKE FRIENDSHIP DIFFICULT

We have discussed ways to attract friends. Perhaps we should discuss some traits that make friendship difficult.

INSINCERITY: No matter how much we like a compliment, we want to feel it is sincere. People who say one thing to your face and another behind your back cannot be counted on as friends.

SARCASM: Some people use sarcasm as a *defense mechanism* (See Chapter 2) to cover up their feeling of insecurity. These people pride themselves on being cynical. They try to feel superior, but inwardly they have a strong desire to be genuinely liked.

BOASTFULNESS: This is another of the reactions we studied in Chapter 2. The boastful person is trying to *compensate* for other shortcomings by "inflating his ego." When he "has his hand called," he becomes nervous and ill at ease.

VULGARITY AND PROFANITY: There are people who seem to have to tell dirty jokes and use profanity. They crave recognition and if they cannot

74

FRIENDSHIP RATING

These traits attract. Are you:		These traits repel. Are you:	
interested in others	sympathetic	self-centered	vulgar
thoughtful	tolerant	selfish	highly critical
kind	truthful	prejudiced	lazy
sincere	patient	bossy	argumentative
modest	dependable	uncharitable	undependable
grateful	neatly dressed	revengeful	insincere
courteous	gracious	moody	sarcastic
cheerful	adaptable	stubborn	boastful
loyal	tactful	conceited	inquisitive
considerate	enthusiastic	a poor sport	a gossip
a good sport		carelessly dressed	
?　　?　　?	?　　?　　?	?　　?　　?	?　　?　　?

get it in one way, they will in another—an antisocial way. This may indicate an inferiority complex. When a person uses profanity for emphasis, he may be attempting to show off, be dramatic, or his vocabulary may be inadequate. Profanity adds neither interest nor emphasis to conversation, and it can soon become a "crutch."

INQUISITIVENESS: No one likes to have people prying into his business. Often, steadies act as if they own each other, and hold each other responsible for every move. A certain amount of interest is fine, but questions should not be asked continually just to satisfy curiosity.

CRITICISM: Even on minor points, people do not like to be criticized. Advice, given tactfully and by the right person at the right time, can be helpful.

UNDEPENDABILITY: Some people never seem to grow up. They cannot be depended upon to keep a promise or do a job. These people take the easy way, avoiding or fleeing from responsibility.

DOMINATION: Friendly discussion is healthy, but when a person insists on having "the last word," friendships can become shaky.

UNREASONABLENESS: We like people who stand up for their beliefs, but we lose patience with those who always have to be right, despite what the rest of the world has proved.

Using the chart above, check yourself by making a *plus* sign for good traits and a *minus* sign for poor ones. (Use separate paper. Do *not* write in this book.) Study the results of this self-check and try to improve.

FRIENDSHIPS AND SOCIAL CHANGE

Our society has changed in many ways, and our patterns of friendship have changed with it. One example is the fact that families move more often today than ever before. Sociologists, people who study our way of life, say that we have become a *mobile society*.

If your class is typical, many of your classmates no longer live where they did ten years ago. When a family moves, is it easy to part with friends and find new ones? If your family has moved, you can answer from experience.

Not too long ago most men worked in small businesses or on farms. Families seldom moved, and communities experienced little change from generation to generation. On Sunday afternoons whole families went to visit friends. This was the highlight of the week. Friendships often lasted a lifetime.

The pace of modern life and the constant uprooting of community ties have given family and community life less stability and made friendships more fleeting. Businessmen's families move frequently as opportunities for advancement occur or as the wage earner is transferred. Families of career military men can expect to move every three or four years. This is what sociologists call *physical mobility*.

Another kind of mobility also affects friendship patterns. As families get more money they tend to become *upwardly mobile*. Because of high salaries and working wives, many families today are upwardly mobile. They may move to a fashionable neighborhood or join an exclusive club. Naturally they want to make friends at their new social level. However, they often learn that it was easier to improve financially than it is to find good new friends.

People feel self-sufficient when they are healthy, busy, and prosperous. At such times they may tend to forget their friends. But when they have to face a crisis—business reverses or a long period of illness—they miss loyal friends and often regret not taking more time to cultivate and enjoy them.

Philosophers and poets have written volumes about friendships. The old adage is as good now as ever, "A true friend is the greatest of all blessings and the one which we take the least thought to acquire."

Words and Phrases to Know

argument	gossip
complement	gracious
compliment	gratitude
constructive	physical
criticism	mobility
conversation	sarcasm
destructive	social
criticism	status
flattery	socio-economic
fraud	trait
Golden Rule	upward
Good Samaritan	mobility

ACTIVITIES

1. Discuss reasons why it is possible to have both friends and enemies, as the little boy found out. Cite instances of changing your mind about persons after knowing them better.

2. Name several popular TV personalities and list their traits that appeal and annoy. Note the number of classmates who agree and disagree. What is the difference between these "picture persons" and people you know? Do you "know" persons on TV?

3. Discuss factors that may cause children to be friendly or retiring.

4. Make a survey in your school to learn about traits that people like and dislike. Publish the results in the school paper.

5. Investigate activities in your community that give persons out of school a chance to meet other young people.

6. As you pass students and teachers in the school corridors, smile and greet them. As you converse with friends, show genuine interest. Discuss the results in class.

7. Appoint a panel to discuss the following topics (this would make a good PTA panel, moderated by a psychologist):
* Ways to make others feel more appreciated.
* Ways parents may help their children to become friendly.
* Advantages and disadvantages of secret societies and cliques.
* Ways to make a new student feel welcome.

8. Have questions for discussion placed in a question box. Discuss as many as time allows.

9. Act out home and school situations based on showing gratitude.

10. On the chalk board, compile a list of current slang expressions. Discuss the origin of each, and when to use and not use such expressions. Single out words or expressions used too often.

11. Spend part of a period citing the origin of common expressions. (See *Why We Say It*, by Robert L. Morgan, Sterling Publishers, 1953.)

12. List the conversation tips, page 73, on the chalk board. Have you heard any of them used or violated in class today? In other recent classes? In clubs or social groups? At home?

13. List on the chalk board the traits that make friendship difficult, and discuss them according to your own experience. Do you think that people usually develop these traits when they are insecure or unhappy and want to feel more important?

14. **Bulletin Board:** Arrange a display showing those traits that repel and those that attract friendships.

15. Review *How to Win Friends and Influence People*, by Dale Carnegie.

16. Discuss problems you have had making friends in a new community.

17. Write a paragraph on what friends mean to you.

18. From any book of quotations, select three on friendship that have the most meaning for you. Read and comment on them in class.

Chapter 4

Food in a Support- ing Role

Have you ever stopped to think of the many roles food plays in your daily life? Food not only satisfies hunger, but it is a very important factor in insuring good health and making life more interesting.

The food industry and industries related to it provide more jobs than any other—growing fruits and vegetables, raising livestock, processing, marketing, and advertising foods, as well as preparing and serving them. About a third of the average family income goes into food, and the average homemaker spends about a third of her worktime providing meals.

When young people marry, the wife is largely responsible for food preparation, while the husband earns the money with which to buy the food, and often helps with shopping. Many young men as well as young women do their own cooking in apartments, or select meals in restaurants or cafeterias. In any case, it is important to know how to select food for adequate nutrition and economy.

A DAILY FOOD PLAN

It is a strange paradox in a land of plenty that many of us are inadequately nourished. Studies reveal that men are more likely to eat balanced meals than women. Teen-agers, especially girls, have the poorest quality diet. The housewife frequently follows a diet far below recommended levels in an effort to reduce. Children between 1 and 3 are often short on proteins, vitamins, and minerals.

A balanced food plan must contain the following nutrients in proper proportions: proteins, carbohydrates, fats, vitamins, and minerals. No one food supplies enough of all these nutrients. Milk is the most nearly complete food, but it is sufficient only for young babies.

The *Guide to Good Eating*, on pages 80 and 81, shows the four principal food groups; the graphs indicate what each contributes toward good health. If you eat recommended amounts of food from each of these groups, you will meet basic nutrition needs. For instance:

Dairy Foods
Proper dairy food diet meets about ½ of the daily calcium needs—600 milligrams of a required 1,000-1,400. Foods from other groups make up the rest. To make it easier to figure your own calcium consumption, let 20 points equal 600 milligrams. Two glasses of skim milk (only 170 calories) supply this. Your diet will be adequate if you eat any combination totaling 20 points.

DAIRY FOODS AS SOURCES OF CALCIUM.

Food	Amount	Calcium	
		Points[1]	Milli-grams
Milk:			
Whole, fluid	1 cup	10	290
Skim, fluid	1 cup	10	300
Buttermilk	1 cup	10	290
Whole, dry	3 to 4 tablespoons	9	260
Nonfat, dry	3 to 4 tablespoons	11	340
Evaporated, undiluted	½ cup	10	310
Cheese:			
Cottage	¼ cup	2	50
Cream	¼ cup	1	40
Natural or processed, such as cheddar or swiss	1 ounce	7	190
Ice cream	½ cup	3	90
Sherbet, milk	½ cup	2	50

[1]One calcium point is equivalent to about 30 milligrams of calcium.

Vegetables and Fruits
This group provides large amounts of vitamins A and C. Although vitamin A itself is not contained in these foods, carotene is, and the body changes carotene to vitamin A. You should eat foods from this group every week equal to a minimum of 140, (or 20 points a day). Points are put on a weekly basis so that a greater variety of foods may be eaten during a week.

You will notice that one serving of any food in this group, except tomatoes and green peppers, more than meets nutrition needs. Therefore on a weekly basis you would want to include a variety such as a serving of kale, sweet potato, tomato juice, and broccoli—totaling 140 points for the week. Yellow and green vegetables should be included.

A medium orange or ½ of a grapefruit will supply all the vitamin C your body needs. This vitamin cannot be stored, so it must be replenished every day. Remember that the point

VEGETABLES AND FRUITS AS SOURCES OF VITAMIN A VALUE.

Food	Amount	Vitamin A	
		Points[1]	I. U.
Beet greens	½ cup	45	5,400
Broccoli	½ cup	20	2,500
Carrots, diced	½ cup	70	9,050
Chard, leaves	½ cup	70	8,500
Collards	½ cup	60	7,250
Cress, garden	½ cup	25	2,950
Dandelion greens	½ cup	110	13,650
Kale	½ cup	35	4,600
Mustard greens	½ cup	40	5,000
Peppers, sweet, red, raw	½ medium	15	1,800
Pumpkin	½ cup	30	3,850
Spinach	½ cup	75	9,100
Squash, winter, yellow	½ cup	50	6,000
Sweet potatoes, yellow	½ medium	40	5,200
Tomatoes, cooked or juice	½ cup	10	1,250
Tomatoes, raw	1 medium	15	1,650
Turnip greens	½ cup	60	7,700
Apricots, raw or cooked	5 halves	20	2,300
Cantaloupe	½ medium	50	6,200

[1] One vitamin A point is equivalent to about 125 International Units of vitamin A.

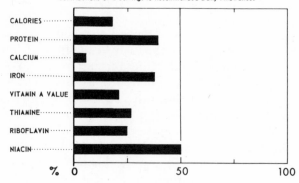

MEAT GROUP
Contributions of 2 Servings to Recommended Daily Allowances ✱

CALORIES			
PROTEIN			
CALCIUM			
IRON			
VITAMIN A VALUE			
THIAMINE			
RIBOFLAVIN			
NIACIN			
%	0	50	100

Charts by United States Department of Agriculture

Meat Group

2 or more servings

Meats, fish, poultry, eggs, or cheese—with dry beans, peas, or nuts as alternates.

Vegetables and Fruits

4 or more servings

Include dark green or yellow vegetables, citrus fruits or tomatoes.

GUIDE TO GOOD EATING
RECOMMENDED DAILY SERVINGS

This Daily Food Guide indicates nutrients in each food group. Asterisks (°) indicate average adult servings totaling 1,250 calories and meeting basic nutrition needs. Other foods may be chosen to contribute extra nutrients, but they should be carefully selected in order not to exceed the individual's calorie needs.
(See detailed discussion on
pages 78 through 83.)

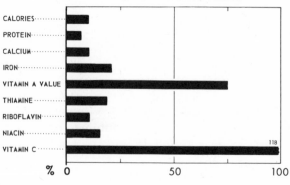

VEGETABLES AND FRUITS
Contributions of 4 Servings to Recommended Daily Allowances ✱

CALORIES			
PROTEIN			
CALCIUM			
IRON			
VITAMIN A VALUE			
THIAMINE			
RIBOFLAVIN			
NIACIN			
VITAMIN C			118
%	0	50	100

BREAD AND CEREALS
Contributions of 4 Servings to Recommended Daily Allowances *

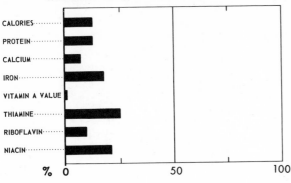

CALORIES		
PROTEIN		
CALCIUM		
IRON		
VITAMIN A VALUE		
THIAMINE		
RIBOFLAVIN		
NIACIN		
%	0	50	100

FOUR FOOD GROUPS
Contributions to Recommended Daily Allowances *

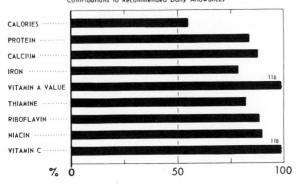

CALORIES		
PROTEIN		
CALCIUM		
IRON		
VITAMIN A VALUE	116
THIAMINE		
RIBOFLAVIN		
NIACIN		
VITAMIN C	118
%	0	50	100

Breads and Cereals

4 or more servings

Enriched or whole grain. Added milk improves nutritional value.

Dairy Foods

3 to 4 glasses milk—children
4 or more glasses—teen-agers
2 or more glasses—adults

Cheese, ice cream, and other milk-made foods can supply part of the milk.

MILK OR EQUIVALENT
Contributions of 2 Cups to Recommended Daily Allowances *

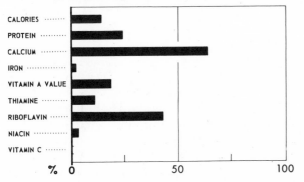

CALORIES		
PROTEIN		
CALCIUM		
IRON		
VITAMIN A VALUE		
THIAMINE		
RIBOFLAVIN		
NIACIN		
VITAMIN C		
%	0	50	100

81

system gives only minimum amounts for health protection. For enjoyment and variety, many more fruits and vegetables should be included in the diet. Foods in this group are low in calories, ranging from 20 to 100 per serving.

The fruit and vegetable charts on this page and page 79 will help you to choose foods in this group to meet your nutritional needs.

Meat Group Protein, iron, and niacin are provided by this group. Two small servings of lean, cooked meat provide 30 grams of protein, representing 20 points. This is the minimum adult daily serving from this group. Other foods provide additional protein if the Daily Food Guide is followed.

FOODS OF THE MEAT GROUP AS SOURCES OF PROTEIN

Food	Amount	Protein	
		Points[1]	Grams
Beef, veal, lamb, pork, poultry—lean, cooked, without bone	2 ounces	10	15
Bacon	2 slices	3	4
Dry beans and peas, cooked	½ cup	6	8
Eggs	1 egg	4	6
Fish, cooked, without bone	2 ounces	10	15
Frankfurters	2 ounces	6	8
Luncheon meat	2 ounces	6	9
Peanut butter	2 tablespoons	6	8

[1]One protein point is equivalent to about 1.5 grams of protein. Because both points and grams are rounded to whole numbers, the equivalent is 1.3 for some items.

Breads and Cereals The value in this group rests in its variety of contributions. For instance, three slices of bread and a bowl of cereal will provide the daily requirements from this group, as well as supplementing the other groups. Other foods in the group may substitute for bread and cereal. No point value has been assigned for this group.

FRUITS AND VEGETABLES AS SOURCES OF VITAMIN C.

Food	Amount	Vitamin C	
		Points[1]	Milligrams
Grapefruit	½ medium	30	76
Grapefruit juice	½ cup	17	43
Orange	1 medium	31	77
Orange juice	½ cup	19	48
Tangerine	1 medium	10	25
Tangerine juice	½ cup	13	32
Cantaloupe	½ medium	24	59
Honeydew melon	1 wedge, 2 by 7 inches	14	34
Pineapple, fresh, diced	½ cup	6	16
Strawberries	½ cup	18	44
Broccoli	½ cup	22	56
Brussels sprouts	½ cup	12	30
Cabbage, raw, shredded	½ cup	10	25
Greens:			
Collards, mustard greens, turnip greens	½ cup	13	32
Garden cress, kale	½ cup	10	26
Spinach	½ cup	9	22
Peppers, green, raw or cooked	1 small	17	43
Peppers, sweet, red, raw	½ medium	31	78
Potato, cooked in jacket	1 medium	8	20
Sweet potato, boiled or baked	1 medium	10	26
Tomatoes, cooked or juice	½ cup	8	19
Tomato, raw	1 medium	14	35

[1]One vitamin C point is equivalent to about 2 or 3 milligrams of ascorbic acid.

If we follow the Daily Food Guide, we can be assured of a balanced diet. Each of its *four food groups* has a special job.

When taken in the amounts recommended on page 81, the *milk group* will provide ⅔ of the calcium, about ½ of the riboflavin, ¼ of the protein and ⅕ of the vitamin A we need each day. The *vegetable and fruit group* will provide all of the vitamin C, ¾ of the vitamin A, about ¼ of the iron, and ⅕ of the thiamine. From the *meat group* we should get more than ⅓ of the protein and iron, ½ of the niacin, and about ¼ of the thiamine, riboflavin, and vitamin A. The *bread and cereals group* will supply us with ¼ of the thiamine and ⅕ of the daily niacin and iron requirements. The graph on page 81 shows how the four food groups combine to give us nearly all our basic daily requirements.

Sunshine and fish oils are the best agents for producing vitamin D in the body. If the Daily Food Guide is followed, vitamins E and K will be included in at least one food group.

Recommended minimum servings from the four basic groups provide only about 1,250 calories a day. Diet specialists frequently recommend more calories than this. You will learn about determining calorie needs according to weight, height, and activity in the following chapter. Perhaps you have noticed that sugars, fats, and oils are not included in the four basic groups. Additional servings from the four groups, or desserts and fats may be added to meet your calorie needs or to add variety to your menus.

SOURCE AND FUNCTION OF NUTRIENTS

This material will serve as a quick check of information covered in other school courses. The study of nutrition and the effects of individual nutrients on health and physical development has been speeded up by experimenting with rats. A rat grows 30 times as fast as a human and will eat the same food. Diet shortages show up quickly because the life span of a rat is less than three years.

On pages 84 and 85 notice what happens when a rat is deficient in any one nutrient. If a child's daily intake of food is off balance for a long time, similar symptoms will develop. Even after a person is full grown, food intake must be balanced for good health, a clear skin, bright eyes, lustrous hair, and resistance to disease.

The source and function of the five nutrients are summarized:

Proteins The word itself is derived from the Greek, meaning "I am first." Except for water, protein is represented in the largest proportion in every living body cell. Proteins build muscles, repair worn tissue, help balance acidity in the blood, regulate the functioning of enzymes and hormones, and provide heat and energy. You can see why proteins are so important.

Protein foods consist of a group of substances called amino acids; ten of these acids are indispensable for building and repairing tissue. Foods containing all of them are called *complete proteins.* These are of animal source—beef, veal, fowl, fish, lamb, pork, glandular meat, cheese, eggs, and milk. Foods containing only some of the amino acids are called incomplete proteins. They are of plant source—beans, peas, and grains. The diets of convalescents should be very high in complete proteins in order to

Well developed rat.

Contrast this healthy rat with the sickly ones pictured here. He has had a balanced diet. The others have been deprived of some necessary food elements.

Generally poor diet caused this rat's bad health. Teeth, hair, and skin have suffered, and the rat behaves listlessly.

DIET DEFICIENCIES AND HOW THEY AFFECT GROWTH AND DEVELOPMENT

If PROTEIN is insufficient or not in proper balance, poor growth results.

Protein

Aids: Muscles, blood, tissues, growth, energy.

Sources: Meat, fish, poultry, eggs, milk, cheese, beans, peas, grains.

CALCIUM makes teeth and bones strong.

Calcium

Aids: Teeth, bones, nerves, blood coagulation.

Sources: Milk, cheese, greens.

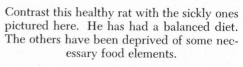

IRON deficiency causes anemia and lethargy.

Iron

Aids: Red blood cells, vitality, growth.

Sources: Liver, lean meat, dried fruits and vegetables, molasses, nuts.

A balanced diet contributes to your health, growth, strength, alertness, and appearance. Experiments have shown that rats are severely affected by diet deficiencies. Your health can suffer the same way if you do not get proper nourishment. Be sure that your meals contain enough of each basic food group.

Vitamin A

Aids: Sight, growth, reproduction, mother's milk supply.

Sources: Yellow fruits and vegetables, milk eggs, tomatoes, glandular meats.

VITAMIN A deficiency leads to night blindness, poor co-ordination, irritability, nose and mouth soreness.

Vitamin B$_1$ (Thiamine)

Aids: Appetite, food assimilation, alertness, calmness.

Sources: Bread, cereals, lean pork, glandular meats, dried and leafy vegetables.

Lack of VITAMIN B$_1$ (THIAMINE) impairs the digestive and nervous systems.

Vitamin B$_2$ (Riboflavin)

Aids: Disease resistance, youthful fitness, skin and hair.

Sources: Liver, eggs, bread, cereals, brewer's yeast, leafy vegetables.

With VITAMIN B$_2$ deficiency, rat seems to age rapidly. Skin becomes diseased, fur unsightly. There is little resistance to infection.

Contrast this skeleton with that on the previous page. Notice how severely a calcium deficiency impaired development of the rib cage and other bones.

Rat skeleton lacking CALCIUM.

Vitamin D (Sunshine vitamin)

Aids: Bones, teeth, blood coagulation, nerves, heart, reproduction.

Sources: Sunshine, fish oils, egg yolk, vitamin D milk.

Vitamin C

Aids: Protection from colds, strong teeth and gums, blood circulation and coagulation, vitality.

Sources: Citrus fruits, tomatoes, berries, leafy vegetables, potatoes.

Poor growth and decline in fertility result from lack of VITAMIN D.

NOTE: Vitamin C (Ascorbic acid) is not illustrated. Rats do not require vitamin C.

rebuild tissue. However, an over-strong protein diet may eventually cause kidney trouble.

Sugars and starches are the two most important sources of carbohydrates. Another is cellulose, a woody carbohydrate. It is not digested, but it stimulates intestinal muscles. Many people are inclined not to eat enough cellulose foods such as leafy vegetables, and cereals containing the outer coating.

Carbohydrates

Sugar is digested very quickly and sent into the blood stream as energy. If you feel fatigue coming on when you are hiking or playing active games, a lump of sugar or small piece of candy may help renew your energy in a short time. *Warning:* Concentrated sugars irritate tissues. You know how candy irritates a cavity. Sweets allowed to stay in the mouth may eventually cause soreness of the gums and roof of the mouth. Moreover, sugar is the favorite food of the bacteria which cause tooth decay. This is why dentists advise eating few concentrated sweets unless you brush your teeth or rinse your mouth immediately.

Starches begin to change to sugar when they encounter enzymes in the saliva. Starches are digested more slowly than sugars, thus providing energy more gradually.

Fat provides 2½ times as much heat per gram as carbohydrates. Fat digests slowly, and slows up the digestive process of other foods. To a limited degree, this is desirable. The body also needs some fat to protect the internal organs and

Fat

meet nutrition emergencies. The Eskimos eat a great deal of fish, rich in oils, and thus store up fat for insulation and vitamins A and D.

In recent years there has been concern over the formation of *cholesterol* in the arteries. This formation may result in part from eating *saturated* fats. These fats, found mainly in animal products (butter and lard) are more likely to cause the formation of cholesterol than are unsaturated fats, found in vegetable products (cottonseed oil, corn oil, and olive oil). Some authorities say that cholesterol, a tasteless, odorless, rather soaplike substance, tends to clog the arteries and to induce coronary artery diseases or heart attacks.

Normal amounts of saturated fat will not harm the average person. In fact, cholesterol has some helpful effects upon the body. Only when the diet contains too much fat do problems arise, including that of obesity (excess weight).

Many factors seem to help determine the amount of cholesterol in a person's body. Besides diet these include emotional strain, heredity, exercise, age, and hormone balance. More research is needed about the exact relationship of saturated fat, cholesterol, and heart disease.

Vitamins regulate body processes and help other foods to undergo chemical changes before they can perform their specific functions. Before 1911 the word vitamin was unknown. That year, Casimir Funk, a Polish biochemist, was puzzling over the problem of why so many Orientals suffered from a strange disease. This disease,

Vitamins

called beriberi, was causing paralysis, a breaking down of body tissue, anemia, and nervous disorders. Funk experimented with feeding the outer coating of rice instead of polished rice to nervous pigeons. The pigeons began to calm down. When people suffering with beriberi began to eat the outer coating of the rice, their nervous symptoms also disappeared. Funk named this unseen, health-giving substance vitamin (*vita* meaning life and *amine* for a nitrogen compound). This first-known vitamin was B_1 or thiamine—the "pep vitamin."

Many vitamins have since been discovered. Some vitamins dissolve in water, others in fat. *Water-soluble vitamins* are C (ascorbic acid), B_1 (thiamine), B_2 or G (riboflavin), and niacin. Foods containing water-soluble vitamins should be prepared in as little liquid as possible, and the liquid should be served with the food to preserve these four very important vitamins.

Fat-soluble vitamins are A, D, E, and K. These vitamins do not dissolve in water. They are found mainly in oily foods but also in green and yellow vegetables, yellow fruits, eggs, milk, cheese, dry beans, and nuts. By serving butter, other fats, or oily salad dressings with these foods, fat-soluble vitamins are utilized.

Vitamin A or carotene helps to prevent or correct certain sight problems such as night blindness; aids in normal growth, reproduction, and lactation; keeps the mucous membranes of the nose, mouth, and throat from becoming dry and sore. *Warning:* Too much vitamin A can be harmful.

Good sources of vitamin A are yellow foods—sweet potatoes, egg yolk, Hubbard squash, carrots, cantaloupe, peaches, butter, fortified margarine, cheese, beans, and tomatoes. Vitamin A may be stored in the body. It deteriorates if foods containing it are exposed to air.

Vitamin B_1 or thiamine stimulates the appetite; aids in the digestion and assimilation of food; helps the nervous system to funtion; aids in keeping the mind alert and free of worry. A serious B_1 deficiency may cause a person to lose interest in life, lack muscular co-ordination, become irritable and slovenly.

Thiamine is found in whole wheat breads and cereals, enriched white bread, lean pork, glandular meats, dried beans and peas, milk, fruits, and leafy vegetables. Thiamine is water-soluble, but is destroyed by long exposure to heat and air. It cannot be stored in the body. Foods containing thiamine should be prepared in very little liquid, kept airtight in a dark place, and eaten daily.

Vitamin B_2 or riboflavin helps the body turn food into energy. A deficiency has many harmful effects on one's health and appearance. For instance, a serious lack of this vitamin may cause the hair to become dry, eyes to burn, lips, nose, ears, and mouth to become sore. The best source of vitamin B_2 is liver. Other good sources are brewer's yeast, leafy vegetables, dairy foods, whole wheat breads and cereals, eggs, and lean meats. This vitamin is water-soluble and harmed by exposure to light; therefore foods containing riboflavin should be stored in a dark place and cooked in very little liquid.

B vitamin niacin has no number. It helps to promote good health and good functioning of the digestive tract.

The best sources of niacin are lean meats, liver, fish, poultry, dried fruits, beans and peas, peanuts, whole grain or enriched breads, and cereals. Niacin will dissolve, but it is not affected by heat. The body cannot store niacin. Foods containing niacin should be prepared in very little water and eaten daily.

A severe niacin deficiency causes *pellagra,* which affects the mucous membranes of the mouth, stomach, and intestines; causes acute nervousness, depression, and eventual loss of mental powers. In milder forms a niacin deficiency shows up in rough skin, digestive disturbances, and listlessness.

Vitamin C or *ascorbic acid* is the vitamin that prevents scurvy. When sailors used to live on salt pork and dried foods, nearly half would die from this dreaded disease. In the 1600's, fresh limes were fed to British sailors, and the disease did not occur. British seamen are still refered to as "limeys." There are certain milder conditions, such as chronic fatigue, aching joints, and frequent irritability, which may also be associated with a deficiency of vitamin C.

Vitamin C is found mainly in citrus fruit, tomatoes, berries, raw leafy vegetables, fruits, and potatoes. This vitamin is water-soluble and may be destroyed by exposure to air. It is not lost in commercial canning. Dried fruits will lose vitamin C unless they are subjected to sulphur dioxide fumes during the drying process. Vitamin C cannot be stored in the body, so it must be obtained in some form every day. For a long time it was commonly believed that large doses of vitamin C were effective in preventing and treating colds, but new research makes this seem doubtful.

Vitamin D is the *sunshine and fish-liver-oil vitamin.* Butter, vitamin D milk, cream, and egg yolks also produce smaller amounts in the body. Ultraviolet (not infrared ray) lamps may be used in winter months to provide vitamin D, but they should be used with caution. They can cause serious burns. Vitamin D is absorbed by the blood and intestines, and stored in the body. Vitamin D helps develop good bones and teeth; aids in blood clotting, normal heart action, and nervous stability. A severe deficiency of vitamin D can weaken teeth and cause rickets—a malformation of the bone structure. This vitamin is essential, especially to growing children, and mothers during pregnancy and lactation.

The function of vitamin E in humans is not fully known, but its lack can harm some animals severely. Humans rarely lack this nutrient which is present in many foods. Best sources include cottonseed and coconut oils, dry beans, wheat germ, leafy greens, and nuts. Vitamin E is fat-soluble, easily destroyed by air and light.

Vitamin K is essential for normal blood clotting. A deficiency may cause free bleeding from a wound. Best sources are green, leafy vegetables, soy bean oil, pork liver, and cereals. Vitamin K is fat-soluble but not affected by heat in cooking.

Pantothenic acid—found in liver, meats, wheat germ, molasses, and yeast—helps to stabilize the nervous system, among other functions.

Folic acid—found in eggs, milk, liver, leafy vegetables, and whole grain cereals—is important in regulating the growth cells and preventing some types of anemia.

Vitamins E and K, and pantothenic and folic acid, will be included automatically if you follow the Daily Food Guide.

Minerals Minerals are necessary for nearly all of life's processes. They build bones and teeth, repair body tissue, influence the development of muscles, help the nervous system transmit messages to the brain, and aid digestion. More than a dozen minerals are used by the body, but we shall discuss only the five most important ones.

Calcium builds and maintains good teeth and bones; helps blood to coagulate; insures normal heart, nerve, and muscle action. A deficiency shows up in rickets, retarded growth, poor teeth, and poor blood clotting after a cut. Best sources of calcium are dairy products. Other sources include nuts, broccoli, cauliflower, beans, and peas.

Phosphorus is comparable to calcium in its function. In fact, most of the calcium foods also contain phosphorus. Protein foods are rich in phosphorus.

Iron is found in the hemoglobin of red blood cells, which carry oxygen from the lungs to all the body cells. These cells constantly wear out, so we need to renew the supply of iron daily. If iron is lacking in the diet, vitality will be low and anemia may result; growth may be curtailed. Best sources of iron are liver, lean meat, dried beans, dried prunes, raisins,

dried apricots, almonds, peanuts, and molasses. Milk, though the best all-around nutrient, is low in iron.

Copper is also essential. It is found in foods containing iron.

Iodine promotes growth and aids in proper *metabolism*, the assimilation of food for body activities. Nearly half of the body's iodine is utilized in the thyroid gland. When iodine is out of balance, people may become very fat, develop a goiter, or become dwarfs or giants. It was discovered that people living along the seacoast seldom developed goiter. The best iodine sources are ocean fish and iodized salt.

Even if you have had no previous study of nutrition, you can see why it is wise to follow the Daily Food Guide. It will indicate all basic nutrition needs for yourself and family.

VITAMIN AND MINERAL REQUIREMENTS

If you pattern your eating habits after the Daily Food Guide, you will most likely meet your needs for vitamins and minerals. The Council on Foods and Nutrition of the American Medical Association backs up this statement. Individuals with poor eating habits, pregnant women, nursing mothers, persons recovering from illness, or emotionally or physically ill persons may need to supplement their diet with synthetic vitamins and minerals.

The labels on vitamin-mineral supplements today will list correct minimum requirements. However, the amounts listed must be added to those from other sources. Vitamins in excess of nutritional requirements are wasted. (Water-soluble vitamins are excreted from the body, and fat-solu-

of calcium deposits in the fetus, which in turn affect the bone structure and functioning of the heart. The body cannot throw off excessive amounts of this vitamin.

Check your *total* vitamin intake, from natural foods as well as synthetic vitamins, against the dietary recommendations. Amounts are indicated on the label.

ble vitamins may be harmfully stored in the body.) Studies have revealed that excessive amounts of vitamin D have been responsible for mental retardation and other abnormalities. During pregnancy women have been known to take 2,000 to 3,000 units of vitamin D when only 400 are needed. It is believed that too much of the vitamin causes unnatural formation

FOOD ADDITIVES

A food additive is any substance combined with basic food items during their production or processing. Common additives are salt, flavorings, spices, and leavening agents. Vitamin and mineral additives are often used in breads, other baked goods, and milk.

Chemical preparations are added

FOOD AND NUTRITION BOARD, NATIONAL ACADEMY OF SCIENCES—NATIONAL RESEARCH COUNCIL*
RECOMMENDED DAILY DIETARY ALLOWANCES, REVISED 1964

DESIGNED FOR THE MAINTENANCE OF GOOD NUTRITION OF PRACTICALLY ALL HEALTHY PERSONS IN THE U.S.A.

(Allowances are intended for persons normally active in a temperate climate. Women during pregnancy and lactation need greater allowances, which a physician may prescribe.)

	Years from to	Protein gm.	Calcium gm.	Iron mg.	Vitamin Value (I. U.)	Thiamine mg.	Riboflavin mg.	Niacin Equiv. mg.	Ascorbic Acid mg.	Vitamin D (I. U.)
Men	18–35	70	0.8	10	5,000	1.2	1.7	19	70	
	35–55	70	0.8	10	5,000	1.0	1.6	17	70	
	55–75	70	0.8	10	5,000	0.9	1.3	15	70	
Women	18–35	58	0.8	15	5,000	0.8	1.3	14	70	
	35–55	58	0.8	15	5,000	0.8	1.2	13	70	
	55–75	58	0.8	10	5,000	0.8	1.2	13	70	
Children	1–3	32	0.8	8	2,000	0.5	0.8	9	40	400
	3–6	40	0.8	10	2,500	0.6	1.0	11	50	400
	6–9	52	0.8	12	3,500	0.8	1.3	14	60	400
Boys	9–12	60	1.1	15	4,500	1.0	1.4	16	70	400
	12–15	75	1.4	15	5,000	1.2	1.8	20	80	400
	15–18	85	1.4	15	5,000	1.4	2.0	22	80	400
Girls	9–12	55	1.1	15	4,500	0.9	1.3	15	80	400
	12–15	62	1.3	15	5,000	1.0	1.5	17	80	400
	15–18	58	1.3	15	5,000	0.9	1.3	15	70	400

*See pages 107-112 for height, weight, and calorie correlation.

Abbreviations: gm. means gram, mg. means milligram, I. U. means International Units.

to potato chips, cheese, bread, crackers, and shortening to keep them from spoiling. Gum arabic is used to preserve the flavor in cakes and pudding mixes. Other chemical compounds are added to salad dressings, chocolate candy, and ice cream to help them keep the desired consistency (thickness). Substances are added to coconut and marshmallows so that these foods will not dry out. Non-fattening sweeteners are used in low calorie foods.

Without the use of additives many foods would be lacking in flavor, nutrition, and eye appeal. Pure food legislation protects the consumer against the use of harmful additives.

BUYING AND STORING FOOD

Market research has become a big business. Perhaps some of you have participated in market surveys aimed at finding out what new items and services shoppers want. Others of you without knowing it may have been watched by unseen eyes and your behavior tabulated on computers as you pushed a cart through the aisles of a supermarket. Landscaped parking lots, piped-in music, and attractive displays are some of the results of consumer surveys.

To further attract customers, stores conduct games and contests, and hand out trading stamps, tickets for popular entertainment, and other "giveaways."

The psychology behind these attractions is to make your trip to the market a pleasant experience rather than a chore. When shopping is enjoyable, the shopper is likely to spend more money.

It is natural to enjoy the cheerful surroundings and all the other extras connected with modern supermarkets. Remember, though, that their main purpose is to get you to spend more money. Don't let frills lead you to buy items you don't need, pay high prices, or put up with poor service or discourtesy from store employees.

Market surveys have shown that the typical supermarket shopper is in her mid-thirties, has two children, and her husband earns between $6,000 and $7,000. She changes brands frequently, shops without a list, spends about a third of her food budget on meat, and does a lot of impulse buying of items at eye or waist

Attractive, wholesome, economical meals are easy when you understand nutritional needs, meal planning, shopping, and proper food preparation. The breakfast and two lunches shown on these pages are well balanced.

91

Photographs by National Dairy Council—Shigeta-Wright Studios

level. These are favored locations for merchandise.

It is interesting to note that in one way modern supermarkets are turning back the clock. In the late 1950's these markets began adding drug items and soft goods, to compete for more of the consumer's dollar. Thus the new supermarket more and more resembles the general store of a century ago.

Here are some suggestions to further facilitate food purchasing and handling:

* Locate a market or grocery store you like; find out the day, and the time of day, when fresh meats, fruits, and vegetables arrive. If possible, plan to shop at these times.
* For efficiency, limit your shopping to one or two days a week, with the exception of "pickup" items such as bread, ice cream, and fresh fruits.
* Read the daily newspapers for special sales on frozen, canned, and pantry shelf foods; buy in quantities you can store and use to advantage.
* Keep a permanent shopping list, and a record of foods that are running low, in a convenient place. For greater efficiency, list foods according to departments where they may be found.
* Compare the costs of serving canned, fresh, and frozen foods; buy items in container sizes best suited to your needs.
* Have a supply of quick-to-prepare foods on hand for emergencies.
* For special meals, make out menus ahead of time. Otherwise, keep a supply of staples for a week or ten days on hand and plan meals each day according to how much time you have, how many people you are serving, and what you feel like preparing. Few people find it desirable to plan a week's meals in advance before shopping. Substitutions often have to be made; family members may be unexpectedly absent from some meals, and appetites may vary.

* Buy grades of meat, poultry, butter, and eggs according to use. Consider tougher cuts of meat—they are nutritious, inexpensive, and may be tenderized and used in appetizing casseroles, stews, and other dishes.
* Store perishable foods as soon as possible after purchasing.

Wrap meats loosely and store in coldest part of the refrigerator.

* Wash vegetables quickly — except potatoes, onions, and corn—and store in bins, or cover in plastic bags and keep on refrigerator shelves. Vegetables need not be washed again; repeated washings partially waste vitamins. Store fruit and berries in bins while still cold, and wash as used. Wash berries *before* stemming to save nutrients.
* Make sure the food is fresh. Store foods no longer than the recommended number of days for safety and maximum retention of flavor and texture. The accompanying chart will guide you in planning storage time for many common foods.
* Store frozen foods as soon as possible. Thawing and re-freezing will cause a change in texture and flavor, and in some instances may cause food poisoning, especially with poultry, variety meats, and fish.
* Freeze foods quickly. You may freeze all foods except vegetables that are to be eaten firm or crisp—lettuce, radishes, tomatoes, green peppers, cabbage, cucumbers. You may freeze

92

meats, poultry, fish, butter, cheese, fruits, and vegetables (except the above), cakes (better iced with egg white icings after defrosting), pies, breads, casseroles, and sandwiches. Chill pie crust, cakes, and casseroles before wrapping.

• Use suitable wrappings and containers for freezing. Household waxed paper is *not recommended* for packaging foods to freeze. Locker paper with a heavy wax coating may be used for *short-time freezing only.* For longer periods, use the following:

LAMINATED PAPERS: These are moisture-vaporproof, greaseproof, puncture-resistant, and non-transparent. They may be of plastic film or aluminium foil, laminated to good quality paper. Place the film side next to the food, and seal with *freezer locker tape.* Aluminum foil may puncture, so for long-time storage, a stockinette should be pulled over it.

NON-LAMINATED PAPERS: These are transparent wrapping materials in sheet or bag form which may be sealed with a warm iron. They include cellophane with a special code number, polyethylene, and pliofilm.

CARTONS AND JARS: Use special glass that is not affected by sudden freezing, plastic jars, and upright or collapsible cartons. Clean, undamaged coffee cans may be used. Seal with freezer locker tape if the carton is not airtight.

Dangers of Food Spoilage Microorganisms such as bacteria, yeasts, and molds cause some foods to spoil. These same microorganisms, however, may help to preserve other foods. For example, lactic acid *bacteria* are used to make

ITEM	NUMBER OF DAYS
Cold cuts and frankfurters	7
Cheddar and processed cheese (keep tightly wrapped)	until used
Canned meats—after opening	3
Steaks, chops, roasts	3
Turkey	3
Freshly ground meat	2
Liver and variety meats	2
Fish and chicken	2
Eggs	14
Butter—tightly wrapped and covered	14
Cottage cheese—covered	7
Fresh fruits—lightly covered (apples, oranges, lemons longer)	7
Fresh vegetables—in hydrator (carrots and cabbage longer)	7
Fresh milk—covered	5
Canned foods opened, including baby foods*	2

*Lift from can only portion to be used; avoid warming and chilling contents. Keep all containers, especially metal, air-tight, to avoid change in flavor. Leftover custard and similar foods become watery when allowed to stand for a day, even if kept in a refrigerator.

sauerkraut from fresh cabbage; a *mold* is added to the curd to produce Roquefort cheese; *yeasts* are used in making breads and some beverages.

Chemical substances called *enzymes* are necessary to the ripening process of certain foods. However, unless their action is curtailed, enzymes also hasten food spoilage. Enzyme action aids in the production of wine by converting the sugar into alcohol; enzymes are also important in the production of vinegar. When butter becomes rancid, it is because enzymes have been at work.

Two harmful kinds of bacteria are *salmonella* and *staphylococcus*. Salmonella infection causes severe cramps, nausea, diarrhea, and vomiting. These bacteria are sometimes present in eggs, poultry, and meat from animals whose feed has been contaminated. Salmonella germs are usually killed if the food is cooked long enough, but if not they multiply rapidly at room temperature. This is why refrigeration is necessary when storing cooked foods.

Staphylococcus bacteria may cause food poisoning with symptoms similar to those of salmonella infection, but the sickness usually does not last as long. These bacteria are apt to be found in sandwich spreads; salads such as tuna, chicken, and potato; cream puffs, and creamy pies and puddings. These items must be refrigerated and should not be kept over a day or two.

Infections from salmonella and staphylococcus bacteria are not generally fatal, but *botulism* kills about two out of every three persons infected. A few years ago a Michigan woman died after eating tainted tuna, and several persons died in Tennessee after eating smoked whitefish. If these harmful germs are not killed in the canning process, they become active and multiply. Fortunately, the danger of botulism is no longer as great as in the days when more families canned meats at home.

Pork sometimes contains the germs of *trichinosis*. In this serious disease tiny worms multiply in the intestines and are carried to the blood stream, causing muscular pain and diarrhea. Pork must be thoroughly cooked to destroy the harmful germs.

PROGRESS IN FOOD PROCESSING

Traditional Methods of Preservation
Research is constantly introducing new ways of preserving foods as well as improving the established methods. Our forefathers depended upon preserving meat and fish by drying, smoking, or pickling with vinegar, spices, and brine. Root vegetables were buried, apples and corn were dried. Other foods were preserved with spices and sugars.

A Frenchman, Nicholas Appert, was the first person to can food successfully toward the close of the eighteenth century. William Underwood established the first cannery in America in 1817. In 1856 Gail Borden developed a method for canning milk.

At the start of the twentieth century American families were buying canned products in larger quantities, and food standards were becoming of national concern. In 1906 Congress passed the Meat Inspection Act, the first federal law related to food. In 1938 this act was replaced by stronger legislation, the Food, Drug, and Cosmetic Act. This act made it a federal offense for any manufacturer to ship harmful or useless foods, drugs, or cosmetics across state borders. The act has since been amended to cover additives. The Wheeler-Lea Act of the same year gave the Federal Trade Commission power to stop false and misleading advertising.

New Processes
Until Clarence Birdseye introduced quick freezing methods for preserving foods, no dramatic changes were made in food processing for over a century. Early freezing processes

U. S. GRADES AT A GLANCE

Condensed from Shopper's Guide to U. S. Grades for Food (Home and Garden Bulletin No. 58,
U. S. Department of Agriculture).

	1st Grade	2nd Grade	3rd Grade	4th Grade	5th Grade
BEEF.....	USDA Prime Top quality mainly for restaurants.	USDA Choice Very good grade for dry heat.	USDA Good Less juicy may be used for moist or dry heat.	USDA Standard For stews, ground beef.	USDA Commercial Long-time moist heat cooking or soups.
VEAL.....	USDA Prime	USDA Choice	USDA Good	USDA Standard	USDA Utility
	From animals 3 months old or less; higher grades more thickly fleshed and more tender than lower grades—roasts best cooked by moist heat.				
CALF.....	USDA Prime	USDA Choice	USDA Good	USDA Standard	USDA Utility
	From animals 3 to 8 months old; intermediate between beef and veal in color, texture, flavor and tenderness; comes in small cuts.				
LAMB.....	USDA Prime	USDA Choice	USDA Good	USDA Utility	USDA Cull.
	About 90 per cent of sheep in the U.S. is marketed as lamb; little demand for mutton; roasts best cooked by dry heat.				

BUTTER[1]..	U. S. Grade AA (U. S. 93 score)	U. S. Grade A (U. S. 92 score)		U. S. Grade B (U. S. 90 score)
		Grades AA and A have fine flavor and keep longer.		Less flavorful and will not keep as well.
POULTRY[2].	U. S. Grade A Highest proportion edible meat.	U. S. Grade B Not as fleshy as Grade A.		U. S. Grade C Less meaty and less flavor— good for soups and stews.
EGGS.....	U. S. Grade AA U. S. Grade A Large and firm with fine flavor—good for boiling, poaching, frying, custards.		U. S. Grade B U. S. Grade C Whites and yolks less firm, good for baking, scrambling, puddings.	

[1]Unless butter has U.S. prefix, the markings are only those of the manufacturer.
[2]All poultry moving in interstate commerce must be federally inspected. Poultry moving within a state may have voluntary inspection.

An entire meal may be prepared in an electric fryer.

H. J. Heinz Company

have been improved to maintain natural flavor, texture, and color. Freezing has reached a place where gourmet foods featuring Oriental, Parisian, and Scandanavian meals are available in large supermarkets. A new process promises quick frozen tomato slices for salads.

A new method of canning, called *Flash 18*, uses pressure cooking and sealing to reduce cooking and cooling time. The process preserves the texture of starchy foods such as spaghetti, noodles, and potatoes which are often overcooked in hash and stew. Partly cooked bacon can be canned, stored, and quickly heated.

Through the use of a new *liquid nitrogen process* which freezes foods almost instantly at minus 320 degrees F., shrimp and other seafood, mushrooms, and fruit may be quick frozen to retain better flavor and texture. Many of these foods may be heated for serving in the bags in which they come.

Freeze drying is a modern way of dehydrating foods. In this method the food is frozen and its moisture is removed in a vacuum, allowing the food to be stored without refrigeration. You have probably eaten freeze-dried berries or fruit with prepared dry cereals. Foods preserved in this manner are also very popular with campers. However, such foods can be rather expensive.

By the process of *nuclear irradiation* foods can be sterilized and pasteurized so that refrigeration is not necessary. When perfected, this process will make many fruits, vegetables, poultry, and seafood easy to store at room temperature.

Low-Calorie Foods   With the emphasis upon slimness and reducing diets, low-calorie foods have skyrocketed into popularity. With these new, low-calorie foods weight-watchers can "have their cake and eat it too." In 1965 the sale of low-calorie beverages was 15 times higher than in 1960, and the sale of low-calorie foods was five times greater.

The *cyclamate sweeteners* have an advantage over traditional synthetic sweeteners such as saccharin in that they do not leave an after taste.

Meals can be nutritious yet lack interest. To be appetizing, foods must have contrasts in color, texture, and flavor. The meals shown on this page would be about equally nutritious, but note the difference in eye appeal.

96A

When you have more guests than you can seat at a table, a *stand-up party* is the solution. The lazy susan offers tempting treats: *pastry boats* filled with seafood salad; *deviled eggs; rounds of pastry* filled with tomato paste, cheese, and seasonings; and *kabobs* of pastry squares, sausages, and olives, to be dipped in the seasoned cocktail sauce.

Good food is only a part of mealtime success. Careful thought should be given to the appearance of the table settings and other accessories. Notice how the golden brown rolls and almond oven-fried chicken fit in with the color plan. The twisted white and gold candles repeat the colors in the china. Jellied madrilene and tomato aspic add the final color note.

96C

Even when camping out you can follow healthful meal practices. Modern food preservation methods and containers make it possible to take along a variety of foods that are not only easy to prepare and serve but nutritious and tasty as well.

Baked products and ice creams with cyclamate have become popular low-calorie items, and so have salad dressings in which starch, water, and vegetable gums replace oils for maintaining texture. The calorie value of nuts is also being cut by a process which involves roasting.

PREPARING FOODS TO RETAIN NUTRIENTS

It is unwise to spend money for food, then, in preparing it, lose healthgiving vitamins and minerals by improper preparation and cooking.

For the greatest benefit from nutrients, observe the following suggestions:

MEAT: Meats are cooked by dry or moist heat. Dry heat means cooking meat without a cover, in an oven, under a broiler, or in a frying pan—roasting, broiling, or pan frying. Moist heat means cooking meat surrounded by hot liquid in *covered* roaster, or steam in pressure cooker—braising, stewing, or boiling.

In general, tender cuts of meat are better cooked by dry heat at a low temperature (300 to 325). High temperatures make meat tough and may cause shrinkage up to 30 per cent.

Steaks and chops less than 1 inch thick may not be as juicy broiled as pan fried over higher heat and *turned frequently*. Tough cuts of meat become more tender when cooked for a long time by moist heat. You can cook tough cuts under a broiler or by dry oven heat in about half the usual time if they have been marinated from six to eight hours in vinegar, wine, sour cream, or other sour liquids, or treated with commercial tenderizers.

Salting thinner cuts of meat *before* *cooking* will cause a loss of juice, but virtually no juice is lost in salting a roast because salt penetrates very little.

ROASTING: Season with salt and pepper, place on a rack in a roaster with fat side up, and insert a meat thermometer which must not touch the bone, if any. Do not add water, do not cover, and do not baste. Roast beef, veal, lamb, and smoked pork at an oven temperature of 300°; roast fresh pork at 350°. For rare beef, the thermometer reading will be 140°, medium 150°-160°, and well done 160°-170°; for well done smoked pork 160°-170°; well done veal 170°; lamb 175°-180°, fresh pork 185°. Only beef should be eaten medium or rare.

As mentioned earlier, pork often carries germs of *trichinosis*. People who eat pork that is not well done risk contracting this disease.

Roasts and whole fowl are more easily carved if allowed to stand for 10 or 15 minutes after roasting.

PANFRYING: Brown meat on both sides in a small amount of fat in a heavy frying pan. Do not cover. Cook at moderate temperature, turning occasionally until done. To retain juices, serve at once.

BROILING (INDOOR): Place meat 2 to 4 inches from heat, depending upon thickness of meat and degree of heat—the thinner the meat, the closer to the flame. Trim fat to reduce smoke. Clip edges of the meat to prevent curling. Broil on one side and then the other until done. Use a meat thermometer for especially thick cuts. For charcoal broiling, have coals red hot and turn the meat frequently.

BRAISING: Using fat, brown on all sides in a heavy utensil; then add a

Casserole and salad meals are appetizing
and economical.

small amount of liquid. Cover and
cook at low temperature (300-325)
until done. Use cooking liquid for nutritious gravy. If excess fat is removed
from the meat before cooking, or
skimmed off, the gravy will not be too
fattening.

STEWING: Using fat, brown the
meat on all sides in a heavy utensil.
Cover with liquid and cook below
boiling point on a burner or in the
oven. Add vegetables long enough
before serving to be cooked. Use
cooking liquids.

BOILING: Cover meat with water;
salt; bring to boiling point and lower
heat to hold at simmer point. Use for
soup, stew, meat pie, or serve in thickened broth.

POULTRY: In the United States all
poultry may be purchased ready to
cook and inspected for wholesomeness. Poultry should be firm, evenly
colored, and practically free of pin
feathers. In a young bird, the breastbone is flexible. Chickens come in the
following classes: broiler or fryer,
roaster, capon, caponette, and stewing chicken. Turkeys may be had
eight pounds and under for frying or
roasting, or up to twenty pounds and

over for roasting. Hen turkeys are
smaller than toms. Other fowl include
duck, goose, squab, and Rock Cornish hen.

Fowl as well as meat has less
shrinkage, is more tender, and tastes
better when cooked at low temperatures. However, quick cooking at high
temperature may be all right if the
bird is wrapped air-tightly in heavy
aluminum foil. Excess fat may be
skimmed off and cooking broth used
for gravy.

FISH: Some familiar *fresh water
fish* are black bass, carp, catfish, pickerel, pike, sunfish, whitefish, and
trout. Some familiar *salt water fish*
are bluefish, flounder, cod, haddock,
halibut, herring, mackerel, mullet,
red snapper, salmon, and tuna. Fish
may be purchased whole, drawn,
dressed, in fillets and steaks; all methods of cooking may be used.

Shellfish include clams, crabs, lobsters, scallops, shrimp, and mussels.

Fish is so perishable it should not
be allowed to stand at room temperature long before cooking. Frozen fish
should be cooked as soon as it thaws.

EGGS: Quality is judged by firmness. The white and yolk of a highquality egg that has been kept in the
refrigerator will be firm when broken
into a pan. The color of the shell is
not important. Eggs vary in size from
extra large to small. Therefore egg
recipes that give measurements rather
than number of eggs may turn out
more satisfactorily.

Bedfast persons should not be
served raw egg whites, such as in meringue. The white is difficult to digest. Although eggs cooked in the
shell are referred to as "boiled eggs,"
they should be called *soft, medium,*

or *hard-cooked* eggs. Keep the water below the boiling point and the utensil covered to prevent protein in the white from becoming tough. If the heat is turned off when the water reaches boiling point, and the pan covered for 10 minutes, the white will be tender; the yolk will not have a green tinge.

BUTTER: Butter will become stale or rancid if it is transferred in and out of the refrigerator often. Butter may be kept fresh over a long period by freezing. Margarine will keep longer than butter without becoming stale. Margarine should be fortified with 15,000 International Units of vitamin A per pound.

MILK: When milk is exposed to light, riboflavin is destroyed. An hour's exposure destroys one-third. Cooking in a covered metal utensil is preferable to cooking in glass. Keep dry milk *tightly* sealed, because exposure to air makes the powder lumpy and decomposes the protein.

You may have heard that chocolate flavored milk is not good for you. Research shows that unflavored milk does provide more calcium and phosphorus, but the difference is probably not enough to discourage the use of chocolate milk or cocoa.

FRUIT: No fruit should be cut, peeled, or squeezed until just before it is used, if you are to receive full benefit of the vitamins. Exposure to air increases the loss of vitamin C in citrus fruits. If orange juice must be prepared in advance, be sure the oranges have been chilled, extract the juice quickly, use an airtight cover on the container, and store in the refrigerator. Little vitamin C is lost in cooking sour fruits such as green ap-

ples, rhubarb, and plums, because the natural acid retards enzyme action. When frozen fruits are thawed in contact with air, vitamin C is lost.

If fruits are cooked in a minimum amount of water, their natural sugars will be retained, and less sugar will be required for sweetening.

All kinds of berries should be refrigerated as soon as possible—unwashed and unstemmed. Handling and shaking bruises the fruit, stimulating enzyme action and the loss of vitamins. The chilled fruit should be *washed quickly in cold water and kept cold until serving time.*

VEGETABLES: Vegetables lose a great deal of their flavor as well as from half to almost all of their vitamins and minerals by improper care in preparation and cooking. Fresh or frozen vegetables should be cooked in as little water as possible until done but not soft. In cooking canned vegetables, boil down the liquid; add vegetables; heat, and serve in the cooking liquid.

The loss of nutrients is hastened when tomatoes, cabbage, and leafy vegetables are chopped, peeled, or shredded, unless they are eaten soon afterward. Soaking may destroy vitamin C. Hard water and the addition of soda, or cooking in iron or copper utensils also destroys vitamin C.

Vitamin A in sweet potatoes, Hubbard squash, and carrots is not easily destroyed in cooking. Vitamin B_1 in dried beans and peas and leafy vegetables is weakened or destroyed when the water boils fast or vegetables are overcooked.

Foods prepared according to these suggestions will not only be more nutritious but will also taste better.

Finger salads for a buffet or barbecue.

Food must have aesthetic appeal . . .

A bowl of salad greens.

A fix-it-yourself salad tray.

ADD THE MAGIC TOUCH

Colorings, flavorings, spices, seasonings, herbs, and garnishes cost little, but make foods more appetizing, and they are fun to use.

A little yellow coloring in chicken gravy, creamed chicken, and lemon icing, or a little red in canned pie cherries or sallow looking tomato juice will improve the appearance.

Flavorings, if used properly, can give many ordinary dishes an inspired touch. Smoke flavoring adds zest to the taste of bean and split pea soup. Peppermint flavoring and red coloring *or* nuts, maple, and butter flavoring beaten into vanilla ice cream can lend glamor to an ordinary dessert.

Cooking wines, spices, and herbs give everyday meats and casserole dishes a special appeal. Cooks who want to impress their guests should learn to use these items:

COLORINGS: red, yellow, and green.
CONDIMENTS: ground horse-radish,

Hawaiian luncheon salad.

. . . to be fully enjoyed.

Grapefruit flower salad to accompany a heavy meal.

Luncheon salad with pineapple slice, jellied cranberry slice, cottage cheese, peach half, and cherry.

Photographs by H. J. Heinz Company

SEASONINGS AND SEEDS: pimiento, celery seed and celery salt, garlic and garlic salt, onion flakes, chive, leeks, dried parsley, poultry seasoning, caraway, and sesame.

SPICES: nutmeg, cloves, ginger, cinnamon, allspice, and pickling spices.

HERBS: mint, marjoram, dill, basil, savory, rosemary, oregano, bay leaves, thyme, sage, and tarragon.

GARNISHES: parsley, celery leaves, water cress, olives, lemon slices, pimientos, green pepper, maraschino cherries, candied fruit, chopped nuts, and grated cheese.

FOOD PATTERNS AND CULTURE

Your food habits and eating behavior are influenced by your culture, family customs, social status, food

curry powder, cayenne, chili powder, pepper, dry mustard, and paprika.

EXTRACTS AND FLAVORINGS: butter, banana, peppermint, rum, brandy, vanilla, lemon, almond, and maple.

101

supply, income, and the emotional atmosphere in which you eat your meals.

The basic foods in a nation or other area depend upon the climate, soil, type of plant and animal life, extent of technology, and communication. In northern Europe and North America wheat, rye, beef, and pork are plentiful and popular. In other areas rice, maize, oats, or barley may be easier to raise, and people may eat the meat of horses or monkeys. Seafood in many forms is plentiful along lakes, rivers, and oceans. The popular fats in temperate climates are butter, lard, beef suet, and margarine, and in warmer climates olive, corn, and peanut oils.

If you were to eat a typical German dinner it might be planned around a heavy soup, boiled potatoes, rye bread, sausage, cabbage, and pickled foods. A typical Italian dinner might include minestrone soup, Italian bread, spaghetti and tomato sauce, tossed green salad, and fresh fruit.

Food patterns are established not only by the availability of certain foods but by religious customs as well. Since the dawn of civilization prayers, songs, and dancing have been associated with the harvest. These ancient customs are reenacted when we ask a blessing at mealtime on the food we are about to eat.

Religious customs related to food vary within our own country and throughout the world. For example, some Roman Catholics do not eat meat on Friday in commemoration of Christ's suffering on the cross. Many Jews do not eat pork, wild animals, or scaleless fish because the ancient Hebrews considered these unclean.

Hindus consider the cow sacred and therefore do not eat beef. Buddhists eat no meat at all because they do not believe in taking any kind of life.

Not only do foods differ from nation to nation, but so do mealtime customs. As travel becomes easier, more Americans are apt to find themselves in places where dining practices are very different from what they have always known. If you were to dine with an Arab family you might eat while sitting on the floor, use your fingers rather than a knife and fork, and dip bread into a common bowl. In Japan also you would probably sit on the floor, around a very low table, and use chopsticks. Even in England, where many customs are similar to ours, you would see people eating from forks held, prongs down, in the left hand.

In some societies a dinner guest is expected to eat noisily to show that he enjoys and appreciates the food. Eating quietly would be considered impolite. Also there are cultures in which a plump figure is admired. In such places it is customary to eat greater quantities of food than Americans usually eat.

Naturally most people favor the customs and manners they have always practiced. But should this mean making fun of others whose ways are different? Is it better to be critical of other cultures, or to try to understand and appreciate them?

Over the years many mistaken beliefs have been associated with certain foods. For example, at one time tomatoes were considered poisonous. Even today there are people who believe that fish should not be served with milk, that celery and fish are "brain foods," that beets build blood, that brown eggs are more nutritious than white eggs, or that yogurt is more nutritious than milk. These beliefs have no scientific basis.

In most civilizations the dinner hour has a social importance. As far as possible the entire family should try to make it a time for being together and enjoying one another. The emotional atmosphere has a great deal to do with the enjoyment and digestion of food.

FOOD PREFERENCES

Studies of the eating habits of Americans indicate that vegetables—especially cooked vegetables—are the least popular of foods. Most frequently rejected are cabbage, carrots, squash, and parsnips. High on the food preference list are milk, meat (except lamb and organ meats such as liver), fruits, most breads and cereals, and practically all desserts. The eating habits of parents, especially fathers, exercise an influence upon the eating habits of children. Whether they eat with the family or alone, children should be fed in a relaxed, quiet atmosphere. They should be given small portions, suited to their needs, and allowed to feed themselves when old enough. When nagged to eat, they will rebel; when bribed or given too much attention, they will demand still more.

Words and Phrases to Know

additive	hemoglobin
avocado	iodine
beriberi	iron
botulism	laminated
braising	marinate
broiling	mineral
calcium	niacin
calorie	nuclear irradiation
carbohydrate	nutrient
cellulose	pan frying
cholesterol	phosphorus
condiment	pliofilm
cyclamate	protein
sweeteners	riboflavin
deficiency	rickets
drawn (referring to	roasting
chicken and fish)	salmonella
enzyme	staphylococcus
fat-soluble	stewing
fillet	thiamine
foil	thyroid
fortified	trichinosis
garnish	vitamin
glassine	water-soluble
goiter	yogurt

ACTIVITIES

1. Discuss your own eating habits in relation to the Daily Food Guide. What foods are you eating in smaller or greater amounts than recommended?

2. Make a list of foods under each of the following headings, then discuss each group of foods in relation to nutrition, storage, preparation, and cooking:

Foods with water-soluble vitamins.
Foods with fat-soluble vitamins.
Foods with vitamins or minerals affected by light and air.
Protein foods.

3. Before class, plan to have meat cooked fast at high heat and slowly at low heat. Taste and judge according to tenderness, flavor, and shrinkage. Record weights before and after cooking.

4. Demonstrate the use of a meat thermometer. Why is a thermometer more accurate than timing roasts according to weight?

5. List the least expensive cuts of beef, pork, and lamb. Girls: Begin collecting recipes you might want to use.

6. Discuss experiences members of the class have had catching or cleaning fish, raising or cleaning poultry, raising cattle, hogs, and lambs.

7. Study meat packers' charts showing meat cuts.

8. Arrange a display of various kinds of fowl, or visit a meat market where such a display may be arranged. Discuss each in relation to preparation and cost.

9. List the kinds of fish commonly available in your community. How do fresh fish compare with frozen fish in taste and texture? Discuss ways of preparing fish. If possible, plan to have fish prepared various ways before class. Members may compare flavors.

10. Display egg cartons showing various grades and sizes. Discuss uses for each grade. Examine and taste eggs cooked by being dropped into boiling water; compare with eggs cooked by putting them in cool water, bringing water to a boil, and turning off heat. Be sure eggs are hard cooked for easy tasting.

11. Conduct a taste test for milk. Chill each of the following kinds of milk: ordinary pasteurized; homogenized; skim; evaporated or condensed (diluted for serving); dried or powdered (with water added); yogurt. Discuss the food value, uses, and taste of each.

12. Discuss the ways you prepare fruits and vegetables at home in relation to what you have learned here.

13. Discuss your family's methods of buying and storing food.

14. **Bulletin Board:** Arrange a display of foods grouped under proteins, carbohydrates, fats, and individual vitamins and minerals.

15. Arrange a display of one or two foods to show *can* or *package* sizes, *grades* and *varieties*. Compare costs, quality, number of servings, and uses.

16. Discuss meal preparation with ready-to-heat-and-eat frozen foods and mixes, in comparison with meal preparation in your parents' and grandparents' early days.

17. **Bulletin Board:** Arrange a display showing how garnishes add interest to foods.

18. Make some comparisons between shopping at a neighborhood grocery store and at a large food market.

19. Discuss some symptoms, dangers, and treatments of food poisoning.

20. Arrange a display of low-calorie foods and compare with the same servings of regular food in calorie value.

Correlation

SCIENCE: Arrange with the chemistry or biology teacher to give an illustrated talk on the digestive process.

LOCAL NEWSPAPER OR SCHOOL PAPER: Prepare several articles under titles similar to the following:

"Eat Your Way to Health."

"Why Pay for Food and Discard the Nutrients?"

"Read Labels and Reap Dividends."

"Sharp Shopping."

Home Experiences

Have your parents read the chapter and discuss their methods of shopping for food and preparing it, in relation to the information in the chapter.

Type and post these charts on a cabinet door near your food preparation center—Table of Equivalents; List of Meats and Vegetables (with cooking time and temperature figures).

Prepare several dishes with a "foreign flavor." Discuss them in committee meetings out of class, and prepare some of the foods in class for members to taste. Start a recipe file of foreign dishes.

Chapter 5

Keeping Physically Attractive

Weight, well-being, and recreation are closely related. Attaining and keeping a good, young figure and active zest for living will help you contribute to the adult world, as well as to your personal success, by boosting your chances for physical and mental health. You actually *owe* this to your loved ones, business associates, and friends.

EXCESS WEIGHT IS A HEALTH PROBLEM

How do we decide if we are overweight? Some young adults, who think they are overweight, seriously endanger their health on self-made or fad diets. Unwise reducing can also cause skin troubles, fatigue, and other physical disturbances.

Height-weight charts for teen-agers are not perfect criteria for determining your ideal weight. Available tables are based upon average weights for boys and girls according to a *height and age* scale. It is not unusual for a boy 10 to be as big boned as a

boy 15, or a girl 14 to be as mature as another girl 16. Body framework is a necessary consideration in determining weight. Even when weight charts are based upon small, medium, and large frames, few teen-agers can identify their frames. It is easier to classify persons according to frame and weight after the growing process is complete. Girls usually reach their maximum growth at about 17; boys may grow until they are 20.

Although there are many underweight people, we are concerned much more about those who are overweight. To carry around ten or more pounds of excess fat is like living with bags of sand strapped to the body. More work is placed on the heart, blood vessels, joints, and muscles. An overly fat person is almost five times as likely to have diabetes, four times as likely to have high blood pressure, three times as likely to have heart diseases. He is more accident prone, and takes twice as great a risk in a major operation as a person of more normal

105

weight. The mortality rate of obese men in their 20's is 80 per cent higher than men of normal weight. Although a gain of 20 to 25 pounds is not unusual during pregnancy, an abnormally overweight woman may have difficulty during childbirth.

What makes people overweight? In a few cases, glandular condition may cause poor metabolism, but usually, eating habits are responsible.

• Some people overeat because it is a family tradition to enjoy good food.

• Others may eat too much just to be sociable without realizing how quickly pounds can be added.

• Many people establish eating habits while young, and fail to reduce food intake as they grow older and become less active. A person in the fifties may need only half as much food as he needed in his early teen years. A person whose weight is right at eighteen cannot be sure of maintaining his figure and health even at twenty-five if he continues eighteen-year-old eating habits. Child bearing, and less exercise after the school years, have "weighty" results.

• Emotionally disturbed people may eat to compensate for not fitting in with a crowd, achieving desired success, or finding love.

Some people simply let weight creep up by reducing their activities but not reducing their calorie intake.

CASE STUDIES: Bill Jennings, who had been accustomed to walking to school—a total of three miles a day—started riding but did not change his eating habits. Bill no longer energized (used up) the calories he had been using on his walks. His body stored the excess calories as fat. In a year he gained 13 pounds.

Peggy Simons started taking a glass of whole milk (170 calories) and two saltines (30 calories) at bedtime in addition to her normal diet. In four months she gained over five pounds.

You may ask what's the limit on gaining? You might compare the body with a business. As a business expands it takes more dollars to run it, and still more to expand further. As weight increases it takes more calories to maintain the new weight and still more to increase it. Up to a certain point you will continue to gain before leveling off, but if you continue to increase calorie intake gradually, it is frightening to think of what you could weigh.

PROPER DIET AND WEIGHT CONTROL

When our blood sugar runs low, we get hungry. Blood sugar is at its lowest in the morning, and if raised then, it is easier to maintain a good level all day, without overeating. This is important to remember on a reducing diet. Furthermore, studies show that students who eat a well balanced breakfast experience less fatigue by noon and do better school work. Too many people in high school and college, especially girls, either eat a poor breakfast or skip it entirely. A breakfast of coffee and doughnuts lacks vitamin C and protein which the body needs daily.

Sweets are assimilated quickly, but their effect soon wears off. Starches take longer than sugars to be assimilated, and protein foods take still longer. That is why protein foods keep you from becoming hungry.

People attempt to control appetite in many ways. Not all are good.

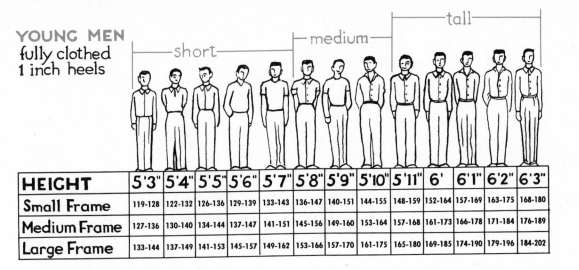

YOUNG MEN
fully clothed
1 inch heels

short — medium — tall

HEIGHT	5'3"	5'4"	5'5"	5'6"	5'7"	5'8"	5'9"	5'10"	5'11"	6'	6'1"	6'2"	6'3"
Small Frame	119-128	122-132	126-136	129-139	133-143	136-147	140-151	144-155	148-159	152-164	157-169	163-175	168-180
Medium Frame	127-136	130-140	134-144	137-147	141-151	145-156	149-160	153-164	157-168	161-173	166-178	171-184	176-189
Large Frame	133-144	137-149	141-153	145-157	149-162	153-166	157-170	161-175	165-180	169-185	174-190	179-196	184-202

YOUNG WOMEN
fully clothed
2 inch heels

short — medium — tall

HEIGHT	4'11"	5'	5'1"	5'2"	5'3"	5'4"	5'5"	5'6"	5'7"	5'8"	5'9"	5'10"	5'11"
Small Frame	104-111	105-113	107-115	110-118	113-121	116-125	119-128	123-132	126-136	129-139	133-143	136-147	139-150
Medium Frame	110-118	112-120	114-122	117-125	120-128	124-132	127-135	130-140	134-144	137-147	141-151	145-155	148-158
Large Frame	117-127	119-129	121-131	124-135	127-138	131-142	133-145	138-150	142-154	145-158	149-162	152-166	155-169

Metropolitan Life Insurance Company

For girls between 18 and 25, subtract 1 pound for each year under 25.

• Some smoke cigarettes to take the mind off food. Smoking may tend to slow up the stomach's demand for food to a slight degree, but there are dangers in heavy smoking, one of the worst of which is lung cancer. The death rate from lung cancer is 12.8 per 100,000 for non-smokers, against 95.2 for heavy smokers.

• Reducing drugs are popular with some dieters. These drugs depress the appetite temporarily and dehydrate the tissues, causing a quick—but not often permanent—loss of weight. The sale of prescription drugs for curtailing the appetite doubled in a recent five-year period.

• Those who can afford the costs go to reducing salons or buy expensive exercise equipment. However, reducing salons will not usually guarantee loss of weight except to those who follow rigid diets. Many of these diets are deficient in one or more nutrients. Exercise keeps the body in tune and holds weight to a level, but it is not a quick way to reduce. Do you know that you would have to walk 35 miles to energize 3,500 calories, the equivalent of one pound of body fat?

• Many people, with or without the advice of a doctor, substitute a low-calorie formula in liquid, powder, or solid form for one or more regular daily meals. Although partially fortified with essential nutrients, these formula diets should not be used over a long period of time without medical supervision.

People who really want to reduce will use will power and count calories. They do not follow fad diets for a week or two but *establish a new pattern for eating,* minus pastries, candy, ice cream, cake, rich salad dressings, and gravies, except in small amounts and on special occasions.

Eating vegetable and fruit snacks and using skim milk will satisfy the appetite and provide valuable nutrients without adding many calories to the diet. Any food eaten between meals or at bedtime, of course, must be counted in the day's calorie total, whether you are trying to gain or lose. Even though the mind may ignore these significant snacks, the body registers every calorie.

Inadequacies of Fad Diets

In the desire to find some "magic" way to reduce, people are inclined to take counsel from newspaper advertising and TV commercials.

Certain *900-calorie formula diets,* available in liquid, solid, and powder form, were extremely popular in the early 1960's, but only two brands were on the market five years later. Most people do not stay on these diets because they offer no variety of flavor or texture and, unless other satisfying foods are eaten, they may make a person quite irritable.

The term "magic diet" has been applied to such combinations as cottage cheese and peaches, or lamb chops and grapefruit. Reducing diets of this sort become popular from time to time. However, most of them are fads and are deficient in essential ingredients.

The *low-carbohydrate diet,* under many popular titles, advocates counting grams of carbohydrate instead of calories. Followers of this diet claim that calories do not count and that they can eat all the protein and fat they want. They forget that calories, when not needed, are stored up in body fat, and excess protein may overtax the kidneys.

The low-carbohydrate diet is no more effective and far less safe than the 1,250-calorie diet which you would follow if you ate the recom-

The Calorie Line-Up.

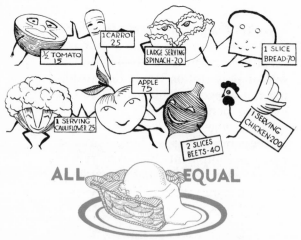

1 CARROT 25

½ TOMATO 15

LARGE SERVING SPINACH-20

1 SLICE BREAD-70

APPLE 75

1 SERVING CAULIFLOWER 25

2 SLICES BEETS-40

1 SERVING CHICKEN-200

ALL EQUAL

APPLE PIE ALA MODE ~ 470 CALORIES

108

mended servings from the four basic food groups.

Nine out of ten persons on fad diets do not stay reduced; many even gain back more than they lose. Fad diets can undermine physical and mental health because, as mentioned previously, most are deficient in essential nutrients. *No quick way to reduce is safe.* It may take a long time to lose ten or twenty pounds, but think of how long it took for that much weight to accumulate! The safest and surest

way to lose weight or avoid gaining weight is to establish an eating pattern that fits your needs. By eating three well balanced meals a day in average portions a person can reduce and stay reduced. Furthermore, such meals can be not only nutritious but can have variety, texture, and flavor.

Weight, Activity, and Health A person 10 per cent *over* or 20 per cent *under* the desired weight should consult a phy-

If you have a weight problem, learn to spend your calorie allowance for the best nutritional results. Concentrated sweets are *high in calorie value*. Omit rich desserts, gravy, cream and sugar in coffee.

1200 CALORIE DAILY MENU

BREAKFAST

ORANGE JUICE-60 + BOILED EGG-75 + THIN SLICE BREAD-70 + TEASPOON BUTTER-25 + SKIM MILK-85 + COFFEE-0 = **315 CALORIES OR ONE PIECE OF PIE**

LUNCH

LETTUCE 5 / 5 T. COTTAGE CHEESE 100 / ½ PEACH 60 + CREAMED ASPARAGUS ON THIN TOAST* 118 + ½ GLASS SKIM MILK-45 = **328 CALORIES OR TWO CUPCAKES**

*1 t. BUTTER (25)

DINNER

3 OZ. LEAN MEAT-200 + ½ CUP BEETS-40 + ½ CUP SPINACH 20 + BAKED POTATO 1 t. BUTTER-125 + COFFEE-0 + FRUIT JELLO-87 + BEDTIME SKIM MILK-85 = **557 CALORIES OR ONE MALTED MILKSHAKE AND CRACKER**

sician. The person who is greatly underweight may have less endurance and less resistance to infection. Tuberculosis may strike underweight persons more frequently. Many people are underweight because they do not have much interest in food, strange as it may seem to most of us.

We cannot see a calorie, but we determine energy in calories, just as we determine height in inches and weight in pounds. If your weight is normal for your height and body frame, the number of calories you need will be determined by your age, activities, appetite, and perhaps by whether you want to gain or lose a few pounds. You need fewer calories normally in a warm climate or during summer months, because you will not draw upon your supply for keeping your body warm. You need more calories during your growing years, and for active sports. Energy requirements gradually decline after early adulthood because of a decrease in metabolism and lessened physical activity.

The Food and Nutrition Board of the National Academy of Sciences— National Research Council compiles nutritional information. In 1963-64 this group revised its dietary allow-

A person uses up six times as many calories in active exercise as sitting in a chair.

ances, decreasing the number of calories needed by the average person. This was done because the automobile and other mechanized equipment have steadily reduced the amount of physical activity for most people.

In setting up requirements the Food and Nutrition Board speaks of the average or *reference man and woman.* The *reference woman* is 64 inches tall (without shoes) and weighs 128 pounds. The *reference man* is 69 inches tall and weighs 154 pounds. It is estimated that the *reference woman* needs 2,100 calories daily between the ages of 18 and 35; 1,900 between 35 and 55; and 1,600 between 55 and 75. The *reference man* has a daily requirement of 2,900 calories between 18 and 35; 2,600 between 35 and 55; and 2,200 between 55 and 75.

The body frame is another important consideration in counting calories. A shorter person would require fewer calories and a taller person more. Special conditions can also change calorie needs. For instance, during the last six months of pregnancy a woman needs 200 more calories a day and during lactation about 1,000 more.

Here is the latest Food and Nutrition Board Chart for calorie allowances:

	Age	Weight	Height	Calories
CHILDREN	1–3	29	34	1,300
	4–6	40	42	1,600
	7–9	53	49	2,100
BOYS	10–12	72	55	2,400
	13–15	98	61	3,000
	16–18	134	68	3,400
GIRLS	10–12	72	55	2,200
	13–15	103	62	2,500
	16–18	117	64	2,300
MEN	18–35	154	69	2,900
	36–55	154	69	2,600
	56–75	154	69	2,200
WOMEN	18–35	128	64	2,100
	36–55	128	64	1,900
	56–75	128	64	1,600

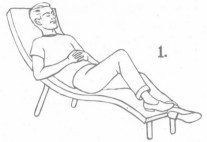

Calorie needs in relation to activity.

Activity	Calories per pound per hour
Sleeping, lying still watching television, reading in bed	0.42
Sitting at home, in a car, school or church—reading, talking, watching television, listening to records.	0.65
Light exercise in sewing, playing the piano or other musical instrument, typing, playing cards and table games, laboratory work, dressing, slow walking, driving car.	1.10
Moderate exercise in ordinary walking, daily cleaning and meal preparation, laundry work with equipment.	1.88
Active exercise in heavy cleaning, scrubbing, laundry work with little equipment, house painting, dancing, gym class, heavy lifting, brisk walking, walking up hill, playing golf, working on a car or in a workshop.	2.92
Very active exercise in running, swimming, tennis, horseback riding, bicycling, playing football, basketball.	3.90

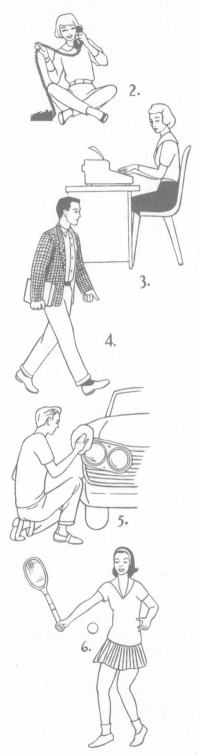

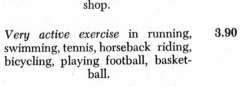

As you see, the chart on page 110 is based on average persons. The chart on this page treats calories differently. It relates calories to physical activities. By estimating the number of hours you spend in various activities, you can use this chart to determine your own calorie needs.

Let's suppose you are a girl 18. If you are 5'6" (with 2" heels) and of medium frame, you should weigh about 7 pounds less than the recommended weight in the illustration on page 107, or between 123 and 133 pounds. Let's say you weigh 125 pounds. By using the data with the illustration on page 111 you can figure your calorie needs thus:

Activity	Hours	Weight	Calories per Pound per Hour	Calorie Needs
SLEEPING	8	125	0.42	420
SITTING	8	125	0.65	650
LIGHT EXERCISE	6	125	1.10	825
MODERATE EXERCISE	2	125	1.88	470
TOTAL	24			2365

In one way, counting calories is simple arithmetic. Feed 2,600 calories into your digestive system, use or dispose of only 2,000 and what happens? The 600 excess calories tuck themselves away as 1/6th of a pound of fat. (As mentioned earlier, 3,500 calories represent about one pound of body weight.) Continue this eating habit for one year and you will need an entirely new wardrobe! It will take just as long to lose the excess weight, but instead of allowing yourself 2,000 calories a day, you will have to cut down to 1,400 to lose 1/6th of a pound per day.

However, diet is more than counting calories—it is selecting foods wisely. Recommended allowances are given in Chapter 4, page 90.

KEEP IN TUNE WITH EXERCISE

Many people think they can lose weight by exercising; but when they try, they often find out that this is hard to do. Of course, exercise does affect weight, as Bill Jennings found out (page 106). However, it takes a great deal of regular exercise to result in permanent loss of many pounds.

For example, it takes a five-mile hike to work off the calories in a typical fudge sundae, and a brisk 35-mile walk to lose one pound, when the temperature is at 70 degrees. (A large person tends to use up more calories than a small person.) When you lose a lot of weight after heavy exercise, much is just water loss which you quickly replace.

Still, the benefits of regular daily exercise to persons of all ages are undeniable. Without exercise an individual's muscles become so soft that he experiences chronic fatigue. Regular exercise geared to one's general health reduces the likelihood of heart attack, lowers cholesterol level, and clears fats from the blood faster after meals. Exercise also helps to slow down the aging process. Furthermore, moderate exercises followed regularly will help keep weight *under control*, even if they won't result in spectacular weight *loss*. In some businesses, instead of coffee breaks, employees are given exercise breaks.

National attention was called to the weakness of our youth some years ago

Swimming is excellent exercise. It can contribute to good health for the entire family.

when the records of physical fitness tests were compared with those of other countries. The Kraus Physical Fitness Tests were given to 7,000 youths between six and sixteen in the United States, Austria, Italy, and Switzerland. About six out of ten American children failed on one or more of the six basic strength and flexibility tests, whereas fewer than one out of ten European children failed.

As mentioned earlier, increased use of automobiles has reduced the amount of exercise most people take. Worksaving devices in the home as well as automation in business and industry also make life easy but deprive us of the kind of activity needed for good physical condition and mental health.

You do not have to leave your room or even your desk to benefit from *isometric exercises*. These are simple muscle tensing activities you can do throughout the day. For instance, sit up straight and draw in your abdominal muscles, or hold your legs out

straight tensing the muscles, or hold the muscles of your arms tense for six or eight seconds from time to time.

All through the day you can get the benefit of "hidden exercises." Stand as you put on your shoes and stockings, balancing on one leg. Walk up several flights of steps instead of using an elevator. Walk rather than ride short distances.

For picnics select foods that will satisfy hearty appetites, but don't forget to count calories.

113

SAFE REDUCING MENUS*

	1,000-Calorie† Diet	1,200-Calorie† Diet	1,500-Calorie† Diet
BREAKFAST	Fresh fruit or juice..........1 serving—½ cup	Fresh fruit or juice.......1 serving—½ cup	Fresh fruit or juice.......1 serving—½ cup
	Egg—cooked without fat......1	Egg—cooked without fat..1	Egg—cooked without fat..1
	Bread or cereal...............1 slice of bread or small serving of cereal	Bread or cereal............1 slice of bread or small serving of cereal	Bread or cereal...........1 slice of bread or a serving of cereal (1 cup, prepared or ½ cup, cooked)
	Butter or margarine..........1 level teaspoon	Butter or margarine......1 level teaspoon	Butter or margarine......1 level teaspoon
	Skim milk or buttermilk......1 glass—6 ounces	Milk...........................1 glass—6 ounces	Milk...........................1 glass—8 ounces
	Clear coffee or tea	Clear coffee or tea	Coffee or tea
			Cream.........................1 tablespoon
DINNER	Lean meat, fish, or poultry....3 ounces (average serving)	Lean meat, fish, or poultry. 3 ounces (average serving)	Lean meat, fish, or poultry. 3 ounces (average serving)
	Vegetables......................½ cup Group I and ½ cup Group II	Vegetables.................½ cup Group I	Vegetables.................½ cup Group I and and ½ cup Group II
	Skim milk or buttermilk......1 glass—6 ounces	Potato or bread...........1 small potato or 1 slice of bread	Potato.......................1 small
	Fruit—raw, or cooked or canned without sugar.......1 serving—½ cup	Butter or margarine......1 level teaspoon	Butter or margarine......1 level teaspoon
		Milk...........................1 glass—6 ounces	Milk...........................1 glass—8 ounces
		Fruit—raw, or cooked or canned without sugar...1 serving—½ cup	Fruit—raw, or cooked or canned without sugar...1 serving—½ cup
LUNCH OR SUPPER	Cottage cheese, meat, or eggs.........................½ cup of cheese, 2 ounces of meat, or 2 eggs	Cottage cheese, meat, or eggs.........................½ cup of cheese, 2 ounces of meat, or 2 eggs	Cottage cheese, meat, or eggs.........................½ cup of cheese, 2 ounces of meat, or 2 eggs
	Vegetables......................½ cup Group I and ½ cup Group II	Vegetables.................½ cup raw Group I and ½ cup Group II	Vegetables.................½ cup Group I and ½ cup Group II
	Skim milk or buttermilk......1 glass—6 ounces	Milk...........................1 glass—6 ounces	Bread.........................1 slice
	Fruit—raw, or cooked or canned without sugar.......1 serving—½ cup	Fruit—raw, or cooked or canned without sugar...1 serving—½ cup	Butter or margarine......1 level teaspoon
			Milk...........................1 glass—8 ounces
			Fruit, plain custard, or plain cookies..........½ cup of fruit or custard, or 2 cookies

*Some people cannot lose weight satisfactorily on a 1,200-calorie diet. A doctor may cut their daily allowance to 1,000 if progress is too slow, or increase it to 1,500 if they lose too rapidly. Diets below 1,000 calories require very close medical supervision. †Approximate.

FOODS AND CALORIE VALUE

Food	Size of Serving	Approximate Calories	Food	Size of Serving	Approximate Calories
BREADS AND CEREALS			Cherries	15 large	75
Bread, white	average slice	75	Grapefruit	½ fresh	50
Bread, whole wheat	average slice	70	Grapes	22–30	75
Corn flakes	½ cup	40	Orange juice	½ cup	60
Crackers	1 about 2″ square	15	Orange	1 medium	80
Macaroni—cooked	¾ cup	100	Peach and pear	½ in juice	60
Muffin	1 medium	100		½ large, in juice	100
Noodles—cooked	¾ cup	100	Pineapple	1 slice in juice	50
Oatmeal—cooked	¾ cup	100	Plums	2 medium (fresh)	50
Pancake	1 (4″ in diameter)	75			
Waffles	1 (6″ in diameter)	250	MEAT, POULTRY, FISH, AND EGGS		
			Bacon	2 strips	85
DAIRY PRODUCTS			Beef	3–4 oz. (average serving)	150–250
Butter	1 tablespoon	95	Chicken, turkey, and sweetbreads	3–4 oz.	175–200
Buttermilk	1 cup	85	Eggs	1 medium	75
Cheese			Fish	3 oz.	100–200
American	1 cube (1⅛″ square)	110	Frankfurter	1	100–125
cottage	5 tablespoons	100	Ham (smoked)	3 oz. (average serving)	260
Cocoa	1 cup liquid	150	Lamb	3–4 oz.	100–200
Cream—light	1 tablespoon	65	Liver	2 oz.	120
Milk			Pork	3–4 oz.	200–400
whole	1 cup	170	Veal	3–4 oz.	100–200
skim	1 cup	85			
yogurt	1 cup	160	SWEETS		
			Candy bar (chocolate)	small size	200
VEGETABLES			Cider	1 cup	100
Asparagus	4 spears	20–25	Fudge	average square	100
Beans			Fudge sundae	average size	400–500
snap	½ cup	25	Ice cream	½ cup	200
canned with pork	½ cup	150	Ice cream soda	fountain size	325
lima	½ cup	100	Jams and jellies	1 rounded tablespoon	100
Beets	2 slices (2″ diameter)	40	Malted milk	fountain size	460
Broccoli	3 stalks—large	100	Soft drinks	6 oz. bottle	75
Brussels sprouts	6 average size	50	Sugar		
Carrots	1 (4″ long)	25	brown	1 tablespoon	35
Cabbage—raw	1 cup	25	white	1 tablespoon	50
Cauliflower	1 average serving	25			
Celery	2 stalks	15	CAKE		
Corn			Angel	1/10 large cake	155
canned	½ cup	70	Iced butter cake	average square	200
fresh	1 ear	85	Iced cup cake		250
Lettuce	2 large leaves	5			
Olives	4–5	50	PIE	3″ section	200–300
Onions	1 (2½″ in diameter)	50			
Peas	½ cup	65	SOUPS, CONDENSED		
Potatoes			Mushroom	11 oz. can	360
white	1 medium	100	Noodle	(usually two	290
sweet	½ medium	100	Tomato	servings)	230
mashed	½ cup	100	Vegetable		200
salad	½ cup	100			
Potato chips	8–10 large	100	MISCELLANEOUS		
Spinach	½ cup	20	Beer	8 oz.	120
Sauerkraut	½ cup	15	Boiled dressing	1 tablespoon	25
Tomatoes	1 medium	30	French dressing	1 tablespoon	90
Turnips	1 medium	25	Gravy	Depends on amount of fat	
Turnip greens	½ cup cooked	30			
FRUIT			Mayonnaise	1 tablespoon	100
Apple	1 medium	75	Whisky, rum, gin	1½ oz.	120–150
Avocado	½ medium	265	Wines	1 oz.	25–60
Banana	1 medium	90			
Berries	1 cup	90			
Cantaloupe	½ average	50			

The President's Council on Physical Fitness, aware of the importance of exercise, has prepared a booklet entitled *Vim*, with exercises for girls, and one called *Vigor,* for boys. These may be ordered from the U.S. Government Printing Office, Washington, D.C. 20402, for 25 cents each.

The exercises are of three types: *warmup* exercises to stretch and limber muscles and increase heart and lung action; *conditioning* exercises to tone up major muscles in the abdomen, arms, back, and legs; and *circulatory* exercises to stimulate and strengthen the respiratory and circulatory systems. A 10- or 12-minute workout three or four times a week will do much toward helping to keep you physically fit. Make regular exercise a habit.

For a simpler exercise, try the 52 *pick-up*. Scatter a deck of cards on the floor, then pick them up one at a time, bending only one knee each time—first one knee then the other.

The Kraus Physical Fitness Tests. Can you pass them?
(1) Touch toes without bending knees and hold 10 seconds.
(2) Lie on back, lift legs 12 inches from floor, keeping knees straight. Hold 10 seconds.
(3) Lie on back, hands under head, with someone holding your feet. Rise to a sitting position as you pull toward your knees.
(4) Lie face down with a pillow under lower abdomen. While someone holds your feet, raise your trunk and hold 10 seconds.
(5) Lie on your back and rise to a sitting position without raising your legs.
(6) Lie face down with pillow under lower abdomen and as someone holds your trunk, raise legs and hold 10 seconds.

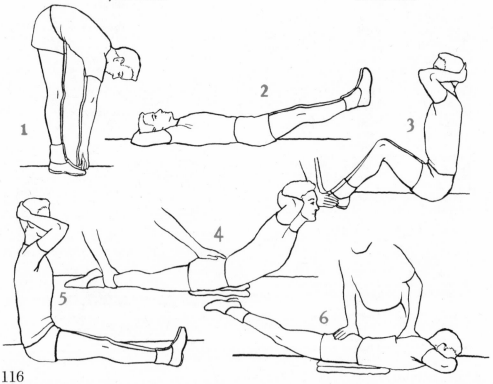

116

1. TUNING AND TOUGHENING
ABDOMINAL MUSCLES

Gene Tunney's exercises for men to stay
physically fit.
 (1) Raise hands to front and above
     head, inhaling deeply. Lower arms,
     keeping them stiff and straight until
     they touch knees. Drop head until
     chin touches collarbone. Bend at dia-
     phragm and draw stomach up as
     hands touch knees. Exhale. Repeat
     20 times.
 (2) Clasp hands behind neck. Draw up
     diaphragm and relax shoulder mus-
     cles. Swing upper body in a circle.
     Exhale on way down. Inhale on way
     up. Circle to right 10 times and left
     10 times.

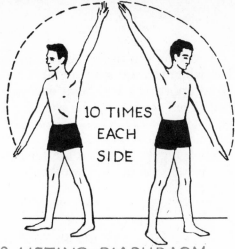

3. LIFTING DIAPHRAGM,
WAIST AND SHOULDERS

 (3) Extend arms sidewise at shoulders.
     Drop right hand 10 inches and raise
     left hand 10 inches. Draw stomach
     in. Swing right hand behind and
     down, left hand going forward and
     up. Let head follow hand that goes
     back and down. Inhale as head
     comes up. Exhale as head follows
     left hand. Repeat 20 times.
 (4) Stand with heels 15 inches apart.
     Inhale while rising on toes and
     reaching arms over head. Bring arms
     down stiff and straight between legs,
     exhaling, bending knees and touch-
     ing floor with back of hands as far
     back as possible. Repeat 20 times.

2. EXPANDING CHEST AND
LIFTING DIAPHRAGM

117

4. STRETCHING BACK, HIP
AND ABDOMINAL MUSCLES

Next time you cannot solve a problem while you are studying at home, stand up, stretch and bend over several times, stretch out on your back on the floor, and your chances of solving the problem will increase.

Brief, regular exercises are far better than occasional long workouts.

You may have heard middle age defined in terms of the *Four B's* from head to toe — baldness, bridgework, bay window, and bunions. Your knowledge and self-discipline concerning diet and exercise can do much

Figure Improvement Exercises for Women.

1. TO REDUCE HIPS

2. TO REDUCE WAIST

3. TO FLATTEN ABDOMEN

118

When you practice good posture you feel better and look better. Which silhouette looks like you?

him. Men who sit at a desk most of the day tend to walk with their chins out, shoulders bent, and abdomen sagging. If a person constantly suffers defeat or submission he will slouch and lean against things. A man happy at home, successful on his job, and willing to take moderate exercise, will walk with rhythm, hold his head up, and look chipper. Posture is affected by poor diet as well as emotional upsets and careless habits. You may acquire a more graceful carriage by calisthenics or joining a class in dancing —any kind of dancing.

Girls will appear more graceful when they walk if they keep one arm bent and one hanging. Try it before a mirror. In many high schools mirrors are placed conveniently so that pupils will notice how they dress, walk, and stand. The results have been amazing. Do you bounce, shuffle, jerk, walk stiff

to make middle age more pleasant.

"Straighten your neck and you straighten all." If you stand and walk with your head up, you will improve the tone of your whole body. Notice how out-of-position the body framework is when you are slouching. When your body is not receiving its proper support, you tire more easily and look slovenly in your clothes. Poor posture prevents your lungs from getting enough oxygen, tires you, makes your intestines sluggish, and can produce swayback and a hump on your shoulders. Good posture and carriage help you to sell yourself because you not only look better, you feel better.

Posture experts claim that they can look at a person and tell a lot about

119

Bayer Aspirin

When a person feels inadequate and unable to cope with ordinary situations, mental health may be threatened.

left instep, and flex the right knee slightly (or vice versa). Take a slightly diagonal position in your chair, crossing your ankles. If you must cross your legs, be sure your skirt is wide enough to cover your knees. Hands at rest look better if they are in profile and not flat or held in a fist.

For Young Men Men may sit with legs or ankles crossed, but they should sit up straight, back in the chair. They should stand without slouching and walk with a lilt.

GUIDES TO GOOD MENTAL HEALTH

Good mental health means being able to get along with yourself, with others, and with daily circumstances. Most of us never give mental health a thought. The possibility of having even a mild emotional disturbance seems remote.

As life has become more complex and pressures have increased, the percentage of persons suffering nervous disorders has been on the upswing at all ages. Strangely enough, a person can be mentally ill and sometimes appear to be in good condition.

In research among military personnel, psychiatrists found that the health of some apparently well adjusted young men was undermined when they had to do jobs for which they were not suited; were treated like machines instead of humans; were kept too long in combat, or had trouble at home. With this knowledge, military leaders have changed some of their ideas on leadership training,

legged, swing your hips, bob your head, swing your arms, turn your toes in or out? If you do, you need to practice walking on a straight line, toes pointed out only slightly. Walk to music. When you stand, place one foot slightly in front of the other but close to it.

For your own well-being and to prevent fatigue, practice good posture in all your daily activities — sitting, bending to pick up something, getting in and out of a chair.

For Young Women As you sit down, make sure the calf of your leg touches the edge of the chair. Hold the chair lightly and lower your body without throwing your head over too far. Sit so that your back is supported. Angle your feet so that your right heel fits near your

120

tried to fit the man to the job, and lifted many other pressures.

Dr. Jules H. Masserman, Professor of Psychiatry at Northwestern University, lists three general causes of nervous disorders:

INDIVIDUAL INADEQUACY: When a person is somewhat under par physically and must assume sudden responsibility, do extended strenuous physical work, or make many continuous decisions, he may "go to pieces."

STRAINED RELATIONSHIPS: If a person is deserted by those upon whom he has learned to depend, he may experience a sense of inadequacy and loneliness. For instance, an emotional reaction occurs when a child feels neglected by his parents; a young person is left out of a social group; a wife is ignored by her husband or vice versa; a mother or father is neglected by the children.

THREATS TO DEEPLY CHERISHED BELIEFS: A person who feels that he must compromise by casting aside some of his ideals in order to be identified with a group may succumb to a nervous illness.

With rest, love, understanding, and easing or removing anxieties, mild nervous disorders tend to disappear.

In your present state of youthful health, you may have no fear of stomach ulcers, high blood pressure, and nervous tension. You can continue to feel safe for many years if you recognize the conditions leading up to poor mental health and try to avoid them. Some of these conditions are:
• Declining interest in people and activities.
• Prolonged irritability and restlessness.
• Inability to sleep soundly.

Bayer Aspirin

Acting natural and becoming interested in others is better for one's mental health than trying "to keep up with the Joneses" or being self-centered.

• Tendency to find fault with people.
• Increased use of profanity or abusive language; growing fondness for alcohol, tobacco, or both.
• Frequent headaches, excessive fatigue, dizzy spells.

When symptoms of distress occur, there must be causes. Like any other illness, if a nervous disorder is diagnosed early, the cure comes soon.

Have you ever reached the point where you wanted to give up after a hard day in school? To help avoid harmful nervous tensions, be sure you practice the following:
• Face your responsibilities and act promptly. When you put off doing unpleasant tasks, you become more nervous about them, and they begin to seem even harder.
• Give yourself time enough to do things well. Pressure is unbearable if

121

you are in a continual rush. Try working for shorter periods, resting in between. Deliberately relax when you feel the urge to hurry.

* Learn to put first things first. You cannot do everything or please everyone. It takes judgment to know what is important, and to avoid getting yourself involved with a lot of trivial activities. Advice and the good example of others can help, but good judgment is something you eventually will have to develop for yourself.

* Forget about *keeping up* with anyone. Why try to imitate your classmates? As long as you are honest with yourself, and set your goals according to worthwhile standards, you don't need to worry if your acquaintances are setting a faster pace socially. But when you stop being an individual and just follow the crowd, you may be pushing your personality into a groove it won't fit—into a rut. Nervous strain and frustration come from trying to be someone you are not meant to be.

* Avoid bottling up your feelings. This is very important. If you have problems, talk them over with someone—parents, an older friend, or someone your age whose judgment is trustworthy. *Physical exercise* also will help you to release nervous energy and bottled-up feelings.

* Get enough sleep. Rest relieves tension. The necessary amount of sleep differs with individuals. However, most people need at least six hours of sleep a night. People who get along on less, often take light naps during the day to increase vitality.

CASE STUDY: Julie Blanchard constantly amazed her parents, teachers, and friends with the way she could take part in so many activities, get excellent grades, and never seem upset or nervous despite all the work she did. It was even more amazing because, being so busy, she rarely got enough sleep. Besides her nearly straight "A" average, she was editor of the yearbook, and leading lady in the class play. She was a member of a dance group which rehearsed and performed frequently, and she played the piano in church school. In her first year of college, Julie kept up the same pace until just before exams. Then she collapsed. Luckily, all she needed was complete rest for a month; her condition could have been much more serious.

Dr. and Mrs. Graydon L. Freeman, psychologists at Northwestern University, made a study of sleep habits and their effects upon mental and physical functions. Some of the conclusions reached from the Freeman study and studies at Yale and Syracuse universities are as follows:

* People "hunger" for sleep as they hunger for food. This hunger must be satisfied.

* One good night's sleep is not enough to make up for a prolonged loss of sleep. It takes two or more nights to recover completely.

* After loss of sleep during exam periods, a student may do well on short exams, but it will take much more energy than usual. This is because loss of sleep tightens nerves and muscles for quick but limited spurts of thought. On a long exam, fatigue will interfere greatly with thinking.

LEARN TO HAVE FUN

This may seem ridiculous to some

If you work with people all day, choose quiet recreation such as painting, music, or working with your hands.

parents, who may think that your greatest concern right now is having fun. However, many active persons do not have fun.

Relaxation and recreation are important to our well-being. The person who neglects to take out time for some form of recreation is neglecting his health—both physical and mental.

CASE STUDY: Ed Burns had no time in high school for play. He belonged to everything, studied hard to maintain high grades, and worked at a filling station during his spare time. He won a scholarship to college, joined a fraternity, and continued working after school and on week ends. After finishing college he took a job and through hard work and tireless social activity, managed to get one promotion after another.

Ed thought that someday he could relax with a hobby and ordinary friendly companionship, but that time never came. At 39 he suffered a heart attack. He needed to relax but did not know how. During fifteen years of married life, Ed and his wife, Martha, had very little fun. Martha centered her interests in the chil-

dren, school organizations, swimming, bridge, and church affairs — waiting until Ed's schedule would lighten. Instead of enjoying many activities, Ed had to eliminate all active recreation and work, and resign himself to life as a semi-invalid.

When people in their youth do not take time to enjoy sports, good music, beauty in nature, creative work with their hands, reading, and the pleasures of companionship, they are not likely to do so later. This is one thing that makes our American educational system superior to that of many other countries. It balances study with recreation. This balance becomes more and more necessary as cities absorb rural areas, and city life grows more mechanized and complex.

Your recreation should complement the type of work you do. For instance:
• If you take up work isolated from others, choose recreational activities involving people—card playing, spectator sports, bowling, choral singing, theater or concert groups, golfing, "chauffeuring" the children, or helping raise funds in church and community.
• If you spend all your time *working*

123

indoors, choose outdoor activities such as walking, swimming, golf, tennis, skating, helping with community athletics, camping, or scouting. Active indoor recreation is also good.

* If you *work with people all day,* you can relax in quiet activities such as painting, playing a musical instrument, hunting, reading, fishing, boating, hiking, listening to music, playing cards, or taking a walk.

* If your job *requires strenuous physical work,* you might enjoy playing cards, working puzzles, pondering over collections, painting, model building, any form of crafts, or music.

* If you have a *routine job* requiring that you sit at a desk all day, you will need active exercise such as swimming, table tennis, gardening, and boating; plus *creative activities* like community betterment, photography, crafts, "ham" radio, or woodworking and carpentry at home.

* If your job involves *heavy responsibility* all day, you will need physical activities and relaxation in light reading, television, or playing cards.

Health is a most valuable asset. Guard it well!

Words and Phrases to Know

inadequacy   psychiatrist
mortality rate   psychologist

ACTIVITIES

1. Make a list of items, including advertisements, in newspapers and magazines, radio and television, that stress weight control and physical improvement. Discuss them in relation to the way we live.

2. Demonstrate among members of your class the relationship between bone structure or framework, and weight.

3. Collect reducing menus from magazines and discuss them in terms of the Daily Food Guide.

4. Measure and weigh yourself in heels as referred to in the illustration on page 107. Compare your weight with the chart.

5. Using the Daily Food Guide, plan menus for any diet you choose between 1,400 and 3,400 calories.

6. Use the chart on page 112 to determine your calorie needs. Are you eating too much or not enough?

7. Demonstrate and practice graceful walking, sitting, and bending.

8. Observe students in classes, in hallways, and on the streets; comment on their posture.

9. Discuss how mental pressures affect your well-being. Do you agree completely with the advice on how to avoid tension? Discuss.

10. List activities in high school that you will continue to practice for relaxation and recreation later.

11. Discuss activities which you can do now that will help to prepare you for the job you are considering.

Correlation

PHYSICAL EDUCATION: Ask the physical education instructors to demonstrate exercises that are recommended for keeping the body in tune.

Take the physical fitness tests in the gymnasium. Practice until you can pass them.

ART: Make posters to demonstrate dieting or exercising. Keep them on the comical side.

Chapter 6

Dressing Right— Economically

Your appearance gives another person his first impression of you. If you are poised, well groomed, and pleasingly dressed, you will impress others in school, and receive attention from clerks in stores and waiters in restaurants. If you apply for a job properly dressed and appearing poised, you will find it easier to impress a potential employer.

CASE STUDIES: Steve Williams was one of 35 young men who applied for a job as an electronics technician. When he saw the number of applicants he wondered what chance he would have.

The employment manager walked around the room and jotted down the name of each man. Shortly afterwards all but five men were dismissed. The five men were interviewed and Steve was offered a chance to show what he could do.

Several weeks later, upon meeting the employment manager again, Steve remarked about how lucky he was. "That wasn't luck," replied the manager. "When I sized up that group of

applicants, there were only five who impressed me at all, and in the final interview you seemed to have what we needed."

"But with so many applicants, how did you pick out five so quickly?" Steve asked.

"When I select a prospective employee," said the manager, "I look for poise, neat clothes, a smooth shave, trim hair cut, polished shoes, and clean fingernails. You qualified on every count. Frayed collars, off-center ties, shabby shoes, and poorly shaven faces help to eliminate many prospects."

Jean Burton, Alice Delancey, and Betty King, all business graduates, were interviewed for attractive jobs at the same advertising agency. Jean planned to meet a date for dinner later, so she wore a floral print dress, rhinestone earrings and necklace, shoes with very high heels. She used melon-colored nail polish and carried a large white purse adorned with a perfumed rose. Alice decided to hurry in to the city after school, wearing a

125

blouse and skirt, shoes with flat heels, gloves but no hat. Betty spent an evening pressing a dark tailored linen dress, shampooing her hair, washing a white collar and cuff set, manicuring her nails with clear polish, cleaning her shoes and planning the accessories she would use — white gloves, dark purse, and small dark hat; no jewelry except a pin at her collar. She took time to go home to change clothes after school. She was not as naturally pretty as the others, but she was offered the job.

DRESS FOR THE OCCASION

School Dress Codes Some years ago certain high school students, parents, and teachers began to feel a need for higher standards of dress at school. A "Dress Right" program was started in the Buffalo, New York, high schools. Many other schools around the nation soon adopted similar codes of dress. *Acceptable for girls,* under these codes, are skirts, jumpers, blouses,

You spend much of your day in school. Good grooming, good posture, attractive but conservative clothes will make you look and feel better.

H. Armstrong Roberts

sweaters, jackets, and tailored dresses. Considered *unacceptable* are Bermuda shorts, kilts, slacks, and dressy clothes. *Acceptable dress for boys* includes shirts and ties, sports shirts, sweaters, suit jackets and trousers, and clean, pressed, casual trousers. Considered unacceptable are dungarees and unpressed slacks. Girls and boys are discouraged from wearing T-shirts, sweat shirts, and extreme fashions of any sort.

Clothes you wear to school may also "double" for many social occasions. *Informal parties* and *movie dates* call for casual clothes—slacks and jackets (white shirt and tie in cities) for boys and casual skirts, sweaters, and blouses or tailored dresses for girls.

Formal dances call for a dark suit (or tuxedo), dark socks, and dark shoes, for young men. If a coat is needed, a topcoat with solid color scarf and gloves should complete the formal outfit. Young women usually wear sleeveless dresses in prevailing silhouettes and lengths. Shoes dyed to match the dress are preferable to dark shoes; short white gloves and a short wrap are usually formal enough. Long gloves and more dressy wraps should be worn on very formal occasions. A small beaded or cloth clutch purse is almost a must to carry a compact, lipstick, handkerchief, and small change.

Dress conservatively for *church.* Casual shoes, white socks with dark shoes, sweaters, and open neck sports shirts for young men are taboo—except that sports shirts might be used in resort areas. Young women should not wear extremely low neck dresses or too much jewelry. A hat should be worn and gloves kept on during the service.

Utility clothes should look good on you. When you clean house, work in the yard, wash the car, or play after school, wear clothes that are meant for this kind of use. Utility clothes should be colorfast and shrink-proof. They should be kept neat and mended. Outdated dress clothes and soiled, ill-fitting discards should not be worn. Why not look your best at all times?

Slacks for young women as well as young men, if becoming and well fitted, are acceptable on certain occasions and advisable for many household activities. It is preferable, however, not to go shopping in either slacks or shorts. You may dress less formally at a resort, or on a quick trip to the corner grocery or suburban shopping center, but not to a downtown shopping area. Whether you are wearing shorts, slacks, or a skirt, be sure that you look well groomed on the street—your clothes are becoming, clean, and neatly pressed. Our casual way of living has made many people careless about everyday dress. But carelessness can spread to bigger things. You will find pleasure, and the respect of others, among the rewards of wearing proper, neat clothing even for routine tasks.

Employers are concerned about the way some young people dress for business. For young women, *business clothes* mean a suit with a becoming, tailored blouse, or a tailored dress, shoes with moderate heels, and a minimum of jewelry. Make-up and nail polish should not be glamorous. Hair should be clean and becomingly styled. During an interview, a young woman should sit up straight, keep her gloves on, avoid crossing her legs, and even if a cigarette is offered, refuse politely. The general effect is striking, in this casual age.

For young men, *business clothes* mean a white shirt, tie and coat (not a sport or knitted shirt, except perhaps in parts of the country where dress customs are very casual), dark shoes and dark socks. Sweaters, white bucks, and sports shoes are not recommended. Even when a young man is applying for a laborer's job, he should wear a neatly pressed suit, or slacks and sports jacket, polished shoes, and have a fresh shave, haircut, and trim, clean nails.

WHY WE DRESS AS WE DO

Along with considering *what* is proper to wear, it is interesting to think about *why* we favor certain clothing styles.

Psychologists say that in the way we dress we are constantly torn between a desire to *conform* and a desire to *differ from the group*. In other words we want to dress *similarly* to our friends, but *not exactly* as they do. In trying to balance these desires most people conform more than they differ from society.

Have you ever stopped to think about how much your choice of clothing is governed by what your friends are wearing? Studies show that until children enter school their use of clothing is chiefly influenced by the attitudes of parents. However, by the time children are eight they are more concerned about the attitudes of their friends. (Of course, parents' attitudes remain important, as you may have learned if your parents disapprove of current fashion fads.) It is generally

127

agreed that when children are permitted to dress the way their friends do, they adjust better to school.

Although most people tend to be conformists in clothing behavior, some do not. There are a few persons to whom clothing is merely a covering for the body. Such persons show little concern about what others are wearing. There are others with a strong urge to differ from the crowd in order to win attention. Some choose unusual clothing styles in order to appear sophisticated. Others believe that if they make themselves look odd, they are showing disapproval of society. Still others adopt strange clothing and hair styles to identify themselves with some musical or artistic group or movement. Then there are those who select their clothes mainly to attract members of the opposite sex.

As you can see, a person's choice of clothes reflects his personality. Sometimes this process can be made to work in reverse—by changing a person's dress habits his personality can be changed as well. A shy person may become more relaxed and friendly when he wears informal clothes. Someone who is depressed may be helped by changing from drab to bright clothes. Social workers often urge delinquents to improve their appearance. Can you see why?

The relationship between clothing and behavior is also recognized in military organizations and in many private schools. Authorities in such places feel that the use of uniforms erases class barriers and makes discipline easier. Can you think of other advantages and disadvantages of wearing uniforms?

How Styles Change

Clothing that is considered proper at one period in history or in one part of the world may seem very odd at other times and places. Even in our own country today, some styles come and go in a matter of months.

One reason for this is that people like variety. What is fresh and pleasing today may seem boring next week. The more unusual a new style seems, the sooner it may become tiresome.

Fashion designers and advertisers know this and take advantage of it. Magazines, television, and other media keep the latest fashions before our eyes. An advertisement may make us feel "out of it" if we do not have the newest style hat. Or we see a glamorous celebrity pictured in an unusual skirt and we want one like it.

Is it wrong for designers and advertisers to keep stirring our desires for new things? Or are they just trying to satisfy our basic need for variety?

Fashion is also affected by technology—new fabrics, new methods of garment construction. Your grandparents can probably tell about some major changes they remember—for instance, when nylon began to replace silk. Perhaps someday you will tell your children about an era of change when paper clothing replaced cloth garments for many purposes.

KNOW BECOMING LINES AND COLORS

Whether you are a young man or a young woman, you appear taller in a solid color suit, matching slacks and shirt, or matching skirt and blouse. You look shorter when you use *contrast* in your outfit.

Six basic combinations of hair, skin, and eyes are shown here, with some of the colors they can wear best. The *Blonde* (top left) can wear navy blue or very dark brown, as well as the medium and light shades shown. The *Brownette* (center-left) looks best in subtle, slightly grayed tones such as the apricot, aqua, and yellow shown here. For the *Redhead* (bottom left), copper, yellow, and warm grays may be suitable, as well as the tones pictured. The *Vivid Brunette* (top right) may choose strong colors, especially reds, blues, yellows, and purples. Medium color values with a bronze cast are best for the *Latin Brunette* (center right), bringing out the similar bronze tones of the skin. Very pale colors are not good. The *Dark Brunette* (bottom right) often looks attractive in pearl gray, off white, or slightly grayed blues, reds, or yellows.

128A

When you know you are well groomed and attractively dressed, your evening is already a success. The faille alpaca bolero dress and matching purse may be worn on semiformal or formal occasions. White gloves, pearl earrings, and a pearl bracelet or necklace are always in good taste.

(left)

Celanese Fibers Company

You can look your best in casual clothes. These girls have chosen tops and A-line skirts which are well coordinated as to color and line. Simple outfits like these are likely to remain in style longer than more elaborate garments.

(right)

Simplicity Patterns

128C

Pendleton Woolen Mills

Advice about combining blue with green has traditionally been, "Don't do it." However, Mother Nature went right on filling her landscapes with green grass around blue lakes and green trees rising against blue skies. Now fashion designers have come to agree with her, as shown, for example, in this plaid suit with striking accent sweater. A word of caution: Not *all* shades of blue and green go well together.

128D

Use Line to Add or Subtract If you are tall and slender or short and stout, you can give the illusion of more regular proportions by using the following suggestions:

Young Women

LINES THAT ADD HEIGHT

Princess, sheath
Narrow, matching belts
Vertical and diagonal lines
Coats as long as dress
Boleros (as a rule)
Matching colors in outfit
Single-breasted jacket
One-piece dresses
Narrow, close hats
High or V-neck, pointed collar

LINES THAT SUBTRACT HEIGHT

Full or pleated skirts
Wide, contrasting belt
Horizontal and curved lines
Short coats
Tunics, peplums
Contrast in outfit
Double-breasted jacket
Blouses and skirts
Broad hats
Yokes, square necks

Young Men

LINES THAT ADD HEIGHT

Solid color, dark suits
Single-breasted coats
Matching belts
Overcoats or topcoats
Welt pockets
Narrow lapels
Firmly woven fabrics
Stripes
Plain trousers

LINES THAT SUBTRACT HEIGHT

Contrast in jackets and trousers
Double-breasted coats
Contrast in belts
Suburban or short coats
Patch pockets

Wide lapels
Coarse tweeds
Plaids
Pleated trousers

Use Line to Modify Minor Defects Young men with large hips and waist look more streamlined in well-fitted (not tight) trousers without pleats. Young women with large hips and waist should avoid tight skirts and wide belts. Young men who have a broad chest and shoulders can use pleated trousers to balance their proportions. Young women who have a large bust measurement and narrow hips should wear skirts with some fullness, and diagonal, loose lines in a blouse rather than horizontal, snugly fitted lines.

Use Line to Improve Facial Features Hair styles and neck lines affect the shape of the face, as shown on page 130. Even if your face is a nearly perfect oval, you may have features which you want to minimize. If you are a young lady with more or less sharp features, use soft hairlines. If you have a *receding chin,* avoid closely cut styles. If you have a *prominent chin,* or *large nose,* avoid flat haircuts; don't comb your hair straight back.

Young women, of course, may do a great deal more than young men to bring out their best facial features because they have a wider choice of hair styles and necklines.

Young men, as a rule, settle for a flat-top or rolled, longish style regardless of how becoming it may be. Sometimes it is becoming, but more often a personal hair style is better.

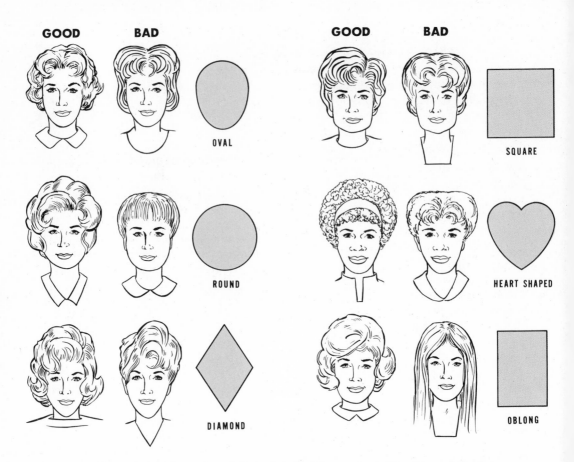

Choose hair styles and neck lines that do not accentuate the shape of the face.

Choose Colors That Are Right For You   Men usually are less concerned about gaily colored clothing than women are, but designers of men's wear are introducing more and more colors in sweaters, shirts, jackets, sportswear, and dress clothes. California, Florida, Texas, and other southern play areas probably set the vogue for sports shirts.

Your skin, hair, and eye coloring determine your choice of colors. Of the three, your skin is usually (but not always) your first consideration.

If your hair or eyes are especially attractive, choose colors that will do the most for them.

Generally speaking, we have six basic color types:

BLONDE: The semi-blonde has fair skin with blue undertones, beige or yellow hair tones, and blue or gray eyes. The rare, pure blonde has wheat yellow hair, blue eyes, and very fair skin. Almost all colors are good for blondes except washed-out or very intense hues.

BROWNETTE: We have many types between blondes and brunettes. Some have blonde skin coloring and medium or light brown hair, and others brunette skin tones with light or medium brown hair, and either light or dark eyes. Skin tones usually determine whether to choose colors of the blonde or brunette.

REDHEAD: Skin usually has a fair, bluish cast, although it may have warm tones, especially with brown eyes. Eyes are usually blue, hazel, or gray. Reds are not recommended, especially if skin is florid, but apricot pinks are becoming. Purples and lavenders may emphasize sallowness. Cool blues and greens, grays, and browns are the best choices. Black can be striking.

VIVID BRUNETTE: This is a striking type, especially if the skin is fair. Hair is dark brown or black, and eyes blue, hazel, or brown. Black or bright colors, grays, and beige are all good. Subdued, pastel colors are the least becoming.

LATIN BRUNETTE: Latin or Oriental brunettes have skin with a yellow bronze cast, very dark brown hair, and dark eyes. Warm, slightly neutralized colors are very good. Pastels and colors matching the skin should be avoided. Off-white is good.

DARK BRUNETTE: Skin tones may range from olive-tan to very dark brown. Hair is near-black and eyes usually very dark brown. Warm colors in most values, off-whites, warm grays, and cool blues or greens, grayed slightly, are good. Black, unless relieved, browns, and sharp green or yellow green are not advised.

Hues should never make your own personal coloring appear monotonous by repetition. For instance, if you are pale-haired and sallow, beige may not suit you. If you have very dark skin and hair, browns matching your coloring are ill-advised. "To win a smooth fellow, corn blondes avoid yellow." If you have a ruddy complexion, reds and strong colors weaken natural coloring. Pink tones are usually becoming to every type. Peach (a warm pink) is more becoming to people with vivid coloring, and orchid (a cool pink) to persons with more neutral coloring.

Opposite tones emphasize each other. For instance, blues and greens are suited to blondes and redheads because they complement the pink in the skin. By the same principle, yellow is not good if one has shadows, or purple tones in the skin, because it will make the purple too noticeable. Skin tones are also emphasized by *repetition*. Pink clothes may accentuate pink in the skin; purples,

This child can learn not only from books but also from her mother's good taste in clothing and grooming.

H. Armstrong Roberts

grays, and tans may exaggerate skin shadows.

Strong colors eclipse pale blondes; pastel shades (except off-whites) do very little for brunettes; bright reds and oranges often "cheapen" copper-colored hair. Pure, strong colors are less suited to Latin types than medium, slightly bronze colors.

Only by experimenting before a mirror can you determine your best colors. Even young men will notice that charcoal and pearl-gray tones in a suit may be better than browns and beige tones—or vice versa.

"New" Colors   There are actually no *new* colors. However, old colors may assume new names. For example, oxford gray, ashes of roses, and ivory may become charcoal gray, dusty rose, and winter white. Orange or purple variations may be unpopular for years, but come into fashion as we tire of other hues.

For relaxing out-of-doors choose informal clothes that do not sacrifice neatness.

ACCENT WITH ACCESSORIES

Accessories are a barometer of your taste. They need not be expensive, but they must be well styled and harmonize with the outfit. They should be chosen to go with major pieces in the wardrobe.

Young Women   Some girls wear the wrong jewelry at the wrong time. Rhinestone decorations and other pins, earings, or necklaces that glitter should not be worn before six in the evening. *White cloth gloves* and a *string of pearls* are good for semi-dress any time of day and in any season. Having two or three pairs of white gloves makes it possible always to have a clean pair. Choose hats, purses, and gloves in *harmony* with your outfit. Buy good gloves and a good purse for winter because you are likely to use these items more than one year. Keep accessories *in scale with your size.* A tall girl may use an oversize purse, for instance, that might overwhelm a short girl.

132

Study construction of suits and coats; become a wise consumer.

Young Men Accessories for men are limited. A *tie* must be in style. If narrow ties with subtle stripes are popular, why wear a broad tie with a floral pattern? Colors must blend with the outfit. If a sports jacket has a pronounced plaid, a solid-color tie is best. *Socks* should harmonize with sports shirts or with the tie if a white shirt is worn. If a man's suit and topcoat are in the tan or brown color group, *gloves* should be tan; if in the gray or blue color group, gray gloves are a good choice. A *scarf,* whether solid or figured, should not clash with the topcoat.

SHOPPING FOR OUTER CLOTHING

Garment Alterations Have you ever bought garments that needed so much altering that you either let them hang, useless, in the closet, or sacrificed much of their style in altering them? When trying on clothing, stand, sit, bend, and walk as you would in normal use of the garment. Study these effects in a *three-way, full-length mirror.* Be sure the garment suits your color plan and activity needs.

Alterations are usually "free" on men's clothing, although they represent from four to seven per cent of the cost. (This cost is already included in the purchase price.) Trousers, if altered at the waistline more than one inch, will hang awkwardly. Coats are altered at shoulders, sleeve, cuffs, or across the back. Extensive alterations may change the lines of a coat.

In women's clothing, alterations are on a cost-plus basis; if extensive, they can be very high.

Buying a Woman's Dress or Suit The fit at the top of the sleeve is very important. Bend your arm to make sure the sleeve is full enough and the back wide enough for comfort. Notice the waist line all around, and the length of the belt. Be sure the neck line (or collar) is comfortable at the back and lies gracefully in front. Sit down to be sure the skirt has enough fullness. Look for wide seams, full pleats, well matched plaids or checks, a good hem, and firmly woven lining.

Buying a Man's Suit The fit across the shoulders and at the top of the sleeve is very important. Make sure the collar feels comfortable at the back of the neck and lies flat in front. Bend your arm to be sure you will be comfortable at a desk or driving a car. The sleeve should be long enough to permit your shirt cuff to show only slightly. The suit coat length should come to your knuckles or perhaps to your fingertips, when your arms hang free at your sides. Sit down to make sure the trousers are large enough. The cuff should have a slight break in front and hang straight at the back, with about 1 inch of your shoe showing above the heel.

133

HAT: head diameter

DRESS SHIRT: neck measurement, sleeve length

SPORT SHIRT: small, medium, large, extra large; sometimes neck measurement

SUIT COAT: chest measurement; short, medium, long

TROUSERS: waist measurement; inseam measurement

PAJAMAS: A through D according to chest measurement

ROBE: chest measurement and length; also small, medium, large, and extra large

UNDERSHIRT: chest measurement

Men's and women's garment sizes. These are convenient for your own shopping and to send to friends and relatives who might want to send you gifts.

SWEATER: chest measurement, similar to sport shirt

GLOVES: measurement around open palm of hand

BELT: waist measurement

TOP COAT: chest size over suit coat

SOCKS: inches heel to toe

SHOES: length and width of foot, measured by special gauge

BRIEFS: hips measurement

SHORTS: waist measurement

T-SHIRT: chest measurement or small, medium, large, extra large

Summary of Measurements

Belt	_____	Shoes	_____	Top Coat	_____
Briefs	_____	Shorts	_____	Trousers	_____
Gloves	_____	Socks	_____	T-shirt	_____
Hat	_____	Sport Shirt	_____	Undershirt	_____
Pajamas	_____	Suit Coat	_____	White Shirt	_____
Robe	_____	Sweater	_____		

BLOUSE: bust measurement

COAT: bust and waist measurements, one size smaller than dress

SWEATER: bust measurement; sometimes two sizes larger than dress

SKIRT: natural waistline and hip measurements

SLACKS: waist and hip measurements

GOWN: bust and length measurements

GIRDLE: waist and hip measurements

HAT: head circumference

DRESS: bust, waist, and hip measurements. Dress variations: misses, junior, and half sizes

GLOVES: measurement around open palm of hand

BELT: waist measurement

HOSE: inches from toe to heel; short, medium, long

SHOES: length and width of foot, measured by special gauge

PAJAMAS: bust measurement

ROBE: bust and length measurements

PANTIES: hip measurement, small, medium, and large

BRA: bust measurement; chest measurement above bust and under arms

SLIP: bust measurement; short, medium, long

———————————Summary of Measurements———————————

Belt	_____	Gloves	_____	Robe	_____
Blouse	_____	Gown	_____	Shoes	_____
Bra	_____	Hat	_____	Skirt	_____
Coat	_____	Hose	_____	Slacks	_____
Dress	_____	Pajamas	_____	Slip	_____
Girdle	_____	Panties	_____	Sweater	_____

135

MEN'S CLOTHING SIZES
(BASED UPON CHEST, WAIST, AND HEIGHT)

SUITS	*Height*	*Waist less than chest measurement*
Short...............	5′5″ to 5′7″	5″ to 6″
Regular.............	5′7½″ to 5′10″	5″ to 7″
Medium Long........	5′10″ to 6′1″	5″ to 7″
Long...............	6′1″ to 6′3″	5″ to 7″
Stout..............	5′5″ to 5′9″	same
Portly.............	5′5″ to 5′10″	3″

SPORT SHIRTS	*Weight*	*Neck size*
Small..............	125–145 lbs.	14–14½
Medium............	150–165 lbs.	15–15½
Large..............	175–190 lbs.	16–16½
Extra Large........	195–220 lbs.	17–17½

PAJAMAS		
Small..............	A	110 to 135 lbs.
Medium............	B	135 to 165 lbs.
Medium Large.......	C	165 to 185 lbs.
Large..............	D	185 to 220 lbs.
Extra Large........	E	220 to 275 lbs.

SWEATERS	
Small..............	Size 36
Medium............	Sizes 38–40
Large..............	Sizes 42–44
Extra Large........	Size 46

SHOES AND SOCKS	*Shoe size*	*Sock size*
	6 and 7	10
	7½ and 8	10½
	8½ and 9	11
	9½ and 10	11½
	10½ and 11	12
	11½ and 12	13

ROBES	
	Small........... up to 150 lbs.
	Medium......... up to 170 lbs.
	Large........... up to 190 lbs.
	Extra large...... over 190 lbs.

UNDERSHIRTS............. (According to dress shirt size.)

Undershirt	*Dress shirt*
36	14½
38–40	15–15½
42–44	16–16½

SHORTS................ (Sized by waist measurement.)

WOMEN'S CLOTHING SIZES
(BASED UPON HEIGHT, WAIST, BUST)

Item	Description	Sizes
DRESSES		
Junior's..............	5'2" to 5'6"—small to medium frame, defined waist, shorter from shoulder to waist.	7–15
Petite..............	Under 5'4"—of medium or small frame.	10–20
Misses'.............	5'3" to 5'6½"—well proportioned, medium frame.	8–20
Tall Misses'.........	5'7" to 6'—tall, well proportioned, medium to slender frame.	8T–20T
Women's.............	5'4" to 5'6½"—mature figure, fuller bust, hips, and waist than average.	18–44
Half sizes...........	5'3½" and under—medium heavy frame, shorter waist to shoulder.	12½–26½
BLOUSES...............	(According to bust measurement.)	
Misses'...............	....	30–38
Women's...............	....	38–44
SKIRTS AND SLACKS.......	(According to waist measurement.)	22–40
SWEATERS...............	Slip-ons....................................	34–40
	Cardigans.................................	34–40
SHOES AND HOSE..........	*Shoe size* *Hose size* 5 and 5½ 9 6 and 6½ 9½ 7 and 7½ 10 8 and 8½ 10½ 9 and 9½ 11	
GLOVES................	(Sold according to measurement around hand at knuckles.) Sizes 6½ and 7 most popular.	6–8

Buying a Man's Shirt Most dress or business shirts come in broadcloth and oxford cloth, in all-cotton or in a cotton blend. Other materials are madras, poplin, and dimity. Most collars on broadcloth shirts are permanently stiffened. A shirt collar fits well when you can

Shirt collar styles. Round or short point collar, worn with a pin, is good for dress wear. The button down collar may be worn for business.

ROUND WITH EYELETS   SHORT POINT SPREAD   ROUND SPREAD   TAB   POINTED SPREAD   BUTTON DOWN

137

Women's dresses and suits come in petite, average, and tall models. Similarly, men's suits are made in short, regular, and long models.

hook your finger under the collar and slide it around. The sleeve, with arm bent, should extend a little below the coat sleeve. Better shirts have gathers in back, on each side of the yoke. See the illustration on page 137 for collar styles.

KNOW FIBERS AND FABRICS

The fiber story is long and getting more complicated every day. For hundreds of years there were only four familiar fibers—silk, wool, cotton, and linen. Rayon, first produced commercially in the United States in 1911, became popular during the 1920's. Nylon, introduced by DuPont in 1938, was considered a $30,000,000 gamble, but turned out to be one of DuPont's best investments. Now new fibers, fiber blends and special finishes come into being so rapidly that manufacturers of soaps, detergents, and laundry equipment, as well as dry cleaners and launderers, have many problems

keeping up with methods of cleaning them.

The government has tried to clear up some of the confusion resulting from the use of so many new fabrics. The Textile Fiber Products Identification Act was passed in 1958 and has been kept up to date by amendments. It requires that the names of fibers used in a product be shown on the label. Also the label must tell what percentage of the product is made up by each type of fiber—for instance, 90 per cent wool, 10 per cent cotton. Trade names are not used for giving this information, so to read fiber-product labels correctly you must understand generic names. Wool, silk, acrylic fiber and polyester fiber are examples of generic names.

There is no perfect all-round fiber. Each has its own job to perform. Textile engineers may blend four or five fibers in one yarn to produce the end results desired for a specific use. *Silk* is the strongest natural fiber, and *nylon* the strongest man-made fiber —in fact, the strongest of all fibers. That is why any fiber is reinforced when blended with nylon. *Cotton* and *linen* are the cool fibers, with *rayon* coming close. *Wool* is the warmest natural fiber, but the acrylics can be as warm as wool. Polyester is the most crease-resistant fiber, but wool runs a close second.

Wool is warm and wrinkle resistant. It cleans easily, and tailors better than any other fiber. Wool takes dye well and is very resilient, which lets it keep a press well. However, wool pills, collects lint, felts, shrinks, and is attacked by moths unless special finishes are given in processing the yarns.

138

Since wool suits, slacks, and jackets are big items in men's wear, you should understand certain terms.

Wool suiting is referred to by ounce weight, i.e., the weight of one running yard of 54″ material. A 12-ounce material is average; 10-ounce or under is summer weight; and 14-ounce or over is heavy. A *tropical worsted* is 8 to 9½-ounce weight. Tropical worsteds are gaining as year-round suiting fabrics because they resist wrinkles and wear well. *Flannel* comes in woolen and worsted. *Worsted* flannel is finer, looks better, and wears better than woolen flannel.

Tweed, except in cold climates, may become uncomfortable because it is rough and bulky and has a prickly texture. *Cheviot* resembles tweed, but is finer, more springy, and lighter in weight. It will not hold a crease, and tends to pull out of shape. *Shetland* also looks like tweed, but is softer and lighter in weight. It does not keep its shape or a crease. *Sharkskin* is a hard, worsted twill, very durable; it comes in solid colors, stripes, and patterns, and wears well. *Gabardine* is a worsted twill that wears well, holds a crease, but shows spots, worn areas, and will develop a shine with wear and cleaning. *Napped* worsteds hold up well, take a press, and are slow to develop a shine. *Twist* is a firm, rather stiff worsted resembling a tweed. It resists hard wear, holds a crease, and does not develop a shine.

Woolen yarns are blended with acrylics for flannels, and worsteds are blended with polyesters for gabardines and other firm textures. Acrylics and polyesters both reduce shrinkage; polyesters also add crease resistance. Wool naturally resists creases, so that in a polyester-wool blend the polyester must be over 50 per cent of the blend to be more crease resistant than wool. A 55-45 polyester-wool blend is popular.

COTTON is absorbent, airy, nearest ideal for men's shirts, underwear, and athletic garments. It dyes and launders well, and comes in unlimited weaves and finishes, so it is good for warm-weather garments, children's clothing, and sportswear. Cottons may be given treatments to resemble wool, silk, acetate, or rayon, and to resist soiling and wrinkles. Dust and sunlight are harmful to cotton—one reason why cotton curtains deteriorate in a south window.

LINEN is especially cool, absorbent, and hygienic, but it wrinkles and soils easily. Finishes may be applied to make linen wrinkle- and soil-resistant. The natural luster of linen makes it desirable for table use, dresser cloths, and guest towels. It takes embroidery, cutwork, and block or silk-screen printing better than any other fiber.

SILK is strong, wrinkle resistant, drapes very well, and takes dyes beautifully. Nylon is the only fiber stronger than silk. White silk tends to become yellow, yet it may not be bleached. Metallic finishes and sunlight will cause silk to deteriorate. Silk comes in a variety of weaves, and needs no finish to improve its appearance. All pure dye silk is labeled as such. Formerly popular only in ties, hosiery, lingerie, dresses, drapery fabrics, and cushion covers, it is now blended with man-made fibers and wool for men's and women's suitings.

RAYON is made from regenerated cellulose derived from trees and cotton. It may be treated and woven to resemble almost all others. It is cool and absorbent; it dyes well. Inexpensive to produce, it is frequently blended with one or more fibers. Its weak points—stretching and shrinking—have been largely overcome. Labels such as Avoset and Sanfoset indicate controlled shrinkage.

Pajamas and slips of rayon tend to open at the seams. Rayon shirts and dresses will acquire a permanent shine if ironed on the right side.

ACETATE AND TRIACETATE (made from cellulose treated with acetic acid and other chemicals) drapes and dyes well, and somewhat resembles silk. It wrinkles easily, but wrinkles tend to "hang out." It is thermoplastic, which means it will take permanent crinkle or embossed finishes. It is not attacked by moth or mildew, but will melt under a hot iron. Formerly, atmospheric conditions caused color changes, but improved dyeing methods have corrected this fault. Labels indicate color fastness. Acetate is used mainly in lingerie, dresses, and in blends for suitings, trousers, and drapery fabrics.

Arnel (Celanese), *Acele* (DuPont), and *Estron* (Eastman), are triacetates. They are stronger and more wrinkle resistant than acetates. In blends of cottons or rayon, triacetate adds wrinkle resistance. It will take permanent pleating, and does not pill in sweaters.

NYLON is the most wear-resistant, and one of the strongest, most elastic fibers. It will not stretch, shrink, or mildew; moths will not attack it. Even a weak chlorine bleach will not harm it. It will pill in sweaters, and pressed wrinkles are difficult to remove. It gathers much static electricity, so it attracts dirt from other fabrics in the same wash. This fiber, which is made by a chemical process, came into common use in the 1940's. *Caprolan* is Allied Chemical's nylon fiber.

ACRYLIC fabrics are weather- and sun-resistant, light in weight, bulky, soft, and warm. They hold pleats and resist wrinkles, but not as well as wool or polyester. Blended with wool, they decrease wool's tendency to shrink and attract moths. Trade names of acrylic fibers are *Acrilan* (Chemstrand); *Creslan* (American Cyanamid); *Zefran* (Dow), and *Orlon* (DuPont).

POLYESTER fibers resist wrinkles and retain creases the best of any fiber. Polyester fabrics will not tailor as well as blends. A small percentage of polyester will increase the wrinkle resistance of cotton. With wool, however, over 50 per cent polyester is required. Polyester fabrics dry fast, need little ironing. Polyester fibers include *Dacron* (DuPont), *Kodel,* (Eastman), *Fortrel* and *Teron* (Celanese), and *Vycron* (Beaunit).

MODACRYLIC fibers, *Dynel* (Union Carbide) and *Verel* (Eastman) are warm and strong, resistant to sunlight, moths, and wrinkles; they launder easily and dry quickly. They are similar to acrylic fibers but more flame resistant, making them desirable for blankets and draperies in institutions. People with sensitive skins may prefer them to wool. Too much agitation in washing will cause modacrylic fibers to pill; a hot iron will make them harden. In furlike form, they should be treated like fur.

Metallic fibers usually are made of colored aluminum filament, encased in plastic. Gold and silver are popular tones. These decorative yarns give interesting effects in dresses, suits, household linens, drapery fabrics, and similar articles. They are not harmed by moths or mildew, and may be laundered and dry cleaned, but a hot iron will melt the plastic coating.

SPANDEX under familiar trade names such as DuPont's *Lycra* and U. S. Rubber's *Vyrene* stretches and returns to shape better than any other fiber. It may be used alone, in woven or knit fabrics, or as a core around which any fiber may be twisted.

Fiberglas and *Saran* are not used for clothing. Fiberglas is used mainly for window curtains, stage curtains, and ship or hotel draperies because it is flameproof. It is *harmful to the skin.* Saran is popular for outdoor furniture, luggage, and awnings because it has high abrasive qualities.

Yarn Types The type and twist of yarn used in fabric construction influence the surface texture. A tightly twisted yarn and close weave produce a firm, smooth texture such as gabardine suiting; loosely twisted yarn and loose weave produce a porous texture common to tweeds. The texture found in shantung comes from the use of irregular yarn. A yarn with random loops produces a texture similar to Turkish toweling. Yarns may be varied by blending natural and man-made fibers.

Stretch yarns are produced by three common methods: *Mechanical crimping,* in which the yarns are made to buckle and expand in a mesh effect. (Not very elastic.) *False-twist,* in which a yarn is kinked and the kink is set by heat. (A popular form of stretch.) *Elastometric stretch,* in

Common Weaves: Plain, basket, twill, herringbone. The weave affects the wear.

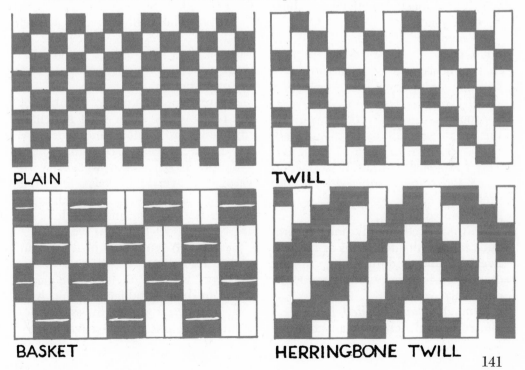

PLAIN

TWILL

BASKET

HERRINGBONE TWILL

which spandex forms the core for the twisted yarns. (A true stretch yarn.)

Fabric Construction
Do you understand the difference between a fiber and a fabric? A fiber is just a thin strand of material. When many fibers are joined together they form a fabric.

Probably the first fabric was made when man learned that wool placed between his foot and his sandal would felt (mat together) and provide a soft padding. That discovery was made in prehistoric times.

The search for better ways to make fabric has been constant. Weaving, knitting, braiding, and netting were other early methods. The invention of a knitting machine, in the 16th century, was an important breakthrough. So was the making of fine lace, which dates from about the same time, although it is partly based on netting which had been practiced for hundreds of years.

As mentioned, the first fabric was not woven. It is interesting to note that some of the most modern fabrics—for instance, rubber and sheet vinyl—are also *non-woven*.

Among the newest non-woven fabrics are those made by fastening web-like layers of fiber with an adhesive. These materials are used as facings and interlinings. (Adhesives are also used with certain woven goods, as will be explained later.)

Knitting is commonly done to produce fabrics for such items as hosiery, sweaters, and underclothing. Among other good features, knitted goods are not easily wrinkled.

Laminated and bonded fabrics resemble a sandwich with an adhesive for filling. Examples would include jersey, semi-sheer, or lacy fabrics bonded to a backing which might be a woven, non-woven, or knitted fabric. Such combinations tend to be versatile, lightweight, warm, wrinkle-resistant, and easy to tailor.

Weaving is the most common form of fabric construction. Familiar weaves are:

PLAIN: Found most often in gingham, percale, chintz, taffeta, crepe, and suiting. Slub (yarns with small loops) and multicolored or knotted yarns change the appearance of the plain weave. Firmly woven, a plain weave is very durable. If a slub is used, the loops tend to catch on rough surfaces.

BASKET: A variation of the plain weave is the basket weave. It is found in such material as monk's cloth and often in misses' coats, and sports jackets for men. This weave is less useful than the plain or twill.

TWILL: The twill weave is a firm, diagonal weave found often in worsted fabrics such as gabardine, woolens such as flannels, tweeds, and in cotton denim.

HERRINGBONE TWILL: A variation of the twill. It comes in wide and narrow wales in woolens and worsteds. Twill weaves wear very well.

SATIN: In the satin weave, warp yarns float over filling yarns to give a lustrous surface. It is not a durable weave. Rayon, silk, and acetate satin are examples of the satin weave.

SATEEN: A variation of the satin weave, for cotton.

Other weaves include *jacquard*, found in damask tablecloths and brocades; *lappet*, in dotted Swiss; *dobby*, in huck toweling; *gauze* weave, in curtain fabrics and dish cloths; *pique,* in pique, and *pile* weave, in velvets and corduroys.

Fabric Finishes Finishes are either *routine* or *special.* They are done for various purposes, such as to increase wear and give the fabric resistance to soil, moisture and mildew, moths, fading, or shrinking.

Some routine finishes are:
* Beetling, the pounding of cotton fabrics to make them resemble linen.
* Bleaching, to whiten natural fibers.
* Brushing, to produce a nap on cotton, wool, or rayon.
* Mercerizing, to give cotton a luster.
* Sizing, to add weight or crispness.

New *special* finishes are constantly being developed. Textile companies have their own trade names for their special finishes. In some instances a special finish destroys the original properties of the fabric. For example, a crease-resistant finish makes a fabric less absorbent and often less durable. However, many people are willing to sacrifice some of the coolness and absorbency of cotton to eliminate ironing.

Wash-and-wear garments are popular, but most need some touch-up pressing.

The newest process for no-iron fabrics is *durable* or *permanent press.* Although these fabrics need no ironing, they are not problem-free. They must be tumble-dried or hung up dripping wet; spin drying tends to set wrinkles. Alterations are difficult because the creases, as on trousers, may be in the wrong place after the garment is altered. When some of the problems are eliminated, permanent press will have wider use.

Printing is done by various methods. One of the most common is direct printing with steel rollers. Another is silk-screen printing, in which the design is produced by squeezing paint or other coloring agent onto the fabric through a stencil and a piece of fine-mesh silk. Still another process is flock printing in which the design is printed with an adhesive, and fine particles of fibers (called *flocks*) are dusted on.

TEN SHOPPING SUGGESTIONS

1. *Take Stock:* Go through your closets and drawers and separate items according to *unusable, wearable with alteration,* and *new.* Give or throw away unusables, clean and alter wearables.

2. *Relate Purchases to Activities:* Correlate colors for school and spectator-sports wear, *and* for street,

Good grooming and appropriate clothing are assets in business, on campus, and in social gatherings.

Richman Brothers

143

Simplicity and neatness are hallmarks of good grooming and dress for school.

church, and social occasions. List clothing needs for special activities.

3. *Study New Fashions:* Look through magazines and newspapers and go window shopping. Pay special attention to lines and colors that you can wear.

4. *List Anticipated Purchases:* Use a copy of the wardrobe form (page 145) to indicate your needs.

5. *Plan Outfits:* Instead of shopping for isolated items such as sweaters, dresses, or skirts, shop with complete outfits in mind.

6. *Plan Around a Basic Color:* Select an easy-to-match color for major items and plan other purchases accordingly.

7. *Shop Early:* Don't wait until the day before you need a new garment to buy it. Often clothing bought hastily is not satisfying. You may save money on end-of-the-season sales but sizes, styles, and colors will be limited.

8. *Buy Familiar Brands:* "Name" brands are usually dependable. Avoid others unless you are a sure judge of quality.

9. *Buy Accessories Last.* Be sure they will complement your basic outfits.

10. *Retain Labels and Sales Slips:* These will help the dry cleaner and make exchanges easier.

BUYING GUIDES

Have you ever bought garments which needed so much altering that you either let them hang, useless, in the closet, or sacrificed much of their style in altering them?

Alterations   Alterations are usually free on men's clothing, although they represent from four to seven percent of the cost—included in the purchase price. Trousers often need altering at the waistline, but an alteration of more than an inch may make them hang awkwardly. Coats often need to be altered at the shoulders, sleeves, cuffs, or across the back.

In women's clothing, alterations are on a *cost plus* basis; extensive alterations may spoil the style of the garment and represent too high a cost in proportion to the purchase price. It is far easier and less expensive to alter the skirt of a dress or suit than to alter the shoulder or neckline. Therefore it is wise to buy according to bust rather than hip measurement and take in or let out the skirt.

Comfort   Before you buy any garment try it on. Stretch, reach, bend, and sit as you would when giving the garment normal use. It is very uncomfortable to have to drive a car in a garment with tight sleeves or to have to keep pulling at trousers and skirts when you sit down.

SEASON'S WARDROBE

Item	Have	Need
COATS		
Dress		
Casual		
School		
SUITS		
JACKETS		
SLACKS		
SKIRTS		
OR		
TROUSERS		
BLOUSES		
SHIRTS		
Dress		
Sports		
SWEATERS		
HOSIERY		
SHOES		
Dress		
School		
HATS		
ACCESSORIES		
Ties		
Belts		
Gloves		
Purse		
Jewelry		

Also list your undergarments, sleeping garments, and clothes for special activities—skating, square dancing, swimming skiing, tennis, and so on.

Construction   In buying most outer garments here are some points to check:

· *Seams* should be wide enough to let out, if necessary, and treated so they will not ravel.

· *Hems* should hang evenly, be securely stitched; on straight skirts they should be deep enough to let out.

· *Fastenings* such as buttonholes should have a firm edge; zippers should be neatly applied.

· *Linings* should be firmly woven and guaranteed to withstand the same wear as the garment.

Fit   If a garment fits well, the perpendicular lines of the fabric grain should be at right angles to the floor. When the sleeves or skirt twists, the garment is off grain. *Sleeves* should conform to the shoulder curve, and the grain of fabric should run perpendicular from the highest point of the shoulder to the wrist. There should be little if any wrinkling, *across the shoulder* in back. The *neck line* should fit smoothly without appearing to gap or stretch out of shape.

A *skirt* should not be so tight at the hips that you appear to be stuffed into it. *Slacks* should fit smoothly at the hips and firmly at the waist. Stretch pants should not be too snug for comfort and good appearance. *Trousers* should have a slight break, just above the cuffs in front, and be long enough so that socks do not show in back. A man's *suit jacket* should come to the knuckles or perhaps the finger tips. The jacket collar should permit the shirt collar to show slightly, and the sleeves should allow the cuffs of the shirt to show a little.

Also see charts, pages 134-137

ANTICIPATE NEEDS AND GIVE YOUR CLOTHES GOOD CARE

Many of the clothes you buy now will last several years. This is another reason for developing a good basic wardrobe. You may be working or attending a college where you must dress as you would for business; or perhaps the dress customs at your college will be no different from high school. Many girls may marry, settle down to a full-time career of homemaking and raising a family; others may combine outside work with keeping house. You may live in the suburbs or in the city, in a cold climate or a warm one, in a locality where people dress very casually, or in a section of the country where they dress more formally. So always leave definite openings in your plans for future buying to meet changing conditions.

Use the chart on page 145 to indicate your present clothing list and needs for the coming season. (Do not write in this book.)

"A penny saved is a penny earned." With good care your clothes will last much longer, you will feel better in them, and you will appear better groomed.

Daily Care   The more frequently a garment is washed and ironed or cleaned and pressed, the shorter its life becomes. You must keep your clothing clean, of course, but you need not abuse your clothes and increase the need for cleaning. For example, changing right after school will save your school clothes.

New habits may take hold slowly, but they can become as much a part

146

YOU CAN RELAX.....THIS IS

ARNEL®

IN A FABRIC OF CELANESE® ARNEL TRIACETATE AND COTTON

57% CELANESE" ARNEL" TRIACETATE & 43% COTTON · EXCLUSIVE OF DECORATION

—ARROW—
WASH and WEAR
100% COTTON

■ Permanent collar stays that insure lasting neatness.
■ "Sanforized"... fabric shrinkage not more than 1% for lasting fit.
■ Exclusive Arafold collar for best comfort and appearance.
■ Chip-proof buttons won't come off.
■ Fabric selected for luxurious feel and ease of laundering.
(See washing suggestions on back)

BELGIAN
LINEN

A FIBER CONTENT
NATIONALLY ADVERTISED
BY **DU PONT**

This fabric contains
65% or MORE
DACRON*
REG. U.S. PAT. OFF.
with COTTON

*DU' PONT'S REGISTERED TRADE
MARK FOR ITS POLYESTER FIBER

This is
genuine
Leather

TOP GRAIN SNUFFED

Printed in U.S.A.

Pure Silk

WASHABLE
WRINKLE-FREE

FORMAT

AN INTIMATE BLEND OF
65% DU PONT DACRON*
AND 35% PIMA COTTON
YARN-DYED

by
FABREX

Silversheen
75% LAMBS WOOL · 15% FUR · 10% NYLON

FORSTMANN
Piquette
100% VIRGIN WOOL
LOOMED FOR
Monarch

Make a habit of reading labels. Some labels identify fiber content while others indicate special finish. Note also that some give instructions for garment care.

147

Young people especially can look smart in well-chosen casual clothes.

of your life as eating and sleeping. Here are a few good daily habits to form:

* In the morning, before your night clothes are out of your hand, hang them up. Don't stuff them under a pillow; they need to air. Step out of your bedroom slippers near the closet and slide them inside or place them on a rack.
* Unfasten all buttons, hooks, and zippers *completely* before you put on a shirt or blouse, skirt or trousers.
* Avoid forcing your arms into the sleeves or jerking garments unnecessarily. Such carelessness leads to ripping and stretching out of shape.
* Avoid jamming your feet into your shoes and breaking down the heel counter. Loosen laces, buckles, or buttons first. Use a shoehorn if shoes do not slip on easily.
* Young women—gather up the sides of your socks or hose between your thumb and fingers almost to the toe before pulling them on. Make sure *seams* are straight in hose. *Long nails* and *rough heels* are hard on hosiery. Keep your toe nails trimmed, and rub hand lotion into rough heels.

* Young women—ease your fingers into your gloves, and work each finger in place.
* Use deodorant to avoid perspiration odors and stains on clothing.
* When you go to bed, undress near the closet; as you take off clothes you expect to wear again, hang them up. Suit coats should be hung on large *wooden hangers.* Many dresses require *padded hangers.* Sweaters should be *aired, folded,* and *placed in a drawer* or over the *padded bar* of a hanger. Never dry a sweater on a hanger. Toss dirty clothes in a bag or hamper.
* Clip skirts to hangers or make your own hangers with spring-back clothespins. Use cuff-clamp trouser hangers.
* Place shoe trees in shoes every night if the toes tend to turn up. Wood trees are better than metal ones. If shoes are wet, dry them away from the heat and rub saddle soap into the leather.
* Leave your closet door open a little at night or part of the day for clothes to air.
* Remove spots and stains as soon as they occur.
* Young women—before you go to

148

bed, wash out *socks or stockings* and *underwear*. Partially dry these garments in a towel and finish drying them over a portable towel rack, or any place that will not interfere with other persons.

• Keep plastic covers over garments you wear only occasionally.

Occasion- al Care Occasional care refers to spot and stain removal, pressing, mending, and weekly laundering.

SPOT AND STAIN REMOVAL: Agents for removing spots and stains are *absorbents, solvents,* and *bleaches*. Many grease spots can be removed with an absorbent or chalky substance. Stick spot remover is inexpensive and effective. To use, spread the garment on a table, and rub the absorbent lightly into the fabric. After a few minutes, brush off the chalk. Repeat if necessary. Absorbents are most effective on woolens.

Solvents are liquids, such as water, gasoline, benzol, and denatured alcohol. In using a solvent, *turn the fabric soiled-side-down on a piece of folded soft cloth* (old sheeting is good). Apply the solvent with a soft cloth and work toward the center of the spot—moving the garment as the cloth under it becomes wet. Tap the fabric gently around the edges of the spot to prevent a ring. Best practice is to avoid using flammable solvents. If you must use one, be extremely cautious; never work near flames, and warn smokers to stay away.

Bleaches include lemon and salt, chlorine, solvents, hydrogen peroxide, and Javelle water. They are effective on white cotton, linen, and nylon. Read directions carefully before using a commercial bleach. Many stains on white fabrics can be removed with soap and warm water — butter, tea, coffee, candy, cream, egg, glue, iodine, milk, mud, and fruit juice.

Common stains that require special treatment are listed below:

BLOOD: Soak in cold water and wash in suds. Rinse.

CANDLE WAX: Place blotting paper on both sides of spot and press with a warm iron. Remove remaining stain with a bleach, if the fabric will take a bleach, or try denatured alcohol.

CHEWING GUM: Sponge with a good, modern cleaning agent.

CHOCOLATE: Wash and bleach, or use denatured alcohol or equally good cleaning agent.

FRUIT: Soak in cold water, wash, and stretch fabric firmly over a bowl. Pour boiling water over stain from a distance of 1 foot.

GRASS: Wash. Remove traces of stain on white cotton with bleach. Use denatured alcohol on other fabrics.

INK: The composition of inks differs. Try soaking in sour milk, buttermilk, or lemon juice and salt. Wash. Repeat.

LIPSTICK: Rub petroleum jelly or cold cream into the stain. Dab with good cleaning solvent, placing fabric soiled-side-down on soft cloth.

MILDEW:	Soak in sour cream, or salt and lemon juice.
PAINT:	Place fabric soiled-side-down on pad and use paint thinner or turpentine. Remove while fresh.
RUST:	Moisten with lemon juice and salt. Rinse and repeat.
WATER:	Place on soft pad. Scratch gently with fingernails around edge of water spot to spread sizing. Hold under steam iron and rub lightly from underside.

To get the best results with pressing, use the proper equipment: a well padded ironing board, sleeve board, pressing mit, regular iron, steam iron, commercial press cloth, sponge, and bowl for water.

It is usually safer to press dresses and trousers *on the inside first*. This way you can press seams flat. Touch up the garment on the right side with a steam iron, or iron and press cloth. Dampen the press cloth with a sponge to control the amount of water. Use a sleeve board for pressing sleeves and a pressing mit for shoulders and neck. Trousers keep a crease better if a dampened commercial press cloth is used, rather than a steam iron.

Dry Cleaning Make a practice of sending woolens and silks to a dry cleaner. It is *extremely hazardous* to dry clean at home, and results usually are not good. With the wide variety of fibers and finishes, a dry cleaner needs the label information, so include it. If you do not have a label, tell the cleaner the composition of the fabric, as well as kind and age of spot. Remove all buttons or trimming that may not clean well, or see that the cleaner removes them.

Mending Mending is not difficult if done promptly, before laundering. Think about the old adage, "A *stitch in time saves nine*." Catch a small run in a stocking or mend a small hole in the toe of a sock and it will give many more wearings. (With nylon toes and heels in men's socks, holes do not appear as soon as when socks were made entirely of wool or cotton.) Keep a needle and thread near the ironing board and catch up rips in seams of trousers or skirts while they are small. Sew on buttons before you put away shirts, blouses, or pajamas after laundering. *Here is a hint:* keep a small pair of scissors and needles threaded with black, white, tan, and navy blue thread in a box top in your dresser drawer, and you will find minor repairs simple.

Seasonal Care Woolens, furs, rubber articles, leather, and rainwear require special *seasonal* care. Here are a few suggestions:
• Never store woolens unless they have been dry cleaned or washed. If garments have been cleaned and allowed to stand in a closet, examine them carefully, brush, and air before storing. Use a moth spray or moth crystals. Airtight containers are best.
• Wash cotton garments that have been starched before storing, because starch attracts "silver fish."
• Keep rubber garments away from heat, light, cleaning fluids, grease, and

oil. Girdles and athletic supports should be washed often for sanitation and because the oils in perspiration weaken the elastic.

• Have furs or fur-trimmed coats cleaned carefully, and store them in a cool, mothproof area. If a fur garment is very valuable, have it insured and placed in storage.

• Have cloth raincoats cleaned before they become badly soiled; ask the cleaner to restore the water-repellent finish.

• Keep saddle soap on hand for treating leather shoes, purses, and belts frequently to prevent drying out.

Laundering The fabric, amount and kind of soil, and hardness of the water will determine the type of detergent or cleaning agent, temperature of water, washing and drying method, and bleach to be used in *laundering*. Separate all items carefully. Do not wash napkins or dish towels with wearing apparel, or white things with colored items. Observe the following suggestions for different fibers:

COTTON: Soak white cottons 10-15 minutes in water at 160° F., and machine-wash with heavy-duty soap flakes or syndet for 10-15 minutes. Use bleaches according to directions. Wash sheer fabrics in a net for half the time. Do not soak colored cottons; wash in water 120°. Dry colored cottons out of the sun or in the dryer until *almost* dry. Use *high heat* setting for all cottons except knitted garments. These dry better at *medium* setting. Dampen and use hot or moderately hot iron. Iron dark cotton dresses and trousers on the wrong side; flatten seams and touch up on right side with a steam iron.

LINEN: Treat the same as cottons, but wash only half as long. Wash fine linens at 120°. Use a very diluted bleach. Dampen and iron seams and hems on wrong side until dry. Touch up on the right side. Linen does not require starch.

SILK: Have silk outer garments dry cleaned. Hand-wash lingerie in lukewarm 100° water and mild suds. Rinse in cool water and squeeze out (don't wring). Do not dry in automatic dryer unless at *low* setting, for a short time. Damp-dry in bath towel, shake, and iron on wrong side. Avoid sunlight and hot iron.

WOOL: Dry cleaning is usually preferable for all but sweaters, scarfs, and blankets. Soak five minutes in mild suds and *lukewarm* water at 100°. Squeeze out. Avoid rubbing or agitation because of wool's tendency to shrink and felt. Rinse in water of the same temperature. Avoid any sudden change in water temperature. Dry small items partially in a towel, and block sweaters for drying. While they are slightly damp, press dresses or trousers on the wrong side with iron set for wool. Press seams on the right side with a steam iron or dampened press cloth and dry iron. Never use a chlorine bleach.

RAYON AND ACETATE: Machine-wash heavy white rayon and acetate at 160°. Dry at low setting. Hand-wash sheer fabrics in 100° water, unless washer has special setting. Dry partially in towel, shake out, and iron on the wrong side while wet. Touch up on the right side with a steam iron.

NYLON: Wash separately from other fibers; do not mix white and colored

151

nylons. Use 160° for white fabrics, 120° for colored. Use mild syndet and wash 3-5 minutes. Avoid wringing. Rinse well. Dry partially in a towel or an automatic dryer at low setting. Press lightly with a steam iron. Mild chlorine bleach may be used.

POLYESTER: All-polyesters and cotton blends may be dry cleaned, but they are easily washed. Treat the same as nylon. Drip dry or use automatic dryer if setting for polyester is indicated. Use low heat ironing.

ACRYLIC: Soak and machine-wash all acrylic fabrics with mild suds, or hand-wash. Use 160° water for white garments, 120° for colored. Damp-dry sweaters in a towel; block, and dry away from direct heat. Do not bleach; use low heat in ironing.

METALLIC FIBERS: These decorative yarns may be laundered or dry cleaned, but a hot iron or very hot water will melt their plastic casing.

FIBERGLAS: Although it is not a clothing fiber, you should know how to launder it. People who have laundered Fiberglas find that the fibers disintegrate and impregnate the entire wash with fine glass. *It must be washed alone.* Fold lightly and pull gently through suds. Rinse gently. *Do not* wash *or* dry automatically. Do not wring or pin on clothesline. Hang over line for a short time and hang up at windows.

WASH-AND-WEARS: Most wash-and-wear fabrics need touch-up pressing, although some may be washed in automatic washers with accurate water

Packing to eliminate creasing.

(a) Fold suit skirt lengthwise with bottom hanging out. Place jacket with shoulders toward rear of bag on top of skirt, with sleeves folded across jacket. Fold skirt end over jacket, and bottom of jacket over skirt.

(b) To pack suit, or slacks and a sport coat, lay trousers out flat and put buttoned-up coat on top. Then fold trouser legs over.

(a)

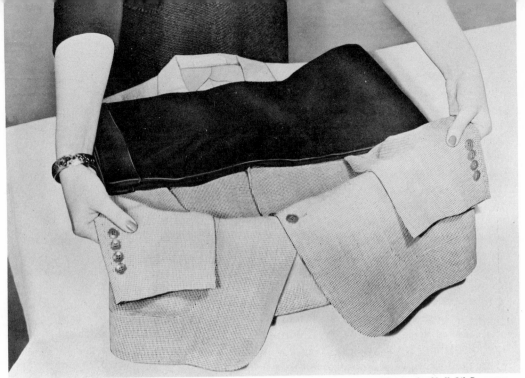

(b)

temperature controls, and dried in automatic dryers that specify wash-and-wear. Especially good blends are: 65% polyester and 35% cotton; 50% polyester and 50% acrylic; 80% acrylic and 20% cotton; 70% acrylic and 30% wool, cotton, or rayon.

Wash-and-wear garments are affected by the amount of agitation, water temperature in washing and rinsing, and method of hanging. White and colored garments should be laundered separately and the washer should not be crowded. Moderately cool water will produce fewer wrinkles. If garments are allowed to soak for ten minutes the washing cycle may be cut to five minutes or less. Avoid overdrying; wrinkles that "dry in" are difficult to remove. Garments should be shaped while slightly damp and hangers that may leave marks or stains should not be used.

Permanent press, as mentioned earlier, is a finish that never requires pressing, provided care is taken in laundering. This type of finish is baked into certain fabrics. All-cotton permanent-press garments tend to hold their shape better than cotton-polyester blends. Washing in extremely hot water or prolonged drying in a hot dryer can cause wrinkles which are very difficult to remove.

LEARN HOW TO PACK FOR A TRIP

A few tips and a little time spent in packing will add to your travel pleasure. With the new fibers you can pack lightly. This is important in plane travel because excess poundage is costly. Here are a few good ideas:
• Decide upon a basic clothing color; select shirts or blouses, ties, belts, and other accessories to harmonize.

• Choose fabrics that pack well, launder easily, and dry quickly — nylon, polyester, acrylics, silk, processed cottons, and rayons. Knitted, printed, seersucker, or tweed-like fabrics do not show wrinkles.

• Pack seldom-used items, such as bathing suits and rainwear, underneath other things.

• When packing, place your suitcase on a luggage rack, bed, or card table, to avoid stooping.

• Use cellophane bags of different sizes for separate items—one each for underwear, night clothes, shirts, blouses, hosiery, and handkerchiefs. This makes it easier to use each without disturbing your packing.

• Pack shaving equipment or cosmetics, washcloth, soap, and other grooming items, in waterproof containers—plastic bottles are good for liquids.

• Include the following: mending kit, medical kit, toothbrush and paste, stick spot remover, and soap, in plastic zipper bags.

• Young women — lay dresses and blouses flat on your bed; then fold each with tissue paper between the folds. Fold so that the garment will fit evenly into the section allotted. Young men—fold shirts over lightweight cardboard, with a narrow piece of cardboard under the collar. Avoid placing heavy items on top of clothing that wrinkles easily.

• Place jewelry, cuff links, manicure items, a small clothesbrush, shoe polish, and other small things in little plastic bags, and tuck into the side pockets.

• Lock your suitcase and keep the key in your handbag or pocket. *Don't leave it on your dresser.* Tie an identification tag, with your name and address, onto your suitcase.

Words and Phrases to Know

concept	perception
exotic	social
generic	stratification
optical	textile
illusion	engineer

ACTIVITIES

1. Plan a "Dress Right" fashion show for a school assembly. Arrange scenes according to the occasions for which you need clothes. Comment on the relationship between the way you dress and the way you feel and act.

2. **Bulletin Board:** Mount clippings of garments good for young people who are very tall or very short.

3. Study the shape of your face and determine where it fits in the illustration on page 130. What styles of necklines suit you best?

4. List your class members according

to color types. **Young Women:** Assemble color capes or triangles, and try on different colors. Make a note of your own best colors. **Young Men:** Try on different suit coats—beige, tan, gray, charcoal, brown, and so on, to determine your best colors.

5. **Young Men:** Bring to class some suits and slacks; discuss the fiber content, cleaning directions, and construction.

6. Make your own list of items recorded in the illustrations on pages 134 and 135. Take your measurements and fill in your chart accurately.

7. Examine variously priced garments to determine differences in workmanship and quality of fabrics. You may secure the co-operation of a shop or department store in this.

8. Wear to class a garment you think fits (1) very well, or (2) not so well. Separate into two groups according to sex and discuss.

9. **Bulletin Board:** Mount neatly trimmed swatches illustrating as many fibers, weaves, and finishes as you can. Label each.

10. Discuss experiences you have had with fabrics pilling, shrinking, stretching, fading, or developing a shine. Offer solutions to problems.

11. Arrange an exhibit of rainy-day clothes for young men and young women. Collect water-proof and water-repellent labels and discuss their significance.

12. Make a study to find out what it would cost to provide a capsule wardrobe—low, average, high cost—for a young woman and a young man. Divide into groups for this. You may use prices in magazine and newspaper ads, and those in the stores.

13. Demonstrate how to remove the stains listed on pages 149 and 150.

14. Arrange an exhibit of equipment for pressing, and demonstrate how to use each item.

15. Arrange a limited exhibit of items required in laundering, and treatment for storage — soaps and detergents, bleaches, absorbents, solvents, moth crystals and spray, saddle soap, and other items. Discuss.

16. Give demonstrations showing how to pack a woman's suit; a man's suit.

Home Experiences

1. Check your clothes against the recommended lists. Have you too little, too much, or just enough?

2. Go through your wardrobe with a list of all the fibers, weaves, and finishes you have studied in class. See how many you can recognize.

3. Make a list of all of the occasions for which you need clothes. Plan a wardrobe for the coming season, considering your best colors, lines, and the clothing you have on hand. Estimate the cost of supplementing your present wardrobe. Discuss plans with your parents.

4. Have someone type or mimeograph the tips on *Daily Care of Clothes* and post a copy in your bedroom where you can see it. Try to improve your own habits.

5. Prepare a small mending kit in a box lid, to keep in your dresser.

6. Show the Laundering Guide Chart to your mother and discuss your special home laundry problems. Discuss adding to your home equipment for ironing if you do not have the recommended items.

Chapter 7

Manners in the Adult World

Manners, like clothes, change with the times, and differ greatly around the world. In seventeenth-century England, a dinner guest was expected to smack his lips loudly to express appreciation to his host. This is true in some countries today. In Burma, a woman walks behind her husband as a sign of submission to him. In European countries at present, food is transferred to the mouth with the left and not the right hand. A toothpick shielded behind a napkin may be used to remove a bit of food lodged between the teeth, but in America, we feel we should suffer the discomfort until finding privacy. In Italy and France, men often embrace male relatives and friends and kiss them on both cheeks. During World War II our servicemen were instructed to remove shoes before entering a Japanese home, Buddhist temple, or Mohammedan mosque.

What is right to do is determined by where you are. The origin of the word *etiquette* is interesting. When French court life was at its height, guests were given etiquettes or tickets, on which social rules of the court were printed. Not to know these rules meant dismissal from court functions.

PROTOCOL IN INTERNATIONAL RELATIONS

A breach of etiquette can be a serious thing in diplomatic relations even today. Diplomats, military officers, and their wives, are drilled in protocol. If any of you should be sent to a foreign country in military service, or as the wife of a serviceman, you should learn the customs and etiquette of the country. As representatives of the United States, you will have an opportunity to encourage good relationships by adapting yourselves graciously to new situations. One slip in diplomatic behavior, or a thoughtless act in foreign social circles, can undo years of hard work toward good international relations. Just as we would misunderstand the customs of people in other countries, those people can

Presbyterian Life

A Korean custom. Two country gentlemen, in traditional mesh hats and white robes worn by family heads, kneel and bow to greet each other. Instead of asking, "How do you do?" it is the Korean custom to inquire, "Are you living peacefully?" If the men had not known each other, they would have touched foreheads to the ground three times.

misunderstand us, although we try our best to make a good impression.

President Coolidge established an Office of Protocol when the wife of a Belgian ambassador refused to sit next to Germany's ambassador after World War I. Anyone entertaining dignitaries at an official function must know who precedes whom, who sits next to whom, in what order people are introduced, the length of gloves for a formal evening reception, and who should pour coffee or tea—coffee takes precedence over tea!

MANNERS AT HOME

Natural graciousness is more important for everyday living than practiced protocol. Many people with very little education or world experience may have better manners than those who are always aware of their conduct.

If you make a habit of saying "Good morning," "Please," "Excuse me," and "Thank you," in your daily associations with your sisters, brothers, father, and mother; if you do kind, thoughtful things for members of your family and guests in your home; if you remember to observe the Golden Rule, your courtesy will become a habit everywhere you go. You cannot be rude, thoughtless, and selfish at home, and conceal these habits in public.

Here are some family courtesy rules we all may know, but often fail to put into practice:

· Wear presentable clothes to meals; greet your family with a smile.

Monmouth College

Usually a boy opens a door, but there are times when it may be a gracious gesture for a girl to do so.

· Be on time for meals, and contribute your part to mealtime conversation.

· While you are at the table, avoid reading, humming, watching television, or arguing, if you want to be a desirable dinner companion.

· Be orderly, especially in a room shared by the entire family. This means keeping clothing hung up; books, magazines, furniture, records and music in place; ash trays emptied; towels and bathroom supplies in order.

· Be considerate of how loud you play television, records, or the radio. Noises may interfere with what others are doing.

· Knock before you open a closed door, especially to a bedroom. People like privacy and a little warning.

· Use the expressions "Please," "Thank you," "Excuse me," and "I am sorry," as naturally with your family as with outsiders.

· Don't raid the refrigerator, unless you understand your privileges, and under no circumstances open the refrigerator away from home.

When you leave a dance or party, be sure to pay your respects to the host and hostess or chaperones.

• If you have had "the crowd in," be sure to tidy up before you go to bed.
• When someone comes to call, open the door graciously and *if it is someone you know,* say "Good morning," or "Good evening," according to the time of day, and "Will you come in?" Once in, ask the caller to be seated until you summon the person he wishes to see. If there is going to be a delay, offer to take the guest's wraps. You may offer him the newspaper with, "Would you like to read the paper while you are waiting?"

SCHOOL MANNERS

In many southern colleges it is the custom for students to speak to others, even to strangers, when they pass on campus. It is the mark of a real leader to smile pleasantly and say, "Good morning" to any student or teacher in school. Younger students appreciate it especially. When you were an underclassman think of how good it made you feel when an upperclassman smiled and spoke to you. Little courtesies and attentions make the day more pleasant for others and make you happier with yourself.

John Farrand was voted the most courteous senior for *Who's Who* in the school yearbook. Good manners had become a habit with him. For instance, if John met a teacher or student with an unwieldy armload of books, he offered to help with them. If he started through a door at the same time as a teacher or a girl, he stepped aside and held the door open. In class or at a meeting he respected the person who had the floor. In the corridors, lunchroom, and restrooms, he avoided throwing papers around.

Not everyone will be honored for courtesy as John Farrand was, but everyone can be courteous. You may ask, "Exactly what can I do to practice greater courtesy around school?" Here are some suggestions:
• Help to keep the corridors open so others can walk. Have you ever been in a hurry to reach your locker or to get to class, only to find your way blocked by a group standing idly in the hall? If so, you know how irritating this can be. Avoid being a part of such groups. If for some good reason you have to wait with a group in a corridor, try to stand where you will not be in the way, perhaps next to a wall. When in a line that extends into a corridor, as at a drinking fountain,

When students are mature and interested the stage is set for education at its best. With such a group the teacher may permit a certain amount of informality. He knows that the rules of courtesy will be observed.

Merriam-Webster

159

be willing to step aside for a moment so others can pass through.

* Do your part to keep the building clean. Some students attend all the school's games and brag about their school spirit, but think nothing of scattering papers around a restroom or lunchroom. Would you say their idea of school spirit is a bit mixed up?

* Losing a book or a garment can cause real problems, as you may know if you have ever lost something of value. If you find an item which someone has lost, take a few minutes and turn it in to the lost-and-found office. This is both courteous and honest, and you may be certain someone will appreciate your effort.

* Pay attention in class and do your schoolwork assignments. You know that these things are important if you are to get good grades. But have you ever stopped to think that they are also acts of courtesy to your teachers?

It is as easy to form good habits as bad ones if we make the effort.

INTRODUCTIONS

Many people feel awkward at making introductions, and often avoid them. The rule is easy—mention the name of the older or "key" person (your mother or teacher) first and introduce the other person *to* her or him. However, if you do it the other way around, do not worry. People will remember your poise longer than whose name you mentioned first.

Your *mother, father,* or any other *adult* takes precedence over your friends; a *girl* over a boy or a *woman* over a man, an *older woman* or *man* over a younger woman or man, the *host, hostess,* or *teacher* in her classroom over a guest (even though the guest is distinguished), an *individual* over a group of individuals. For instance:

"Mother, this is Margery Davis." (If your mother's name is different from yours, you say "Mother, this is Margery Davis. Margery, this is my mother, Mrs. Sloane.")

"*Miss Perkins* [teacher, at a school affair], may I introduce my mother and father?" You may say, "These are my parents," if you wish.

It is more gracious to introduce in-laws as "my husband's sister" and not "my sister-in-law" *or* "my husband's mother" and not "my mother-in-law." The term "in-law" sounds cold and formal.

When you introduce strangers, make a few remarks as a basis for starting a conversation, such as, "Mary Ann is one of the artists in our class," and "Jack's in charge of the stage crew." Immediately, Jack and Mary Ann have a common meeting ground.

If you are introducing a friend, it is preferable to say, "This is *one* of my classmates," or, "*a* friend from our church group." To say this is *my* friend implies that you have only one friend. You may say, "one of my best friends," or in other ways honor your friend, if you wish.

If you are in a small group and have not met one of the other members, ask someone who knows that person to introduce you. If you are attending a large party and find yourself with a guest you do not know, introduce yourself: "I don't believe we have met. I am Helen Jennings," (not Miss Jennings) or, "I am Helen Jennings—Mrs. John Jennings." The other party replies, "How do you do, Miss [or Mrs.] Jennings? I am Becky Morrow."

160

You assume it is Miss Morrow and not Mrs. Morrow in your response.

If you forget a name temporarily, don't worry—anyone may have this experience. Say, "I am sorry your name has skipped my mind for the moment." An alert person will anticipate another's lapse of memory and mention his name without being asked.

Introductions are usually acknowledged with a smile and, "How do you do?" or, "How do you do, Mrs. Macky?" If you *really mean it,* you may add, "I have been looking forward to meeting you," or, "Jean has told me about you and all the interesting things you do," or something similar. If the introduction is strictly informal, "Nice to know you" or other substitutes for, "How do you do?" are acceptable in meeting someone your own age.

Upon introduction, men always shake hands with other men or boys. A hostess offers her hand to all guests as a sign of welcome. Women in general need not shake hands, but if a hand is extended, a woman should be quick to accept it.

In shaking hands, avoid using a "dead-fish," "iron-grip," or "pump" handshake. Use a warm, firm grasp.

Men remove gloves unless caught in such a position that to remove them would seem awkward. Women do not remove their gloves.

A man always rises and remains standing until the person to whom he is introduced sits, or until he is asked to be seated. In fact, *a man should rise when any woman, girl, or man older than he first enters the room, regardless of introductions.* A woman rises for an older woman, and remains standing as long as she is talking to the woman or until the other woman seats herself. A woman does not rise when a younger man or woman is introduced to her, but should rise to speak to the hostess, host, or a distinguished guest.

After an introduction at a party, either person being introduced may take leave with a smile and a polite remark: "It has been nice to talk with you," or, "I hope we shall see each other again."

TELEPHONE TIPS

For the sake of good home telephone manners as well as efficient

Make your phone calls reasonably short, and leave time between them for possible incoming calls.

Bell Telephone Company

service, it might be wise to review the following tips:

• Avoid mumbling, and talking with food in your mouth. Enunciate clearly.
• When you answer the telephone, simply say, "Hello." You may repeat your telephone number or announce your residence, such as "Wilson's residence," but these responses are a little formal. However, if you answer the phone at a friend's home, announce the telephone number or name of the residents.
• If the person calling asks for you and does not recognize your voice say, "This is he speaking," or, "This is [your name] speaking." Never say, "This is him."
• If the caller asks for a member of the family, summon that person to the phone quietly. Only if the person wanted is out should you ask, "Who is calling?" or, "Is there a message?" Take messages accurately, and establish a definite place to leave notes for family members. When you phone someone and are told he is not at home, it is polite to identify yourself and indicate whether the call should be returned. You may say, "If Tom comes in before 10 o'clock, will you please have him call me?" or, "Don't bother to have Tom call me back, Mrs. Arvin. I will talk to him tomorrow at school."
• If someone calls for one of your parents while they are entertaining dinner guests, it is proper to say, "May Mother call you later? She is busy just now." Or you may say briefly that you have dinner guests and ask if the call may be returned later. A *long distance call* justifies calling a person away from the table.
• If you make a social or committee call, announce yourself as, "This is Helen James," or, "This is Jim Clarke," not, "This is Mrs. James," or, "This is Mr. Clarke."
• Try to limit all conversations to five minutes, especially if you are on a party line. Pause between calls to give others a chance to use the phone or to contact your home. Houses have burned down and lives have been lost because of telephone thoughtlessness.
• Eavesdropping, interrupting a conversation while listening in on another

Don't ride the horn. Showing impatience by blasting your horn is rude. Two or three *light taps* are sufficient to indicate you want to pass or to warn pedestrians.

Consider your passengers when you open windows or tune in the radio.

phone, discourtesy to someone who has called the wrong number, and saying, "Guess who this is!" are irritating signs of bad manners.

Knowing how to use the telephone is extremely important in a place of business. Those who employ skilled clerks, stenographers, and secretaries are often surprised at their lack of telephone poise. A salesman usually sets a good example to follow. A person who is inefficient, discourteous, abrupt, or too talkative can lose business and create poor public relations. On the other hand, a person with a good telephone personality may be of great worth to the business.

Those of you who are ready to follow a business career will want to observe the following rules:

• Answer the phone promptly. Announce the name of the firm or office. If the person being called is out, reply, "I'm sorry, Mr. Allen is not here. May I take a message or have him call you?" If it is possible to transfer a call, do so.

• Speak directly into the phone in a normal voice, with your lips an inch or so from the mouthpiece. Neither shout nor whisper.

• Give the caller your undivided attention. If that is impossible at the moment, offer to call back at a time convenient to the party.

• If you do not understand clearly, say, "I am sorry, I did not hear you clearly," and not, "Whajasay?"

• Take notes, including the person's full name, phone number, time of call, and message.

• Avoid "Yeah," "Uh-huh," "Hum," "See you," "Bye now," and other slang.

• Take time to be courteous and sincere, but avoid being personal: "Thank you" (not "Thanks" or "Thanks a lot"), "I am sorry," "I'll be glad to," and "Please," make pleasant relations with the person on the other end of the line. Do not argue, interrupt, or show impatience. Be attentive, alert, and interested. The telephone creed, "Courtesy Is Contagious," has much to recommend it.

CAR MANNERS

A *driver* should think of the comfort and pleasure of others before lowering windows, smoking, tuning in the radio, or overcrowding the car. Polite *guests* refrain from back seat driving.

A person in the front seat can be of great help by reading maps, checking highway signs and names of streets, operating the radio, adjusting sun visors, and sometimes just being quiet. No passenger should urge the driver to speed. From the many serious consequences of picking up riders, you should avoid doing so, and do not "thumb" rides. A generation or so ago it was a popular thing, but now it is too risky.

Usually, dates or husbands and wives sit together rather than women in one seat and men in the other.

CORRESPONDENCE

Letter writing, like home repairing, is less work with proper equipment and a place to keep it. Items for your *correspondence kit* should include:

Paper—white paper and envelopes for business letters;
   —white or tinted for personal letters (tints for men are limited to gray and beige).
   —note paper 5 x 3¾, for invitation acceptances and regrets.
Cards—informal as well as special occasion.
Stamps—general and airmail.
Erasers, paper clips, scissors, transparent tape.

Here are some suggestions to help you write pleasant, personal letters:
• Write as you would talk. People like to picture *you* as they read your letter.
• Express your thoughts clearly. If you can get an idea across in ten words, do not take forty or fifty.
• Write about cheerful things. If you must talk about your disappointments and sorrows, be brief.

• Avoid boring people with excuses and complaints. Taking a whole page to explain why you have not written sooner does not excuse you, and often makes dull reading. Lack of time is never a good excuse.
• Be sympathetic with someone in sorrow, but don't overdramatize. Express your sympathy and then recall some special occasion you have enjoyed with the person who has passed on.
• If you are provoked at someone or your feelings have been hurt, write a letter, if you must, but postpone mailing it long enough to decide whether you really want to send it. You may wish later you could take back some of the things you said.

INVITATIONS, ACCEPTANCES, AND REGRETS: Informal cards may be used as shown on page 165.

Who Writes First? The person who leaves town writes first; i.e., if you go away to college, to work, or on a trip, you write home first; if you visit a young lady or young man at home or on campus, you write first. You may write a short note following a dinner, but it is not always necessary if you have been gracious in expressing your appreciation in person.

Writing to Titled People At one time or another, almost everyone needs to write a letter to a titled person. Clergymen and government officials are probably the most common examples. If you were writing to a clergyman who was not of your denomination, would you know for sure whether to call him

Buffet Supper
Sat. Feb. 8th at 7

Dr. and Mrs. F. Sargent Cheever

R. S. V. P.   *10 Park Lane*

To meet
Miss Lynn Williams

Mrs. Wilbur James Hawkins, Jr.
Tea 3-5
Sat. Apr. 14
College Club   R. S. V. P.

Invitations

Mr. and Mrs. Robert Arthur Licht
accept with pleasure
for the 8th at 7

Mrs. Sam Baughman Craig

accepts with pleasure
for the 14th

Acceptances

~~Miss Louise Lee~~
Sorry to miss your lovely
supper, but I will be out
of town on the 8th
Louise

~~Miss Theresa Rolshouse~~
Sorry I cannot be
with you on the
14th -- expecting guests
Theresa

Regrets

Informal cards (fold-overs) may be used for invitations to buffet suppers, teas, and similar social functions. A reply should be as formal as the invitation. If you sign your name, you may wish to draw a line through the printed name. This is optional. Some authorities say that visiting cards may also be used for informal invitations and replies.

165

Accepted table manners.
(a) Tilt your spoon away from you when you eat soup.

(b) Hold your knife and fork in this position when you cut food.

(c) Lift food to your mouth like this (American custom). . .

(d) Or like this (Continental custom).

the Reverend Mister, or Pastor, or Father? If you want your letter to show intelligence and good taste, it is important to be accurate about even the smallest details. Webster's New International Dictionary lists proper forms of address for the more frequently used titles. For less common titles, much help will be found in *Styles of Address*, by Howard Measures, published by the Thomas Y. Crowell Company, New York, 1947.

TABLE MANNERS

Table manners are important; don't let anyone tell you they are not. If you practice the following rules at home, you will feel at ease when you go out.

· Eat slowly. Eating too fast is not only bad manners, but also can result in poor digestion and overeating.

· Place luncheon napkins on your lap fully opened, dinner napkins folded once.

· *Before* you drink from a glass, wipe your mouth with your napkin to avoid making a mark on the glass rim. Hold large-stemmed glasses at the base of the bowl, small-stemmed glasses by the stem.

· Tilt soup bowls or plates *away* from you, lifting spoon toward the outside of the plate. Transfer the liquid quietly to your mouth from the side (not end) of the soup spoon.

· Test hot foods by tasting. Never blow on hot foods.

· Avoid *noticeable* stirring or mashing. Although most people put gravy on potatoes, it is actually not proper to ladle gravy onto anything except meat. On very formal occasions you may want to observe this rule.

166

• If you must cough, sneeze, or blow your nose at table, turn your head and hold your handkerchief to your face. You need not, but you may quietly say, "Excuse me," and you should not refer to your discomfort. If a bad coughing or sneezing spell comes on, excuse yourself from the table.

(e) Spread butter on half of a small biscuit or a small portion of bread at one time.

• Remove fish bones or olive seeds from the mouth with the fingers. However, if you are eating cherries for dessert, remove the seeds with a spoon to the plate under the dessert dish.

• Do not reach across the table to spear a piece of bread, or use your own knife or spoon to take butter or jelly.

• Break a slice of bread in two and then in two again before putting butter on it. Break a biscuit in half and let the butter melt between halves, but lift only a small portion to your mouth at one time.

(f) Leave knife and fork parallel and toward one side of your plate when you have finished the main course.

• Take a portion of everything served. Eat it if you can. If you cannot, leave it with no comment.

• Silver is usually used in the order in which it is placed—from outside in. If in doubt, watch your hostess. Use butter knives for spreading butter or jams, and steak knives with a sawtooth edge for cutting steak.

• When you have finished eating, place your knife across the rim of the plate, sharp edge in, and the fork parallel to it. Never rest a knife and fork on your plate "gangplank" fashion. If you *have not used* your knife, you may leave it where it was placed. After each course, the person clearing the table should remove all items not used.

(g) Take no more dessert on your spoon than you can eat in one bite.

(h) When you have finished eating, your place setting should look like this.

• Never leave a dessert spoon standing

When you eat in a car, be careful not to spill food on clothes or upholstery.

"flagpole" fashion in a sherbet glass *or* bouillon spoon inside a bouillon cup *or* teaspoon in a teacup.

• Avoid resting your arms on the table while you are eating. Never shove your plate away to indicate you have finished eating, or turn your cup upside down to indicate you do not want a beverage. Say, "No, thank you," and if a beverage is poured anyway, leave it.

• If you are a house guest you may fold your napkin. Otherwise, lay it casually to the left of your plate. Never fold a paper napkin, or a cloth napkin in a restaurant.

• *Never* hold a spoonful of ice cream or fruit, sipping at it. Take only enough for one bite and eat it all at once.

• Last but not least, a gentleman holds the chair for the woman nearest him on his right or occasionally, his left. He should not make himself conspicuous by trying to hold chairs for too many persons. Doing the thing that creates the least confusion is best.

• Guests should wait for the host and hostess to dismiss the table.

When passing dishes around the table, it is a good idea to pass them all in the same direction, and usually they are passed toward the right. At a fairly crowded table, you may find it helpful to receive dishes with your right hand, and pass them on with your left. At first this may seem awkward, because you are reaching across yourself, but it keeps your arm from bumping the person next to you.

The chart on page 169 tells how to eat various foods. Few people may have special spoons for cereal, fruit, and creamed soups, so we shall mention only the spoons most people own —tea, soup, and bouillon spoons.

MANNERS IN PUBLIC PLACES

Whether you are on the street, at work, at a drive-in or a first class restaurant, in church, at a dance, or at a college weekend event, someone is noticing you. The way you act can reflect upon your family, and influence your social or business success. The following review of manners is brief, but it will help to bring up interesting questions for discussion.

On the Street and in Places of Business Manners here may begin with dress and grooming. In our busy way of life, people — especially young women — have become careless about dress. What excuse is there for appearing at shopping centers with soiled shorts and slacks, and hair in curlers? Be sure to follow *best* practices of your own group and locality.

It is bad manners to eat or chew gum on the street, talk loudly, and show affection. A young man does not

168

HOW TO EAT DIFFERENT FOODS

Spoon Foods	Finger Foods		Fork Foods
TEASPOON	Apples	Crisp bacon	DINNER FORK
Apple sauce (if thin)	Artichokes	Grapes	Most foods
Cereals	Bananas	Nuts	FISH FORK
Custards	Bread	Olives	Fish cocktail
Fruit cocktail	Cake (small and firm)	Pickles	Lobster
Grapefruit	Cheese—firm	Potato chips	SALAD FORK
Oranges	Celery	Radishes	Salad
Soft cooked egg	Cookies	Rolls	Pie
Stewed or canned fruit	Corn on cob	Sandwiches	Cake (sticky)
Stewed tomatoes	Crackers	Toast	Moist sandwich loaf
BOUILLON SPOON			
Bouillon and soups in bouillon cups			
SOUP SPOON			
Soup in large bowl			

even take a young woman's arm unless assistance is necessary. A young man usually tips his hat when he speaks to a girl or older woman on the street. However, it is not necessary for a boy to remove his hat if a lady enters an elevator *unless* it is in a hotel or apartment house. Hat tipping stems from the medieval practice of lifting a face visor to identify yourself to a friend.

If you are on the street with your parents, be as courteous as with a date. Treat your mother like a lady and your father like a gentleman. Your self-respect will rise, along with your parents' pride.

In Restaurants and Other Places to Eat *Eating* out and *dining* out are quite different! Many of us eat out in unpretentious drive-ins. Even so, there are rules to observe. A young lady orders first; usually she gives her order to the young man. Eating in a car requires good manners. Carelessness with milk shakes and moist sandwiches may ruin

When dining in a restaurant, the boy holds his date's chair and sits on her left.

Good Housekeeping

a good suit, dress, or the car upholstery.

Dinner in the home of friends is perhaps the first experience in dining out. Although mentioned in Hospitality Highlights, a few pointers are given here that are omitted in that chapter. If you are invited to dinner, you wear exactly what you would wear to a restaurant. While waiting for dinner, a young man rises each time a young lady or older woman enters the room, and sits only after requested to, or after all the women have been seated. Young women rise for the hostess or older guests. If the hostess must move often in and out of a room, she should motion to her guests not to rise each time. Ladies precede men in and out of the dining room. The hostess indicates the seating arrangement.

The first experience in *dining out* at a first class restaurant, hotel, or club dining room is usually a little easier if two couples go together.

A young lady should wear smart but not frilly clothes. Gloves and a small purse are a must, and in some sections of the country a small hat is in best taste. Large hats are seldom worn after dark. A young lady should carry small change for rest-room facilities. She need not check her coat, but a young man always checks his top coat.

If the restaurant is likely to be crowded, reservations should be made in advance. Once inside the restaurant, the head waiter or seating supervisor asks the number in the party and selects a table to allow the best service for your party. The waiter leads the way to the table, with the young lady following, then her date.

Her date helps her to remove her coat, seats her, and then sits either opposite her or on her left. If there is no one to seat you, one young man leads the way and the young ladies follow. Women are given the most attractive view, whether it is facing inside or outside a window. A woman removes her gloves after she is seated.

The waiter should hand a menu to each person. If not, young women in the party should see the menu first. Prices vary considerably; it is well to observe the price range which your host chooses or discusses. If the appetizer is expensive and not included in the price of the dinner, a guest may say, "I don't believe I care for a first course." It is not good taste to be eccentric and order either the highest or lowest priced dinner. In order to save himself embarrassment, the host should know about prices and cover charge in advance.

A young man may take a young lady's order and repeat it to the waiter, or she may consult with him before ordering. A young lady talks to a waiter *only* when asked a direct question. If something is missing, the young man, in an inconspicuous manner, motions the waiter or tells another waiter, "Will you please ask our waiter to come here?" The host *never* snaps his finger.

If a young lady drops a piece of silver or a napkin, the waiter will pick it up and replace it with a fresh one. If she drops her purse or gloves and the waiter is not available, her date should come to the rescue. If he fails to notice, a girl may say, "I believe I dropped my purse."

If a lady stops to speak to someone at your table, all the men rise and

170

remain standing until she leaves. Make dinner interruptions very brief. If a friend talks for more than a few minutes, one of the young men should say, "May I offer you a seat?" This is usually the signal to start moving. If, for any reason, a young man's date leaves the table, he rises when she leaves and when she returns. Young women rise if an older woman stops to speak, but the thoughtful visitor will say, "Please don't rise. I don't want to interrupt your dinner."

If a young man does not know whether to pay the waiter or cashier, he may ask the waiter. If the waiter is paid, he will return the change on a tray. A tip of approximately fifteen per cent of the bill is left on the tray. If the cashier is paid, the same tip is left at the table. Tips are not always given for light snacks at a counter or drive-in.

A young lady precedes a young man out of the restaurant. A young man leaves a twenty-five cent tip for a coat and hat, ten to fifteen cents for a hat only.

In Church When you go to church, you go to worship. Conversation, making notes, and reading unrelated material are not a part of worship. Have you ever been annoyed by people whispering or chewing gum during the worship service, or distracted by someone dressed as if she were going to a cocktail party?

If attending a service that differs from your own, rise and sit with the congregation, but if it is not your custom to kneel or genuflect, you need

A young man assists a young lady with her coat.

Robert L. Brooks

171

Make hospital visits short. Appear cheerful and interested.

not do so. If you do not know the prayers and responses, simply listen. If communion is part of the service in the church you are visiting, you need not participate unless you wish. (In some churches, communion is intended only for members of that faith.) There is usually an opportunity to leave quietly before the communion service, or you may remain until the service is over.

In a Hospital Many people think they are being friendly when they make a long visit with a hospital patient. Visitors often are more helpful to patients if they limit calls to ten or fifteen minutes. With the many necessary interruptions by the hospital staff, a patient has actually very little time for rest and personal needs. Doctors often find patients more upset on Monday morning than any other day of the week because of long Sunday visits.

Middle to late afternoon and early evening are the best times to call. If you find out-of-town callers present, pay your respects and offer to come another time. Avoid talking about your troubles. The patient is more interested in his own. Listen sympathetically and do not belittle an operation or illness. Be cheerful.

If you send flowers, put them in a container in which they can stay. Sending flowers in a box makes a problem. Someone at the hospital has to find a container for them. Plants last longer than cut flowers and make less work for hospital attendants. Books, magazines, candies, toilet articles, and cookies are acceptable gifts. A card every few days with a personal message is just as welcome.

At Dances   Except for special proms, dances are usually informal.
Even at an informal dance, couples are expected to speak to the host and hostess or chaperones as they come and leave. It is very bad manners to slip out as if you did not know how to act. Gloves are usually worn by the ladies at very formal dances and kept on all evening. They are removed only to drink punch or eat refreshments.

Although it is the present custom to dance with your date all evening, it can be much more fun to exchange dances. The procedure is easy—a young man asks his date if she would like to dance with a friend and the two young men arrange to exchange dances, walking back with the girls to where they met.

If there is a "stag line" of young men, the social committee should urge sociability between them and the unescorted girls. Girls should never dance with other girls.

Except at some weddings, people in this country seldom think of "duty" dances, but it is, nevertheless, a courteous custom. Duty dances at weddings are mentioned in another chapter.

When a group entertains, it is very thoughtful for the officers to ask chaperones for a dance. All officers, of course, need not dance with all chaperones. Also, if your parents are chaperoning a dance, it is gracious for you and your date to dance with them.

Campus Week End   A young lady who is invited for a college week end is the envy of all her friends. Here are a few rules to follow to assure a second invitation, whether you are a young lady or young man.
• College men should invite girls far in advance, because arrangements must be made about missing classes, finding transportation, and assembling clothes.
• Young ladies should answer invitations as soon as they are certain they can make all the necessary arrangements.
• Young men should give young ladies some idea of the week-end schedule so they will know what clothes to bring.
• A young man usually locates a place for his date to stay, and vice versa, unless the guest has some connection with a fraternity or sorority.
• A young lady pays for her own room. A young man, if he is the host, pays for all other expenses connected with the week end. If the young lady is hostess, the young man, as guest, pays for his room and any meals eaten out. The young lady provides tickets for games and dances, and may arrange for a picnic or buffet supper.
• Young ladies should arrive with clothes appropriate for all activities, packed in not more than one suitcase. Girls who keep changing clothes to show off usually make themselves unpopular with other girls in the crowd.
• Young people—men and women—who do not want to drink should not feel they must keep up with the crowd. Drinking spoils many otherwise wonderful college week ends.
• Guests should take care not to be too critical. Any trip usually causes

certain discomforts, but complaining about food, rooming facilities, or other guests will only hurt the feelings of your host.

• Any guest should write to the host within a week, graciously but not too profusely expressing thanks.

Wherever you are, if you dress and act the part, you will feel the part; you will make a better impression on others, and be pleased with your own "know how."

Words and Phrases to Know

a' la carte	manners
canapé	parfait
cover charge	protocol
entreé	
etiquette	smorgasbord
frappé	salutation
hors d'oeuvre	table d'hôte

ACTIVITIES

1. Ask someone in your school, who has lived in another country or another part of the United States, to tell about differences in customs and manners.

2. Investigate and discuss the origin of our social customs such as shaking hands, rising when someone enters a room, men walking on the outside of the sidewalk, tipping hats, and using the letters "RSVP" on an invitation.

3. Discuss your contribution toward good manners at home. Are you cheerful at the breakfast table? Do you help to make family activities such as a drive, a picnic, or an evening out as interesting as you would for a date? Are you considerate of others when it comes to using the telephone, television, radio, bathroom, or car? Are you as careful to say "Please" and "Thank you" at home as you are away from home?

4. Practice making introductions, and put your practice into use outside class.

5. Dramatize dining at a friend's home and in a fine restaurant.

6. **Bulletin Board:** Mount menus from various types of restaurants. Compare menu forms, types of food served, and prices.

7. Discuss tipping in restaurants, taxi cabs, hotels and other places. When and where is tipping not good manners?

Correlation

ENGLISH: Half the class may write an *invitation* to a party, dinner, visit to a college campus, or other social function, and the other half *reply* to the invitation.

Select a titled person to whom to write a letter; send the letter, requesting some information.

JOURNALISM: Conduct a question and answer column on manners in several issues of the school paper.

Home Experiences

Prepare a list of frequently-called telephone numbers and mount it in your telephone directory, or file it near the telephone. Use the following as a guide:

air lines	gas company
beauty parlor	grocer
bus depot	hospital
car service	laundry
church	library
dentist	long distance
department stores	milk man
doctor	police department
drug store	school
dry cleaner	TV repair man
electrician	theaters
fire department	friends

Practice family courtesies. Discuss the chapter some evening at the dinner table.

Chapter 8

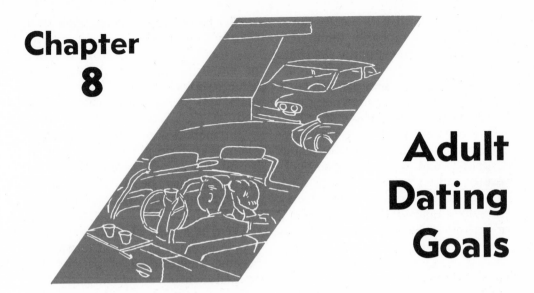

Adult Dating Goals

Dating customs in America differ greatly from those in other parts of the world. Exchange students from foreign countries find it difficult to understand the emphasis on early steady dating here.

In European and South American countries, boys and girls attend separate schools where extracurricular and social activities are not a part of education. Most families in other countries do not own cars. This greatly affects dating. Young men meet young ladies in the late teens through families, friends, at churches, swimming pools, tennis courts, and other social gatherings.

In the United States, steady dating often begins in junior high school. Although few older people approve of early marriages, many teen-agers marry before finishing high school. Steady dating has contributed to early marriage.

If you are going steady, you probably meet before and after school, at your lockers, at the corner drugstore,

and even schedule classes together. Few husbands and wives show such "oneness." It is like a hypnotic trance! Regardless of how you feel about steady dating, it might be a good idea to discuss the subject from different angles.

STEADY DATING

According to a Gallup Poll taken during the mid-1960's, the majority of young people approved of steady dating, although only twenty per cent of those interviewed actually "went steady." By the time people are entering their twenties, steady dating leading to marriage is expected; however, steady dating in the early teens is questionable. The opinion poll indicated that steady dating was most popular in the South and least popular in the West.

The poll revealed that by the sophomore year about three fourths of the girls and half of the boys were dating frequently. By the senior year about eighty per cent of all students were dating, but not all with steady dates.

As you have probably found out, many young couples simply drift into steady dating. A chain reaction begins. A young lady accepts a date. It is easier next time for the young man to ask the same girl. The young lady asks the young man to a vice-versa dance, and by this time other boys hesitate to cut in. A few more exposures and it's a "take." How long it will last neither person knows. It may end with a quarrel, through boredom, or interest in another person. It may lead to marriage.

How Did Steady Dating Begin?

During the "Roaring Twenties" and into the Depression years of the 1930's "going steady" would have been considered as old fashioned as "keeping company" in the Gay Nineties.

Some people trace the "going steady" custom back to the mid and late Depression years preceding World War II when a young man showed willingness to marry a girl if, after several dates he spent the equivalent of a day's pay on an evening's entertainment. Such investment in time and money was expected to have some future guarantee.

War came along and young couples, out of loyalty, pledged themselves to each other to the exclusion of all other dates until they could be in a better position to marry. After the war, a shortage of men made competition keen, and when a young lady found a young man interesting and attentive, she made every effort to hold him. Young men, after being away, looked forward to marriage, a home, a family.

Why Has Going Steady Continued?

Have you ever stopped to think of why you like or do not like to go steady? Here are some reasons sociologists give to explain why steady dating has continued:

• Our mobile population has robbed many young people of the sense of belonging to a community, and "steadies" may be a substitute for strong family roots or a feeling of security.

• There is a natural urge for young people in their early teens to want to become independent of parents. Increased school activities and local amusements have offered excuses for boys and girls to be away from home, thus offering opportunities to meet members of the opposite sex and select one of special appeal.

• Some parents, too anxious to relive their own teen years, have pushed their children into advanced social situations, encouraging early dating. In some communities, mothers campaign for community-organized social activities in the evening for grade school children, yet a year or two later bemoan the fact that Susie has a steady and wants to act like a sixteen-year-old. This is like "green house forcing" of young plants.

• The social status that is given to "going steady" has made young people cling to the system whether they are altogether happy about it or not. Most teen-agers and people in general want to do what others do.

• It is convenient always to be sure of a date.

• National prosperity makes early marriage financially possible for many couples.

Going Steady—   Many of you whose
  Pro and Con   parents object to
                  steady dating may
have heard remarks similar to the following:

"Going steady, in my day, was only
for those who had had the experience
of dating a lot of people until they
had singled out the one they liked
best, with matrimony the object. Any
fellow who got trapped at your age
was making a fool of himself."

"When you took a girl to a dance
your stock went up if all the boys
rushed up to sign her up for a dance.
If you got stuck with the same girl
all night, the girl wondered what was
wrong with her and so did the boy."

Such arguments seem old fashioned
to young people who want to go
steady. On the other hand, the opinions of young people are likely to
seem immature to their parents. Too
often each side thinks the other is all
wrong, and that is not the best way
to discuss a delicate question. Actually the pros and cons of steady dating
are numerous. Few persons of high
school age are sure which choice is
the best. What are the reasons given
on both sides? Let's examine the
points *against* steady dating first:

• It can become a mere habit, to the
point that even when two persons become bored with each other they lack
the initiative and confidence to break
the ties.

• It may encourage questionable relationships.

• Often steady dating is based on
what others are doing rather than on
preferences of the persons involved.
Think about this. If you had been
born thirty years earlier, you would
have "gone along with the crowd" by
dating anyone you liked. The "crowd"
generally considered steadies as a
kind of lonesome twosome with no
other friends. Of course, this was
wrong. The standard was too rigid to
fit everyone. In other words, the opinion of the crowd means nothing if you
become a slave to it.

• The teen years are a time for developing a sense of independence and
freedom. Going steady has the opposite effect. It reduces freedom.

• A variety of wholesome experiences
will help you develop an interesting,
well-rounded personality. Steady dating limits variety.

• Pretense—a form of dishonesty—
often occurs in steady dating. You
have heard friends say, "I know she
goes with him, but she really likes—."
We have strong age-old beliefs that
any form of dishonesty will turn out
badly because it leads to a chain of
pretense that hurts everyone concerned. According to this standard,
you should like a person a great deal
before you go steady with him.

• Another objection to steady dating,
as a general practice, is that it *defeats
its own ends*. In order to keep from
being permanently involved with
someone, teenage boys tend to stay
aloof from all girls. High school and
college "mixers" do not solve the
problem.

• A girl who has a steady in the class
above hers may cut herself out of a lot
of fun during her senior year.

• Boys and girls constantly going
steady lose out on friendships with
members of their own sex.

• Frequent steady dating may leave
no time for advantageous pursuits or
hobbies outside school which could
mean more to you than the memory

of a date every other night. This may not be true if two people make an effort to plan beneficial activities.

• Young people who limit their friends of the opposite sex to one person are limiting their sights and lowering their future prospects for a successful marriage. Few people buy a house without looking over a number of places. A date who looks good at sixteen may look quite different at twenty or older, and may not be as easy to dispose of as a house!

• When two people break up, someone is usually hurt to the point where grades fall off, dispositions become surly, and family relationships are upset.

The Roman Catholic and Mormon churches openly disapprove of steady dating. Bishop Fulton J. Sheen has said, "Going steady puts permanence at the wrong end; it hitches colts to wagons, calves to a milk bottle and puts the flower seeds in the vase . . .

A more normal fellowship between growing boys and girls develops poise and stability . . . This immature commitment used to be called 'puppy love'—and maybe it should still be so called, for those who fall for it generally end by leading a dog's life." This may be a severe observation, but statistics prove that teen-age marriages are less secure than marriages at a later date.

On the *positive* side of "going steady" might be the following:

• It gives a comfortable feeling to know there is always someone to date without worrying about asking or being asked.

• It provides social prestige—real or imaginary. However, no one should go steady merely for the sake of being "on the band wagon."

A steady should not take up all of a young man's time. It is important to have time for other young men and their interests.

Edgewood High School

178

• It may be more economical and require less effort to go steady because simply being together is usually sufficient without entertainment.

• Going steady is natural as people approach their late teens and early twenties, in this era when early marriages are common. It may be desirable if it helps a serious couple to understand each other and themselves better.

• When college separates a couple, they may look forward to "importing" their steadies for special week ends on campus. However, there are obvious hardships involved in separation. Often it is necessary to spend considerable time and money traveling to be together for just a brief time. Also, it may mean passing up some enjoyable school activities, if the other person is unable to attend.

• Many students who go steady and later marry have satisfactory marriages. This is not necessarily the result of going steady, but of two well-adjusted personalities learning to give and take. Sometimes, when high school seniors who date steadily go

Informal gatherings at a favorite spot can be pleasant. Would you feel free to join such a group if your "steady" could not be there too?

away to college, to work, or to enter military service, they find out that they have not really been in love. If they do continue their relationships after a temporary separation, they are likely to be sure of their love for each other.

WHAT ATTRACTS A DATE?

Some people have so much attraction for the opposite sex that they create envy and jealousy. It is difficult to define all the magnetic traits they possess. Girls are more likely to attract boys physically than boys are to attract girls. However, in both sexes, appearance is the initial attraction, even though surface appeal may wear off soon with nothing to back it up.

Have you ever heard someone say, "What in the world does he see in her? She isn't even pretty!" In a number of studies, boys and girls in their late teens tend to place less value on

179

pure physical beauty, extremely stylish clothes, the possession of a car, and lots of money. A good mind, good health, sex purity, cleanliness, and dependability take precedence over many of the traits people in their early teens often consider important.

Of foremost importance to nearly all boys and girls are the following:
• A neat, well-groomed appearance. This does not imply qualities of glamour but natural freshness and physical fitness.
• An alert, interesting personality—someone each can be proud to introduce to friends and family.
• A companion who can be a good listener and a good conversationalist without feeling he or she has to chatter all the time—one who has a sense of humor without being silly and loud.
• A dependable person, considerate of the feelings and comforts of others.
• A person who is versatile, adaptable, stimulating, and friendly.

Young men are almost unanimous in their agreement about girls they dislike: *gold diggers; girls who pout, sulk, talk about other dates; girls who tell shady stories, use heavy make-up talk baby talk, or swear.*

Young women prefer young men who do not drink, swear, brag, or act conceited; who do not sponge off other boys, tell vulgar stories, or ask for last-minute dates.

A new method for finding dates is by computer. It started when students at a men's college and a neighboring women's college "told" a computer about themselves and let it match them up for dates. The practice quickly became nationwide, and some businesses began selling this service.

Given honest information, a computer can match persons of similar interests and backgrounds. Of course, there have been mixups, such as the young man who was matched for a date with his sister. As to how romantic these computerized courtships are, you may form your own opinion.

DATING AND FAMILY COMPLICATIONS

You know many of the issues upon which parents and teen-agers disagree and you may have felt that your parents have been too strict or too interested in you. Or you may have wished your parents had been more strict and more interested. One 16-year-old mother remarked: "I wish my parents had laid down the law. I wouldn't have liked it, but I would have done what I was told about places to go and time to come home."

An extensive study was made in California to determine the home factors most likely to lead to social misbehavior. Slum neighborhoods and broken homes were important, but just as important were parental attitudes. If discipline is too strict or not strict enough, the study showed, trouble is likely to follow. (You see, it is hard for parents to know just how strict to be.)

Most parents try to understand the differences that exist between their generation and yours. Communication is often difficult, but it is interesting that 70 per cent of young people take problems first to their parents, according to a Gallup Poll.

Young people, the majority of them, are concerned about adult opinion of their behavior. Parents who expect their children to make their own decisions must provide values and stand-

180

ards for decision making. In many parts of the country teen-agers and their parents have established codes of behavior regarding *drinking, driving, weekday and weekend curfews, party crashing,* and *supervision during parties at home and away.* Rules save arguments and make decisions easier.

It is not "kid stuff" to phone your parents if you cannot be in when you are expected. Even parents extend this courtesy to each other and their families to relieve members from worry!

It is not childish to stay home to study week nights and to be in at a reasonable hour week ends, except for special occasions. Your body can take only a certain amount of physical abuse and emotional strain during your teen years without affecting your health and mental powers. You will function better later if you get proper rest now. Knowing when to study and being able to get good grades is not "sissy." On the other hand, your whole future may be at stake. Business men and women—and certainly the better models, TV and movie stars, and professional athletes —make a special effort to get enough rest and eat proper food. Their success depends upon keeping fit.

PETTING AND POPULARITY

Petting is a weak prop upon which to build popularity and a poor choice as a means of entertainment. In spite of new emphasis on sex education, some people still learn this too late.

You know that your parents and religious leaders urge you to practice chastity, and you know their reasons, based on moral teachings which have

Bell Telephone Company

If you expect to be out far beyond your planned time, phone your parents to relieve them of worry, or if you expect to invite the crowd in for a meal, give your mother some warning.

been accepted for centuries. But have you ever thought about the common sense reasons for purity, the ones based on human nature?

Psychologists say that a woman especially tends to be *monogamous*— that is, she wants a lasting relationship with one man. Sex, rightly understood, is part of such a relationship, a way for a man and a woman to show the affection, happiness, and trust they share only with each other. Petting ignores this true meaning of sex. It does nothing to satisfy the deep craving for a permanent relationship, so it does not bring lasting happiness. (Usually it does not even bring a few moments of real pleasure, as will be explained later.)

A worse result of petting is that it makes true happiness in marriage later hard to find. Intimacy in marriage does not mean as much to one who has let relationships with others become too close.

A well-known psychologist and

writer says that he has yet to find a girl who was happy to have lost her purity. Intimacies outside of marriage seldom bring the expected thrill, especially to a girl, partly because such acts are accompanied by feelings of guilt and worries about pregnancy.

Another common idea is that petting leads to popularity. Many studies have shown that this is false. For instance, *Seventeen* magazine questioned six young men, high school seniors, to find out what they expected on a date. One replied:

"I'm looking for a good time—good companionship, somebody to make me feel at ease. And of course, I'm a human being. I have certain physical desires but if I can squelch them with a good-night kiss, that's all right until I'm ready to get married."

Other surveys have shown that this young man's high ideals are not uncommon. What would such a boy think of a girl whose standards were much lower than his?

Wholesome ideas about the opposite sex can be formed in many ways. In responding to the *Seventeen* survey one of the young men, a Roman Catholic, indicated that the sex education he had received through his church had given him a very high regard for moral virtues. Another student credited his father with his understanding of the real place of sex in dating.

Taking older persons' advice is often difficult. The student just mentioned was fortunate because his father could talk to him well. A parent may not always be able to say what he feels in a way that will convince a son or daughter that his experience means anything to them.

Nevertheless, the parent who tries sincerely to offer behavior guides does so because of his great interest in the future of his children. If he has made mistakes, he does not want his son or daughter to suffer the same effects. Love and concern for your well-being are the basis for most parental advice. You can be assured of one thing: If your own conscience tells you that you are pursuing the right gains and goals, no one will hound you with advice and warnings!

According to a recent Gallup Poll the highest goals of most young people are a happy home and family life. Such mature aims speak well for today's teen-ager. By adhering to the highest standards you will have the best chance of reaching these goals. Therefore when the question of petting comes up remember that the adult role you are striving for is one of lasting happiness, not deceptive, momentary "kicks."

This discussion is meant to defend ideals that have led others to maturity and happiness. You are not expected to give the "right answers" just to get a high grade. By examining your own opinions about behavior on a date you can match your ideas with those that have been expressed. *Knowing* the values most important to you, and putting them into practice, will result in an important step toward a responsible adult role.

DATING AFTER HIGH SCHOOL

The staff of *Teens Today* surveyed college men, men in military service, and young men who went to work after high school to find out what counted most in dating. Their replies differed as the following summaries indicate.

In Col-
lege First of all, most college men feel that there is little basis for sharing interests with girls still in high school. Furthermore, beauty alone is not enough—*a girl must please the ear as well as the eye.* She must have a pleasant personality, dress smartly, and have healthy, intelligent interests.

In college, a young man usually limits his dating to week ends and feels much less dejected if a girl turns him down. College men often have to get a date on short notice, because study schedules do not always permit making dates in advance.

When asked about what to expect of a girl on a date, a typical remark was, "I'm more interested in what kind of time we have together during a date than if she will neck, or pet." College men have no real feeling for a date who is a pushover, and certainly marriage with her is far from their minds. The majority of college men felt that marriage and studying were difficult to manage and more than half of the college men said that they would prefer to postpone marriage until two or three years after college. This does not mean that they will wait that long.

Young men in military service like girls whose background is similar to their own.

Teens Today

H. Armstrong Roberts

Men in college like young women who enjoy talking about and doing the things that interest them.

In Military
Service Frequently you hear that men change their moral codes after entering the military service. From the remarks of young men in their first year of service, this is not true. Even though they may be miles from home, and what they do may never get back, few men act differently with a date near a military base than with one back home.

Servicemen who liked wholesome girls at home still do because they feel more comfortable with them. They like sincere, genuine attention on a day off, after being regimented and taking orders all week. They like girls who can have a good time without spending a lot of money. Two servicemen made this comment about two sisters they dated—"We only went to a carnival and ate pizza but it was a kick every minute. Those two girls had a real talent for making things fun."

Loneliness is the biggest problem for a young man away from home, in service or on a job. Often, a young man in service will propose to a girl

183

Teens Today

The young man in business likes a girl with good social understanding—one who is interested in making a good home.

after a few dates. A lonely sailor, Paul Symons, proposed to a lovely looking girl on his third date. She turned him down. Paul remarked, "She was a sweetheart—darn bright too. She told me she'd been dating sailors for two years and I was the *thirteenth* guy who'd proposed. I remember she gave me a real nice kiss and said, 'Some other girl might not understand that you are lonely, not in love.'"

Sometimes real romances that lead to happy marriages do occur on military bases, but young men more often marry the girls back home.

On the Job   The young man, out of school and earning enough money to support himself and a car, is the most serious about dating. He has marriage on his mind. He can afford to take his girl to dinner and a show or to the beach for a day to impress her. A young man who is working full time is looking for a young woman, not a girl. He wants someone who is mature and capable. For in-

stance, Norm Brinker had two girls and could not make up his mind which one he liked better. About Sue he said, "Take what happened two months ago: Sue's mom had a heart attack and Sue had to take over things at home, plus managing her job at the office . . . Like I said, she took it all in stride."

Terry, his other girl, was equally capable. Norm remarked, "Maybe some nights I'll say I'm in the mood for a fat steak, and she'll say, 'Why should you spend ten dollars to eat out when I can cook a steak at home for a third of that?'" Norm added, "Terry's great with kids, too. I've watched her with her kid brother, and she is as good with him as her mother is."

The majority of working young men have no regrets about not going to college. They felt that specialized courses would make up financially for a college education. By far the majority expressed a desire to marry a year or two after being on a job.

From these remarks, you can see that it is more important to show a date a genuine good time than to resort to petting as an only means to win a man—or a woman.

ENTERTAINING A DATE

Some communities have teen-age centers offering week-end entertainment. Many homes have recreation rooms where young people enjoy table tennis, chess, darts, cards, or dancing.

Some groups may enjoy music. For instance, four young people in one school have a band, and like to play while others sing, dance, or just listen. Instrumental clubs are popular. Many young people discover interests that stem from class activities.

CASE STUDIES: Jane Drury and Tom Grimm found out in art class that they both liked designing and silk screen printing. Setting up equipment in Jane's basement, they began printing Christmas cards for themselves, and later took orders from friends. Other couples helped with cutting, folding, and packaging the cards. Their hobby became profitable.

Charles Cole and Carol Newsam became interested in a project in physics and spent many evenings developing a prize-winning exhibit at a tri-state science fair.

Other couples get together and compare stamps, coins, or records. Four couples became so talented at square dancing that they were in popular demand as entertainers and earned spending money during their junior and senior years in high school.

Often, young people fail to take advantage of the many worthwhile opportunities in their home town—flower shows, art exhibits, outdoor concerts. You might try substituting some free community activities for an expensive evening "on the town" or a "lonesome-twosome" date.

Ginny Allison, whose home has a large backyard, has only to say, "Come over for a barbecue. I'll supply the entertainment if the crowd will bring the food." To add to the fun of cooking outdoors, she has a badminton set, a shuffleboard painted on the garage drive, croquet, darts, and ring toss.

Study the chart on page 186 and see how well you can do in planning entertainment for a couple or a group.

A picnic date in the park is a relaxing, inexpensive, and enjoyable way to spend a Sunday afternoon.

H. Armstrong Roberts

185

Eastman Kodak Company

When "going out" for an evening becomes routine—or too expensive—try double dating at home. Simple games, conversation, and a snack make a pleasant evening for mature young couples.

THINGS TO DO ON DATES

Indoors at Home	Activities
Bridge	Church youth
Box hockey	groups
Canasta	Future Farmers
Checkers	Future Homemakers
Chess	Future Teachers
Table games	Hi-Y
Table tennis	Junior Achievement
Scrabble	Orchestra
	School choir
Outdoors Away	School clubs
	Y-Teens
Concerts	
Fishing	**Indoors Away**
Hiking	Art exhibits
Ice skating	Ballet
Movies	Bowling
Outdoor operas	Concert
Picnics	Dancing
Rowing	Flower shows
Square dancing	Opera
Swimming	Plays
	Roller skating
Outdoors at Home	Square dancing
Badminton	**Miscellaneous**
Barbecue	Astronomy
Croquet	Drama groups
Darts	Photography
Ring toss	Reading groups
Shuffleboard	Silk screen work
Volley ball	Sketching

WHAT IF YOU DO NOT HAVE DATES?

Frequently the girl who has few dates in high school because she is too tall, too mature, or not very competitive, reaches college and becomes popular. The girl-shy fellow or the fellow who was too busy with sports or a part-time job in high school may also be a "late bloomer" and a successful husband.

In a 300-item check of 15,000 students in grades 9, 10, 11, and 12 over the country, the Purdue Opinion Poll found that 48 per cent of boys and 39 per cent of girls seldom date. In the *senior class*, a third of the students seldom have dates. How do you believe a poll of your own high school would compare with these findings?

Let's consider two young people who seldom dated but took advantage of an opportunity to broaden their interests.

CASE STUDIES: Ed Hurley, one of a family of four boys, looked upon dating as a waste of time and an unnecessary expense. He considered parties and dances as trivial affairs. He preferred to hunt, fish, hike, tinker in his workshop, or go out with a gang of boys.

Marianne Pressler did not get off to any kind of social start during her sophomore year, and as a result she became more engrossed in piano practice and sewing. She voluntarily limited her social life to girl-group and family activities—reading, movies, listening to records, bridge, and weekend trips.

Ed and Marianne will, no doubt, catch up socially later. In the meantime they have made good use of their time. They did not put in *all* their time watching TV or movies, or just loafing. Their experience in activities will pay them dividends later and make it easier for them to fit into many groups.

Even though you may not date, it is a good idea to attend group social gatherings and *appear friendly* and interested in what others do.

If you do not have all the dates you would like to have, consider the following:
• Act natural without trying to be somebody else. If you are the quiet type it would be as much of a strain to be lively and quick witted as it would be for a very lively, active person to be quiet.
• Know your shortcomings; if you can improve, you will find the effort worthwhile. The chapters on Personality Patterns, Manner Minimums, and Hospitality Highlights should help you.
• Be friendly. Do not expect the other person always to take the initiative in being friendly. Avoid feeling sensitive if someone you like fails to speak to you. Learn to smile *as much as other persons you like* and appear happy even though you do not always feel that way.
• Set your own good standards about grooming, dressing, behavior, and spending money. Trying constantly to keep up with *everyone else* will make

If you do not date regularly, take advantage of opportunities to work with members of the opposite sex in school activities.

you feel uncertain about how to behave.
• Expand your interests, read more, so that you can share experiences with others. Learn to talk about the things other people talk about—a job, college, school sports, the school publication, attractions in town, travel, the space age. You will be surprised at how this will broaden your interests and skills, and relax you when you have a date.
• Join clubs, which have members of both sexes. If you are on a food committee, and do not have a date for the dance, go anyway! Dress up, smile, and take every opportunity to serve others. Avoid overplaying, yet if you are a boy in the stag line, do not run home if the first girl refuses to let you cut in. Try again.
• Observe others in the classroom, at church, during games, and on other occasions, and make mental notes of the traits that the best-liked persons have. Try to work some of them into your pattern of living. Observe objectionable traits and eliminate them.
• Above all—get your mind off yourself. This takes discipline. Focus your attention on other people and new interests. If you are not having many dates, learn new skills, read, be

SELDOM DATE

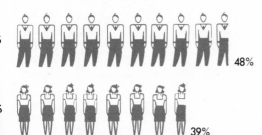

s

48%

s

39%

187

friendly with others, and these new experiences will make you a more interesting person in the future. Frequent dating is no guarantee of marriage *or* happiness after marriage. Social experiences are very desirable to develop poise, but you can get these experiences from a group, as well as by dating.

A SUMMARY OF DATE TECHNIQUES

Asking for a Date Have you learned not to say, "Ellen, what are you doing Saturday night?" This puts you and the girl on the spot. A girl neither wants to say "Nothing," or "I'll be busy."

After a few friendly remarks, ask for a date to a specific event, for instance, "Ellen, would you like to go to a party at Jim's Saturday evening?" or "Ellen, would you like to see a movie Saturday evening?" Later — "*Haunted* is playing at the Regent and *Play Ball* at the Garland. Any choice?" If the boy mentions neighborhood shows, Ellen should not suggest a more expensive downtown movie.

Ellen may accept with, "Sounds like fun, I'd love to," or regret, "I'd love to, but I have already made other plans for Saturday." If she seriously wants the young man to try again she may add, "Do call me another time,

A boy appreciates a date who is on time and who shows that she is glad to see him.

Singer Sewing Machine Company

Ralston Purina Company

though," or, "I hope you'll give me a raincheck."

A young lady who is stalling, hoping someone else will ask her, may say, "I am not sure of my plans for Saturday; can I let you know later?" Such a response is justifiable if the girl is sincere, but it is not fair to keep a boy guessing just because you have a faint hope that a more desirable date may phone.

At the close of the telephone conversation, a young man should repeat the day and time to avoid misunderstanding.

Calling on a Date Under usual circumstances, a young man calls for his date in person. If it is his first call, the girl (let's

A young man usually gets party snacks for his date, but if a young lady wishes to help herself, she may.

call her Jane) should make a special effort to answer the door. Jane should introduce her parents and anyone else in the room. If Jane's father or mother should answer the door, the date (let's say Jack) might say, "Good evening, Mrs. Davis [or Mr. Davis]. I have come to see Jane." If he does not know Jane's mother, he introduces himself. "Good evening, I am Jack Courtley. I have come to see Jane."

The young man should set a time for a date and be there promptly. A girl should be ready on time also. When a date or her mother comes into the room, the young man should rise

189

and remain standing until she sits down, leaves the room, or offers him a seat. It is thoughtful for a young couple to say "Good-by" to parents, if present when they leave.

A young man opens and closes the car door for his girl. The girl accepts the gesture with a "Thank you," and does not say, "Never mind, I can get it myself." If traffic is heavy on the street, the young lady should say, "There is so much traffic, don't you want to slide through first?" It is annoying if a girl does not give her escort time to be courteous.

Only under unusual conditions does a young man arrange to meet a girl anywhere except at home. Can you think of any circumstance when it might be difficult for a boy to call for a girl?

Breaking a Date It is unkind as well as bad manners to break a date unless unavoidable. The party with whom the date is broken may have difficulty in getting a last-minute substitute. If you have a good reason for breaking a date, break it as early as possible. It will save embarrassment and "face" to explain truthfully but *briefly* why you cannot keep the date. Don't become fussed and go into detail. Be sincere in saying you are sorry, without overdoing the act.

Girl Asks Boy There are many occasions when a young woman may ask a young man for a date. It is usually to a group affair—party or dance—not for a date alone together. She invites the young man to something definite, and she pays for the tickets. The young man provides transportation, and perhaps a snack, although the girl may invite a few couples to her home afterward.

Pick-ups and Blind Dates It is foolish to make an impromptu date with a person you meet on a bus, at a movie, or on the street. *Blind dates* are in a different category. Many people have met their future mates on a blind date. If you can trust the person who makes the date for you, it may turn out to be fun. A *planned activity* makes an evening with a blind date less of a strain.

Playing "Second String" If it hurts your pride to play second to anyone, you may be permanently on the losing end. If you can have a good time with your date, even though you know another person has been asked first, what do you really have to lose? By showing your date a good time, you may play "first string" some day. You get a chance to meet others on the date; you are number one for the evening; you don't have to "get serious" every time you go out, but you can't get anywhere by staying at home every night.

Going Dutch This social custom became acceptable and popular during the Depression of the 1930's. If a young man asks a young lady for a date, she is never expected to share the expense. But if a group attends a movie or other entertainment that is understood to be all Dutch—very well, why not? If two young people are going steady and an overwhelming chain of events is going to cause a definite financial strain on the boy, the girl may sug-

190

gest, "Jim, I'm such an expense this weekend. If it's all right with you, I'd like to share in something." A young man may still be touchy about chivalry, so be tactful if you make such a suggestion. Girls may share expenses by suggesting snacks, dancing, or games at home.

It is in better taste to give impersonal, inexpensive gifts unless **Gifts** you are engaged and marriage is near. Gifts for *girls* may include a compact, bottle of perfume, charm for a bracelet, pin, simple bracelet or necklace, jewelry box, or small purse for dress occasions. For *boys:* sweater, tie, tie clip, cuff links,

key case, pocket knife, tie rack; for *either boys* or *girls,* books, records, personalized book marks, picture album, grooming or manicure case, book ends. Gifts related to a person's interests, perhaps sports, photography, needlework, or cooking, usually are pleasing.

If expensive gifts are given and a couple later breaks up, these gifts should be returned immediately, the same as an engagement ring, school ring or pin, or portrait photograph. Return them with a friendly note; avoid displaying hurt feelings, spite, or sarcasm. It is wise to avoid sentimental engravings on gift jewelry.

ACTIVITIES

1. Compare your dating privileges and customs with those of your parents, such as use of car, places to go, hour to come home, sources of entertainment, frequency of dating, cost of dates, asking for dates.

2. If there is a foreign exchange student in your school or in a school nearby, ask him to tell about dating customs in his country.

3. Make a class survey to find out the percentage of students who have steadies, wish they had steadies, and approve or disapprove of steady dating; number of dates desirable a week and when; whether or not dating interferes with school work; activities most frequently engaged in on dates.

Publish findings in your school paper. Even your local newspaper might be interested.

4. Discuss the following:

If you like a girl (or boy), should you make it known? How?

Good manners are important to some people but not to others. Why?

Should you make your date feel important? How?

5. Choose a moderator to list on the chalk board in two columns:

"Topics boys like to discuss," and "Topics girls like to discuss."

6. Choose a moderator to list on the chalk board in two columns:

"How to be popular with boys," and "How to be popular with girls."

7. Discuss activities young people may substitute for "lonesome-twosome" dating. What steps can you take toward encouraging wholesome activities among underclassmen?

8. Read again *Petting and Popularity* on page 181. Tell why you agree or disagree with these remarks. Do you know of any instance when foul play or a serious accident has happened to a young couple parked in a car?

9. Is there a recreational center in your community? Would you use one if there were? When? What activities would you like it to provide?

10. Pick a chairman to take a poll of your favorite activities. What two things do you like to do best in each group of activities listed on page 186? Publish results in your school paper.

11. Give your opinions on the following topics in the text:
* Asking for a date.
* Calling on a date.
* Breaking a date.
* Blind dates.
* Girl-asks-boy dates.
* Playing second fiddle.
* Going Dutch.
* Gifts for dates.

12. **Bulletin Board:** Mount clippings from teen-age or dating columns in your local paper. Discuss your reactions to these question and answer columns. Do you think advice from friends, teachers, and parents would be as satisfactory? Why? Why not?

13. Discuss suggestions for increasing dating prospects and add to those listed in this chapter.

14. Review and discuss recent magazine articles concerning dating. Consult Reader's Guide to Periodical Literature.

Correlation

STUDENT GOVERNMENT: Discuss wholesome, standard dating behavior for different age groups in your school.

PARENT TEACHERS ASSOCIATION: Find out how your school's dating standards compare with other schools, and conduct a panel on this topic at a PTA meeting. Use the discussion to form a dating code in your school.

Chapter 9

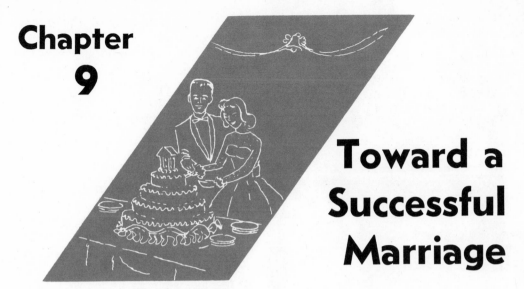

Toward a Successful Marriage

Your marriage may be just around the corner, or still a part of the vague and distant future. In any case it is just as important to study about marriage and all the aspects of family living as it is to study for any career. To be successful as a wife or husband, mother or father, and as a homemaker is one of the greatest of all achievements.

IF YOU HAD THREE WISHES

If you were granted one of the following wishes, after you finish your schooling, which would you choose: (1) an absorbing job; (2) a guaranteed life income; (3) a happy home and family life?

When this question was asked of a cross section of husbands and wives over the United States, eighty per cent chose a happy home and family life. It is obvious that if relationships at home are pleasant, you can take disappointments or hurdle obstacles even though your job may not always be absorbing or your income certain.

Even now you know how much better your day goes if you leave home in the morning with everyone happy. If there is discord and arguing at breakfast, you probably find it interferes with your thoughts all day.

In some marriages, miracles can happen even though two young people may have the odds against them. In other marriages, emphasis upon the wrong values can create a mirage that dissolves in failure with one disappointment after another. You cannot be sure of a successful and happy marriage if you enter it in a hurry any more than you can expect to set up a successful business without study and preliminary planning.

Before discussing some of the more personal aspects of marriage, consider the present marriage laws in the United States.

SOME FACTS CONCERNING MARRIAGE LAWS

Certain marriage laws apply in all states.

193

United of Omaha

A happy home and family life are more important to the majority of young adults than either an interesting job or a guaranteed life income.

• A marriage in all states may be declared void when it involves close blood relatives or when either mate is guilty of bigamy.

• Marriage can also be annulled in all states if one or both parties are under age, or if there has been any fraud or gross misrepresentation of facts beforehand. When a marriage is annulled, it is legally declared never to have existed.

• Common-law marriages, in which husband and wife agree to live together without the benefit of a wedding ceremony, are valid in over a third of our states. Moreover, such marriages in these states may not be dissolved without a divorce.

This custom dates back to frontier days of the early West when there were no clergymen near. Men and women took their own wedding vows and lived together until the circuit rider was able to perform the ceremony. Laws are sometimes slow to change, so a great deal of confusion arises concerning them.

MARRIAGE ODDS FOR MEN AND WOMEN

Sociologists claim that Americans are "the marryingest" people in the civilized world. The most common age ranges for marriage in this country are 18-21 for women and 20-23 for men. In 1967 women sharply outnumbered men in these age groups. One result was a decline in the percentage of teenage women who married. However, the ratio of marriage-age men to women is expected to be nearly even by 1970.

Birth Rate Odds Judging from the fact that for every 1,000 girls born there are 1,055 boys, it would seem that marriage chances favor the girls. But from birth, boys are more vulnerable to diseases and accidents. In their teens and twenties, occupational, highway, air, and military hazards speed up male mortality. At twenty-five the ratio of men to women is equal. From then on the number of women at each age shows a gradual increase over the number of men. At thirty, a single woman has one chance in two of ever marrying, and at forty, one chance in five. A much larger per cent of men will marry between thirty and forty.

Life Span Odds Women are usually referred to as the "weaker sex," but the female is in many ways stronger than the male. Generally speaking, she has greater resistance to fatigue, can go longer without sleep, and stands disappointment, the shock of sudden illness or loss of income better than a man. She is less vulnerable to diseases of the heart, blood vessels, and kidneys. Biologists claim this is nature's way of insuring the preservation of the race.

On the average, a woman outlives a man by more than six years. A white female born in 1965 can expect to live to an average age of 74.7, a male to 67.6. (For non-whites the life span is about six years less.) About two out of every three women sixty-five and over have no husbands. Married people—men and women—tend to outlive single persons. The reason may be selection and not marriage, because the less physically fit are less likely to marry.

Geographical Odds Cupid is always at work regardless of age, occupation, or locale. There are certain geographical differences, how-

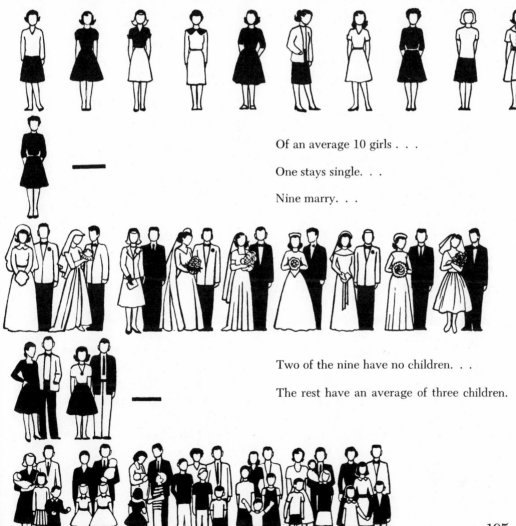

Of an average 10 girls . . .

One stays single. . .

Nine marry. . .

Two of the nine have no children. . .

The rest have an average of three children.

195

ever, for single men and women seeking a mate.

Girls who live in cities have worse odds than those living out of cities; 70 per cent of the unmarried women live in cities compared with 60 per cent of the unmarried men. However, in industrial cities or those near large military bases—for example, Gary, Detroit, San Diego, San Francisco, Norfolk, Sacramento, Youngstown, and Tacoma—there are more unmarried men than women. There are more unmarried men in proportion to unmarried women in western than in eastern states.

Factor of Proximity   Not only are there geographical odds in marriages, but there is also the "factor of proximity." You are most likely to meet your future mate in high school, college, or on a job. Other common opportunities to meet the person you will marry are through friends, church, or club activities.

When women or men work alone or associate with members of the same sex all day, they should make an effort to participate in activities involving the other sex, if they are interested in marriage. For instance, they may join bowling, square dance, little theater, choral, bicycling, hiking, or ski groups. Evening classes are also excellent meeting grounds. Many YMCA's and YWCA's have well organized social activities. Some have clubs for *Parents Without Partners*.

Very few people never have an opportunity to marry. Some prefer to complete their education, become self-supporting, or travel before marrying; others become burdened with family responsibilities. Often when marriage is postponed, circumstances arise to terminate plans. Also, many people set up impossible standards for a mate; the ideal person is never found. These people demand that their mate's standards be higher than their own—which seldom works!

Highly educated and capable single people often render a greater service to society than many of their married contemporaries; in many cases their lives are full, rich, and totally satisfying. On the other hand, some people marry but remain so engrossed in their jobs that their marriage never means what it should to them.

WHAT SHOULD YOU SEEK IN A MATE?

Boys tend to be impressed with a pretty face and provocative figure, and girls with a handsome profile and athletic prowess. As young people mature, a good disposition, good health, ambition, and courtesy often take precedence over a glamorous appearance. Good grooming and becoming clothes, of course, are important at all ages.

Actually, few persons could qualify as beauty kings and queens. Average persons often learn to make up in other ways what they lack in mere physical beauty. The Greek philosopher Socrates called beauty "a short-lived tyranny." Many very attractive girls in their teens turn out to be less attractive as they mature, especially if they neglect other attributes of charm.

The late Dr. Lewis M. Terman, noted research psychologist, studied a large cross section of married peo-

RELATION OF HAPPINESS IN MARRIAGE TO LENGTH OF FRIENDSHIP

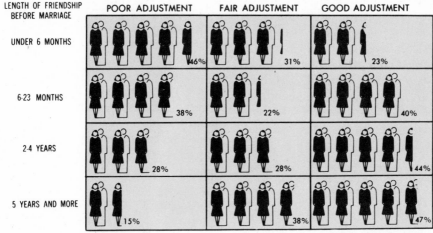

Pictograph Corporation

ple to find out some of the traits that contribute toward a *happy* marriage.

These traits are transposed into questions. It might be interesting to have your classmates score you as you score yourself. The wise comment of Robert Burns, "Oh wad some power the giftie gie us to see oursels as others see us," may be applied here.

1. Are you always considerate of the feelings, opinions, and plans of others?

2. Do you expect a certain amount of consideration from others?

3. Are you slow to take offense?

4. Do you refrain from undue efforts to impress others?

5. Do you enjoy working co-operatively with classmates without always wanting the leading role?

6. Do you enjoy doing things for those less fortunate than you?

7. Have you confidence in yourself and a happy outlook on life?

8. Are your viewpoints on religion, politics, and morals wholesome and orthodox?

9. Are you, as a rule, orderly about your appearance and work?

10. Can you manage money wisely?

The people who seldom find happiness in marriage are those who like to "pick a fight" at every remark made; have a pessimistic outlook; spend too much time daydreaming; are domineering; lack confidence in themselves, and are ardent nonconformists.

HOW WILL YOU KNOW WHEN YOU ARE IN LOVE?

This is a question every young person asks after he or she has been hit by Cupid's first dart. You may have fallen in and out of love one or more times by now. But how will you know when the real thing hits you?

You have already experienced love in many forms:

Love for unattainable personalities— a movie star, for instance.
Love for your mother and father.
Love for your sisters and brothers.
Love for your friends.

197

You may have had the kind of emotional feeling called a "crush"—an infatuation or idealistic admiration for someone. This is a natural emotion in early adolescence. Of course, some of these high school attachments do lead to marriage at an early age. If both parties are stable, with similar educational, social, cultural, economic, and religious goals, their marriage will be successful.

Love is much more than sharing any kind of physical relationship. When two people are in love, they will be proud to be with each other in the presence of family and friends; they will be interested in doing things together; they will be unselfish, and ambitious for each other's future.

You may not be in love enough to be married if you want to rush into marriage mainly because it is what friends are doing. For instance, in Charlotte, North Carolina, two young people, leaders in their class, married at 16 and 15. This caused an avalanche of young marriages, most of which soon failed because the young couples found out that they were short-changing themselves on educational, social, and cultural opportunities. They realized too late that they were poorly prepared for settling down to keeping house, nursing babies, and earning enough money to pay rent and food bills, aside from having any left for clothes, pleasure or savings. Occasionally such marriages are successful. To make them succeed requires maturity, intelligence, and determination on the part of the young people—approval, understanding, and often financial help on the part of the parents.

WHEN ARE YOU TOO YOUNG TO MARRY?

Perhaps you have heard older people say of a married friend of yours: "She is too young. Think of all she is going to miss, tied down with a baby in a year or so—education interrupted!" Parents dislike having a daughter marry while she is still in school, yet they worry if she is not married after passing her middle twenties.

It is often difficult to reason with young people once they have their minds set on marriage, yet many regret hasty decisions later. Here are some things to think about if you are contemplating an early marriage:

• Discuss your plans with your parents sensibly. Parents have the benefit of experience. If you can calmly discuss what you have to gain and lose by marrying young, your marriage will be more likely to work out.

• When you marry against your parents' wishes (unless they are very unreasonable), you may spoil your chances for real happiness.

• Get all the education you can before marrying. A young woman often thinks it is a good idea to quit school, marry, and take a job to help her husband through college. However, this can lead to problems. Consider the life a woman leads if her education is inferior to her husband's. Can she ever become the intelligent companion that he needs? Even worse, instead of helping his career by sacrificing her education, she may become a handicap for him, as in the following story.

CASE STUDY: Tom Lake and Nora Walden married after two years of

198

college. Nora quit school and worked as a typist. By cutting social activities to a minimum they were able to pay for Tom's education. Ed Foltz and Donna Lehman considered doing the same, but finally decided to postpone marriage until both had their degrees. Waiting was hard, but they made the best of it and enjoyed a full campus social life. After graduation Tom and Ed took jobs in the same office. A year later Ed was chosen for promotion. Mr. Conrad, who ran the office, said privately that Tom was a good enough worker, but the new job involved entertaining executives and their wives. Ed and Donna could do this better since they were both well educated and socially at ease.

• Think beyond a beautiful wedding or hasty elopement. What will life be like in two years? If you marry early, many of your friends will still be free from family responsibilities, preparing themselves for a satisfying future and planning marriage when they are better prepared to accept all the responsibilities.

• Give your personality a chance to mature before you marry. Think of how much your tastes and interests have changed since you were a freshman. This will continue in the years just after high school. Your feelings about people will change, too. This is one reason why those who marry young tend to make the worst marriages. When people marry and their personalities then develop along different lines, trouble is the usual result. Statistics show that marriages involving men under 21 and women under 18 are the ones least likely to succeed.

CASE STUDY: No one could see why Laura Vincent, very bright and cute, went with Dick Cousins. Dick was likeable and a good athlete, but one of the poorest students in his high school class. Laura's parents especially could not see it and never quit saying so. This only made Laura all the more loyal to Dick. After graduation Dick went into military service. Laura spent two years in college, then quit school and married Dick a week after his release from service. Their marriage lasted six months. Laura said Dick wasn't the same person any more. In a way she was right. He had changed much since high school, and so had she. They no longer had anything in common.

• If you marry a person whom you have known only a short time, your marriage is much riskier. This fact is shown in the informative chart on page 197.

Despite the statistics mentioned above, some young marriages do succeed. This is because *emotional maturity* is more important than *age* in marriage. Some people are more mature at eighteen or twenty than others several years older. Anyone not aware of the responsibilities of marriage, or unwilling to accept these responsibilities, is too young to be married. You may *not* be too young to marry, if: as a *young man* you can provide a living for a family, be contented to stay home at night; give up personal pleasures to help care for a baby, or as a *young woman* can make up your mind to be happy in all the areas of homemaking, cleaning, cooking, caring for a baby, without feeling sorry for yourself, and satisfied to terminate your formal education should it be necessary.

199

MARRIAGE AND CAREER SUCCESS

A man's marriage almost always influences his chances for a successful career. About 90 per cent of high paying executive positions are filled only after the employer learns something about the wife of the man being hired. The wife's education and social grace can be a factor, as with the couples mentioned on page 198. There are also many other ways in which a wife can help—or hinder—her husband in his work.

Many decisions about a man's career must be made by the wife and husband together. One question which more and more young families must answer is whether to move to another city for a better job.

Moving means tearing up roots—saying goodbye to friends, possibly taking children out of school, giving up a home and finding a new one. If the family has other relatives in the city they are leaving, the decision is even harder. On the other hand, a man often knows that if he refuses a transfer, he may never be offered another promotion.

Obviously there is no easy way to solve such a problem. The answer requires serious thought, based on each family's own situation. Most of all, such a decision requires agreement between husband and wife; otherwise, family harmony may be permanently disrupted.

What can a couple do to avoid such a problem? Before marriage they should discuss this situation as carefully as possible. True, they will not know the specific details of a move they may face in the future, but *if they are mature* their basic attitudes will already have been formed. Is financial improvement more important than keeping up friendships? Would they be willing to move away from their parents for the sake of a promotion? If a couple agrees about these and similar questions before marriage, they can be fairly sure to agree later, when faced with real decisions.

Does this help you to see why emotional maturity before marriage is emphasized so much in this chapter? Mature attitudes are not likely to change and cause disagreements later.

Certainly the best help a wife can give her husband in his career is to excel in her own career—that is, to be a good wife. Specifically, it will help if a wife can develop these traits:

• Flexibility, ability to accept change and to see what is good in a new situation.

• Attention to long-range goals. Willingness to accept hardships when they cannot be avoided or when they are likely to lead to a better future.

• Avoidance of nagging, pushing, unfounded jealousy.

• Avoidance of envy. A wife who struggles daily with dishes and diapers may wish at times that she could trade places with her husband. However, she should remember that his work has its problems, too.

WHY DO SOME MARRIAGES END IN DIVORCE?

After declining for a few years, the divorce rate in the United States is climbing again. Many reasons are offered to explain this sad fact. One psychiatrist says that most people who seek divorces never had much intention of staying married.

Specifically, what causes unhappiness in marriage? Happy marriages seldom result under any of the following conditions:

• If you marry to escape an unhappy home life or job you do not like.

• If you marry on the rebound from a broken engagement.

• If one person has a history of several broken engagements.

• If you marry mainly for social or business reasons.

• If you marry mainly because you feel your parents and friends favor it.

• If you feel you must take the first person who comes along because all your friends are married and you don't want to be left out.

• If you marry because of "love at first sight," with little time to know each other.

• If you feel that sex attraction is something to joke about rather than a special basis for relationship between just two persons.

People who have made a study of divorces have come up with some interesting findings. For instance:

• About 60 per cent of all divorces occur within the first seven years of marriage. By this time, couples have either learned to adjust or have given up trying.

• There are nearly twice as many divorces among childless couples as among those with children. In many instances, however, an unhappy couple will refrain from getting a divorce only for the children or perhaps because of religious beliefs.

• Three-fourths of divorced people marry again in less than five years. At thirty, more than nine of every ten divorced men and women will have married again. These marriages are often more successful than first mar-

A clergyman can often help a married couple solve little problems before they become big ones.

riages because people have profited by early mistakes.

Let's look at some typical cases heading for the divorce court.

CASE STUDY: Jean Scoffield, who eloped, pictured herself as a lovely princess being carried off by a Prince Charming. She thought mainly of the exciting secrecy and carefree honeymoon. Soon she became annoyed by little habits of her husband which she had never noticed during their brief courtship. His table manners were poor. He swore loudly if things went wrong. He continued to flirt with other girls. Jean wanted to run back home and admit it was all a mistake, but pride kept her going until she nearly became a mental case. Nursed back to health, she finally secured a divorce.

CASE STUDY: Ann Wells, who was accustomed to a generous allowance, married Jim Obermann, whose salary barely permitted him to support the two and pay tuition for college classes at night. She came from a family that frowned upon working wives. Ann continued to run up bills, which caused arguments until never a pleasant word passed between them. She would not learn how to manage because she had grown up in a home where there was always money for everything and her spending was never questioned. She finally went home where her sympathetic mother offered to help her apply for a divorce.

CASE STUDY: Allan and Carol Freudlich were young and struggling successfully to overcome a number of barriers—a low income, the arrival of a baby before they were quite prepared, an inconvenient apartment. Carol's parents kept sending them money in hope that Allan would continue his college education on a part-time basis. Instead of graciously accepting the money, Allan became resentful. *His* parents couldn't help, so why should *hers?* Why couldn't *he* run his own affairs? When Allan refused to use the money for his education, Carol decided to spend it for furniture, clothes, and things for the baby. Allan became bitter even about this. Carol and the baby left for her parents' home.

Can you suggest ways these young people might have been able to solve their problems? Mature friends and clergymen, marriage counselors, and family counselors in welfare agencies often help young people solve problems before they become impossible. Most parents are too close to the problem to see all angles.

Lawyers claim that only one out of five wives who apply to them for a divorce ever goes through with the proceedings. Many are simply trying to frighten their husbands, which, of course, is a sign of emotional immaturity. Others recognize their mistake and learn to accept "the bitter with the sweet."

In a recent study, it was found that every couple may find warning signals in a marriage. The wife may threaten to "go home to mother" or even "wish I were dead," so frequently that she shows basic displeasure with marriage. The husband may show signs of growing indifference to real problems at home. Find out early what the causes may be.

You may have heard of the pastor of a large church in Atlanta, Georgia, who has performed over 3,000 weddings in his 37-year ministry, only one of which ended in divorce. Before marrying a couple he talks with them frankly about important matters concerning marriage, many of which are discussed in this chapter. He also urges couples to come back and talk with him if they are not getting along well. Each couple must promise to establish its home according to the teachings of the Bible. Once a year he holds a "Wedding Bells" service, at which time many of the couples he has married renew their vows.

In Los Angeles there is a Conciliation Court which attempts to keep couples from filing for a divorce. Some of the things suggested are.
• **Avoid doing things that irritate**—gambling, the "silent treatment," nagging, bearing grudges, quarreling in the presence of others.
• Bury the past.
• Share interests and hobbies.
• Forget about undesirable friends of bachelor days and make an effort to develop mutual friends.
• Allow each other privacy; refrain from being too inquisitive.

202

• Be considerate and understanding.
• Respect the beauty of love—keep it for each other.

Couples usually agree that it is better to share the same religion, have the husband take the main responsibility for the family support, the wife the leadership in home management, and both assume responsibility for the children and the spending of money.

Marriage counselors have concluded that sex maladjustment is not the principal cause of divorce, but much is lost if sexual love is not shared equally.

Outside troubles such as unemployment, ill health, or a mother-in-law problem are not as serious as *inner* conflicts such as emotional immaturity, inadequacy, and insecurity in meeting responsibilities and personality problems that existed before marriage.

WHAT SHOULD YOU CONSIDER BEFORE YOU MARRY?

There is no perfect blueprint for marriage. Fortunately, no two individuals or two couples are alike, and what makes one marriage succeed, may cause sparks to fly in another. Some people need a clinging vine—a partner whose only satisfaction is to live in reflected glory. It usually works out better if the clinging vine is the wife and not the husband. In other successful marriages both partners may be independent—complete extroverts—and still be very happy.

CASE STUDY: Bob Bourdelais, potentially capable but a little lazy, married Jean Carson—bright, able, and ambitious. Without being aware of it, Bob depended upon Jean to make all of their decisions, plan entertainment, and arrange vacations. Jean liked to study and wanted to work toward a degree in law. Bob agreed to stay with their only child at night until Jean finally passed the bar examinations. Later Jean was earning more than Bob. Bob came to depend upon Jean more and more, but began to resent it. They finally adjusted their marriage after reviewing their real goals when they married. At first they had both wanted more children, but other things seemed to become more important. To regain happiness for them both, Jean offered to give up her job to help Bob feel more secure in his—both hoping to have two or three more children as they had wished earlier. Bob gained confidence in himself as he felt more of the financial responsibility for marriage and watched Jean in her devotion to her family and home. Through willingness to sacrifice, and to admit they had missed their goals, Bob and Jean saved this marriage.

No marriage is a blissful continuation of the courtship and honeymoon. Arguments are natural, but when they lead to saying things that hurt, or carrying grudges, serious trouble is often ahead.

Here are some issues about which you should have some information:

Cultural Background   You have heard the expression, "Water seeks its own level." As a rule, young people tend to marry persons from a similar cultural background—i.e., they have similar living, educational, economic, social, and religious traditions.

Sociologists have found that most people can adjust more quickly to a little higher level of living than to a lower one. They also say that men can adjust to a slightly lower standard than women.

When people come from two entirely different cultural backgrounds, adjustment to marriage may be more difficult. Each brings to the marriage his own background, because no one can be reared in a family without absorbing customs, habits, and attitudes. Little things such as how to decorate a Christmas tree and open gifts may represent big "hidden" adjustments!

CASE STUDY: Let's take the marriage of Dave and Alice Elkins, who eloped at the end of the first year at the state university. They were attractive, bright young people but they did not meet each others' families until two weeks after the wedding.

Dave visited Alice's home first. Her parents were not happy about the elopement but had decided to make the best of things. Dave became uneasy and self-conscious. They had a fine home and two cars. Alice's father was a very successful doctor and her mother, attractive and capable, was a community leader.

Dave immediately felt inadequate and made every excuse not to have Alice meet his parents. Alice insisted on doing so. They drove to Dave's home without advance notice to "surprise the folks." Alice was somewhat shocked when Dave pulled the car to a stop in front of a plain-looking frame house in a mill town. The fat, bald man in his undershirt on the porch was Dave's father. His mother, plump and jolly, came out of the kitchen wiping her hands on her apron, and gave her new daughter-in-law a big kiss.

Alice was torn between two desires —to run off in tears or to throw her arms around Dave's mother because she was such a friendly person. She was *mature* enough to do the latter, but the lack of warning made her mistrust her husband and had a permanently bad effect on the marriage. In many instances, the child of the lower-status family, such as Dave, lets his background bother him more than it does the other party in the marriage. He feels he must constantly defend his family, which becomes irritating to both parties.

CASE STUDY: Art and Betty Thomasson also met in college, married after their junior year, and finished school. Art was good looking and exceptionally able, but self-pitying, self-centered, stubborn, and intolerant. An orphan, he had grown up in institutions and foster homes, where he learned very little religion. Betty recognized Art's faults, but she thought she could change his disposition with tenderness and love, something he had never really had.

Betty tried but failed. Art was too set in his ways. At first Betty suffered quietly, rather than hurt her family. But the situation kept getting worse. She obtained a divorce, but this was no solution to the problem. It simply left the two unhappy apart rather than together.

Common In-   Young adults should
   terests   share a number of in-
              terests. Frequently
after marriage each learns to enjoy many of the other's activities, and often the couple will find new inter-

ests together, especially if they have children.

This is important, but it is also important to be free for individual interests. If a husband likes to watch a ballgame on television, play golf, or talk shop a little, while his wife likes fashion events, talk about babies, or a movie or bridge with the "girls," it may be good for both. If they manage to listen to each other, they may be as happy as if they had shared all experiences together. The danger is that their lives may separate almost entirely.

Hallmark Cards

Military service may influence the age at which you marry. Chances for happiness are better if a man under twenty takes one big adjustment at a time.

Military Service Because we have "Selective Service" instead of compulsory military training, some young men may never be called, although they qualify physically and mentally. Also, some young men may become more valuable to our country if they continue their education or experience in special fields of engineering, physics, chemistry, or mathematics, rather than performing military duties.

However, Selective Service regulations directly affect most young men and, indirectly, many young women thinking of marriage. The questions most frequently asked about the military service are:

Shall I volunteer right after high school or wait and be drafted? In localities where few high school graduates expect to go to college or in times when jobs are scarce, enlistments are high. All of the services offer vocational opportunities; many young men take advantage of these opportunities to train for a specific job. Some find the military service interesting enough to make it a highly satisfactory career.

Shall I continue my education and take a chance on being drafted? The majority of employers, college counselors, and government personnel will advise a person interested in continuing his education to do so, if at all possible, before entering the service. In most areas, a person is not likely to be drafted anyway until after his twenty-second birthday.

A college student who passes the Selective Service College Qualification Test will be allowed to stay in college if he is in the *upper half* of his class during his first year; the *upper two-thirds* of his class during his second year; and in the *upper three-fourths* during his third year. There are deferments also for students in *vocational schools* and for *apprentices* in approved occupations.

Shall I marry before entering the military service? This is an individual matter depending upon many things—age, maturity, ability to adjust to difficult circumstances, as well as the *type* and *length* of service. Generally speaking, the answer is in the negative. Why set up three obstacles to hurdle when even one means a major adjustment: *first*—leaving home, family, and community ties; *second*—facing a new life (often out of the country) that is confining, demanding, and unpredictable; *third*—trying to build a marriage on separate foundations. It is not easy to live at home after marriage while a mate is overseas. Some people can do it, but it takes much love, faith, and fortitude.

A booklet, *It's Your Choice* describing all of the volunteer opportunities for young men, may be had by writing to the U. S. Government Printing Office, Washington 25, D. C.

Most young couples are likely to have a clean bill of health, Health but occasionally an ailment discovered after marriage may cause trouble. Blood tests, required in only a little more than half of our states, reveal very little. The Wasserman or Kahn tests detect social diseases only.

Every prospective bride and groom should have a thorough physical examination. Many illnesses or abnormal physical conditions can be treated or corrected before they become serious.

CASE STUDIES: Marianne and John Ehmer found out that John had a congenital heart condition. It was not likely that he would ever have serious trouble; however, several insurance companies refused to insure him. By knowing this ahead of time, the couple could have adjusted their financial planning better.

Jean and Tom Straub were alarmed when the doctor discovered that Jean had a blood condition which could have a serious effect upon the child they were expecting. This advance examination spared the couple unnecessary worry and perhaps tragedy.

Latent tuberculosis and early stages of cancer, and abnormal functioning of any of the glands or reproductive organs, may show up in an early examination and often can be corrected.

Money Many people believe that Matters finances will correct themselves, yet they are perhaps the most serious cause of misunderstandings.

CASE STUDY: Jim and Sally Newcomb married on a small income but both worked and saved for two years so that Jim might go to graduate school. About the time Jim was to leave for the university, a baby was due. Sally decided to live with her parents while Jim was away. Before Jim left in September, the couple talked over their plans, decided how much Sally would need for board, care of the baby, clothes, and spending money, and how much Jim would need for tuition and other expenses. Sally was to keep the car. They agreed to transfer enough money from their savings account to a checking account in both names, to keep each other informed when they cashed checks, and to balance the books at the end of each month.

But during the first semester Sally overspent for clothes, trips, and baby sitters. At the end of each month she simply stuffed the canceled checks and bank statement into her desk. When the two sat down during the Christmas holidays to check their accounts, Sally knew she had been spending too much but thought she

206

could cut down next semester and balance the books before Jim found out what she had done. She pretended to have "misplaced her checks and bank statement." She was "sure she could remember the few checks she had written." Later, Jim's second-semester tuition check bounced. Jim was not only embarrassed but outraged. Sally finally realized how careless she had been. She borrowed money from her family, got a part time job, while her mother cared for the baby, and soon balanced their account. Their marriage has succeeded only because she recognized individual shortcomings and made an effort to compensate for them.

In this country there is much difference of opinion about whether a wife should work after marriage. A recent study in France indicated that opinion on the matter is not divided there, at least among the women. An overwhelming number of French women told interviewers that they felt a wife's place was in the home, and that they did not envy the financial independence of America's working wives.

Whether there is one income or two, wife and husband must adhere to their plans for spending and saving. Both will have to agree upon savings goals—whether it is more important to save for a house, a car, electrical equipment, an education, a trip, children, or social interests. If one person is extravagant, or suspicious that the other is "holding out," there will be friction. If each demands a detailed accounting for every penny, there will be arguments, too.

CASE STUDY: Gary Breckner happened to find $100 in an envelope when he upset a drawer where Ann kept her sewing supplies. He immediately suspected Ann of falsifying expenditures. His first reaction was, "I'll just have Ann put all her cards on the table." Then he remembered that marriage is a two-lane highway, which means that he should do the same. He had nearly a hundred dollars saved for a watch for Ann for Christmas and did not want Ann to know about that. He decided to let the incident pass.

On Christmas morning they couldn't wait to surprise each other. Ann examined her watch, threw her arms around her husband, and said with sincere gratitude, "It's just what I wanted!" Then Gary began unwrapping the suspiciously large bundle under the tree, and found what he, too, had been wanting most, but never dreamed he could afford—a fine set of golf clubs. Caught between his feelings of happiness with the present, and shame for having suspected Ann, he laughed at himself and said, "Thanks, Honey. I'm going to hang these right over the TV until spring, just to remind me of what a jerk I almost turned out to be—and besides, they're handsome enough to be ornaments." Both Gary and Ann gave up many things for months, to be able to please each other at Christmas. Do you think they would have been happier spending the money selfishly?

Emotional Maturity Do you think Gary showed emotional maturity? This incident may have been his first real test. Had he become suspicious and insisted upon a showdown when he found the $100, he would have felt cheap and Ann

207

Fresh-Start by Pond's

A sense of humor—the ability to share quiet amusement over simple things—is an asset to any marriage.

would never have had the same pleasure in surprising Gary, or in "doing without" so she could please him.

Let's list some symptoms of emotional immaturity. We have just considered becoming suspicious without knowing all of the facts. When you become angry, sarcastic, moody, envious, spiteful, or jealous, or when you carry a grudge or fail to assume your share of work, you are flashing *danger signals* of immaturity. You not only become upset yourself, but you hurt other people—very often those whom you love most.

The "eternal triangle" which you frequently read about or see dramatized on television, often develops because one partner is immature. An ordinary disagreement, which a mature person would quickly forget, may leave a childish person feeling hurt, and carrying a chip on the shoulder. A more serious quarrel is often the next step; then the "offended" person

turns to a third party for sympathy, and the vicious triangle is complete.

Of course, this is not the only way that married couples or steadies break up, but it is a situation to be aware of and avoid. If you tend to be suspicious or jealous, you can discipline yourself so that some meaningless incident doesn't set off a chain reaction and spoil everything.

Marriage is a sacred compact based on child bearing. To the **Children** human race, marriage would mean nothing without the miracle of birth. Normally, children are born within the first year to three years of marriage. For individual reasons, some couples postpone having children. When there are no children within a reasonable period, both husband and wife may begin to worry. Nature may be taking her own time, or either parent may be at fault. Severe emotional strain, chronic illness, subnormal glandular function, or over-anxiety for conception may be the cause. Social diseases or mumps can cause sterility in men.

Some couples do not have children because they do not want to, and others because they are physically unable to have them. You remember from your religious education that Sarah and Abraham were childless until they were far beyond the usual ages for having children. This is particularly striking because childlessness was looked upon as a curse in ancient times, and in later periods as a social disgrace.

A family doctor can usually find the cause of childlessness. In many cases he will also have a remedy.

When a couple considers adopting

a baby, both should weigh the decision from all angles and proceed through proper, legal channels. A few couples, impatient for a child, ignore correct adoption procedures and get a baby from the "black market," then regret their actions later. It is better to wait a year or two and adopt through proper channels than to risk adopting an abnormal baby. Interestingly, it is not uncommon for a couple to adopt a child, and then to start having their own children. Do you know of any such cases?

Where to Live If you are wise, you will avoid starting out your married life with relatives. Very few young people really have to double up. If it happens to you, remember that parents mean well and seldom realize they are interfering. One authority states that parents "do not so much horn in as they are dragged in." For instance:

CASE STUDY: Linda Walfeld never stopped comparing her husband with her father, whom she had over-idealized. Her father always held her mother's chair at the table. He gave her mother flowers or candy on every special occasion. He kissed her mother good-by every time he left the house. Don, Linda's husband, did none of these things and soon Linda began to make comparisons before her parents. They became sympathetic, which was a mistake. The more they sympathized, the more exaggerated the comparisons became. Instead of spending happy evenings together, Linda sulked and Don went out.

A sudden move to another state actually saved Don and Linda's marriage. They became busy with their new home—painting walls, refinishing furniture, and landscaping. When the baby came, Don helped with its care. They set aside a fund for baby sitters so they could spend one evening a week at the theater, movies, or a concert. It finally occurred to Linda that she and her husband were very happy. In his own way her husband was kind, considerate, and courteous. She soon realized that making comparisons between her husband and her father was pointless, because she herself was not much like her mother.

Whether you reside in the city, country, or suburbs is unimportant. Whether you rent or buy, live in an apartment or house, does not matter except financially. The important thing is to make a real home of whatever shelter you choose, so there is as much happiness and as little friction as possible. Allow for differences. They are human!

Sometimes it may be difficult for people to adjust to totally different environments. If a person has spent many years in a rural area, then marries and lives in a large city, the adjustment at first may be difficult. But by trying, a person can find happiness under circumstances not always ideal. Few locations have everything.

Religion When you choose a person to spend the rest of your life with, obviously you want to find someone who agrees with you on important matters, not someone with whom there is bound to be disagreement. If your religion is important to you, doesn't it make sense to want a marriage partner who feels the same way?

Not just common sense, but statis-

Better Living, Du Pont

Marriages are usually happier when the entire family can worship in the same faith.

tics as well, show how important it is for married couples to agree on religion. For example, one independent study of more than four thousand marriages found that 14.1 per cent of Protestant-Catholic marriages ended in divorce; when the wife was Protestant, the rate was a startling 20.6 per cent. Compare this with marriages in the same faith. When two Protestants married, only 6 per cent failed; two Jewish people, 5.2; two Roman Catholics, 4.4.

Even so, mixed marriages take place more frequently now than in past generations. One of the main reasons is our improved means of transportation. Families in former years did not move around the country as much as they do now—groups with similar religious backgrounds tended to live close together. It was natural for young people to meet and marry others of the same beliefs.

Now our society is more mobile— opportunities for advancement keep families with children on the move; as income increases, families move to better locations in the same city;

many more young people go to college where they mix with students of different cultures and religions; more young people leave small towns for jobs in cities. Often friendships, sharing interesting experiences, and the desire for companionship turn into something deeper. Carried away by emotions, a difference in religion may seem temporarily unimportant.

Why are mixed marriages a risk? "My fiance is marrying me, not my church," you may say. That sounds reasonable until you think about it more deeply. Actually, that is the very reason why mixed marriages fail—because your fiance is marrying you, but rejecting something that you value, your church. If you could say "My fiance is marrying me, and *accepting my church, too*," you would have a far better reason for expecting happiness.

Have you ever thought how deeply religion affects the life of a person who really values what he has been taught? Marriage is one of the surest ways to bring this out, because many basic things in married life are covered by church teachings, and there are important differences in belief.

• The marriage ceremony itself is different in various churches. Roman Catholics consider marriage as one of their church's seven sacraments. Although a Protestant wedding may be very solemn, most Protestant churches do not consider marriage a sacrament. Participants in a mixed marriage are apt to dislike this difference and other things that seem strange to them.

• A Protestant who marries a Catholic must take some basic instructions in the Catholic faith, and must agree to train all children as Catholics, or the

210

marriage will not be approved by Catholic authorities.

• If a marriage involving a Catholic is not performed by a priest, the marriage is not recognized by the church, and the Catholic loses his good standing in the church.

• Some Protestant churches, such as the Lutheran and Episcopalian, have forms of worship like those of the Roman Catholic church. Rules may be similar, even though the church organization is not. It is well worth understanding the principles of your church.

People often try to solve interfaith problems by compromise, although they have promised to rear their children as Catholics:

• Alternating the faiths, by training the first child in the mother's religion, the second in the father's, and so forth.

• Attending alternate churches each week.

• Training boys in the father's faith, girls in the mother's.

These methods may work out, but often they cause trouble because the family is divided, and the children are apt to feel indifferent toward all religion.

Love may seem so strong that a person feels he can sacrifice his religion. But early religious training is one of the most powerful influences in our lives. It may be ignored for a time, but it is likely to return stronger, with feelings of guilt for the person who has given up his early beliefs, or simply compromised with them.

Most of us have our beliefs because we were born in a family which taught them to us, or because we made an important, mature decision about what to believe. Either way, it is hard to give up what we really believe. If we know we have hurt our parents by neglecting the religion they taught us, it can be a painful experience. And parents, convinced they are right, may continue trying to influence a mixed couple, adding further complications.

A Jewish-Christian wedding may present even greater problems than a Catholic-Protestant union because culture and living habits, as well as faith, are involved. You may have heard of the play, *Abie's Irish Rose,* the story of an Irish girl who fell in love with a Jewish boy. Although the play was written in a humorous way, it shows the kind of unexpected and perplexing problems which two people face when their backgrounds are so different. Someone in your class may be able to tell the story. Beneath the fun is a significant problem.

In Jewish interfaith marriages, more Jewish men marry Christian women than the other way around. Parents of Jewish children often try to discourage interfaith dating from an early age. Greek Orthodox parents also discourage interfaith marriages.

From these brief remarks you can see why religious problems are difficult to solve. To accept another's religion, if your own religious background has had a deep meaning, is not easy. To marry and attend different churches means dividing your religious emphasis, and also your church contribution. Even though the families of both husband and wife may be reconciled, touchy questions are bound to arise when there are children. You will be smart to think about these things, and decide not to

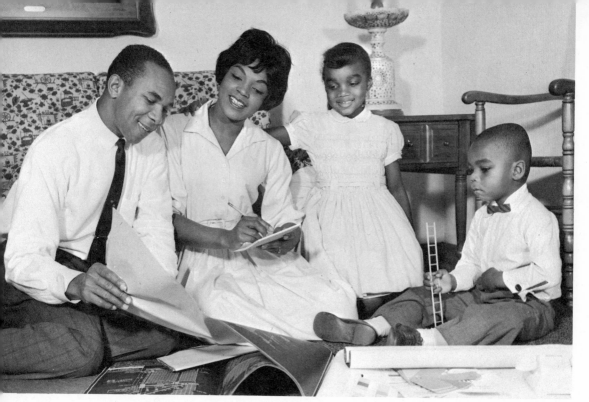

H. Armstrong Roberts

In a successful marriage, the romance of the early months sets the stage for greater happiness in the years that follow. Parents planning for their children's future know one of life's deepest and most meaningful pleasures.

make the same mistakes that others have made.

Until fairly recently, there has been very little understandable literature about marital relationships and reproduction. Few parents have been able to explain such personal problems to their children before they married.

Sex

But now it is difficult to avoid the subject—it turns up in magazines, books, movies, on television, and even in daily newspaper columns. It would be superfluous to attempt to compete with all the literature on the market.

Most people have every hope that their marriage will be ideal. Most of the time a marriage will be successful if both partners really make enough effort. Adjustments are necessary and obstacles can be overcome. One authority suggests a cure for our high divorce rate: "If marriage were made more difficult, there would be fewer divorces." Is he right? A better answer might be: "Study all the facets of adult living. Apply the principles you learn to all adult activities. Marriage is for adults."

Make up your mind that the miracle of a truly successful marriage can be obtained, if you are ready to accept and share adult responsibilities.

ANNOUNCING YOUR ENGAGE-MENT AND MARRIAGE

Soon after a girl becomes engaged, her mother may want to have a party

212

or family dinner to announce the engagement. A young lady may prefer to announce her engagement informally by simply wearing a ring to the office, to a party, or to a gathering in the college dormitory. An announcement similar to the following may appear in the local paper:

"Mr. and Mrs. Robert Crane, 122 Concord Street, announce the engagement of their daughter, Joan, to Allan Rochester, son of Mr. and Mrs. Arthur Rochester of Chicago."

Bridal Showers Showers should be kept in good taste. People in modest circumstances are not expected to give elaborate showers and gifts need not be costly. You may consult the bride-to-be about her preferences and needs. Frequently a shower is given for the couple.

The maid-of-honor or a member of the bridal party usually gives a shower. No immediate member of the family of the bride or groom should give a bridal shower. Invitations may be phoned or written. It is not wise to have more than one shower to which the same persons are invited. The bride-to-be need not write a "thank you" note to anyone she has thanked at the shower, but she must thank people either by phone or note, if they sent a gift but could not come.

Wedding Invitations The bride's family decides upon the number of people who may be accommodated at a reception and asks the groom's family to limit their list to this number. Although it is acceptable to invite some people to the wedding only and not to the reception, some families prefer to have a less pretentious reception and invite everyone to it. When the reception is held "under the same roof" as the wedding, everyone must be invited to the reception.

White, ivory, and cream are the traditional colors for invitations. The address on the outer envelope is hand written. Names, streets, cities, and states are written in full—not abbre-

Gift showers for the couple, not just for the bride-to-be, are becoming more popular in many parts of this country.

The Gorham Company

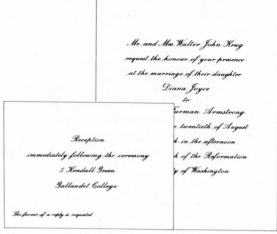

Mr. and Mrs. Samuel Smolar
request the honour of your presence
at the marriage of their daughter
Estelle
to
Irving Lawrence Segal
son of Mr. and Mrs. Louis Segal
on Sunday, the twenty-seventh of November
Nineteen hundred and sixty
at five-thirty o'clock
Beth Shalom Synagogue
Beacon and Shady Avenue
Pittsburgh, Pennsylvania

Mr. and Mrs. Walter John Krug
request the honour of your presence
at the marriage of their daughter
Diana Joyce
to
_urman Armstrong
_ twentieth of August
_k in the afternoon
_h of the Reformation
_y of Washington

Reception
immediately following the ceremony
5 Kendall Green
Gallaudet College

The favour of a reply is requested

Wedding invitations. The invitations at lower left and upper right have enclosure cards for the reception, so that some guests may be invited to the wedding but not to the reception. Cards like these are also used frequently for invitations to wedding breakfasts. The invitation at lower right includes both wedding and reception.

Mr. and Mrs. Lewis Whittaker Morgan
request the honour of your presence
at the marriage of their daughter
Ann Craig
to
Mr. Thomas Newton Slonaker
on Monday, the eighth of September
One thousand nine hundred
at half after eight o'clock in
Edgewood Presbyteria_
Pittsburgh, Pennsyl_

Reception
following the ceremony
Longue Vue Club

Please reply to
510 Maple Avenue, Edgewood

Mr. and Mrs. Alvin S. Vaughan
request the honour of your presence
at the Nuptial Mass uniting their daughter
Betty Jean
and
Mr. Martin Emmett Kenny
in the Sacrament of Holy Matrimony
on Saturday, the eleventh of June
Nineteen hundred and sixty
at ten o'clock
St. Mary's Cathedral
Peoria, Illinois

Reception at two o'clock
Italian-American Hall
Helen and Antoinette Streets

Any invitation to a wedding reception requires a reply. These examples are proper.

Mr. and Mrs. Malcolm Fay
regret that they are unable to accept
Mr. and Mrs. Alvin S. Vaughan's
kind invitation for
Saturday, the eleventh of June

Mr. and Mrs. Gordon Trundle
accept with pleasure
Mr. and Mrs. Alvin S. Vaughan's
kind invitation for
Saturday, the eleventh of June

214

Monsieur Octave Liard,
Monsieur et Madame André Stenuick
ont l'honneur de vous faire part du mariage de
leur petite-fille et fille Andrée avec Monsieur
André de Magnée, Ingénieur civil des Mines.

Madame Lucien de Magnée,
Monsieur et Madame Ivan de Magnée
ont l'honneur de vous faire part du mariage de
leur petit-fils et fils André avec Mademoiselle
Andrée Stenuick.

La Bénédiction nuptiale leur sera donnée
en l'Église paroissiale St. Vaast à Fontaine-l'Évêque
le jeudi 11 juin 1959 à 11 heures.

2, Rue de l'Indépendance,
Fontaine-l'Évêque.

72, Avenue de l'Hyppodrome,
Bruxelles.

The invitation in French provides interesting contrasts to ours. The families of both the bride and the groom, including grandparents, extend the invitation. At lower left and right are informal and formal announcements—not invitations.

June 15, 1960

Dear Sam and Hazel
Endy and I want you to be among the first to know that Judy was married last January to Jerry Kalassay.
As you can imagine this was a great surprise to us but we are happy to have Jerry in our family
Judy and Jerry will live with us until they finish school
Sincerely,
Marjorie Batchelder

Mr. and Mrs. Joseph Carl Rengel
have the honour of announcing
the marriage of their daughter
Susan Judson
to
Mr. James Paul Vinke
on Saturday, the thirtieth of July
Nineteen hundred and sixty
Little Point Sable, Michigan

At Home
after the fifteenth of September
905 Michigan Avenue
Evanston, Illinois

viated. The inner envelope bears only Mr. and Mrs. (last name). Members of a family who are sixteen or over should be sent separate invitations.

Invitations to a wedding alone, as well as announcements of a marriage that has already taken place, need not be acknowledged at all. However, an *invitation to a reception must be ac-knowledged*, even though distance may make attendance impossible. A formal reply (as shown on page 214) is customary, but a personal note may be written to close relatives or friends.

215

Some couples may prefer the intimacy of a wedding *at home,* followed by a small home reception or a larger one at a club or hotel. Guests may be limited to family members and close friends. A similar informal wedding may be held in the church rectory or parsonage. If a wedding is small (under 50) invitations may be hand written. If a wedding is to be held *in church,* someone from the church usually arranges rehearsals, co-ordinates with the florist, and takes care of other details involving church facilities. A wedding performed *in the office or home of a justice of the peace* is not a very solemn affair. Studies reveal that the chances for happiness are lower also.

When young people are married secretly, it is usually because they fear they will not have parental approval, or they do not want the expense and excitement of a big wedding. When two people elope they should be sure they are really ready for marriage and try to arrange to be married by a clergyman. The memory of a bleak office of a justice of the peace — often with strangers for attendants—is not pleasant.

Elopements

After secret marriages, formal wedding announcements are usually sent. A more personal announcement is sent to relatives and close friends. Strictly

The processional. The ushers are followed by the bridesmaids, then the maid of honor, flower girl, sometimes a page, and finally the bride at the right of her father. The minister and groom, followed by the best man, have entered from the vestry. (The order differs in a Jewish wedding.)

216

ALTAR

speaking, gifts are not necessary but are usually sent by relatives and close friends.

By far the majority of wedding re-
Receptions ceptions are informal and many are held in the church social room. Friends often prepare and serve the refreshments. Paper cups, plates, and napkins are acceptable at informal receptions. If the reception is to be held at a club or hotel, there will be some-one to consult about costs and customs. The wedding cake is usually arranged for separately. Refreshments at a formal reception may be similar to those served at a tea, or comparable to a menu for brunch or dinner, with all guests seated at tables. If there is dancing after a wedding reception, guests should not begin until the bride and groom have met their obligation dances. The groom has the first dance with his bride, then with the bride's mother, his own mother, and the bride's attendants. The bride dances with the groom's father, then with her own father, and with the attendants of the groom.

WEDDING COSTS—HOW THEY ARE SHARED

It is in poor taste to plan a wedding so elaborate that it will mean a sacrifice to your parents or to you. Before you plan your wedding, consider the

The recessional. Bride and groom lead the recessional, followed by the flower girl, maid of honor, bridesmaids, best man, head usher, and other ushers. If attendants are paired, the best man walks with the maid or matron of honor, rather than with the head usher.

ALTAR

217

The choice of wedding clothes is determined by individual taste as well as by the degree of formality.

following costs, and plan only the kind of wedding you can afford.

BRIDE'S FINANCIAL RESPONSIBILITIES

Wedding clothes
Wedding photographs
Trousseau
Wedding ring (for double ceremony)
Wedding invitations
Church decorations—flowers and ferns, aisle carpet and canopy (if used)
Fees for use of church
Reception
Gifts to her attendants
Luncheon or party for her attendants
Corsages for attendants—boutonnieres for men
Transportation for bridal party to and from church

The groom and his family pay for items listed in the chart below. Frequently the groom's parents arrange and pay for the rehearsal dinner.

GROOM'S FINANCIAL RESPONSIBILITIES

Wedding clothes (rental of special clothes for formal wedding)
Clothes for honeymoon
Corsages for bride, bride's mother, and his mother
Marriage license
Bachelor dinner (optional)
Gifts for his attendants
Gloves and ties for attendants at formal wedding
Honeymoon (bride's family may lend car, cottage, boat, etc.)

Attendants—bridesmaids and ushers—provide their own wedding clothes, accessories, and traveling expenses. The groom's family may assume the cost of rented clothes for the men attendants.

Gifts If possible, gifts should be sent soon after the invitation is received. The bride often likes to invite her friends in to see her gifts before the wedding. Gifts sent before the wedding should be addressed to the bride. If they are sent after the wedding, they should be addressed to Mr. and Mrs. The bride must write a thank you note soon after a gift is received. If one gift bears a note with several names, each contributor must be thanked.

Dress When the wedding is held in church, the bride may wear a long dress—white, ivory, pale blue, or pale pink—any time of the day, whether the wedding is for-

The receiving line. The bride's mother stands first, then the father and mother of the groom and father of the bride. (Fathers may stand to one side if both are known to guests.) Next, often separated a little from the parents, are the bride, the groom, the maid of honor, and bridesmaids. Ushers do not stand in line.

mal or informal. A cathedral train and long veil or short full veil are worn for a formal wedding, a moderate train and veil for a semi-formal wedding, no train and a short veil for informal weddings. The degree of formality determines the fabric and style of dress. If long gloves are worn, the ring finger of the glove must be split.

During the day, business dress is acceptable for an informal wedding. Men wear a *tuxedo only after six* and if the wedding is more formal. White linen-weave jackets with dark trousers are appropriate for informal daytime weddings in summer. Full dress is worn at a very formal wedding. All men in the wedding party, including the *father of the bride* and *father of the groom* wear suits of the same style and color at all weddings—day or evening—informal or formal.

The mother of the bride and mother of the groom may wear cocktail type

Seating at the bride's table. The bride and groom sit in the center with the best man on the bride's right and maid of honor on the groom's left. Men should sit at the ends of the table. All members of the bridal party (not parents) and the wives and husbands of members sit at the bride's table.

Special wedding dress for men.

Formal Daytime: English cutaway; gray waistcoat (white in summer); gray striped trousers, and silk top hat (top left).
Semiformal Daytime: Morning coat, black or oxford gray; striped trousers, black derby or Homburg hat (top center).
Formal Evening: Full dress, tail coat; matching trousers and opera hat (top right).

Semiformal Evening: Tuxedo with waistcoat or cummerbund (lower left).
Summer Evening Formal: "Summer tux," white dinner jacket, panama hat (lower center).
Informal Summer: White linen or dacron jacket; brown, navy, or gray trousers; narrow stripe or dot tie; straw hat or panama (lower right).
All Year Informal: Dark business suit.

dresses at a formal wedding or long dresses, if the wedding is in the evening. Small hats are worn in the daytime, but no hat with a long dress, unless head covering is required in the church.

Men guests at a formal wedding may wear "tails," a tuxedo, or even a dark business suit and dark shoes. Women guests at a formal evening wedding may wear cocktail-type or long dresses. Men and women guests'

220

attire for informal weddings is similar to that worn to church on ordinary occasions.

For additional information on planning a wedding, write for booklets advertised in one of the bridal magazines.

The groom's hand covers the bride's as they cut the cake together, starting at the bottom tier. They share the first piece to symbolize sharing life together.

ACTIVITIES

1. From the marriage license office in your county court house, or from a reference book, find out what your state requires for marriage—age limit, blood and other tests, waiting period, property ownership rights. What are the regulations in neighboring states? Do you think the requirements are adequate?

2. Discuss the following:
• Reasons why some people do not marry.
• Ratio of girls to boys in your class and school. How does this affect the school's social affairs? The individual's dating chances?
• Why it might be well for men to marry women a few years older than themselves.
• Reasons for people marrying younger than they did a generation or so ago.
• Difference between annulment and divorce.
• Desirable places to meet young people in your city or community.

3. Pick someone to conduct a survey at the chalk board. From the list below, number personality traits in order of importance to the majority of class members.

good grooming	honesty
good health	intelligence
good disposition	sense of humor
ambition	courtesy and kindness
good looks	religious faith
sincerity	any other

4. Answer the questions that refer to Dr. Terman's research on desirable

traits, page 197. Have others judge you. Compare findings.

5. The word *love* can be used in many ways to indicate very different emotions. Substitute another word, or give an explanation of the various meanings of love as used in these sentences.

> I love good music.
> I love to visit my aunt.
> I loved your remark.
> I love oranges.
> I love my dog.
> I love my neighbor.
> I love God.
> I love my family.

6. Debate the issue, "Sixteen is too young for a girl to marry."

7. Give your class members copies of the following list of pastimes. Ask each to check the *six* interests he or she would most like to share with a mate. On the form indicate *boy* or *girl*. Collect forms and tabulate results.

spectator sports	gardening
swimming	picnicking
fishing	shopping
hunting	riding
hiking	bridge
dancing	singing
skiing	household jobs
reading	movies
children's activi-	plays
ties	concerts
tennis	travel
listening to rec-	photography
ords	any other
watching TV	

8. Dramatize the cases described as "headed for the divorce court" and suggest ways these young people might have solved their problems.

9. Invite a marriage counselor to speak to the class.

10. Statistics show that only two-thirds of engaged couples ever reach the altar. Give reasons why so many engagements are broken.

11. List six signs of *immaturity* that often creep into your day—at home or in school. Make up an immaturity test, using three columns for checking immature traits — *frequently, occasionally, never*. Discuss.

12. Do you think a secret marriage is handicapped from the start? Why? Why not?

13. Give some reasons why it might be good for a girl to work for a year or two *before* marrying and *after* marrying. Would your reasons apply to all girls?

14. Discuss the idea: "Children enrich a marriage."

15. What would you want for your first home—furnished apartment, unfurnished apartment, live with parents. Discuss.

16. Invite clergymen from different faiths to discuss marriage before the class.

Correlation

SOCIOLOGY: Study and report on marriage customs in other countries and other periods in history.

LITERATURE: Robert and Elizabeth Browning eloped, yet their marriage was successful. Can you give some reasons why? How was their happiness shown in their writing?

Learn something about the childhood, courtship, and marriage of some of the writers you are studying at present. Discuss your findings in relation to marriage predictions in this chapter. For instance, Charles Dickens and Oscar Wilde had very unhappy childhoods. Were their marriages affected by these experiences?

Home Experiences

Ask your parents to tell you about some of the problems they had concerning their marriage.

Talk with your parents concerning questions to consider before marriage (pages 203 to 212).

Chapter
10

Family
Roles

Studies show that a happy home life is the highest goal of most young people. However, the term "happy home life" does not have the same meaning to everyone.

In the United States young people choose their own mates. Most couples buy or rent a place to live by themselves, and most feel free to go wherever opportunity calls. This is not true everywhere. In India and South America, for example, marriages planned by older relatives are common. Several generations of a family live together in one household.

Family cultural patterns are the result of traditions, geographical location, degree of industrialization, and extent of communication. Your concepts of family life are influenced by your culture, your social and economic position, the neighborhood in which you live, and the specific values emphasized within your home. Some families place a high value

upon efficiency and order, some upon beauty and entertainment, others upon education and travel. In some families children remain at home until they leave to work or go to college. In others they are sent off to camps in the summer and boarding schools in winter at an early age.

Family life in the United States presents a contrasting picture—wealth, freedom, and opportunity on the one hand; numerous problems on the other. The family is the subject of intensive sociological research. Judged on such matters as juvenile arrests, divorce, and high school drop-outs, about 85 per cent of families are rated as "good." Only a small percentage of families fails on all scores. The results of surveys indicate that: (1) juvenile offenders come mainly from families which fail to provide supervision in the home; (2) family friction occurs more often in "mixed marriages" than in marriages of the same faith; (3) non-religious

Outdoor sports such as fishing provide an atmosphere for developing good father-son relationships.

families have higher rates of divorce, desertion, and delinquency than religious families.

The home is the most important institution in any country. When home life is what it should be, problems outside the home are made easier. But we all have to work at making a home successful, just as we do at anything else we consider important. No family runs smoothly all the time, but with patience and understanding we can eliminate much friction, and discover the satisfying rewards which only a happy home can give.

THE NEED FOR LOVE AND DIRECTION

Love Creates Harmony One of the strongest forces in human relationships is love. Without love babies do not thrive, children feel insecure, juvenile delinquents become greater problems, the mentally ill fail to recover, older people waste away. When there is love, almost any obstacle may be overcome.

When love is the guiding power, every family member is interested in the activities and plans of others without becoming envious or jealous; each person sees the good in others, and forgives shortcomings which are unavoidable; everyone enjoys giving an opinion without being ridiculed.

Love means sharing and sympathizing, thoughtfulness for the needs of others, saying kind words or sometimes saying nothing at all. For instance, if your mother or father should appear a little irritable at the breakfast table, it may be wise to say as little as possible. Perhaps they have problems you do not know about, and by evening the atmosphere may be clear again. If occasionally your younger sister begins to brag about her way with the boys, or your younger brother takes all of the credit for winning the ballgame, it may be better to smile and say little than to be critical. To belittle will only start an argument or cause hurt feelings. When one person is out of harmony, a relaxed, happy family atmosphere can suddenly change to one of tension.

Tension Causes Discord Tension makes us impatient and irritable. Problems at home cause accidents on the highway, trouble on a job, and poor grades in school. Reading difficulties among children frequently have been traced to strained home conditions.

Tension increases with fatigue. Some people drive themselves and every member of the family until a relaxed atmosphere is almost impossible. Often a mother must decide whether it is more important to keep the house immaculate every day, or let something go and be more relaxed when her family is together in the evening.

Tension may build up just because of circumstances: when you crowd your days with too much schoolwork and outside activities; when your father works too hard or keeps a job he doesn't like, just to give his family the things they want; when your mother works hard at home and yet adds too many outside responsibilities to her schedule. Friction results when even one person in a family becomes tired and "fed up." It is not always easy to know when a person is trying to do too much, and even harder to know what to eliminate. Nevertheless, whether you are trying to do better at work or be happier at home, you will succeed more easily if you realize that relaxation, not tension, is the atmosphere to strive for.

HUSBAND-WIFE RELATIONSHIP

The husband-wife relationship is not only the closest but continues the longest in most families. If this relationship is to be satisfying and lasting, it must meet emotional, economic, and social needs. Otherwise, frustrations occur. Sometimes a couple believes that having children will solve their problems, but seldom is this the case.

Often a young woman who has given up a promising career to marry, feels deflated and apologetic when she describes herself as a housewife, yet the importance of being a good wife cannot be emphasized too greatly. For instance, the Air Force has found "a direct correlation between aircraft mishaps and unsettled home life . . . The husbands get to thinking about rows with the little woman while they are up there and the first thing you know they press the wrong button."

In business, the kind of wife a man has may affect his whole future. Take the story of Jeff and Connie Davis for example.

A wife appreciates little attentions, and she will show her appreciation in many ways which will bring pleasure to all in the home.

Cuticura

CASE STUDY: After graduating from college, Jeff took a job with a promising future, and shortly afterward he married an attractive but somewhat spoiled young woman. Several years later, Jeff's employer noticed that his work was slipping. The employer began to doubt if Jeff really had the potential to replace a retiring executive. His production had dropped; he seemed irritable and unable to cope with unusual problems.

By coincidence, the employer's wife sat with Jeff's wife at a bridge party. The cause of Jeff's office behavior became evident. Connie's conversation revealed that she gave her husband no peace at home. She expected unusual attention for unimportant reasons. She complained about his long working hours and low pay. In the end, her selfish attitude was reflected in her husband's work. Another employee, with less actual ability, received the promotion.

Many business firms want to know the kind of wife a potential executive has. A woman who makes a good wife and mother at home, and pleasing partner in public, is a great asset to her husband. She should:

• Show him love and attention and once in a while a little "mothering." Men thrive on these things, but they are usually too proud to ask for them.
• Be ambitious for him—not for more money or a higher social position, but to help him meet the good, attainable goals he sets up for himself.
• Allow time for a leisurely breakfast in pleasant surroundings, and avoid bringing up anything unpleasant before he leaves for work.
• Give him time when he returns in the evening to get his breath before telling him unpleasant or troublesome matters that concern the two of them.
• Help him "live with" his faults; use understanding and tact.
• Share his problems and offer advice only when it seems wise.
• Avoid belittling, correcting, or criticizing him in public or private. A man likes to think he is a great guy and thrives on praise if it is sincere.
• Accept gifts graciously.

A mother's job is so complex that she is never through learning about it. Being a good mother and homemaker is a full-time, multi-job business. A mother must be a cook, nursery director, tutor, dietitian, food buyer, laundress, seamstress, housekeeper, nurse, gardener, maintenance man, hostess, chauffeur, dishwasher, and often a part-time secretary.

A young mother once complained, "I have three wonderful children, but I haven't been able to earn a cent since I married." This mother, during a typical week, had papered a bedroom, helped her oldest daughter make a fall formal, typed reports for her lawyer husband, chauffeured the children to scout meetings, music and dancing lessons, all in addition to her regular tasks of shopping, preparing three meals a day, washing, ironing, and cleaning. A friend pointed out to her that although she had not earned any money in the sense of bringing home a pay check, it would have taken more than the family could afford if they had been forced to hire someone to do all these jobs.

Being a good wife is as important as being a good mother, and vice versa. It would take volumes to cover the obligations and responsibilities of motherhood.

226

Marriage is a "two-way street" and a wife likes to be appreciated for her part in homemaking too. A husband can:

• Comment favorably on a good meal, an attractive table setting, a becoming dress, or her way of meeting people.

• Be considerate, especially if the wife holds a job, is confined to the home with small children, or is not feeling well.

• Listen to her problems; try to understand them.

• Help her to plan evenings together.

• Help to correct her faults without being critical, or accept her in spite of shortcomings.

• Confide in her and value her opinions.

• Show her little attentions in social gatherings.

• Bring home a surprise gift now and then.

PARENT-CHILD RELATIONSHIP

Dr. Dale B. Harris, Director of the University of Minnesota's Institute of Child Welfare, has stated: "To be a parent is to be in action; to be in action is to make choices—to consider issues philosophically." Parenthood, Dr. Harris declares, must be positive. "It must commit itself to standards and maintain these standards in the presence of children." He goes on to explain that choices, and the reasons for choices, must be freely discussed between children and parents.

Life involves making many choices, and choices are based upon values. Children absorb their values — opinions, prejudices, religious beliefs, political preferences, and their general pattern of living from their parents.

Parents, therefore, have a tremendous responsibility in establishing values.

One of the basic statements made by the Senate Subcommittee on Juvenile Delinquency was: "Better children can come only from better parents. There is not much that can be done *en masse* for children already badly maladjusted . . . If society is to achieve any really effective curtailment of law violation, it must come largely through the family since it is there that the attitudes and conduct are bred, out of which antisocial lives develop."

Perhaps you have complained that some of the standards your parents have set are too high, but in most cases, parental concern is greater and better founded than children's resentment. Do you think your parents have been too strict about such things as using the car, dating, spending money, and hours to be in? Have you tried to put yourself in their place when you have been out late, spent money foolishly, or insisted on using the family car at inconvenient times? These are some of the biggest sources of disagreement between teen-agers and their parents. A family council approach, and a little "give and take," can eliminate most of the friction.

The relationships between parents and children may be grouped under three headings — autocratic, permissive, and democratic. Of course, in every family all three approaches to meeting problems may occur.

CASE STUDIES: Mr. and Mrs. Samuel Turner believed in *autocratic* family government—"You do as I say or else!" Mr. Turner was the undisputed head of the family. He determined how the children should be disci-

227

The mother who takes time to enjoy her children and share their interests will benefit from this relationship, and so will the children.

plined, set hours to come home and go to bed, handed out allowances, and ignored all suggestions. If young Jerry accidentally lost or broke a toy, he was spanked without question; if Alice came home ten minutes late, she was punished for a week. Neither child felt love or understanding.

Mrs. Turner and the children became submissive and lost their enthusiasm. Among his neighbors, Mr. Turner boasted about how much respect his family had for him, but those who knew him realized that he had mistaken fear for respect.

Mr. and Mrs. W. F. Cramer, deprived of many things as they grew up, adopted a *permissive* philosophy in rearing their children. They thought they could win love and respect by being lenient. They gave their children things they could not afford; they ignored incidents in which the children were disobedient or talked back; they let their children set their own hours and make most of their decisions.

When their children became negligent and disrespectful in their teens, these parents sighed, "But we have given our children everything!" They had certainly tried to give them everything—that was a big part of the problem. Given things too easily, the children did not appreciate what they had. By failing to exercise guidance, by confusing love with overindulgence, these parents kept their children from learning to make wise decisions and from setting worthy goals for living.

Both the Turners and the Cramers felt they were doing what was best. Of course, in every walk of life there must be a head—a president, mayor, chairman, captain. There should be a recognized head in the family, but a successful father, like any other successful administrator, is guided by the thoughts and feelings of others.

On the other hand, in every family children should have certain freedoms if they are to become mature adults. But *freedom without guidance* is as bad as dictatorship in a family.

Research in family living emphasizes the need for love and understanding with the democratic approach, which means giving children certain freedoms but at the same time using direction and discipline. Children feel more secure and truly loved when discipline is firm, reasonable, and consistent. They are quick to take advantage of parental wavering, yet do not realize that getting their own way provides no guidance toward maturity.

The L. J. Clarke family used the democratic approach to family living. When there were problems in school, in social groups, or in the family, Mr.

and Mrs. Clarke discussed their own experiences in meeting such problems, and listened to their children's side of the problem, but did not take sides against a teacher, or other outside party. They pointed out possible outcomes in making decisions. They encouraged each child *to think of others* before making demands. For instance, if a child wanted to buy something that seemed unreasonable with his own money, the decision was *set aside for two weeks* and if he still wanted to buy the item, permission usually was given. Often, in two weeks, the item became unimportant. When a purchase was made, no one criticized, because it had stood the test of thought and discussion. The person making the purchase enjoyed it.

Over a period of twenty-five to thirty years, Dr. Harris conducted research to find out how children reacted to parental training, after becoming adults. He found that children, whose parents used the permissive approach, or expected them at a very early age to make their own decisions, grew up to "lack focus, to be indecisive, to be seeking for something, they know not what." As children, they were permitted to make decisions too early and without direction. They lacked guidance in weighing the values in relation to outcome. Children in autocratic families often became rebellious, sullen, and insecure.

SIBLING RELATIONSHIPS

When there is more than one child in a family, there is bound to be rivalry and jealousy and even real fights. Such behavior is natural, but when rivalries and jealousies are not controlled, children may become too sullen or antagonistic. Even though brothers or sisters may argue and find fault with each other, they will often stick together when someone outside the family mentions the same faults.

Children, especially if they are close together in age, learn much from each other. However, a younger child may appear slow in some learning processes if older children anticipate and fill their needs. An older sister may *tend to mother* a younger child or *become bossy*. When an older child is held up as a model, younger children resent it and there is friction. When an older child is given *too much responsibility*, he may feel imposed upon and compensate by criticizing younger brothers or sisters. On the other hand, younger children often learn to depend too much on older brothers and sisters.

Studies have been made to attempt to determine which child in a family has the greatest advantage—the oldest, in-between, or youngest—but the results have been conflicting. Too many other factors enter. Even in a family with an only child there are no rules. Handicapped children, too, affect families in different ways. *So don't try to set up rules.* Think of each person as an individual.

FAMILY ROLES OF FATHER AND MOTHER

Over the centuries men and women have taken on certain roles in family life. While the man has gone out to hunt, to work, or to fight, the woman has stayed in the home, caring for the children, preparing food, and doing other domestic chores. There have been exceptions, of course, such as some American Indian tribes in which women farmed and did other heavy work. Still, the pattern has remained basically the same in most cultures from primitive times until very recently. Now, however, some students of our society say that a real change is taking place in regard to these roles.

Father's Changing Role

In our own society, man's role has been like that described above—chief wage earner and disciplinarian. Now both of these roles seem to be changing. Under the Nineteenth Amendment women were given the right to vote. The Equal Pay Act of 1963 made it mandatory for employers to pay men and women equally for equal work. Technological progress has lightened work in the home and made it possible for more and more women to hold outside jobs. Additional pay checks have helped to produce an affluent society.

When children are under school age, the mother is usually needed in the home to care for them. This places the whole responsibility for financial support upon the father.

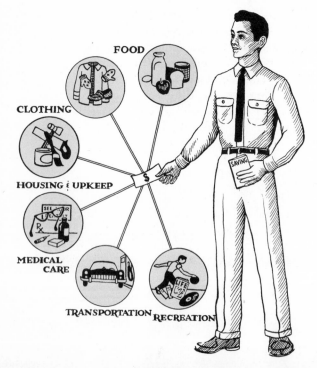

FOOD

CLOTHING

HOUSING & UPKEEP

MEDICAL CARE

TRANSPORTATION   RECREATION

With wives earning even larger salaries, with women away from the home more than in former years, and with men on jobs requiring hours of commuting and travel, the father image has changed. It is no longer what it was when father and son worked side by side in the fields or in a local business.

A great deal has been written about the "vanishing father" and a growing trend toward a matriarchal or woman-dominated society. Many social psychologists are concerned that much of the romance in marriage will disappear as masculine authority is weakened. Also, sons need strong fathers. Besides commanding respect, fathers provide an outlet for the rebellious feelings of their teenage sons. This part of fatherhood is unpleasant but important. Without it the sons will turn their rebellious feelings against something else, perhaps against society and its laws. It is far better, some writers feel, to rebel temporarily against a strong but understanding father.

Whether they like it or not, most men seem to be accepting their changing role. A Gallup poll indicated that 62 per cent of all husbands in the United States take some part in keeping house—six out of ten help with housework, four out of ten with cooking, and about a third help with dishwashing. Rutgers University interviewed a large number of expec-

230

Reproduced with permission of Massachusetts Mutual Life Insurance Company, Springfield, Mass.

One of a father's responsibilities is to spend time with his children, especially his sons, showing interest in their activities.

tant fathers and found that 84 per cent expected to help care for the baby. In another study by the Institute of Matrimonial Research, it was estimated that fathers put in an average of 28 hours a week on jobs at home such as the following: counseling children, baby sitting, tutoring, making home repairs, mowing the lawn, washing dishes, helping with cooking, gardening, and running errands.

Not only have a man's homemaking responsibilities increased but so have his community responsibilities. He may be asked to work for the PTA, church, service clubs, lodge, union, and fund rising drives.

The typical young executive spends about 54 days a year traveling. Wives naturally resent being left alone, as well as the extra work they must do when the husband is gone. In one poll of wives whose husbands travel extensively, 36 per cent seriously disapproved of the situation; the rest said it was something which at best they could only tolerate. Although

there is a certain amount of prestige associated with nationwide and international travel, husbands recognize the possible family conflicts. For example:

CASE STUDY: As the Morrow family expanded, Carl, a commission salesman in a highly competitive field, felt that they should move to the suburbs. This led to placing the children in fashionable schools and buying a second car. Many family heads in the new neighborhood had joined a country club for the advantages it would provide the children—dancing classes in winter and swimming in summer. Carl wanted his family to have the same opportunities. He was sure he could manage if he gave more time to his job.

A troubling incident made him realize that spending more time with his family might have greater benefits. His son, Ted, potentially a bright stu-

When Dad comes home to a warm welcome, he feels the importance of his part in homemaking.

Loft's Candy Shops—Photo by Howard Zieff

dent, had failed to be promoted. The father, tired from intensive work, became very angry and threatened the boy. "I'm through with you; you can quit school and get a job. I drive a thousand miles a week and live in motels so you can learn dancing, go to a good summer camp, attend a fancy private school, have all of the opportunities a boy could want—so your mother can have a car to haul you kids around—and what do I get! A failure!"

"A lot you care!" cried Ted. "Making me do all this junk—dancing classes, snob schools and camps—I told you I didn't fit in that rat race. You wouldn't listen. Why can't we wait till we're rich before we try to act like it? I hate all this phony stuff."

Because of this incident the family reassessed its values. The children really cared more for their parents than for a position among the "ruling class." Public schools were excellent in this new community. Ted had his father's ambitious drive, could not do his best in the role of a playboy, and wanted to work after school and in the summer so he could date and meet his own small needs without "begging." They decided to return to their old ways. As pressures lifted, Dad became more relaxed and found that he enjoyed taking part in family plans. He found pleasure he had almost forgotten existed. His evening work during the summer, tutoring Ted, helped the boy to be promoted in the fall. Oddly enough, his sales increased as his attitude changed, despite less time spent on the road. On the new program, by the end of the year the family actually had more money, and a stronger place in the community.

Wife's Changing Role

The concepts of husband as homemaker and wife as wageearner are signs of changes in American society. However, the traditional roles of husband as family head and wife as chief homemaker need not be discarded if proper attitudes prevail and roles are respected.

When you read about the bored housewife who is wasting her education or the harrassed husband who is tied down, remember that there are far more happily married people than unhappy ones. Many wives prefer not to work, especially while children are in school, and their lives are as rewarding as that of the homemaker on page 226. Many discontented stay-at-home wives might be even more discontented in the dual role of working wives.

Should a wife work outside the home? In deciding, the wife's personality, motivation, and management ability must be considered, as well as the couple's attitudes toward values, goals, and parental roles.

Many young wives with no children work to help their husbands through higher education, or to pay for a home and furnishings. Others simply like to keep busy with a paying job rather than stay at home or take part in clubs and volunteer activities. When children come some women continue to work because they enjoy having the prestige and independence that come with holding a good job.

Many women work out of necessity—perhaps to help with care of a dependent relative or to pay for the bare necessities. When both parents have to be away from home for long

Older persons in the home are happier if they feel needed.

Arvin Industries, Inc.

hours, family life suffers. The thousands of "latch-key" children who come home to an empty house at noon or after school may feel insecure or rebellious unless they are disciplined and loved.

The key to happy family life is not always how much time a family spends together but how well that time is spent. Many employed parents, recognizing the dangers of becoming too deeply involved outside the home, budget time as they budget income. Some families set aside an evening or two a week for family companionship. Entertainment may be dinner out and a concert, a barbecue in the backyard and a game of monopoly, or an evening watching special television programs and popping corn or making fudge.

It is worth sacrificing your individual interests now and then to take part in family activities. In our mobile society, family unity can help overcome the insecurity that comes from moving frequently, having to make new friends, and adjusting to new environments.

WHEN RELATIVES COME TO LIVE WITH YOU

In past generations almost every family included a grandmother, grandfather, older aunt or uncle. It was also common practice for a bride and groom to move in with parents for a few years. Due to social and economic changes, it is no longer necessary for many families to share their homes with others. When they do, studies show that the father has less of a problem adjusting to outsiders than the mother. Not many women can live together and respect each other's roles without conflict.

If the two women can agree about disciplining children, sharing housework, baby sitting, and not offering unwanted advice, happiness may be possible. Adjustments must be made by every member of the family, but if each adjustment represents a sacrifice or barrier, family harmony will become more and more difficult. Children usually accept and often welcome a relative who is happy and adaptable. It is only when they hear a parent's criticism, or when Grandmother or Aunt Agatha begins to show partiality, that they become critical.

As said before, *expecting too much* from an older relative leads to more trouble than we realize. This is an important point to consider.

RELIGION AND THE FAMILY CIRCLE

Do you attend church with your family, observe daily devotions, or seek a blessing before meals?

In our fast-moving world, devotions in the home are less frequent than in the past, yet many of our present-day leaders say that their early religious home training has helped them all their lives in time of crisis. On the other hand, you may hear people who are lax about going to church say, "I'd probably be more interested in church now if I had not been forced to go as a child." They use this more as an excuse than as a reason. Perhaps it is easier than facing the issue

squarely and trying to influence their children the best way.

Numerous studies back up the belief that religion exercises a stabilizing influence on family life. Our democracy was founded partly upon religious freedom. One survey of 25,000 marriages indicated that there were *three times as many unsuccessful marriages in non-religious homes* as in homes where families practiced religion. Another survey shows that marriages performed in a church are more stable than those performed in a non-religious setting.

Some families still have devotions together some time during the day, and many others still ask a blessing before meals. In the majority of American families, individual prayer is more or less a habit and church is attended fairly regularly.

There is an old saying: "The family that prays together, stays together." Family devotions, even in our jet age, can exert a strong family bond. Devotions can become as natural as any other habit. Almost everyone turns to a Divine Power in time of crisis, but we neglect prayer when things are going well.

CASE STUDY: The Armstrongs began family devotions only after their two older boys were miraculously saved when lightning struck a cannery where they were employed for the summer. Their after-dinner devotions lasted just five minutes, but they were shared by all seven family members. Not only did the Armstrongs become more familiar with the teachings of their church, but they also attempted to apply them to daily living. Their influence spread to neighbors; some people who were guests in their home

much fun that you came away feeling almost envious?

Perhaps the best time of day to enjoy family fellowship is during the dinner hour, because this is one time when the entire family is together. Suburban living, with Dad coming home late and children wanting to eat early has threatened this pleasant and extremely important part of family life.

Lester Rand, head of the Youth Research Institute, reported that less than one third of high school students dine regularly (more than three times a week) with their parents. Eugene Gilbert, head of the Gilbert Youth Research Company, says "the family dinner is becoming extinct . . . Young people have too many varied activities."

Marriage counselors, child welfare experts, and psychologists view this new trend unhappily. Some reasons for the decline of the traditional family dinner may be:

Studies reveal that religion exercises a stabilizing influence on the family. We are all free to attend the church of our choice.

Photographs by Better Living Du Pont

adopted their custom. It became a bond that helped overcome discord and bad feeling among them.

Most churches provide helpful literature for family worship. You may want to take advantage of these spiritual guides for individual or family devotions. Many young adults have found that religion has helped them in time of emergency.

One never knows when religious training in the home may help, or when the lack of it may be embarrassing. For instance, Tom Edwards, who appeared to be master of any situation, was called upon, without warning, to ask the blessing at a large dinner. After a horrible silence he could say only, "Bless this and these. Amen." Tom resolved to get a little more religion at home before being embarrassed again.

FAMILY FUN AND FELLOWSHIP

Have you ever been with a family where everyone seemed to have so

235

• Exodus to the suburbs, as stated above.

• Television, with its programs beamed to attract interest at the customary dinner hour.

• Extra leisure time, offering a temptation, especially in summer, to take advantage of daylight for golf, tennis, swimming, and other forms of outdoor, evening activities.

• Emphasis on dieting, which makes weight-conscious teen-agers want to skip dinner so that they can indulge in snacks later with the crowd.

• Using mealtime to reprimand children or conduct family arguments.

• Casual living in general: families seldom dress for dinner; buffet service and eating in the kitchen tend to break up family grouping. *Yet,* such informality may make us participate more.

Fellowship is important, not only in creating family harmony, but for good health as well. When mealtime becomes battle time, fellowship is impossible, emotions are upset, and the digestive system doesn't work right. Nutritious food, served regularly under pleasant conditions, is more effec-

tive than vitamin pills and nerve tonic.

"Conversation is the key to enjoying the family dinners," states James H. S. Bossard, who has written many books on family life. To find out more about family dinner conversation, Dr. Bossard analyzed tape recordings of the table talk of two hundred families.

Can you identify your family with any of these types?

HURRIED MEALS: The main purpose is to re-fuel, with an occasional "yes," "no," "uh-huh," "more," "salt," and so on. After each person has "bolted down" his share of the food, he leaves the table to become occupied with television, the newspaper, or the gang.

DOMESTIC WARFARE: Children are taken to task for misbehavior, parents quarrel, the food is criticized, and there is constant reprimanding about table manners or individual shortcomings. Frequently someone leaves the table in tears or anger.

Dinner time can be a high point of family fellowship. If family members are on time, well groomed, and anxious to share the experiences of the day, dinner will be a happy occasion.

The Gorham Company

236

Boating is a sport that many families enjoy. Powerboat riding, sailing, and rowing all provide different kinds of fun, but they are the same in one important way—the watchword is "safety first."

Sharing work is part of family fellowship. When children can share experiences with Dad as well as Mother, they tend to grow up well adjusted.

CRITICAL CONVERSATION: Family members delight in strengthening their own ego by finding fault with their neighbors, the school program, teachers, the way others handle the scouts, PTA, church activities, or their children. Later these parents wonder why their critical offspring are left out of the crowd.

HUMAN INTEREST TALK: Choice bits of news are saved for mealtime, triumphs and disappointments are shared, topics of the day are discussed —Donnie's scout achievements, Carol's anticipated date for the prom, Mother's experiences at the market, Dad's problems in finding a new employee, or even such weighty topics as attempts to conquer outer space.

FAMILY RITUAL: A formal blessing is asked, candles may glow, people listen attentively, but the atmosphere is very stiff. This kind of fellowship is good once in a while, but too strained for everyday living.

The whole family is responsible for making dinner a pleasant hour. A family council may help to establish the best time for the evening meal and the part each must play to make it a success, whether it is in helping with the preparation or the dishes afterwards. Everyone should make an effort to be prompt and pleasant.

CASE STUDY: In the Magee family, Suzanne tries to keep an attractive

Some families like to surprise Mother occasionally with breakfast in bed. It isn't hard when everyone helps, and what a fine way to let her know she is appreciated.

237

center decoration on the table, varying it frequently to tie in with the season or a special holiday. Jack tunes in the radio for dinner music, and Ed plans the family devotions, passing responsibilities around the circle. Mother is always ready with a puzzle, riddle, or interesting tidbit from the family history.

There are many other experiences that all family members can share. Families who enjoy doing things together occasionally — simple fun like a picnic in the park, or an evening of music at home—store up memories that will mean even more as years go by. What do you remember most vividly about fellowship with your family?

SICKNESS IN THE HOME

Until Louis Pasteur in the 1870's did research on the germ theory of disease, man had to depend upon natural immunity to protect him. Sanitation methods, vaccines, and antibiotic drugs now provide protection against many major illnesses.

Many of the serious childhood diseases have been almost eliminated, but measles, mumps, and chicken pox are as prevalent now as fifty years ago.

Preventive care has eliminated many diseases. We owe it to our family, as well as to ourselves, to have chest X-rays, vaccinations, polio shots, and physical examinations.

Coronet Films

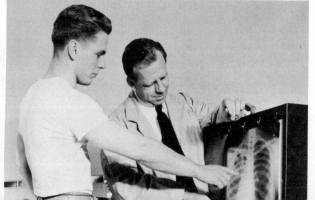

These need not be serious if children are given proper care.

The big killers today are non-infectious diseases of the heart and blood vessels, cancer, and accidents. Other major sources of suffering are diseases of the joints, such as rheumatism and arthritis, diabetes, respiratory diseases such as colds, hay fever, and asthma, and diseases of the digestive tract.

The best ways to take care of your health now and your family's health later are:

· Take advantage of free chest X-rays.
· Have a smallpox vaccination every seven years.

Have *polio* and *flu* protection. Many persons under 40, who need protection most, neglect it.

· Get adequate sleep and rest.
· Eat the right foods.
· Eat and sleep at regular hours.
· Avoid overindulgence in rich foods, smoking, and drinking.
· Drink plenty of liquids — lots of water.
· Practice cleanliness, especially before handling food.
· Get regular exercise — as much as possible out-of-doors.
· Learn to control your emotions.
· Have regular physical check-ups, including teeth and eyes.

By far the majority of sick people in the United States today are being cared for in the home; yet few families have real knowledge of how to care for the sick.

Detecting and Reporting Illness   Some illnesses are short and not very serious. But diagnosing and treating a patient at home can be risky. Even a common cold can have dangerous complica-

238

tions. The doctor should be called as soon as there is even a slight indication that a person may be seriously ill.

You can help the doctor by making the following observations:
· Temperature — morning, afternoon, and evening.
· Quality and duration of sleep.
· Number and type of bowel movements.
· Amount of urine passed in 24 hours.
· Type of food eaten, including amount of liquid.
· Complaints of patient.
· General attitude of patient.

Any person caring for the sick should be cheerful and sympathetic to reduce emotional upsets. He should scrub his hands thoroughly, and observe all possible means of cleanliness, to reduce the spread of infectious diseases. The patient's dishes should be washed, scalded, and stored separately.

Equipping the Sickroom In the case of a long illness, the patient should be moved to a quiet room near the bathroom. The room should be as uncluttered as possible. The following equipment will help you care for a bed patient.

· Comfortable, firm, single bed. It will be easier to care for a patient if rollers are removed and the bed is raised on wooden blocks with depressions for the legs of the bed to rest in.
· Full set of toilet articles — comb, toothbrush, soap, towel, washbasin, shaving supplies—if needed.
· Bed pan and urinal.
· Clinical thermometer. Disinfect *after each use* by wiping with cotton dipped in soap and alcohol, and rinse

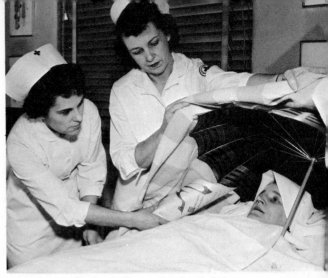

Pittsburgh Chapter, American Red Cross

Sickroom equipment may be improvised. An umbrella may be used as a tent for vapor inhalation.

in cold water. Before using the thermometer for another person, soak it in a solution of iodine and alcohol for 10 minutes, rinse with cool water, and dry.
· The medicine cabinet should contain an antiseptic for cuts and scratches, a salve for burns, a laxative, a stimulant, adhesive tape, absorbent cotton, sterile gauze, tweezers, medicine dropper, eye cup, aspirin, petroleum jelly, medicated alcohol. There should also be a heating pad and an enema bag.

General Care A daily sponge bath is refreshing and stimulating. Areas that support the body weight—back, shoulders, heels, and elbows—should be massaged with alcohol or antiseptic cream once or twice a day to maintain good circulation and prevent bed sores. A public health nurse may be called in to demonstrate special care and bed making.

Special equipment may be rented from a hospital supply house.

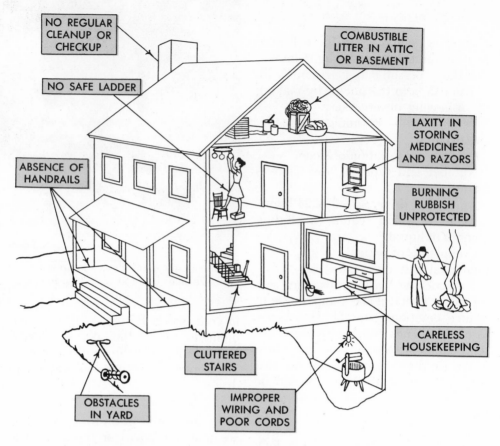

NO REGULAR CLEANUP OR CHECKUP

COMBUSTIBLE LITTER IN ATTIC OR BASEMENT

NO SAFE LADDER

LAXITY IN STORING MEDICINES AND RAZORS

ABSENCE OF HANDRAILS

BURNING RUBBISH UNPROTECTED

CARELESS HOUSEKEEPING

CLUTTERED STAIRS

OBSTACLES IN YARD

IMPROPER WIRING AND POOR CORDS

Look for these causes of accidents in your home and eliminate them.

ACCIDENTS AND THEIR PREVENTION

Motor vehicle accidents are the leading cause of accidental death. In early 1968 the traffic death rate was even higher than in 1967 when 53,-000 people were killed. Another 10,-000 are injured in traffic each day.

Because of this alarming death rate, auto manufacturers are putting more safety features into cars. Some states have raised the age limit for obtaining a driver's license and have placed restrictions on older drivers. Schools are emphasizing driver education.

Because of greater safety precau-tions you are generally safer on pub-lic transportation than in a private ve-hicle. Partly for the same reason a person's place of work is usually safer than his home. Homes rank sec-ond in number of fatal accidents.

Studies show that a large number of accidents happen to children within half an hour of mealtime be-cause they are hungry. They may eat the wrong thing or try to reach for food and fall. This is the time of day when mothers are tired and less alert. If a mother finds she is getting tired, she should find time for a short nap. If the phone rings at a busy time she should offer to return the call later.

240

More than half of home accidents happen outside and near the **Falls** house. Falls account for the major portion. The kitchen is the most dangerous room in the house. Basements and bathrooms vie for second place.

The absence of handrails increases the number of falls. Stairways should be well lighted, with a switch at both top and bottom.

Poor housekeeping accounts for many falls. Make a habit of wiping up grease or water spots and picking up peelings immediately. Avoid a high polish on floors and use skidproof scatter rugs. Keep electric cords out of main traffic lanes and doorways. Use a sturdy, well-balanced ladder to reach high places.

Before dark, make sure that children's toys, brooms, rakes, lawn mowers, and other obstacles are picked up. If there is a temporary hole anywhere near the house, it should be blocked off at all times and well lighted at night. If someone is seriously injured on your property, you can become involved in a heavy lawsuit. (See Comprehensive Liability Insurance, page 395.)

Fire Hazards Electrical fires destroy more property than any other type. The increasing use of electrical appliances overloads the wires in *four out of five* homes in the United States.

The wiring in your home may be inadequate if your lights become dim, your television set begins to flicker, or your vacuum cleaner slows down as you plug in a major appliance. A kitchen panel like the one pictured may take off some of the load, but proper wiring is the best preventive.

According to the National Fire Protection Association, 11,300 persons died in fires in 1957, and *over half of them were trapped in homes.* A fire

An automatic appliance center in the kitchen can increase safety and convenience in the home where many electrical appliances often are used at once.

Westinghouse Corporation, Portable Appliance Division

starts in a residence somewhere in the United States every seven minutes. Toxic, superheated gases often cause death before fire even reaches a room.

Older houses usually have 15-ampere circuits; newer ones have 15-ampere circuits for ordinary needs and 20-ampere circuits (heavy wire) for the kitchen, dining, and laundry area. Your electric company will check the circuits for a small fee.

Overloaded wires become hot inside the walls, where fires can start very quickly. Your TV set may be a fire hazard. One survey revealed that defective TV sets caused 17 times as many fires as careless Christmas practices! In one instance in Pittsburgh, a man noticed smoke coming from a TV set and poured water onto it. The set exploded and injured everyone in the room. Never try the water cure on the TV—or fool with it otherwise, unless you are a professional.

Water and electricity are like dynamite. In the bathroom and laundry, only *rubber-covered cords* and porcelain sockets should be used. Never plug in an appliance with *wet hands* or hold on to anything metal while plugging it in. *Frayed cords* or cords with loose wires at the plug are especially dangerous. If you bend, knot, or wrap electric cords, you may break the fine wires inside, causing a short circuit. Every tiny wire inside a cord must be intact for safety and efficiency.

Fires can start by spontaneous ignition, such as when dirty, oily rags accumulate in basements and attics. If flues and chimneys are not cleaned and inspected periodically, fires can start from combustion of dust particles. Having curtains near electric or gas burners, leaving matches where children can reach them, smoking in bed, keeping flammable liquids in the home, and failing to use screens in front of fireplaces, create fire hazards.

Sharp Instruments and Poisons — Keep sharp knives in a wall rack where children cannot reach them. Dispose of razor blades safely.

Never keep cleaning supplies or medicines in a closet with food. If there are children around, all dangerous items should be kept on a high shelf or in a locked cabinet.

The accompanying list indicates what to do in common emergencies.

Metropolitan Life Insurance Company

FIRST AID FOR THE FAMILY

Note: Sterile gauze compresses to help prevent infection should be kept in the medicine cabinet at all times. If you do not have any, use a clean handkerchief or clean cloth and, if there is time, sterilize by scorching with an iron.

Asphyxiation (breathing stopped): Get patient to fresh air. Send for physician. Start artificial respiration at once.

Cuts, Minor: Wash with soap under warm, running water. Apply mild antiseptic and sterile compress.

Bites, Animal: Wash wounds with soap under running water. Have animal caught alive so that it can be tested for rabies. Take patient to physician.

Bleeding: Press hard with sterile compress directly over wound until bleeding stops. If bleeding is severe, send for physician.

Burns: MILD (skin unbroken—no blisters): Hold burned part under cold running water for 2-3 minutes. If pain persists, apply petroleum jelly or mild burn ointment and bandage.

SEVERE: Send for physician. Apply wet sterile compresses. Do not break blisters or try to clean burn. Keep patient quiet and comfortably warm until physician arrives.

Choking (foreign body in throat or windpipe): Have patient bend forward or lie face down on bed with head and shoulders hanging over the side. Slap his back hard between shoulder blades. If a small child, hold him upside down by the heels and slap his back. If the object is not dislodged promptly, send for physician. If breathing stops give artificial respiration.

Convulsions: Place patient on back on rug or bed where he cannot hurt himself. Loosen his clothing. Turn head to side. Put thick wad of cloth between his jaws so that he doesn't bite his tongue. Raise and pull lower jaw forward. If convulsions do not stop by themselves, sponge patient's head and neck with cool water. Send for physician.

Falls: If patient has continued pain send for physician. Stop any severe bleeding and cover wound with sterile dressing. Keep patient warm and comfortable. If a broken bone is suspected, do not move patient unless absolutely necessary (as in case of fire, etc.).

Electric Shock: Turn off electric power if possible. Do not touch patient until contact is broken. Pull him from contact using rope, wooden pole, or loop of dry cloth. If breathing has stopped, start artificial respiration. Send for physician.

Eye, Chemicals in: Have patient lie down at once. Pour cupfuls of water immediately into corner of eye, letting it run to wash outside of face, until chemical is thoroughly removed. Put a few drops of clean olive oil, mineral or castor oil into eye. Cover with sterile compress. Send for physician.

Eye, Foreign Bodies in: If object can be seen, touch it lightly with moistened corner of handkerchief. If object does not come out after two or three attempts, or if it cannot be seen, take patient to physician. Never rub the eye, as this may force the foreign body in even deeper.

Fainting: If patient feels faint, seat him and fan his face. Lower head to knees. If he becomes unconscious, lay him on his back with coat or blanket under hips. Loosen clothing. Open windows. Wave smelling salts or aromatic spirits of ammonia under nose. After consciousness returns, keep patient lying quiet for at least 15 minutes. If faint lasts for more than a few minutes, send for physician.

Poisoning (by mouth): Call physician. If bottle which contained poison is available, use antidote recommended on label. If patient is conscious, induce vomiting, except for lye poisoning. If antidote is unknown, give patient milk.

Unconsciousness: Keep patient warm and lying down. Send for physician. If breathing stops give artificial respiration. Never give an unconscious person food or liquids.

The Beginning Family

CHANGING NEEDS IN THE FAMILY CYCLE

Over the years, you may have been aware of the changing needs of your family. When you marry and have children, you will become especially conscious of new needs and interests. Nothing is static. A family must be prepared to meet the changes as they occur. Perhaps the two greatest changes in the family pattern are adjusting to the first child, and then, much later, adjusting to the "empty nest." Often, a person leaving home gives little thought to his parents, but it is so much a part of adult living that you might well consider it now.

The family cycle has been divided into four stages: early years or *the beginning family;* crowded years or *the expanding family;* peak years or *the launching family;* later years or *the contracting family.*

The Beginning Family This is the period before the birth of the first child. It usually lasts from one to three years. Emphasis during these years should be on learning how to get along in the new way of life. If routine homemaking skills have been mastered before the first baby arrives, the adjustment to parenthood will be easier. Though the wife may have a job, the couple will probably have more time for social activities, travel, and community or church work than they will after a child arrives. When the wife becomes an expectant mother, periods of irritability and apprehension may follow, but these will be only minor problems for a couple that is mature and truly interested in each other's welfare.

The Expanding Family This is the period from the arrival of the first child until the last child is in school. The length of this period varies greatly, but in most families the first child is born while the mother is still in her twenties, and the last arrives while the oldest is in grade school. During these years the obligations of both parents increase.

Two big problems which parents must face are:
• How to get enough money for necessities, emergencies, and a few luxuries.
• How to find time to do all the work that needs to be done, yet still have a few hours occasionally for recreation and personal enrichment.

Despite these problems, many older couples look back on these years as a happy and rewarding time. Few

The Expanding Family

people ever feel more needed than the parents of an expanding family.

Parents must strive to set values, exercise good judgment in making decisions, show love and interest, and be firm in matters of discipline. There will be sibling rivalry, some of which may be eliminated if parents avoid comparing children with each other and with their friends. Physical, financial, and emotional demands increase. Not only do children crave love and direction but they also want independence and material possessions. Parents need not be rich or famous; if they are respectable and perhaps active in church or civic affairs, children will feel secure and socially acceptable.

A mistake which many parents make early in this period is to spend too much on clothes and furniture for a baby. The garments are soon outgrown, and the furniture can often be borrowed from relatives or friends. Some of the money might be better spent on diaper service which can eliminate a great deal of work.

Another common mistake is for parents to neglect each other, or even to neglect themselves, during these busy years. A woman may become so occupied with her children that she pays little attention to her personal appearance. The marriage will suffer

The Contracting Family

for this. It will suffer also if the husband is always too busy or too tired to take his wife out for an occasional evening of entertainment.

The Launching Family These years begin when the youngest child enters school and end when the children have all left home. During this period, parents must guide their children in many serious matters, some of which will influence their whole lives. Decisions must be made about education, occupation, military service, and marriage. Whether or not a young person seeks advice in these matters, parental influence is bound to be felt.

There may be conflicts over spending money, using the car, behavior on a date, a time to come home after an evening out, and grades, especially if college is in the future. Such complex problems are difficult to solve, but they will not prove impossible if moral, social, religious, and family values have been well established. Parents have the responsibility of knowing when and how far to relax restrictions so that children may grow in independence.

Family relationships can be at their finest during this period. All members

The Launching Family

245

can take part in family fun; conversation can be on a fairly adult basis for the whole group. This is a time when parents usually enjoy their children's friends—when they share deeply in their pleasures and disappointments.

The Contracting Family When the last child leaves for college, a job, or marriage, parents are alone again. Often only one parent is still alive. A major adjustment is sometimes necessary, especially for the mother if she has failed to keep up with her friends and interests. These years can be as rich and rewarding as any, if people are in good health, reasonably free from financial worries, and if they have friends and interests in common. Just as it takes effort to make marriage work, so it does to grow old gracefully, to learn to be a mother- or father-in-law, grandparent, or senior citizen.

With each variation in family living come problems and pleasures, disappointment and joy, challenge and change. Technological advance will influence each stage of the family cycle more and more.

In the future, families will move more frequently. More mothers will work. There will be many more child care centers. Automation will reduce the work week and provide more time for leisure activities. There will be more international travel. Buying on credit will encourage more and larger purchases. Broader social legislation will provide greater health insurance and care for the aged. People will live longer. Taxes will increase! All of us must be alert to our times.

Words and Phrases to Know

affluence	indulgent
asphyxiation	mobility
autocratic	perception
cultural pattern	permissive
democratic	role
human development	socialization
universal trait	

ACTIVITIES

1. Discuss how some causes of family tension might be eliminated.

2. Volunteer for the roles of five family members—father, mother, and children in grade, junior high, and high school, and portray the three types of families described. Discuss allowances, hours to come home, vacation plans.

3. Discuss how your attitudes about parental concern for you have changed in the last few years.

4. As a child, what were you permitted to decide for yourself? What decisions do you make now? Do you prefer making major decisions alone or discussing them with parents? Friends?

5. Show some films related to this chapter and discuss them.

6. Discuss ways in which a wife and husband may help each other.

7. Comment on the following remark made by a parent. "After twenty-six years I know everything about marriage and raising a family. I don't need a book to tell me!"

8. Compare American family customs with what you know of family life in other countries.

9. Take a poll of the young men in your class who help at home now and what they do. Find out if they expect to help after they marry, and how they would prefer to help.

10. Discuss this reaction to receiving a gift: Jane Hurst gave her husband, Allen, a book she thought they would enjoy reading together. Allen tossed it on a chair and said, "Jane, you know I'd never read a book like that."

11. Talk over the responsibilities of a mother and father.

12. Discuss the following statements (you may agree or disagree):

Few families have the time or feel the need for family devotions.

I would like to be a member of a family where daily devotions are still practiced.

I feel a need for religion in everyday living.

13. Pick a chairman to conduct a class study on the status of the family dinner. What things interfere with family dinners in your home? Under which pattern described in this chapter does your family fit?

14. List the ways class members enjoy family fellowship.

15. How many girls in your class plan to continue working after marriage; how many boys would object to wives working; what circumstances might make it desirable for a wife to work.

16. Discuss experiences with sickness in your home, and facilities for caring for the sick.

17. List some accidents that have occurred in class members' homes in recent years. What precautions could have prevented such accidents?

18. Name some families you know that fit into the four periods of the family cycle. Discuss needs at each level. What period seems most difficult? Why?

19. Ask a Red Cross representative to discuss and demonstrate artificial respiration, first aid in the home, and how to make some sickroom equipment yourself.

Correlation

ENGLISH: Write a 400-500 word essay on what you consider to be a good family. Read the chapter first.

JOURNALISM: Summarize the findings of your survey on the family dinner for the school paper.

SOCIOLOGY OR HISTORY: Invite the sociology or history teacher to give a talk comparing family living during colonial days, the Victorian period, post World War I years, and the present.

SPEECH: Find magazine stories of the lives of important people, and tell what influence their home had upon them.

HEALTH: Invite the health teacher to talk about home practices for good health.

Home Experiences

Ask your parents to read the chapter and discuss it with you in regard to the following:

• Making mealtime more enjoyable.
• Stimulating family fellowship.
• Whether to introduce family worship.

Inspect your medicine cabinet and equip it with the supplies suggested.

Observe the behavior of your lights when major appliances are being used. If the electrical current seems inadequate, tell your folks.

Make a list of things you can do to prevent accidents in the home. Do them now!

Chapter 11

Under-standing Children Now

A recent survey showed that nearly half of all teen-age girls, and about a quarter of the male teen-agers, earn money baby sitting. Whether you are a baby sitter, a young aunt or uncle, or simply one of the older students in your block, you will want to know how to get along with children.

As you may have found out, taking care of even a young baby means more than being able to change a diaper, prepare a formula, and give the baby a bath. Taking care of these physical needs soon becomes easy, but coping with discipline problems and emotional upsets, keeping children happy and busy, are more complex.

Years ago, pediatricians discovered that babies kept for weeks in hospitals, where every physical need was met by trained nurses, failed to thrive. They had been deprived of one important ingredient — tender, loving care. You may have noticed this on evenings when you tried to hurry the youngest members of the family off to bed, so you could study for a test

or watch TV. They may have become fretful because they missed your usual affection and attention.

BABY SITTING PAYS, AND PREPARES YOU FOR PARENTHOOD

In years gone by, almost all young married couples settled down in their home towns where relatives and friends were available to help mind the children. More young families today live far from their folks and must depend upon sitters if they want to spend an evening out.

Although you may not do much baby sitting now, in the next few years you hope to have children of your own. Can you recall the first time you were left alone with a baby or several children? Your past experience should be of great value in the future.

It may surprise you to know that there are established baby-sitting agencies in this country that provide professional sitters for homes, hotels, and motels. The number is growing rapidly. On the yellow pages

248

of any medium-sized or large city telephone directory you will find baby-sitting agencies listed. College students and young people with jobs often register with these agencies to earn extra money. Baby-sitting agencies must be state licensed and state bonded. A sitter is usually given a card similar to the following.

SITTER'S INFORMATION SHEET

Phone Numbers:
Where parents will be . . . .
Other relatives . . . .
Neighbor . . . .
Doctor . . . .
Fire department . . . .
Police . . . .

Instructions for Feeding:
Time for feeding . . . .
Menu and how to prepare food . . . . .
How to operate range . . . .

Location of:
Door buzzer . . . .
Light switches . . . .
Diapers, bedclothes, blankets . . . .
First aid kit for minor injuries . . . . . .

Further Instructions:
Time of return . . . .
Favorite story and songs . . . .
Snack or milk habits . . . .
Ventilation for sleeping . . . .
Lights . . . .

Additional Duties (extra pay?)
Washing dishes . . . .
Ironing . . . .
Other . . . .

ADJUSTMENTS WHEN "BABY MAKES THREE"

Naturally, most young couples look forward to starting their families.

Some hope that the first child may be delayed until parents' educations are complete, or money is saved. Sometimes plans go astray, and a baby arrives before the parents are prepared either financially or mentally.

Encouraging a young wife to visit the maternity ward of a hospital before her baby arrives helps to prepare her for parenthood. In many localities, courses for prospective fathers are available. Learning what to expect certainly makes it easier to enjoy the first child.

When mother and baby come home from the hospital, all plans revolve around the new member of the family. The mother must learn to dovetail her work and rest with baby's feeding, sleeping, and bathing schedules. Mother and Father often wonder what it would be like to have a full night's sleep once more!

Meals may be interrupted, Mother may become tired, and Dad may feel neglected once in a while, but these disturbing factors mean nothing compared with holding your child, or

Being interested in the baby is a large part of satisfying his needs. A wise baby sitter or parent makes bigger sister or brother feel important, too.

Gerber Baby Foods

249

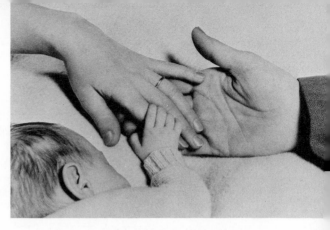

Sharing the joys of parenthood makes temporary inconveniences seem insignificant.

catching the first suggestion of a smile that seems to mean he recognizes you.

When two people are mature and ready for parenthood, there is no greater joy than experiencing the wonder of birth; nothing can be more enriching or rewarding than a happy, healthy baby.

PLANNING AHEAD FOR BABY'S ARRIVAL

Some young adults believe in planned parenthood but others, for religious or personal reasons, object to planned spacing of children. Physicians differ in offering advice on the subject. Some feel that two or three years should elapse between births, whereas others believe that the mother's health may be better when children are born twelve to fourteen months apart. When children are

Baby's debut is awaited by proud father and admiring grandparents.

wanted, welcomed, and cared for lovingly by all family members, the years between make little difference.

Good pre-natal care is more important than the spacing between births. Early and regular visits should be made to the doctor, for the sake of the mother's health, the baby's safe arrival, and the father's peace of mind. A doctor can anticipate irregularities and prescribe diet or treatment to encourage normal birth.

In most cities, there are clinics for families who cannot afford private consultations. Service in all localities is improving yearly.

Arranging for help   Arrangements should be made ahead of time for full or part-time help when the baby arrives.

• In most cases one of the grandmothers is eager to come to the rescue and even more eager to take the entire situation in hand. This is fine if Grandmother's and Mother's dispositions harmonize.

• If outside nursing help is required, a nursing agency, or perhaps the doctor may arrange it.

• Sometimes friends can recommend a good practical nurse.

• If a family cannot afford help, in most cities there are community sup-

250

ported family service agencies that make visiting nurses available for daily calls.

• In smaller communities, fellow church members and neighbors often come to the aid of a young mother.

Providing Supplies Although it may be some time before you are ready to buy clothing, bedding, feeding, and bath equipment for your own babies, you will find the following lists helpful in selecting gifts for friends:

CLOTHING:
3-6 nightgowns (stockinette preferred).
3-6 dozen diapers or *diaper service*.
3-4 sacks or sweaters (easily fastened).
1-2 wool caps (for winter baby).
2-3 pairs booties.
2-3 square cotton blankets.

BED AND BEDDING:
Bassinet (later a crib).
1-2 waterproof sheets.
3-4 square quilted pads.
3-6 sheets (stockinette preferred).
? blankets depending upon climate.

BATH EQUIPMENT:
Tub (enamel tub on card table adequate).
Diaper pail (provided with diaper service).
Bath thermometer (or common sense in judging water temperature).
Rectal thermometer.
Tray for toilet articles.

FEEDING EQUIPMENT:
(To be kept on a separate shelf in the kitchen):
9-12 eight ounce bottles (if bottle fed).
Sterilizer or large enamel pan.
9-10 nipples and bottle covers.
Funnel.
Fine strainer.
Nipple jar.
Measuring spoon.
Tongs.
Quart size enamel saucepan.

As a rule, babies are fed every four hours—more frequently if underweight or born prematurely. Some babies will break themselves of the 2 A.M. feeding at two weeks, others at three months or later. Between ages of three and six months many babies stop needing to be fed at 10 P.M.

Most pediatricians recommend breast feeding. However, it should be done only if the mother is: (1) able to supply enough nourishment to keep the baby contented; (2) free of nervous tension; (3) eager to nurse her baby; (4) not planning to go back to a job soon.

SCHEDULES AND FEEDING

A new baby will sleep almost continuously except for feeding time. However, they do vary in the amount of sleep needed. Some babies as young as two or three weeks get along well on fifteen or sixteen hours sleep

Many babies enjoy bath time. Never leave a baby unattended in his bath.

H. Armstrong Roberts

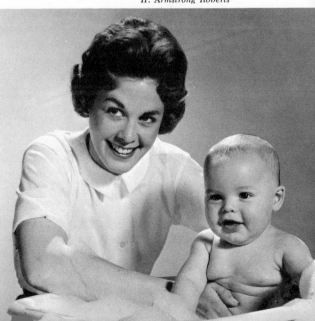

H. J. Heinz Company

Baby should become accustomed to falling asleep in his own bed. If possible, his bed should be moved out of the parents' room when he is six months old.

per day. The baby should become accustomed to falling asleep in his own bed. It is easier to form good sleep habits if the baby is put to bed right after a meal and before he becomes excited with activity.

A baby's sleeping position should be changed fairly often. If the mattress is very firm, he will enjoy sleeping on his stomach, *but be sure he cannot snuggle down and cut off his air supply.* Sleeping blankets are safe but too confining. The baby is better off with a warm garment over his shoulders and light blankets below, well tucked in at the foot and sides.

Never hang anything over a side of the crib. Babies under a year of age have been smothered by pulling down covers left over the crib. Plastic film and other non-porous fabrics should never be used around even an older child. Many deaths have resulted from children pulling plastic film over their heads and suffocating. Babies have smothered also when fatigued mothers have tried to feed them in bed and have fallen asleep. Mothers should put on a robe and sit in a chair for feedings. It's too risky otherwise. If a baby or small child is suddenly

frightened, he needs the temporary security of the parent's bed but only for a short period. In fact, it is advisable to move the crib out of the parents' room at six months.

A baby's feeding should not be hurried; in order to satisfy the sucking instinct, each feeding should consume twenty minutes. The baby should be held in an upright position because air bubbles form on top of milk in his stomach when he is held out flat, making him feel full when he isn't. When a baby cries too long before a feeding, he will have trouble digesting his milk because he will gulp air into his stomach, which interferes with his appetite and digestion.

There is some disagreement about when to introduce different foods to the baby's diet of milk and cod liver oil. Milk, unless it is fortified, is deficient in vitamins D and C. D is the sunshine vitamin and C is contained in citrus fruit. Vitamin C is needed daily because it cannot be stored in the body. These vitamins should be provided early in some form. The following chart is only a rough guide. All foods must be introduced to baby's diet on your doctor's orders.

BABY'S FOOD ADDITIONS

Item	When Added to Milk Feeding
COD LIVER OIL	At 2-4 weeks—best source of vitamin D for prevention of rickets and soft bones.
WATER	At any time. Boil 5 minutes and offer frequently in hot weather.
ORANGE JUICE	At 2 or 3 months—best source of vitamin C to prevent scurvy or soft gums. Usually diluted with sterile water. Heat and exposure to air destroy vitamin C.
CEREAL	At 3 to 6 months with 10 A.M. and 6 P.M. feedings—first solid food. Usually mixed with sterile water, milk, or formula.
FRUIT	After he has become used to cereal. Stewed and strained or mashed ripe bananas at 3 to 6 months. Usually with 2 P.M. or 6 P.M. feedings. Fresh fruit after 1 year. Cherries and berries, melons, after 2.
VEGETABLES	From 2 to 4 weeks *after* introduction of cereal and fruit. With early afternoon feeding. Raw vegetables between 1½ and 2 years. Corn after 2.
EGG YOLK	From 4 to 6 months—valuable for iron for red blood cells. Strained, hard-cooked yolk usually given first. Usually given early morning.
MEAT SOUP AND MEATS	Meat soup is usually given at 6 months. Meat soups contain little meat and should not be considered a meat substitute. Scraped meat at nine months.
PUDDINGS AND JELLO	After 6 months. Good for variety, but less important than other foods.

Three Meals A Day Soon after nine months, babies may be fed "junior" foods that require more chewing. By the end of the first year, a child should be on three meals a day. This menu is typical:

BREAKFAST: Cereal, soft boiled egg, toast, milk.
LUNCH: Vegetable, potato *or* macaroni *or* rice, meat *or* fish, fruit *or* pudding *or* jello.
SUPPER: Cereal, fruit, milk.

Offer orange or tomato juice and crackers between meals.

CHILDREN'S DISEASES AND INOCULATIONS

Although most children's diseases are not serious, it is wise to take every precaution to protect a baby by keep-

A baby's feeding should not be hurried. Each feeding should take about twenty minutes.

H. J. Heinz Company

ing him out of crowds and seeing that he has the usual inoculations. Many diseases begin with a cold and sore throat.

Measles First symptoms resemble a bad cold. Measles occur from nine to sixteen days after exposure. The disease may be especially severe with children under 3 or in a run-down condition. Many doctors now give a vaccine. No booster shot is needed. A similar disease is *rubella*, sometimes called three-day or German measles. This illness is usually mild in children but can have severe complications for an expectant mother. A vaccine is in research stage.

Chick-en Pox The first signs are a few pimples, with tiny yellow centers, on the face and body. Chicken pox develops between eleven and nineteen days after exposure. *Immunization:* None.

Smallpox This is an extremely serious disease. A baby should be vaccinated before the end of the first year, but not if he has eczema. For continued immunity, a person should be vaccinated every three to five years.

Whooping Cough, Diphtheria, Tetanus A series of shots, given in the early months, provides immunity against these diseases. The same vaccine is effective against all three of these once dreaded illnesses. A booster may be necessary if the child is bitten, badly scratched, or injured in any other way that might cause tetanus.

Mumps Symptoms are swollen neck glands and fever. The patient shows signs of illness about twenty days after exposure. He must be kept warm and quiet to prevent aftereffects. The discovery of a vaccine has been announced. Its effectiveness must still be tested.

Scarlet Fever Symptoms include sore throat, fever, and a rash. To prevent aftereffects the patient should be kept quiet in a darkened room and discouraged from using the eyes. There is no satisfactory immunization, but the illness can be controlled by drugs.

Typhoid Fever Inoculations for typhoid fever are given only when a person is going to a country where the water supply and other sanitary conditions may be questionable.

Polio One of the greatest medical success stories is the control of poliomyelitis. Through oral and injected vaccines children in even the earliest months of life can be protected from this disease that cripples and kills.

PLEASURES AND PROBLEMS

If a baby is well and getting proper food, rest, and care, and if his family seems happy, his contentment will spread through the home. A baby can sense tenseness; in spite of good physical care, he cannot help but be affected emotionally by disturbances around him.

As long as a baby sleeps, coos, and gains weight, Mother and Dad are happy, but when problems arise, par-

254

ents sometimes become frightened and forget the old rule: "Be calm and use common sense until a doctor can be called."

Let's mention briefly some of the problems parents face:

Eating The more a parent shows concern over a child's eating habits, the more the child may refuse to eat in order to receive attention. Appetites vary; food likes and dislikes may change every few days. If certain foods are refused, try them a week or so later.

• After a child is old enough to sit up, feed him in a quiet place. Any kind of activity is distracting.

• Let a child feed himself as soon as he can. He naturally likes to pick up things. Serve food in small portions.

• If a child drops food for attention, avoid scolding, or coaxing. Be businesslike; take away his food. Serve him again only when he is convinced he must eat it properly.

• Some children cannot eat three heavy meals and need snacks at mid-morning, mid-afternoon, and bedtime. *Make snacks light*—tomato juice, milk, orange juice, raw carrot, orange sections, piece of an apple, crackers. Avoid sweet drinks, and breads or cookies that stick to the teeth, unless teeth are brushed afterwards.

• If a child wants to eat several servings of one *nutritious* food at a meal and ignore other foods, let him. Even two or three eggs a day will do no harm; serve him less meat. However, avoid imbalance over a long period. Study the Food for Fitness Guide in Chapter 4, and make sure that some foods from each food group are part of the daily diet.

Although his manners may not be commendable, a baby should be permitted to feed himself as soon as he makes the effort.

• Never try to feed a child when he is overtired. Ten minutes rest with a story or music before a meal will relax a child. Avoid showing anger at mealtime.

• If bad food habits cause a child to lose weight or grow flabby, consult your doctor.

The average baby should double his weight at about five months. If quite small at birth, he may more than double it. He should gain about 2 pounds a month for the first three months, then about a pound a month until six months. From this time on the average gain decreases to about ½ pound a month. At the end of a year, a baby will nearly triple his birth weight and be from 35 to 43 inches tall.

Teething Usually a baby cuts teeth at about seven months. He may become fretful at three or four months, and get some satisfaction from chewing on a teething ring. By 2½ years, a child should have twenty teeth. Baby teeth should be kept clean and cavities filled. From the time a child is 2, he should see a dentist every six months. Baby teeth are important in holding the jaw in shape for permanent teeth.

Weaning   A baby should be offered milk or orange juice from a cup at the age of 5 months. Waiting until 9 or 10 months makes weaning more difficult. A child who is put to bed with a bottle becomes used to it, and resists giving it up. So don't start him sleeping with his bottle.

Toilet Training   Dr. Arnold Gesell, founder of the Gesell Institute of Child Development, says that children tend to train themselves at certain ages just as they learn to walk or talk.

When a child is in the second half of his second year, he will be able to control his bowel movements. However, it is possible to "catch" a child after 8 months if he can establish a regular schedule. From 15 months on, many children stay dry in the daytime if they are allowed to sit on a toilet chair every 2 hours. Between 2 and 2½, a child will know when he needs to use the toilet. Most children stay dry through the night between 2 and 3 years.

Training chairs give more support and greater safety than seats on toilets.
• A child should never be left on a toilet longer than five or ten minutes at a time.
• He should be praised for co-operating, but never scolded for being un-co-operative.
• He should never be spanked or scolded for an "accident." He may use this trick later to attract attention when a baby brother or sister comes along.

Thumb Sucking   A baby's natural sucking instinct must be satisfied. If he is *not* permitted a long enough sucking period at feeding time, especially up to three or four months, he will find some way to satisfy his instinct.

Thumb sucking only at sleeping time is of no great concern. Some doctors even recommend pacifiers, long in disfavor, if they are removed frequently, especially when a baby falls asleep. It has been found that few babies allowed to use pacifiers ever become thumb suckers.

There is little evidence on the relation of thumb sucking to protruding upper teeth or other unusual mouth formations. Tying a baby's hands, using special mittens, or putting a bad tasting substance on a child's hands will frustrate him. It is better to divert his attention and keep his hands busy with toys.

If thumb sucking continues after a child is four, there may be some basic disturbance.

Stuttering and Nail Biting   Boys tend to stutter more than girls. Often it is merely part of learning to speak. Most children outgrow it. However, stuttering and nail biting may be the result of nervousness. The following things can make a child nervous: jealousy of other children, frequent corrections, a craving for attention, lack of sleep, rejection at home or school, and family friction. The common-sense solution is usually best. Relieve possible causes — exciting TV programs, fre-

256

quent criticism, insufficient sleep, family bickering, or school difficulties. Many parents simply do not give much thought to the causes. Children need parents' interest in them, or they will not try to help themselves.

Children's Questions on Big Subjects Parents often have trouble answering questions about God, birth, death. At 3, a child is extremely curious about the world. He will ask "Where is God?" "Why did God let my kitty get run over?" Another question is "Why do people die?" These are all very important questions if death has come near. However, the child's span of interest is short; a direct, brief answer is all he needs. You may say that God is in a special world somewhere, and that we are born again into His world.

"Where do babies come from?" should never be answered with the stork story. When a child is taught the proper language concerning sex and given a simple, honest answer, his attitudes in the future will be more wholesome. From 2 to 4 years, a child may be deeply concerned about babies, but he is usually satisfied with, "A little baby grows from a tiny seed inside his mother's stomach or womb." A child learns from watching how a mother dog or cat cares for her young. Also, most libraries have books that give simple answers to questions children often ask.

Emotions An emotion shows in any departure from a quiet state — love, surprise, joy, enthusiasm or fear, anger, jealousy, stubbornness, hate, grief, worry. It is natural and necessary to experience all of these emotions, but when *any* emotion is carried to extreme, there is danger. Children need affection and protection, but when there is over-concern instead of love, a child fails to mature normally.

It is believed that children's experiences until the age of 6 have a profound effect upon their personalities later. How parents handle fears, anger, jealousy, sulkiness, and other anti-social emotions will affect a child's attitudes in later life.

Many things frighten a child—unpleasant noises such as fire alarms, or vacuum cleaners; a barking dog; storms. If parents are afraid, or scold children for being afraid, fears build up and may lead to bed wetting, bad dreams, restless sleep, thumb sucking, or cruelty to pets.

Parents can help children to overcome fear with understanding. Read stories about fire engines; let a child push the vacuum cleaner; perhaps obtain a puppy for him to play with; explain all the wonders of a storm. No child should be deceived by anyone he trusts.

Baby's motor development. Average ages are given. Some babies progress more rapidly than others.

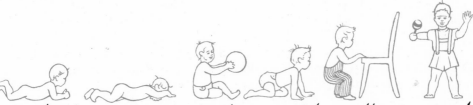

raises head ... *turns over* ...*sits alone*...*crawls*...*pulls up*... *stands*   257
3-4 mos.   *4-6 mos.*   *7-9 mos.*   *6-10 mos.* *10-11 mos.* *11-12 mos.*

H. Armstrong Roberts

Baby will learn to sit without support between seven and nine months. Forcing him to sit alone too early will be harmful.

Until the age of two, a child's emotions are still uncontrolled. Telling him to stop screaming or sobbing, or spanking him, is useless. His attention can be distracted easily with any new trinket or plaything.

When the child is a little older, anger can be controlled by keeping surroundings pleasant, regular meals and sleep, play time with Mother and Dad, and quietly talking to the child. A child needs to fight now and then to wear off bottled-up emotions or to gain a little self-confidence and independence.

Jealousy may begin to show when a new baby arrives. Parents should make every effort to make the older child feel important. Tell him you need him; let him help every way he can. He must not feel like an outsider. Jealousy is not limited to children! An adult can become jealous when a new member joins the staff (business, education, or industry) and receives extra attention.

Discipline Many people associate discipline with, "Spare the rod and spoil the child." Seldom does a spanking do much good. Frequently the child has not meant to do the thing he was spanked for. For instance, a child who breaks a piece of china feels very sorry. Understanding and sympathy may make him more careful than physical punishment.

Mature thinking, tact, and patience are needed for getting along with children, just as with adults. Firm but consistent handling is necessary; a parent cannot keep changing tactics, or the child will not know what is expected of him. Each child is different and must be treated as an individual, but here are a few basic rules which may help in many cases:

• Children react to simple requests and suggestions more quickly and willingly than to demands and commands.

• It is more tactful to say, "Please pick up the book and put it on the table," than to say, "Don't keep throwing your book on the floor." *Don'ts* and *No's,* however, are necessary sometimes because in the world outside the home they will be used.

• Children should realize that Dad is a loving friend and not just the "old man" who deals out allowances and discipline.

258

• Punishment must be associated with the act. It is very bad psychology to say, "Just wait till I tell your Dad." Both parents should agree on all forms of discipline. If discipline is necessary while Dad is away, Mother should know how to handle it.

• If a child is threatened with a spanking, deserves, and expects it for deliberately disobeying, it will clear the air to administer it. Never spank in anger without knowing all of the circumstances, or just to show that you are boss. These are signs of parental immaturity.

• Avoid frequent scolding, yelling, slapping, and nagging. These approaches make children nervous, and they may react by using the same approach with other children.

• Avoid using rewards for eating, or tasks that are part of everyone's family contribution. But, if rewards are promised, be sure to give them.

• Show approval for good behavior.

• When a child is old enough, he should be helped in making choices. At 6 a child begins to reason consciously, and by 9 he is a fairly reasonable person.

BABY'S GROWTH

A baby is a remarkable creature. At birth his heart is nearly twice as efficient as a grownup's. He has a natural immunity to many diseases during the first few months. The soft spot on his skull (fontanel) is covered with such a thick membrane that it is not extremely vulnerable even though it needs to be protected. At birth girls are usually shorter and weigh less than boys, but their bone structure is more fully developed. Girls develop more rapidly and, at 6, many are far ahead of boys of the same age. They may be able earlier to dress themselves, write, and do other things requiring muscular control.

For the first two or three months, every baby is largely occupied with eating and sleeping, but somewhere near the end of this time he will begin to turn his head in the direction of light or sound, and recognize faces.

The ages at which children roll over, sit alone, crawl, stand up, or walk vary greatly. A small, sturdy baby will do these things earlier than a heavy baby. Illness may retard a baby's motor development.

Most babies start to walk at about a year—some earlier and some later. When they become toddlers they are not babies anymore.

Massachusetts Mutual Life Insurance Company

259

Sitting up and Crawling   Between 7 and 9 months, usually, a baby can sit alone without falling. *Do not force it.* At this age, or even earlier, he should start getting accustomed to a play pen. After he begins to creep, it's too late.

Sometime between 6 and 10 months, a baby finds out how to get on all fours, rock, and finally crawl. However, some babies never creep before they start to stand and toddle.

Walking   Most babies start to walk alone between 12 and 15 months, although some start as early as 9, or as late as 18 months. *You do not have to teach a child to walk.* He will do so when he is ready. Walking barefoot strengthens a toddler's arches, but of course this must be avoided if the weather is cold, or ground surface rocky.

The baby's first year is the most difficult one of his entire life. There will never be another time with so many changes and such rapid growth.

Words and Phrases to Know

imbalance	obstetrician
immunity	pediatrician

ACTIVITIES

1. Compare the problems you and classmates have had in caring for children.

2. Conduct a class-by-class survey to find out how many in your school earn money baby sitting; how many hours they average a week; regular pay; extra pay for staying late; other chores expected; privileges granted; problems.

3. Show one or two pertinent films and discuss.

4. Talk with new mothers and tell the class how they provide for help with a new baby. List some of their problems.

5. Form *four* committees to investigate the cost of baby's (a) clothing; (b) bed and bedding; (c) bath items; (d) feeding equipment. Make a budget for a baby's needs.

6. Investigate the cost of diaper service for one year. Compare it with the cost of an automatic washer.

7. Talk with young mothers about introducing new foods and about inoculation schedules.

8. Discuss ways parents have solved such problems as poor eating habits, thumb sucking, nail biting, stuttering, and so on.

9. Investigate the cost of the inoculations listed.

10. Review the suggestions for disciplining children, and recall experiences in your own lives when discipline was justified and unjustified.

11. If you have records, compare your physical development, up to the time you began to walk, with others in the class.

Correlation

JOURNALISM: Publish the findings of the baby sitting survey in the school paper.

ENGLISH: Write a report on any important topic in the chapter, or write a brief biography of Dr. Benjamin Spock or Dr. Arnold Gesell.

SOCIOLOGY: Invite the sociology teacher to talk about the baby in other cultures.

Chapter 12

An Adult View of Children

It was pointed out in Chapter 2 that a child's physical characteristics, mentality, and disposition depend on both heredity and environment. Children, by nature, may be quiet or noisy, contented or peevish, small or large, leaders or followers. Yet all, to a certain degree, tend to follow an established behavior pattern as they pass from one age to another. The pattern is less noticeable in some than in others.

Dr. Arnold Gesell, and his associates Dr. Francis Ilg (pediatrician) and Dr. Louise Ames (psychologist) have studied the behavior patterns of many children from babyhood, through childhood, and into adulthood. They have concluded that "children follow well-defined growth patterns. . . and move from hill to valley to another hill. . . if a child is an angel at 2, swears at 4, obeys at 5 and lies at 6, he is probably just growing up in a normal way."

CASE STUDY: Aunt Jane, who had reared her last child a generation ago,

left her niece's home with very definite opinions of the four children. She liked Peggy and David, but declared to friends, "If I had anything to do with it I'd straighten out Sue and Tommy in a hurry!"

Sue was 2½ and a little tyrant. Tommy was 11—untamed, stubborn, bored with everything. Peggy was 5— reasonable, co-operative, and interested in all kinds of play. Davey was 7 and Aunt Jane's favorite because he was so anxious to please, liked to read and ask questions.

What Aunt Jane did not remember was that at different ages, children go through cycles of being friendly or rebellious, close or distant. Up to adulthood children tend to follow a certain rhythm. Elementary teachers will agree that discipline is more difficult in some grades than in others.

TODDLER AND CLIMBER—1 TO 2

Between 1 and 2 a child is an explorer, seemingly indifferent to dan-

H. Armstrong Roberts

A toddler needs constant watching.

In the first place a toddler is just beginning to explore a whole new world and he has not had any previous experience to connect touching a pan handle with getting scalded, or poking a bobby pin into an electric outlet with getting a shock. Parents should keep pan handles turned, and exposed outlets covered with tape. A child will, no doubt, learn a few things the hard way, because no parent can anticipate everything. When a child does break or spill something, it is best not to shout or scold, but to comfort quietly, repair the damage, and help the child take pride in keeping things in their places. Scolding only makes a child tense and nervous.

In the second place, "No" is poor psychology when used constantly. The understanding young adult will divert a child's attention. Having several baskets of toys and changing them every few days keeps a child's mind on his own possessions. The kitchen is the favorite place for activity but also the room in which most accidents occur. A child will enjoy his own low drawer or shelf in the kitchen with pots, pans, lids, and spoons that are safe.

About the time a baby begins to walk, he will begin to make a few meaningful sounds — mama, da-da, bye-bye, and no. A few toddlers have a fairly large vocabulary at eighteen months. Between 2 and 3, words begin to come rapidly—nouns, pronouns, verbs, and adjectives. If a child is slow talking, a parent should conceal his apprehension. Overanxiety or constant criticism can retard speech. Many children who do not begin to talk until they are 3 may turn out to be just as bright as those who talk earlier.

ger. Shock or startling noise will frighten him; but he might crawl onto a sixth floor window ledge and think nothing of it. During the toddler stage, keep all medicine cabinets locked and razors or nail scissors in a safe place. An ambitious toddler can climb from floor to toilet seat, to bowl, to medicine cabinet in seconds. Keep all harsh cleansers out of reach or under lock. Place lamp cords behind tables. Keep fine china, paint, perfume, pins, buttons, lipstick, and bric-a-brac out of reach.

Some mothers tie a *tiny bell* to the back of a child's garment so he may be heard as he wanders. *Gates* at top and bottom of steps are recommended. See that screens are secure and windows closed.

Have you heard your grandmother say, "When my children were toddlers and into everything, I was mighty strict. When I said, 'No, don't touch,' they knew what I meant."

At 2, baby may be mama's little angel, but in six short months he can become a little emperor. At 2, the goals of babyhood have been met. He has learned to get around, and to ask for what he wants by motions, single words, or perhaps whole sentences. He can eat alone, go to the toilet, and travel about. For a time he is at peace with the world—lovable, affectionate, well adjusted. But soon his emotions begin to show.

At 2½ Junior may be a young Napoleon—demanding and unreasonable. He may insist upon having something one minute, and throw it away the next. The more he has been warned No! No! the more he begins to use "No" as his own response to requests.

Two-and-a-Half does not like to go to bed. He demands the same story every night, and he can tell you if you omit one little thing. He gets along better with one parent at a time—usually Mother.

H. Armstrong Roberts

At 2 a child is usually very affectionate.

Two-and-a-Half is not ready to make choices. Use the *subtle* approach to get things done — "It's time to," "Let's," "How about." Silent strategy gets more things accomplished than force or reason.

By the time he is 2½, a child usually has begun to assert his independence, and may show some signs of aggressiveness.

H. Armstrong Roberts

263

Three years is about the age when children start to help Mother. Newly discovered abilities can have a calming effect on *Three's* disposition.

Spankings may clear the air for a while, but they seem to do little if any real good. A spanking should not be used as a threat. If it seems to be the best solution, it should be administered and associated with the act of misbehaving. Parents should never spank just to relieve their own anger.

Two-and-a-Half is a little young for nursery school, but he will begin to learn social give-and-take by associating with brothers, sisters, or neighborhood playmates.

Sullenness and fears may become more pronounced at 3½.

In showing mental progress, he should be able to place round, square, and triangular blocks into their proper holes without trial and error.

RUNABOUT—3 TO 4

This is an age of exploration and adventure. The child can ride a tricycle, run errands, manipulate crayons, and put away his own toys. He can dress, undress, and hang up clothes if hooks are within reach. With help, he can wash his hands, eat and drink without spilling food.

The urge to grow up is strong. Children often overexert and become nervous or get hurt. They still need close watching and often cry around strangers. See that such an approach is made gradually, quietly, and without forcing the child to be friendly.

At 3 the little emperor changes to mother's little helper. It is not such a rough world after all, and calm prevails. He is more nearly master of his emotions. *Yes* becomes a part of his vocabulary.

264

You can get *Three* to co-operate by saying, "If you get a bath early, we'll have time for a longer story." *Three* tends to wander at night to the bathroom, refrigerator, or parents' bedroom. Some parents tack a tiny bell high on the child's door so they can be alerted. Screens on bedroom windows should be very secure because *Three* is curious and still unaware of many kinds of danger.

This is a "me-too" age. The trait may be utilized in having *Three* copy good habits of older brothers or sisters. At 3 a child may gain a great deal from nursery school.

Three-and-a-Half may begin to feel insecure again and build up fears— fear of the dark, of dogs, of thunder, lightning, and sirens. He may show insecurity by blinking, occasionally crossing his eyes, pulling at his parents' clothing, and in other ways.

If these traits appear, try to find the cause. The child may need only more rest, a snack between meals, more companionship or activity. If he is afraid of the dark, leave a night light burning. Avoid violent television programs and stories, because *Three-and-a-Half* is even more confused about real life and make-believe than some of us adults!

At 3½, a child begins to appreciate his father and will enjoy play periods with Dad rather than being pushed aside to amuse himself. At this age, boys and girls begin to ask questions about physical differences.

THE "WHY" AGE—4 TO 5

Four becomes curious again. He may decide one day to kick over the traces and leave home. He lives in a

Chevrolet

Four's imagination colors many of his activities. It will show in his games, and perhaps in simple desires for adventure.

world of make-believe, and craves to play with other children. He kicks, hits, throws, pouts, laughs in a silly sort of way, and makes all kinds of annoying sounds. *Four* may become defiant, boastful, or even tell lies. He exaggerates to display his imagination, tells stories, true and false. He may even believe some of the things he makes up.

It takes an ingenious person to keep a step ahead of *Four*. The best advice is, "If you can't lick 'em, learn to live with 'em." Take advantage of *Four's* world of make-believe and adventure. "Let's pretend we're beavers and pile up all the blocks like a dam." "I'll bet I can count ten before you brush your teeth." This approach is more successful than a "You-do-it-or-else" threat.

As a child approaches 4½, he may become even more confused about the reality of TV programs and stories. At 4½ boys have nearly caught up with girls in motor and mental abilities. Both are ready to start on the road to greater mental activity, and

265

Simoniz Company

Five is a joyous age for many children. Behavior problems tend to be less frequent because the child understands better than he did earlier, yet does not usually have the rebellious feelings which may come later.

may take to nursery school like a duck to water. If *Four-and-a-Half* is shown three or four objects and turns his back while one is removed, he should be able to tell which one is missing.

THE JOYFUL AGE—5 TO 6

At 5, boys and girls have once more adjusted temporarily to their emotional goals — and it's a wonderful world again. *Five* may enjoy staying near home, co-operating, and showing his skills and talents. At 5, personality is marked, potentials for intelligence show up. A 5-year-old is usually farsighted, and should be discouraged from activities which strain the eyes. *Five* enjoys stories about things around him—trucks, airplanes, steam shovels. He likes to tell stories about happenings at home.

Five has good muscular control but, unless he is watched, he will not stand or sit straight. A boy's height usually will be between 37 and 43 inches and a girl's 36 to 44 inches. Growth begins to slow down.

Five likes rhythmic music, blowing bubbles, and listening to hero stories. He may enjoy one playmate more

than two. He can be reasonable about taking turns, and can enter more into table conversation or help Mother and Dad. He may tire quickly, so he should have a rest period alone sometime in the afternoon. He may not take a nap, but will benefit from quiet periods.

CHILDREN'S PLAY

Children outgrow playthings just as they outgrow clothes. Needs change. If playthings are too simple, they are boring, and if they are too difficult they discourage a child. There are four basic types of play: active, creative, dramatic, and social.

Wheel toys, gym equipment, swings, and ballgames provide *active* play. Building and art materials, hobbies and handcrafts furnish *creative* play. Games and toys that lead the child to imitate grownups supply a basic need for *dramatic* play — cowboy, doctor, Indian outfits, play stores, houses, and airports. Group games of all kinds—table games, dancing, and playground activities — encourage *social* development.

Blocks and pull toys are popular with children between 1 and 2.

Toy Manufacturers of the U.S.A., Inc.

Children enjoy making their own games and toys from boards, string, clothes pins, and other odds and ends. This encourages good creative initiative.

Families often shower children with gifts they are too young or too old to enjoy. The following chart suggests toys and games for children at various ages.

From an early age children enjoy playground equipment. Supervision is most important for the younger child.

National Cotton Council

TOYS FOR CHILDREN 1 TO 6 YEARS*

Boy and Girl 1 to 3	Boy and Girl 3 to 4
Rocking horse Hammer set Cuddly animals Pull toys—trains, trucks Blocks Wagon with blocks Bathtub toys Knock-down toys Strings of large beads	Tricycle Drum and sticks Large truck Large stuffed animals Cars, trains to ride Noah's ark, circus set Peg boards Slide Large picture books Finger paint, modeling clay

Boy 4 to 6	Boy and Girl 4 to 6	Girl 4 to 6
Space-man, cowboy, bandit outfits Wagons Ladders Tool sets Beginners' baseball Large trucks	Creative painting Modeling clay Puzzles Large creative blocks Jungle gym Skates Stilts See-saw Cut-and-paste sets Scooters Bicycle	Items for playing store Articles for playing mother or nurse Dolls and dresses Miniature table and tea sets Imitation carpet sweepers Jump ropes Doll carriage

*Games and activities for older children are discussed under the different ages.

Starting to school is a big change. If *Six* is moody and irritable, it may reflect his slowness in adapting to this new experience.

TRANSITION PERIOD—6 TO 7

The transition from home to school may be easier if a child has gone to kindergarten. Dr. Gesell claims that a great deal of harm is done by starting children to school too early; usually a boy is not ready to concentrate on schoolwork until 7 and a girl until 6½.

Between 6 and 7 the world may seem upside down again. It is an age of turmoil. Life ceases to center around the home, and often Mother is the object of *Six's* resentfulness. Dad may be able to help more than Mother.

At 6 children differ greatly in size, so that too much may be expected of one who is large for his age. Maturity will depend more upon the home and community environment than upon physical growth.

Six is restless—he shuffles his feet, screws up his face when he draws, and throws his arms about. He needs a great deal of activity to work off energy. Pulling wagons, climbing, and ballgames are good. Group activities become popular in the first grade.

Six is moody, may like a fight. If asked to do something he may reply, "No, I won't, and you can't make me!" Yet he resents criticism, blame, or punishment. He may cheat, steal, or cry if he loses a contest, *or* if a companion wins praise and approval, and he does not. Cheating and stealing should be brought out in the open and discussed frankly — the reasons and consequences.

At 6 the best advice to parents is, "Grin and bear it—this, too, will pass." *Six* responds better if met on adult terms in a friendly, matter-of-fact, but positive way. He does not like to be treated as a second-rate human being.

Six delights in receiving praise, and being given small responsibilities. He likes to collect things. He loves Mother and Dad, but he does not like to be kissed in public. He likes gangs, may protest music lessons.

At 6 a child may have a vocabulary of 2,500 words. He knows the value of common coins; can count to ten

From 6 on, children like more challenging playthings.

Eli Lilly and Company

Seven still may be moody at times, but he is usually anxious to please, and becomes absorbed in many activities.

detoured often. He needs constant re-assurance and soft-spoken reminders. He wants to know how things work. Do not impose on his eagerness to please. He tires easily and needs as much as eleven hours sleep per day. He may develop nervous habits. *Seven* can count coins, and may be started on an allowance. On mental tests he can tell what is wrong with an absurd picture such as a man pouring milk into a wastebasket. He is becoming more aware of sex differences.

You should sympathize with *Seven*, but avoid taking his problems too seriously. Take care not to turn religious training entirely into "busy work," such as pasting cutouts and making posters. Head him toward knowing the ideas of your church, and participating in the activities.

and give his full address; is learning to read and to doubt the existence of Santa Claus. Religious convictions should be taking form. Keep such training simple. Vague talk will be wasted.

AGE OF ABSORPTION—7 TO 8

Seven is much more cautious than *Six*, withdraws more from the family, becomes more absorbed in his own activities. He has his good and bad days. He tends to choose friends and to notice the difference between his home and the homes of others.

He may say, "I wish I was dead." He will stand up for his just rights, and should be encouraged to do so. He craves adult approval, may tattle on his friends to win it. Listen to him, but don't reward him for tattling. He likes to be first and best. He gives in more readily than *Six* to adult authority.

Seven may worry about being late for school, winning his teacher's approval, and getting homework done. He means to obey, but seems to get

HAZARDOUS AGE—8 TO 9

Eight wants to appear grown-up but does not feel that way *inside*. He likes to give and take but he likes to take more than give. New tasks are begun with enthusiasm, yet tears come readily if success is not achieved.

Eight is full of life—most susceptible to accidents. Parents may enjoy a good give-and-take relationship with *Eight*.

Del Monte Foods

269

H. Armstrong Roberts

Nine has a growing awareness of the world. He tends to like competitive games, but school work may worry him.

Eight enjoys a chum or best friend, although the two may quarrel and call each other names. Boys enjoy boys and girls enjoy girls. *Eight* will argue about doing tasks but finally obey with, "Well, if I have to." He likes to feel his worth by running errands, cutting grass, and washing dishes for pay, or having an allowance related to work.

Baseball and football may interest an eight-year-old boy, but he needs adult leadership. Girls want and need a close relationship with their mothers. Both boys and girls enjoy group games. It is a peak age for TV, comics, competitive games in arithmetic or spelling. Girls like paper dolls. *Eight* can tell time and relate dates. He likes fairy tales and stories about people in other countries. This is a good time to start permanent collections of anything that interests the child.

You should discourage him from attempting too much, and not be too critical of failures. Be sure that his religious training is supported by family participation, rather than leaving everything to outside leaders—if you wish him to grow religiously.

AGE OF CONCENTRATION— 9 TO 10

Nine tends to withdraw and live within himself, but distinctions in personality begin to strengthen.

At 9 a child is more interested in friends a year or two older, than a year or two younger. In many ways nine is a wonderful age, dependable and reasonable. At 9, a child may be skillful with his hands, and can spend longer periods in concentration.

Many children at 9 read as well as an adult. This is a good year to encourage reading, and, if a child is not reading well, to take him to a reading clinic. For most children, being held back in school now does more harm than at any other time. *Nine* likes to read about people, adventure, and travel; comics reach a peak in popularity. He likes clubs, gangs, and friendships. Small babies hold a fascination for these boys and girls.

Nine can spend many hours on puzzles, collections, bead looms, construction and chemistry sets, tools and handcrafts, working hard to perfect a skill. Boys like to box and wrestle. Girls enjoy roller skating, jacks, and jumping rope.

From nervous causes, *Nine* may twitch, blink, sniffle, or shrug his shoulders. He may complain that his eyes hurt if he doesn't want to study, that his hands hurt if asked to practice the piano, or that his stomach aches if he doesn't want to help at home. When parents are overly strict or tense, *Nine* may become more nervous, yet keep his feelings bottled up because in most families he has been trained not to talk back.

Nine enjoys clubs and gangs, so being identified with a group is very important. At 9 children often have their first experiences away from home at a camp. Boys and girls develop different reading interests and many children will begin to show enthusiasm for some special field.

Avoid bossing or criticizing *Nine* too much or probing too far into his affairs. Encourage him in any wholesome hobbies or interests he develops, because his improving mind needs "feeding" now.

THE FRIENDLY AGE—10 TO 11

Ten is friendly and willing to share his possessions. He worries less, usually likes school, but does not seek lavish praise. Parents attain a new role, and even brothers and sisters may be respected. It will pay dividends later if Dad will take time to enjoy *Ten* on hikes, picnics, fishing trips, or any other activity. Ten loves "corny" jokes, and laughs at his own jokes regardless of the point.

Ten is concerned about right and wrong, and puzzled about sex. If possible, *Ten* should have a room to himself. This is a good time for educational TV programs and simple literature about the birth of a baby. Biographies, mystery, adventure, horse stories hold a real interest for a boy.

Clubs, scouting, collecting as a hobby, and using strange passwords and mottoes are part of *Ten's* world. Most girls and some boys like to be consulted about clothes and help select them.

Enjoy *Ten* and be reasonable about scheduling duties, meals, or baths that might interfere with his strongest interests.

PRE-ADOLESCENCE—11 TO 13

From 11 to 13 physical differences between children of the same age become more marked. Some girls may begin to mature even before eleven. Boys mature later.

The interests of boys and girls are

Ten's activities are varied. Dad and Mother can take a larger part in the child's interests than ever before. Collecting things is a popular pastime.

H. Armstrong Roberts

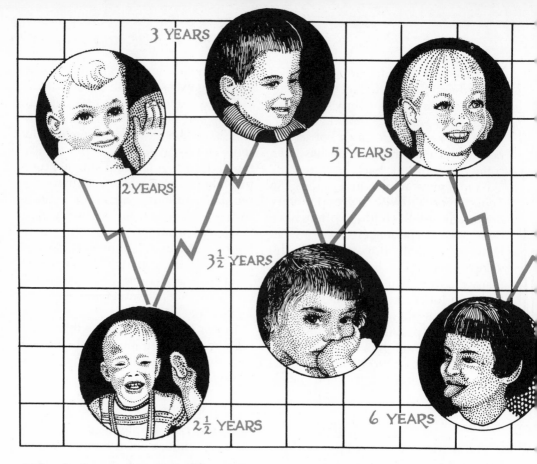

3 YEARS

2 YEARS

5 YEARS

$3\frac{1}{2}$ YEARS

$2\frac{1}{2}$ YEARS

6 YEARS

at the farthest poles. Girls like quiet activities, boys very active ones. Girls are becoming aware of boys, but boys *seem* oblivious to girls. Group identification is important to both sexes, and skills in sports, sewing, art, and music are becoming noticeable.

Pre-adolescence is an age of disorganization when urges to show inde-

Eleven lives in a world of competition.

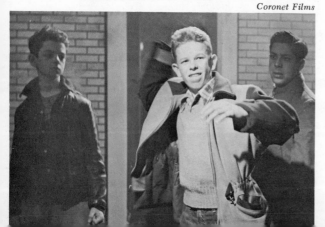

At some ages children are better adjusted to their surroundings than at others.

pendence becomes strong and restrictions are difficult to take. Teens, on the verge of maturity, need parent understanding — an opportunity to gain independence, approval of their desire to dress and be like the gang. They need wholesome homelife and social acceptance.

Although behavior patterns vary more during pre-adolescent years than earlier, a large majority still shows typical behavior patterns.

Eleven's world is topsy-turvy again and many undesirable traits may pop up. He may argue, act rude, and become jealous at home, but he can be an angel away from home. It is a

272

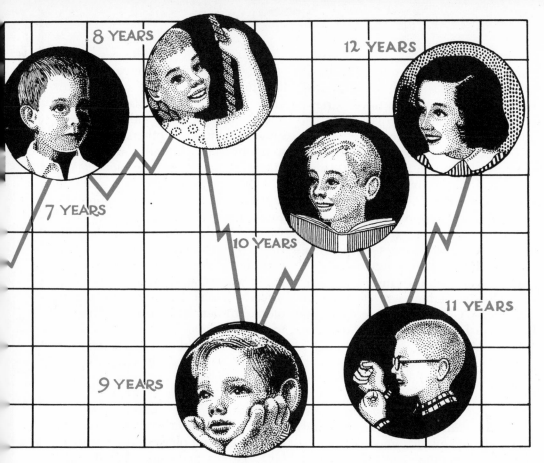

period of, "Other kids do it, why can't I?" and of wanting to disagree with habit patterns at home and in school.

TV programs may lose some of their importance, but radio music or records usually accompany the doing of homework. Movies become more interesting and many 11-year-olds enjoy the pictures and some of the simpler stories in adult magazines *Life, National Geographic, The Saturday Evening Post,* and others.

Eleven wants to know more about religion, but standard group study may not satisfy his need for personal investigation. He likes people — parents who make few but wise demands; teachers who are challenging and firm but not domineering. He likes team games. This year a child may want to

skip classes often. Physical changes are taking place within, which influence emotions.

This is a good time to show selected

At 12, girls often are ready to associate with the opposite sex. Boys generally still prefer companionship with other boys, but their awareness of girls is growing.

Elliott Erwitt, Magnum Photos

273

movies on sex. Boys and girls are at an age to watch such films and discuss them. It is advisable to have parents see the same films so that they can answer further questions.

Twelve typically is warm and bubbling, uninhibited, extremely solicitous, and tactful, but at this age lots of rest is needed.

As puberty approaches, a child tends to want more time alone. He may show a new concern for parents, a more adult sense of politeness.

Hero worship and crushes are evident. Kissing games will be popular with some. Girls *seem* more aware of boys than boys do of girls. Girls also may be self-conscious if they are taller than boys of the same age, as they often are. *Twelve* favors group activities such as picnics and camping. Boys and girls enjoy tennis, skating, and horseback riding. Boys like to build radios, model planes and cars. Girls also like to do things with their hands —cook, sew, and paint.

At 12, a girl likes plenty of time to prepare for bed; both boys and girls may dream they are heroes. *Twelve* enjoys watching adults at any kind of interesting job. He wants to know more about religion, moral codes, and sex.

Twelve worries about irregular home situations, is critical of parents and teachers, but will work hard if he likes them. Delinquency may begin at 12 if a child is insecure or too idle.

Although *Twelve* is usually happy, he is headed toward the turbulent teens. From 13 to 16, he has many problems; parent sympathy and understanding are essential. At 16 there may be another period of security.

Although certain behavior patterns are followed, no two children are alike. Some are responsible, others are not; some sociable, others distant; some ambitious, others apathetic; some are self-centered and stubborn; others outgoing and affable.

As a rule, the oldest child in a family receives the most discipline, because his parents are inexperienced yet very dedicated to doing the right thing. The oldest child may go to two extremes—take too much responsibility or not enough. Younger children often will secretly or openly admire older brothers and sisters, and want to be like them.

Parents should avoid making comparisons among children, either in their presence or in the presence of others, unless the comparisons are pleasant. If parents appreciate the differences in children's personalities and understand the phases of growing up, both parents and children will enjoy happier family relationships.

WHAT TO DO ABOUT AN ALLOWANCE

Although there is disagreement as to the best age to start an allowance, child experts agree on one thing—an allowance should be based upon *need* and not given as a *reward* or withheld as punishment. As needs increase, allowances should be increased. This may be necessary every year or two.

Ages
6-8   When a child starts to school he will appreciate having an allowance. In starting an allowance there should be some understanding as to what it is to cover.

Parents should try to guide spending but not be dictatorial or critical about how money is spent.

At six most children need no more than thirty-five cents a week for sweets, comic books, and simple toys. The amount may be increased to sixty-five cents by age eight when more money is needed for special hobbies. Even in these early years a child can gain valuable experience in the handling of money.

Ages 9-11 During this age allowances will vary considerably according to locality, family social and financial status, and the child's interests. Money is needed to pay for sweets, magazines, hobbies, sports equipment, tickets to movies, and school activities. It is advisable to have children at this age help to determine their money needs.

It may surprise you to learn that some grade school children have charge accounts. However, this practice is not recommended. Neither is it a good idea to deduct a large portion of the allowance because of poor grades or to pay for items accidentally damaged in the home. It is a good idea to have children of this age help with simple housework or yard chores whether or not it is in exchange for pay.

Ages 12-14 During this period money needs increase. It is impossible to say how large an allowance should be. This will depend in part on the community and the type of entertainment available there. Money will also be needed for grooming aids, gifts for friends and family, and school supplies.

By this time many young people have a clothing allowance. Under this arrangement clothing costs should be averaged because needs are seasonal. In other words, a person does not spend the same amount each month on clothing. When major purchases are needed, the money should be "borrowed" from the allowance for future months when clothing needs will be light. Here again the allowance is an individual problem that must be worked out between the teen-ager and parents.

Ages 15-18 A poll of 500 high school students in a large eastern city showed that they were earning money in over fifty different ways. Their jobs included baby sitting, lawn mowing, house cleaning, repair services, and even raising pets for sale. Some energetic students earned $20 a week at odd jobs.

The emphasis upon getting into college has led some parents to offer their children financial rewards for high grades. In fact, a number of psychologists have indicated that a bright teen-ager represents a family status symbol; such a student may use scholastic achievement to bargain for a higher allowance. What do you think of this practice? Should parents place this type of value on school status? Should students seek money for improving their own minds?

To make good decisions about money you must have a sound sense of values. Will the things you want now help you reach your long-range goals? Usually there is a good way to get what you want without causing your family to sacrifice, *provided that your wants are reasonable.*

275

1. Observe the children in your own family, or those of relatives or neighbors. Make notes, and come to class prepared to discuss your observations. Which traits appealed to you? Which annoyed you?

2. Do you know of any children who are suffering from lack of affectionate care, or are overshadowed by their brothers or sisters? How would you feel toward a child who is an ugly duckling, crippled, deaf, or blind? Discuss.

3. Divide the class into three groups and observe children in a *nursery school, kindergarten,* and *first grade.* Take notes on the size of the class, how children play, what stories they like to hear, how they co-operate, and how the teacher handles problems. After separate group discussions out of class, appoint a chairman for each group to give a class report. Do you notice many differences from age to age? How do behavior patterns of the children compare with patterns given in the text?

4. Talk with teachers in elementary school and find out the ages at which discipline is most difficult. Compare your findings with behavior patterns in the text.

5. If there are any nursery schools for crippled, deaf, or blind children in your community, observe these children and compare their behavior patterns with those of normal children of the same age.

6. Discuss the following statements:
• You can reason with any child at any age.
• There is never any excuse to spank a child.
• Discipline is the father's responsibility.
• Children should be required to put away toys at bedtime.
• A child should not be punished for thumb sucking, nail biting, bed wetting, or stuttering.
• Punishment is in order when a child insists upon striking matches.
Name some other common ways that children misbehave and discuss suitable kinds of punishment.

7. Conduct a panel on child behavior for a PTA meeting.

8. Assemble toys, grouped under *active, creative, dramatic, social,* for kindergarten and first grade children. A local store will probably co-operate.

9. Arrange a display of books for different grades. Teachers and the librarian will help.

10. Sponsor a contest for making safe and useful games. Arrange an exhibit and award ribbons for the most original, most attractive, etc.

11. Discuss your own experience as you approached adolescence.

Correlation

ELEMENTARY SCHOOL: Arrange to set up some toy exhibits in an elementary school to be viewed before or after a PTA meeting. The panel on child behavior may be conducted at the same time.

Invite an elementary school principal to give a talk on children's behavior and special discipline problems at different ages.

Make a list of action games such as "London Bridge," and if possible, volunteer to help with nursery school or kindergarten classes during your free period for a week.

Home Experiences

Use some of the suggestions in the text for dealing with children. Report to class.

Chapter 13

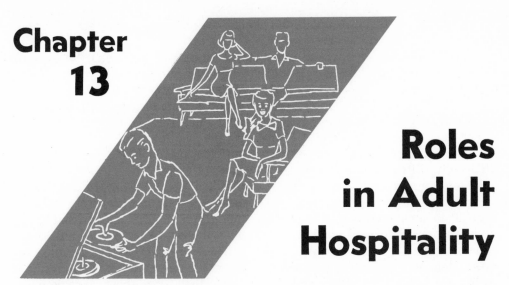

Roles in Adult Hospitality

Hospitality is something anyone can offer, because it is based upon a sincere interest in making people feel welcome. In extending hospitality, it is the spirit that counts—not the desire to make a display.

HOSPITALITY COMES FROM THE HEART

Money, household servants, and fine table appointments do not, in themselves, mean hospitality. Hospitality may be warmly given and received by serving inexpensive snacks at a simple card party.

When hospitality comes from the heart, anyone can be as gracious as a king and queen. Sometimes we are self-conscious about entertaining others of better means, or we think we are too busy to make a big effort needed to entertain. Entertaining can be simple. There are few things more pleasant than sharing a few congenial hours in the home of friends. When people visit foreign countries, they feel as if their visit has been more complete if they have had a chance to share in the hospitality of a home. In our country, too, hospitality is a cherished tradition.

CASE STUDY: Students from seven or eight large cities were attending a crafts workshop in the North Carolina mountains several summers ago. One afternoon, Mrs. Bernice Evans, a gracious but not well-to-do widow in her seventies, invited the group to have tea at her small cottage. Everyone accepted with enthusiasm, yet wondering what to expect.

The white-washed frame dwelling with red rambler roses covering the picket fence looked like something out of a fairy story. Her hand-hooked rugs, handmade quilts and skillfully tended plants in the windows gave her home an individual charm.

The tantalizing odor of hot gingerbread came from the kitchen. As Mrs. Evans greeted her guests, she made them feel as if just being there was a wonderful experience. While the visitors chatted on the porch she served cold buttermilk and fresh milk from the spring house, and hot ginger-

277

bread on crazed china plates. Of course, she made no apology for the smallness of the place. That would have detracted from her self-confidence and charm. Some people apologize, when inwardly they are seeking praise. The atmosphere that afternoon was alive with warmth and friendliness. The memory of the visit in its exquisite setting lingered with everyone present.

It is far better to entertain graciously in your own way than to try to *imitate* or *outdo* another. When you plan entertaining that involves more work than you can manage comfortably, you become too tired and nervous to enjoy your guests. On the other hand, don't be too casual about entertaining; the best things take interest and effort.

SUCCESSFUL ENTERTAINING TAKES PLANNING

Having the crowd in for soft drinks, snacks, and records or dancing may not require as much planning as a dinner or barbecue, but previous planning will always help make the party. A little extra attention on a dinner for two—candlelight, music, and a party dress make an ordinary dinner at home something special.

Setting for two by candlelight turns an ordinary evening into a gala occasion.

Consolidated Trimming Corporation

To quote the opera star, Blanche Thebom: "When you entertain, give a little of yourself—you'll have much more fun and so will your guests." When you spend all day cooking a meal that is consumed in less than an hour, you may wonder if it is worth the effort. But part of the fun is in anticipating, planning, and knowing that you have done a job well.

When you plan a dance or party at school, isn't getting ready often as much fun as the event itself? You have more fun and so do all others.

There are two kinds of people who might be better off not entertaining at all—the couple that makes no effort and the couple that is simply paying off an obligation. Let's call the former Mr. and Mrs. Casual and the latter Mr. and Mrs. Grippe.

CASE STUDY: The Casuals enjoy people but are lazy and admit it. They invite another young couple in for the evening, saying, "Come on over. We'd love to see you . . .No, we won't go to any trouble!"

When the guests arrive Mrs. Casual may still be washing noon dishes and Mr. Casual may be working in the garden. Neither goes to the trouble of changing clothes. After a few remarks they may remember their favorite TV programs and without consulting their guests, lead the way to the living room and turn on television, leaving the others to shift for themselves.

For snacks, Mrs. Casual suggests: "Help yourselves out of the refrigerator—we don't go for formality around here." No entertainment has been planned, so the men wander into the garden and the wives talk. The "party" breaks up early, of course.

278

This case may be slightly exaggerated but there are such people. It is not necessary to "knock yourself out" to be hospitable, but it is no compliment to your guests to be utterly casual. What do you think?

CASE STUDY: Mrs. Grippe does not really enjoy people; any extra work, although she may do it well, seems to be a burden. Her husband phones home in the morning, explaining that he is obligated to entertain a certain businessman. "Shall I bring him home or eat downtown?" Mrs. Grippe replies, "You know we can't afford *not* to entertain your best accounts. What choice do I have! Bring him on home!" She may bang down the phone loudly enough to be heard by both men at the other end.

She complains to herself all the time she is cooking and cleaning the house. Still, she makes elaborate preparations, invites extra guests, and serves lavishly. Then she acts over-apologetic for what is really fine food. Her husband and guests feel ill at ease. The card party she has arranged is spoiled by the way she makes excuses for every detail that isn't perfect. No one enjoys himself.

Unless we entertain graciously, find pleasure in it, and make guests feel welcome, an obligation had better be forgotten.

Most of you have helped with entertaining at home. However, you may need a few reminders to make it easier, better, and less work for your parents. Later you will want to remember these suggestions if you have a stag party or invite several couples to your apartment; or if you have a shower or dinner party. When you marry and entertain friends in your

Towle Silversmiths

Setting for a buffet supper. Salad and a casserole dish make a simple, satisfying meal.

home the following suggestions will be especially useful.

Inviting Guests No more guests should be invited at one time than you can take care of with ease— as far as your own personal strength and facilities are concerned. Invite your guests in person, by phone, or written invitation. Be sure to make clear the date and time. Invite persons you know will be congenial with all the others who will be present.

Setting the Stage Plan where you will have the party; note the food you will serve, decorations, and other appointments you will need, and what you will do to entertain your guests. Provide a place for wraps and sometimes umbrellas or overshoes. The bathroom should be in order, including fresh towels. Having a good selection of records on hand helps any kind of party—for background music, listening, or perhaps dancing.

Preparing and Serving Food Finger foods, paper cups, and paper napkins may suffice for some parties, and save dishwashing.

279

Children practice hospitality by asking friends in to play. This mother knows how to supervise without interfering.

Refreshments served in little baskets or attractively decorated boxes add interest and variety. If bottled drinks, cups, or glasses are served with plates, you will need individual tables or lap trays. Prepare ahead of time all food that will not lose flavor or good appearance. Arrange with friends to help serve. Set out plates, silver, bowls, and other things you will need, so that neither host nor hostess need be away from guests for very long.

Receiving Guests The host or hostess should receive guests as they arrive; refrain from monopolizing the party; help to make shy guests feel at ease. If congenial persons have been invited and the "stage" well set, the host and hostess may enjoy the evening as much as anyone.

While you are still entertaining at your parents' home, you will show wisdom as well as good manners to have an older person somewhere in the house, until you are out of high school. Guests enjoy chatting with parents for a few minutes. However, the sensible parent does not intrude

on the fun, even though Mother can be of much help.

If guests do not seem to know when to go home, you may have to use tact. You can say, "Dad says the curfew's at twelve." When you have a home of your own you may look at your watch and comment, "How fast the evening has gone," hoping guests will take a hint. Some people do not know how to leave without help. On the other hand, do not insist that everyone remain, just because you want them to. Be sensitive to the group's desires about going home.

Tidying up No matter where you entertain, there is always cleaning up to do. Some of your close friends should offer to help, unless you prefer otherwise. You or your mother will feel better if the house is in order, even if dishes are simply stacked in the sink to be washed next morning. When you have your own home handle these matters as you wish, unless it causes arguments.

Food Ideas for Special Occasions Almost anytime you have guests in your home, it will be an occasion for serving food. Whether the situation calls for formal entertaining or just a snack, you will enjoy knowing you have served the appropriate foods, and served them well.

BARBECUE: This is where men often excel as chefs. With paper plates and cups, very little dishwashing is involved, so the girls really get a break. Grilled hamburgers, hotdogs, meat kabobs, plus finger salads are favorite choices. For heavy eaters, potato salad or baked beans may be added. A tray of fruit, assorted tarts from the bakery, or homemade cake can finish off the meal. When you barbecue, use charcoal and trim most of the fat off meat to reduce smoke.

BUFFET SUPPER: A buffet supper is an easy, informal way to entertain. A meat, poultry, or fish casserole, salad, some kind of bread, and dessert may all be prepared in advance. Cold cuts and molded salads are nice in warm weather. Card tables may be set up with silver, cups, and saucers, *or* all these items may be picked up at the buffet table. Lap trays may be used in place of tables for a large party.

PICNIC: Picnic food is often cold, with one hot dish. Most of it may be eaten with the fingers. Many young adults like to pack a picnic basket for a swimming, boating, hiking, or fishing party. You can have a simple picnic with two kinds of bread, canned meats and spreads, a beverage, and fruit. Add personal favorites according to the time you have for preparation.

LUNCHEON: Luncheon may be served on table mats on the dining room table, or card tables. Fruit salad and cold meat *or* a generous fish or chicken salad and spiced fruit may be served on the same plate and placed on the table before guests are called. Prepared rolls or bread eliminates a lot of work, if time is important. Parsley, pimiento, or a cherry adds eye appeal. Any dessert is appropriate except a repetition of the main course. For instance, do not serve a fruit dessert with a fruit salad or spiced fruit.

BRUNCH: This is a meal often served on holidays to combine breakfast and lunch. Serve fruit juice from a tray, rolls in a basket, coffee from a carafé, to add individuality to the meal.

INFORMAL GET-TOGETHER: After a game, movie, or informal dance, it's fun to have the crowd in for snacks and records. Bottled drinks, or punch, with potato chips and a dip, pretzels, crackers, cheese, and cookies are always popular. For something heavier, serve buns from a basket with cold cuts, spreads, and cup cakes arranged

Setting for guest luncheon or informal dinner.

Towle Silversmiths

attractively on platters or trays. An appropriate centerpiece adds interest. You may have had experience with this kind of entertaining.

OPEN HOUSE: Open house is popular after the prom and during the holiday season. Individual invitations may be issued or a group of people—club or class—may be invited. The awkward thing about an open house is the uncertainty of requirements, but leftovers are always enjoyed by the family.

Food is similar to that served at an informal get-together, if it is for the school crowd. If the open house is a little more formal, a variety of sandwiches, cookies, tiny iced tea cakes, nuts, and mints makes an attractive table, and tastes good. For a more elaborate affair, serve shrimp, deviled eggs, sliced ham and turkey, moulded salads, and tiny rolls with beverages.

TEA: Tea is served any time between three and six. An announcement party or a party to honor a special guest may take the form of a tea. Teas are more popular with women than with men. A simple tea may be served from a tray in the living room. It may consist of tea and strips of cinnamon toast, or may be similar to the open house, with an attractive centerpiece and cloth or small, decorative paper napkins. The more formal the open house or tea, the more elaborate must be the tablecloth, china, silver, and centerpiece.

COFFEE: Many young married women prefer something less formal than a tea, such as coffee between 10 and 11:30 in the morning while children are in school. This is a nice time for neighbors and friends to get together for a chat. A simple service may consist of coffee and sweet rolls. A tablecloth and centerpiece are not necessary unless the food is elaborate, but a flower or fruit centerpiece on an attractive table mat always adds interest.

DINNER: Many hostesses like to serve a first course in the living room —hot, spiced tomato clam broth, a fruit drink, or tomato juice with or without crackers, chips, a dip, and relishes. This gives the hostess time to put the finishing touches on the dinner. Dinner plates, especially in winter, should be warm. Dinner may be

A foursome setting followed by cards.

Towle Silversmiths

282

This hostess planned well. She invited congenial guests —not too many for her rather small but well chosen site. The hamburgers are easy to prepare and serve informally, and not too hard on the purse.

Tupperware

served from the buffet or it may be carried on plates from the kitchen to the dining table, just before calling guests. The host may serve the meat and vegetables at table if the group is small. For a large group the food can be served hotter if someone helps the host serve either the meat or the vegetables. Such items as bread and butter may be placed on the table and passed. The hostess usually serves a hot beverage at table.

When service is not buffet style, all dishes—including bread, butter, and relishes—should move around the table in the same direction.

A male guest of honor sits at the right of the hostess and a woman at the right of the host. The next in rank sits at the left of host or hostess. When there are four couples at the table, the hostess sometimes asks the favored male guest to sit at the head of the table on her right, opposite her husband, to balance men and women.

Order of Dinner Service The most important female guest is served first and then the other women, followed by the most important man. The host is served last and hostess next to last. However, if there are more than eight at the table and no help, it may save confusion to serve one side of the table and then the other.

It is usually easier to pass food to the person on your right. Plates are served and removed so as to avoid reaching across or in front of someone. Main dishes are removed before individual plates. Plates are removed with the left hand and not stacked at the table. However, the dinner plate may be lifted and salad plate placed on top of it to be carried away. Trays and carts should be stacked *outside* the dining room.

Before dessert is served, the table should be clear of everything that will not be needed with the dessert course. If there are crumbs on the table, they should be removed with a brush for the purpose (silver crumber if a tablecloth is used) onto a small tray or plate.

Coffee may be served with dinner or only with dessert (after dessert, in demitasse cups, if the dinner is formal). Some people like to serve coffee in the living room after dinner.

It is considered bad manners to

start smoking before the dessert course. Small ash trays should be provided for cigarettes to avoid use of cups or saucers.

The hostess nods to the host when it is time to leave the table. As a rule, the hostess tries to eat as long as her guests are eating, even if she just nibbles at celery or bread. A course is not changed until all guests have finished eating. The polite host or hostess does not urge guests to eat something they have refused, no matter how good the food is supposed to be. On the other hand, a guest should take and eat a little of everything.

DINNER SERVICE FOR ENTERTAINING

You will receive china, silver, crystal, and table linens as wedding gifts, but perhaps not all you need. You may want to keep your best things for special occasions and use inexpensive substitutes for everyday.

Give a lot of thought to planning a purchase of fine china, crystal, silver, and linens. Your place settings will look more attractive if they harmonize in line and form, and if the colors in

A formal dinner requires careful planning. This is the time to use your best wedding crystal, china, silver, and linen.

Towle Silversmiths

china and linen blend with the colors in the room.

Most couples accumulate table appointments over a number of years, with a service for twelve as a goal. If possible, you should try to buy all items in "open stock" and inquire how long the stock will be open. Open stock means that you can buy in odd lots, not sets, but *does not guarantee how long a crystal or china pattern will be available.*

For the normal amount of entertaining, you will find the following linens adequate:
• 1-2 tablecloths (linen damask, lace, or embroidered linen)
• 3 sets of table mats (plastic, woven, and cloth) with matching napkins
• 2 dozen tea napkins
• 2-3 breakfast cloths
• 2-3 bridge sets
• 1 dozen dinner napkins to match or harmonize with cloths.

Although paper napkins are acceptable for family meals and informal entertaining, cloth napkins are preferable for a guest dinner or bridge party.

Several pictures in this chapter illustrate how to set a table for different occasions. Silver is placed in order of use from outside in. Keep pieces parallel, and 1 inch from the edge of the table. The open corner of the napkin is placed near the edge of the table toward the plate.

It may be some time before you can really put this information into practice. But if you take every opportunity to develop skills in entertaining, you will find it genuinely rewarding as a host or hostess later.

Here is a plan for building your dinner service:

284

BUILDING YOUR DINNER SERVICE

Begin with	4 dinner knives 4 dinner forks 8 salad forks 8 teaspoons 1 sugar spoon 1 butter knife 2 serving spoons	4 dinner plates 4 cups and saucers 4 salad plates 1 vegetable dish 1 meat platter	8 dessert plates 8 water glasses 8 sherbets 1 pitcher (1) 2 relish dishes
Add	4 dinner knives 4 dinner forks 8 teaspoons 8 butter spreaders 1 pickle fork 1 gravy ladle	4 dinner plates 4 cups and saucers 4 salad plates 8 bread and butter plates 1 vegetable dish 1 gravy boat	2 large cake plates 4 dessert plates 4-8 water glasses 4-8 iced tea glasses salt and pepper shakers
Add later (2)	8 bouillon spoons 8 demitasse spoons 1 carving set 1 lemon fork 1 jelly spoon 1 pie server	1 large meat platter 8 cereal bowls 8 luncheon plates 8 bouillon cups 8 demitasse cups and saucers	relish trays large fruit bowl

(1) Need not be crystal.

(2) Add gradually on anniversaries and birthdays until you have a service for twelve. You may want other things such as a coffee and tea service, punch bowl and cups, glasses for special drinks, special platters, candle sticks and candelabra.

HOW TO BE A THOUGHTFUL HOST OR HOSTESS

Be Ready to Receive Your Guests Make guests feel welcome as they arrive; be sure that everyone is introduced. (Introductions are discussed under Manner Minimums.) Avoid appearing hurried or tired, and making profuse apologies.

If overnight guests arrive a little early for dinner and the weather is cold, you may suggest that you will have tea ready shortly and ask if they would rather have it in their rooms and rest a while before joining the family in the living room. If it is a warm day, you may serve a cold drink.

Assure Privacy If there is no guest room and a guest must sleep on a sofa or couch in the den, living room, or dining room, the host may make a portable folding screen from two plywood panels with racks for towels, clothes, and magazines, and place a bridge lamp and TV table near the bed. Arrangements about using the bathroom should be made, if everyone must share it.

Provide Essential Equipment Make sure there is some place to hang up clothes, even though it may be only part of a closet or even a clothes rack in the corner of the room. Clear out one drawer, at least, and line with shelf paper or

285

Polite treatment of callers, whether in person or on the telephone, is an important part of hospitality. Even small children can learn this skill.

wallpaper. Other essentials are: a clock; water glass; ash tray and matches; recent magazines and perhaps a light novel; cleansing tissues; good reading light; hangers for clothes; luggage rack or bench for suitcase; towels and washcloths on a separate rack in the bathroom, or portable rack in the bedroom.

Add the Little Extras Providing guests with thoughtful extras can turn a routine visit into a memorable experience. A guest might like a bowl of flowers, a tray of fruit, or a dish of candy. Other extras may be a note pad, pencil, pen and stamps, needles threaded with black and white thread, pins, small scissors, and a tin of aspirin. Male guests may like an extra pillow for use while reading.

Extend Extra Courtesies Indicate where guests may find extra towels or blankets, outlets for a razor, and perhaps a full-length mirror. You might also mention that there are bottled drinks in the refrigerator. If your guests should ask to be awakened, offer a small tray with hot coffee or fruit juice on it as you call them. A tap on the door signals your presence best.

Think of how important you would feel if someone offered you such extra attentions!

HOW TO BE A GRACIOUS GUEST

Whether you are a guest for a party, dinner, or week end, here is a set of good rules to follow:

Answer Invitations Promptly A guest should express regret if acceptance is impossible, or otherwise accept enthusiastically. If the invitation is for longer than an afternoon or evening, the guest should indicate when he will arrive and depart, and not keep a host guessing.

Avoid Retracting an Acceptance Have you ever accepted a date and later wished you could retract it when something more interesting turned up? This may happen to anyone. Sincere people meet their first obligation once they have accepted, and go with the idea of having a good time. Occasionally, circumstances may make it necessary to cancel an engagement. In this case, the host should be notified as early as possible. When you are invited to any social occasion, you are being honored, so why be impolite? Children, too, feel that appointments with them should not be treated lightly. Be considerate if you have to break a date with a children's group.

Arrive on Time If a time is set, be punctual. If unavoidably detained, call the host or hostess, indicate how late you will be, and urge that others not wait for you.

Dress the Part It is an insult to the host to come to a dinner party in plaid shirt and slacks, or everyday blouse and skirt. It may be just as embarrassing to come to a barbecue or picnic in business attire or party finery. If you are not sure what to wear, ask the host what others are wearing.

Don't Be a Sponge Check ahead of time to be sure what necessary grooming aids and other personal items you will need. If you are invited for a week end, leave at the appointed time. Many hosts may urge you to stay, but you should be firm if you do not want to wear out your welcome.

Enter into Activities Once you have accepted any hospitality, make up your mind that what you are doing is important. Be interested, participate in conversation, and show enthusiasm if entertainment is pro-

Towle Silversmiths

Table set for guest breakfast.

vided. Act the way you would want *your* guests to act. Be acceptable—not critical!

Help in Any Way You Can If you are a house guest, you should make your own bed, hang up your clothes, and keep your room tidy. Ask to help with cooking, serving, or dishwashing, but if your hostess prefers doing these things herself or having outside help do them, do not be a nuisance about it. Leave your room and bathroom in order. When you leave, fold up soiled bed linens and leave them on top of the made-up bed.

Don't Expect Constant Attention If things are dull, and you are left alone for a while, pick up a magazine or book, write a note, or take a stroll. Do not make the host feel that you must be entertained all the time.

Be Considerate If you are a house guest, find out what time meals are served, and be on time. Guests who sleep late in the

Settings for children's parties should be simple but gay.

The Paper Cup and Container Institute

287

morning may upset plans for the whole day. Avoid leaving magazines and newspapers lying carelessly around. Throw candy wrappers or other papers in the wastebasket. Take used bottles, cups, or glasses to the kitchen. Avoid keeping your hosts up later than they wish, whether you are a guest for an evening, a week end, or a week. Be careful not to monopolize the bathroom at busy times of the day, especially if there is only one bathroom.

Be Cour- When you depart, express
teous your thanks warmly. If you have been an overnight guest, write a note of thanks within

Inviting neighbors in for coffee is a gracious way to introduce a newcomer to 'the neighborhood.

a week. You may send a little gift. (Some people like to bring such a gift with them and present it at a convenient time.) When leaving, do not be either too abrupt or too long winded about saying farewell.

Words and Phrases to Know

brunch	porcelain
buffet	pottery
china	sherbet dish
earthenware	service plates
formal dinner	silver plate
goblet	solid silver
hospitality	tumbler

ACTIVITIES

1. Discuss the meaning of hospitality. Recall visits you have had in the homes of relatives or friends, and guests you have had in your own home.

2. Comment on the remarks: "When you entertain, give a little of yourself—you'll have more fun and so will your guests," and "Do not apologize profusely

when something is not quite up to your usual standards."

3. Act out the references to Mr. and Mrs. Casual and Mr. and Mrs. Grippe.

4. From your own knowledge of friends who have been married, discuss the type of entertaining most young married people do. How do they compensate

for a limited supply of service items?

5. Select the type of party you would like to give and make a list of things to do ahead of time to guarantee the success of the party.

6. Form a panel to discuss the following:
• Presence of an older person in the home during a party.
• Favorite parties.
• Popular party foods.
• Time for party to start and end.
• Greetings and departures.

7. **Bulletin Board:** Arrange clippings of interesting parties and party foods.

8. Make a class survey to find out the kinds of parties people like best; times for a party to start and stop; how classmates feel about home parties.

9. Arrange clippings of table settings for the types of entertaining described. Name the silver, crystal, and china patterns, if possible.

10. Demonstrate serving and removing dishes, from soup to coffee. Do not interrupt the person serving, but note mistakes and discuss later.

11. Discuss how you feel about accepting and then retracting an invitation.

12. Tell about experiences you have had as a guest in the home of friends or relatives, or in having visitors in your home.

13. Assemble china, silver, crystal, and linen for several place settings. Consider color, design, texture, and occasion. (This may be combined with activity 7.)

14. Discuss "ice breakers" in getting a party off to a good start.

15. Suggest ways in which a host can add to the success of an evening's entertainment.

16. After viewing a film on carving, have a young man volunteer to demonstrate how to carve a roast and a chicken. Let other young men take turns.

17. Discuss all-night-after-prom parties from (a) student's viewpoint; (b) parents' viewpoint.

Home Experiences

Help with plans the next time your folks have guests.

Ask your parents to tell you about their experiences in hospitality when they were younger.

Invite a small group of friends for snacks and games, TV, or listening to records.

Chapter 14

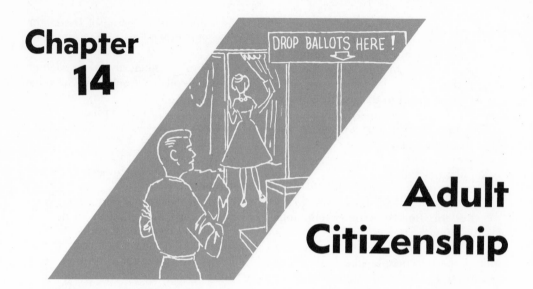

DROP BALLOTS HERE !

Adult Citizenship

Citizenship carries with it responsibilities as well as privileges, yet many of us are much more interested in the privileges.

• We covet certain freedoms but we forget the meaning of patriotism.

• We value our rights in a democracy, but we are lax about voting.

• We like the protection and conveniences afforded by government, but we resent high taxes.

• We refuse to compromise on spending, and let inflation continue.

• We boast of our high standard of living, but we depend upon someone else to deal with problems of delinquency and blight.

• We are aware of the value of community contacts, but overlook opportunities for creating international good will.

Most of us take our present way of life for granted. It is a good idea once in a while to review our history, our government, and the lives of the men whose foresight made our great democracy possible. The better we understand our country's past and present, the better we can determine its future.

THE MEANING OF PATRIOTISM

If you look up *patriotism* in the dictionary, you will find that it means "devotion to the welfare of one's country." This is well expressed in the Preamble to the Constitution of the United States.

How well do we live up to that definition today? Some people say that our nation has lost its spirit of patriotism. News reports might seem to support that view. However, in judging our nation as a whole, many events and opinions must be considered, not just the unusual ones which make the news.

Few people would deny that our outward expressions of patriotism have changed. Many of our ancestors came to this country seeking a better way of life. It was natural that they wanted to show feelings of devotion toward their new country. Flowery speeches and parades on national holidays were much in style. However, customs change. Many young people today are ill at ease when asked to talk about their patriotism. Does this indicate a lack of respect for their country? Or do young people show their patriotism in other ways, such as the Peace Corps?

Certainly we have every reason to respect our nation. America's role in the world has been not to conquer but to help. Germany and Japan, our enemies in World War II, are now our allies. Millions of American dollars have been spent in foreign aid to these and many other nations. At home there has been steady progress toward full equality for all citizens. Although some problems remain, still our record of social reform and widespread prosperity is one that any nation might envy.

Proper respect for our country is necessary if we are to carry out our roles as responsible members of society. For deeper awareness of what it means to be an American, take notice of the many symbolic reminders of our nation's heritage. The American flag waves from public buildings. The Great Seal appears on many important government papers. The Statue of Liberty holds her torch high as a beacon of freedom. The Liberty Bell rests as a mute reminder of our Declaration of Independence. Coins and bills bear likenesses of our great leaders and symbols of our democracy.

When you pledge allegiance to the flag, do you ever stop to think of what the flag symbolizes? Do you know how to respect it? Have you ever wondered why certain designs were chosen to embellish our money?

By which document are we guaranteed the right to representative government, freedom of worship, freedom of speech, the right to security from intrusion by persons without warrant, and public trial by jury? These are privileges enjoyed in only a few countries. On occasion it has become necessary to fight to preserve these rights, but every day we have the responsibility of guarding them by becoming more active citizens.

VOTING IS A PRIVILEGE AND A DUTY

When we criticize our government and political leaders for high taxes, inflation, or laxity in law enforcement, we criticize ourselves. *We make the laws under which we live.* By voting or failing to vote we elect our leaders to public office.

Although we cherish our way of life, we are less interested in voting

Freedoms we should cherish—to worship as we wish; to lock our doors against illegal force and violations of privacy; to speak and write what we feel is the truth; to choose the people who govern us.

The Independent Electric Light and Power Companies

The Great Seal.

Symbols of our democracy.

than our forefathers or citizens in free European countries. Only 59 out of every 100 eligible American voters cast ballots in the 1964 presidential election, whereas eight out of ten eligible voters voted in the 1880's. Some of these people worked twelve hours a day, and had no cars!

False Ideas About Voting Richard M. Scammon, Director of Elections Research at the Government Affairs Institute, has suggested some reasons why people fail to vote. (Voters between ages 21 and 29 have a poor record in this regard.)

• Many people feel their vote is insignificant among the millions of votes cast. This is not true. A change of just one vote in each precinct would have reversed the outcome of many elections, not only at state and local level, but congressional and presidential contests as well. A mere handful of voters in key states could have made

Richard Nixon the winner over John Kennedy in 1960. In the same election, the electoral votes of California were won by absentee ballots, cast by persons away from home who realized that their vote was too important to waste, no matter where they were.

• A few feel there is something crooked about politics, and they refuse to have anything to do with elections. This is shallow thinking. Most people in public office are sincere and capable; otherwise our nation never could have prospered as it has. If there are a few bad spots here and there, responsible citizens must clean them up by voting intelligently. Ignoring trouble only makes it worse.

• Some people cannot decide between opposing candidates. Newspapers, radio, and television provide extensive coverage of campaigns. Both parties distribute free literature presenting their viewpoints. Libraries stock books about leading candidates. Anyone who is not just plain lazy can learn the differences between candidates and the parties they represent.

• Women may be tied down with families, and sometimes lack transportation. A phone call to the local headquarters of either party will usually bring a free ride to the polls, and in many communities baby sitting service is also provided.

• A voter may be away from home at the time of registration or election. Except in emergencies, you can usually plan your trips so that you do not lose your chance to vote, or you can use an absentee ballot. When a person becomes 21, or changes his name or address, he should contact local election authorities about registering.

To be able to vote properly, you must be informed on the issues and the character of the persons on whose shoulders you place so much responsibility. Learn to differentiate between propaganda and truth; high pressure politicians and conscientious leaders; what political machines want and what people need. A person who votes blindly is not exercising his full rights.

TAX SOURCES AND BENEFITS

Have you any idea what taxes your parents pay and what you and your family in turn receive from those taxes?

The High Cost of Taxes According to figures from the Bureau of the Census, Americans paid an estimated $60.5 billion in income taxes for 1967. This is roughly $1,200 per family in federal income tax alone. Besides this there are many other local, state, and federal taxes which are paid by private citizens. Even taxes on corporations are passed along to the customer. Directly or indirectly, all taxes are paid by individuals like you and your parents. Since taxes represent a high percentage of your family's income, you are entitled to know what you are getting for your money.

Sources of Taxes In 1913 the *individual income tax* was written into the Sixteenth Amendment to the Constitution. Nearly everyone 293

Liberty Bell.

Coronet Films

Statue of Liberty.

National Park Service

This is America!

The rugged New England coast.

pays an income tax. Even though most of it may be withheld at the source, many families have an additional tax to pay on earnings from other sources. As incomes increase, the percentage for taxes expands greatly. Federal government gets half of its revenue from its share of the individual income tax, and states get a tenth of their revenue.

In 1966 *corporation income taxes* accounted for 30 per cent of federal, state, and local revenue. To show how this tax has increased, the comparable figure in 1956 was 20 per cent. Your share of these taxes is hidden in everything you buy.

Sales taxes make up a large part of state revenue. Some states have taxes as high as 6 per cent on taxable merchandise. In many instances necessities such as food eaten at home and most items of clothing are not taxed.

Gasoline taxes may run as high as 15 cents on the gallon. The average motorist pays between $75 and $100 a year in gasoline taxes alone.

An *excise tax* is placed on so-called luxuries—furs, jewelry, automobiles, entertainment, toilet articles, and telephone calls, among others. These taxes are changed according to the state of our national economy. They account for about 8 per cent of the federal budget.

Property taxes are levied to pay

Deserts of the Southwest, lonely and excitingly strange.

294

This is America!

Mountains and lakes — the powerful beauty of the Pacific Northwest and Alaska.

National Park Service

state and local expenses, but the local community receives the highest percentage.

School taxes are included in the property tax. In many communities this is a very expensive item.

Social security taxes are paid by nearly every employed person in the United States. They are usually paid by means of a payroll deduction, with the employer paying a portion of the tax.

Many taxes vary considerably from one locality to another. For instance, licenses for cars cost much more in some states than in others. States which have had expensive road construction projects tend to charge more for licenses. Hunting and fishing licenses, inheritance tax, and property transfer tax are others which vary widely.

What We Receive from Taxes *Federal taxes* provide an army, navy, marine corps, and air force for defense. Funds are used also for scientific experiments such as those at Cape Kennedy, medical research and hospitals, a postal system, social security benefits, parks and monuments, guaranteed loans for housing, subsidies for farmers and students, a network of roads and bridges, power and flood control projects, foreign aid.

Semi-tropical areas are found in the South, Southwest, and Hawaii.

National Park Service

295

This is America!

Peaceful scenes are found
from coast to coast.

State taxes provide money for universities and special schools for the handicapped, hospitals and institutions, roads, bridges, and parks.

From *local taxes* we receive police and fire protection; streets, roads, and sidewalks; garbage and sewage removal; street lights, bridges, parks, and playgrounds; health protection and sanitary inspection of public places; street cleaning; libraries, and many other things.

Government has, step by step, assumed responsibility for many social and economic programs, many of which have been valuable, but as voting citizens we should question how far this should go. None of us wants *socialism*. How our government spends income is the concern of us all. It's our money!

INFLATION

When people speak of inflation, what they usually mean is higher prices. Actually, inflation is not that simple. However, rising costs are part of inflation—perhaps the part that affects us most.

On the average, in mid-1968 it took $1.43 to buy goods which would have cost only a dollar in 1947-49. According to some economists, the rate of decline in dollar value—currently about 4 per cent a year—will become more severe by 1975.

Big city turmoil—a way of life for millions of people.

296

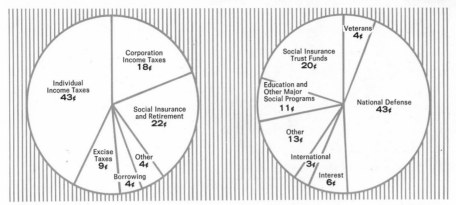

A dollar in the federal budget. The drawing at left shows where the federal government gets its income, and the one at right shows how the money is spent. Notice that the largest source of revenue by far is the individual income tax. Among expenditures, that for national defense is more than double any other. Figures are based on the estimated budget for fiscal 1969.

Obviously, as prices go higher, it takes more money to live. Many Americans have been able to increase their incomes fast enough to keep pace with the rising cost of living. For them, inflation may not seem to be a serious problem. In fact, some people claim that a little bit of inflation is good for our nation's economy.

However, there are many people who are not so fortunate. Most retired people, for example, have what is called a *fixed income*. This means that they get the same amount of money every month, no matter how much their cost of living may rise.

Another way that inflation can hurt us is in competition with other nations. As our prices rise, we have a harder time selling American goods in foreign countries. Imported products become more popular in our country because they cost less. This is a serious problem, not only for companies which sell goods overseas, but for our entire national economy. Can you see why?

Even people with good incomes are affected by inflation. For instance, many people decide against saving money. They say, "Why put a dollar in the bank today if it may be worth only 70 cents in ten years? Why not spend it now and get the full dollar's worth?" Inflation naturally leads people to think this way. What do you think of this attitude? What are some points for and against it?

To protect our country against excessive inflation, here are a few things we can do:
• Study government spending. Read what intelligent men have written about our national economy. Discuss these ideas with others, so that more people will become interested.
• Make these attitudes part of our own thinking—give a dollar's-worth of work for a dollar's pay; save for the future rather than piling up debts that even future generations won't be able to pay; stop waiting for the *other fellow* to act; don't let speculation overrule good sense.
• Elect congressmen who have shown good judgment in financial matters.

Boys' Club of Carnegie, Pa.

Giving children a chance to develop creative skills teaches them values and appreciations which will be useful all their lives.

Remember that although the President can suggest and use influence, the senators and representatives really make the laws.

• Investigate such controversial issues as governmental price supports, import duties, and wage regulations. Don't take these things for granted. Look at both sides of these questions, decide what policies will serve our nation best, and vote for men who agree with you.

Since you will be responsible for our economy a few years hence, you need to put much thought and study into government economics now. Public education and communication systems would cease if it were not for taxes. We would be defenseless against attack. But we cannot expect our elected officials to do all our thinking for us.

DELINQUENCY IS EVERYBODY'S BUSINESS

An exceptionally small percentage of our population could be called criminals or delinquents, but just one criminal in a community where otherwise law and order prevail can change the whole character of living for those he hurts.

Many young adults think our courts are too lenient on juvenile delinquents. When students have sat in on juvenile hearings, their recommendations often have been more severe than older judges and jurors. Typical remarks of students have been, "If you do something once and get away with it, then you think you can get away with it all the time." "Kids. . . know they can play on adult sympathy."

On a Gilbert Research Opinion Poll of 5,065 high school students in 35 cities, between 80 and 85 per cent voted to jail any person under eighteen who took part in a street fight, smoked marijuana cigarettes, took narcotics, vandalized property, or drove a stolen car.

Traffic accidents involving teenagers were cut considerably in Pocatello, Idaho, after high school students began to sit in on traffic court trials and issue some of the verdicts.

Legal authorities agree that it is better to prevent crimes than to solve

Youngsters are not likely to become delinquent when adults take genuine interest in them and help them in wholesome activities.

The Salvation Army of Pittsburgh

them. In many communities police now use computers, closed circuit television, helicopters, and other modern devices to curtail crime and delinquency, preferably before it starts. You can help in many ways, both now and in the future when you become community leaders. For instance:

• You can be an example to others. If your actions are good, your associates will be influenced.

• You can be "a friend in need." Kindness and sympathy at the right time can help a boy avoid delinquency.

• Through your student government and the PTA you can establish a teenage code concerning hours to come home, driving limits, and places to go.

• You and your teachers can help direct young people who come from underprivileged homes to the programs of boys' clubs, the Y, scout groups, or to jobs in the community. In the meantime, a kind word and smile can work wonders.

• You can talk with your parents, and men's business groups, suggesting that campaigns be organized to clean up and improve the poorer city areas where delinquency is worst, or to raise funds for needy young persons.

• You can spend some of your free time helping with recreational programs in your community. Young people need such programs. In one suburb vandalism increased greatly when houses were built on a lot where youngsters had been playing ball.

• You can help your parents take the following precautions at home: Lock all doors and windows securely, especially at night and when your father is not at home; when going out of town, stop all deliveries, arrange to have grass cut or snow removed, and

Mexico, Mo., Junior Chamber of Commerce

Many organizations in Mexico, Mo., cooperated in constructing this outdoor theater which has become a cultural and religious center.

notify neighbors and police; list fire, police, and other important numbers near the phone.

• You can notify police if you are approached about illegal matters such as gambling or drugs.

To combat the need for better recreational facilities, Mexico, Missouri, accomplished one of our most successful civic programs. The Junior Chamber of Commerce organized a townwide do-it-yourself project enlisting newspaper editors, storekeepers, carpenters, painters, plumbers, electricians, teachers, parents, and high school students. When the project was completed the town had children's playgrounds, tennis courts, a swimming pool, golf course, outdoor amphitheater and parks with benches.

• You can petition contractors to provide temporary interest areas while they are building on vacant lots, until new recreational facilities can be provided. For instance a Junior Conservation Corps with clubhouse and refreshments was set up in one community to watch over building projects. In still another area, youngsters were given building material and supplies to construct small buildings under supervision. In another community, trade organizations and builders

299

One of Pittsburgh's successful slum clearance projects:
the same intersection, before
and after renovation.

sponsored radio give-away programs
to keep children home during the
hours when vandalism was greatest.

TURN BLIGHT TO BEAUTY

Notice the corridors, classrooms,
and cafeterias of your school. When
you leave after classes, take a look at
the steps, pavements, sidewalk, and
lawn. Are you proud or ashamed?
Have you helped to keep papers and
bottles picked up? What can you do
to call attention to neglected features?
Communities are often judged by the
appearance of school buildings and
grounds.

We have the best sanitary conditions of any country in the world, yet
the fact that we package everything
produces litter on our streets and
roads. In a remote town in the wide
open spaces of Wyoming, the Elks
Lodge offered Boy Scouts a penny
for each beer can picked up along the
roads near town. In a short time, 7,400
were turned in!

In many states "litterbugs" can be
fined as much as $100 or even jailed.
If this seems severe, consider that it
costs taxpayers—including you and
your parents—millions of dollars every
year to deal with this problem. Litter
is both unsightly and unsanitary.

Our country has some of the most
beautiful national parks and forests in
the world, but if we do not take care
of them, they will not offer much for
future generations to enjoy. People
are careless about tossing out matches
and starting fires. Many visitors to the
unusual petrified forest in Arizona
think they own a part interest in it
and brag about sneaking out pieces of
petrified wood. Other abuses to our
national and state parks include
throwing cans and bottles into springs
and streams, hacking marks on stately
old trees, carving names on rustic picnic tables, debasing beautiful stone
formations with paint. Oddly enough,
young people, who use our outdoors
the most, and should be very appreci-
ative, cause much of the damage.

300

Why not lead your group into a new point of view?

Slums, long a major problem, are discussed more than ever these days. Perhaps the reasons for inner city problems are: (1) many people have moved to the suburbs, leaving their fine, old, city homes to be converted into apartments which often are allowed to deteriorate; (2) because we can travel so quickly, and many families move frequently, our population has lost the sense of pride in local conditions. By the mid-1960's the suburban population exceeded the city population for the first time.

Besides local programs such as the one in Mexico, Missouri (page 299), the federal government has taken steps to remedy the situation. President Dwight Eisenhower started the American Council to Improve Our Neighborhoods (ACTION). This organization inspired clean-up campaigns in many neighborhoods.

In the late 1960's more than 800 cities were participating in urban renewal projects under the Federal Housing Administration. Still others were to be helped under the Model Cities Program announced in 1967 by President Lyndon Johnson.

Despite local and federal programs, many problems remain. Here are some signs of blight that may require action in your own community.
* Cracked masonry walls and foundations, loose bricks, paint peeling off, splintered window sills and frames.
* Rusted down spouts, leaking roofs, loose shingles.
* Old homes converted to rooming houses.
* Broken sidewalks and rough streets.
* Porches and steps in need of repair.
* Trash piled up at doorways.

The best way to start is by helping to maintain the beauty of the home in which you live and the highways over which you drive.

COMMUNITY CONTACTS

If you have been active in Boy Scouts or Girl Scouts, Red Cross, 4-H Club, Future Farmers, Future Homemakers of America, Future Teachers, Junior Achievement, the Y, Glenn Club, an orchestra, debate society or athletics, you will probably be active in community organizations later.

There is a limit to what anyone should undertake in addition to homemaking and a job. You should choose community organizations which fit your talents. It is often better to be active in one or two groups than merely a member of many. The following organizations offer opportunities for service, enjoyment, and making friends.
* *Civic* or *national* organizations such as The American Legion and The American Legion Auxiliary; Veterans

The American Red Cross offers opportunities for people of all ages to help with vital service projects.

Pittsburgh Chapter, American Red Cross

A civic symphony gives enjoyment to members as well as audience, and stimulates community pride.

Take advantage of local cultural opportunities such as museum exhibits, lectures, educational films, concerts, plays, and recitals.

of Foreign Wars; Catholic Veterans; CYO; the Y; civic clubs; historical societies; garden clubs; women's clubs; boosters' clubs.

• *Service* clubs such as Rotary, Kiwanis, Lions, Optimist, Sertoma, Junior League, and others.

• *Business* groups such as junior chamber of commerce, chamber of commerce, sales and accounting clubs.

• *Cultural* participation such as little theater, civic orchestra, literary and choral groups.

• *Political* groups such as party committee work, League of Women Voters, forums, and discussion groups.

• *School* organizations: Parent Teachers Association, school boards, and adult education classes.

• *Social* groups such as school and sorority alumni clubs, card clubs, dancing classes.

• *Church work* in men's and women's organizations, teaching in church school, or serving on various committees at local, state, or national level.

• *Professional* affiliations such as with medical, engineering, or educational organizations.

• *Volunteer work* in hospitals, the Y, schools, community drives, city betterment.

INTERNATIONAL RELATIONS

Until air travel became common, and our military men were sent to many places abroad, we felt isolated from other nations and saw little need for speaking another language. Now, with people in distant lands only hours away, with brothers and friends serving overseas, we are becoming more aware of the need to understand customs and languages of nations all over the world.

The Peace Corps offers opportunities not only for service but also for deeper understanding among nations. A training period acquaints members with the language, customs, and conditions of the country where they will serve. Then for about two years the volunteers live in a foreign country, usually one where the way of life is very different from ours. There are many opportunities for people with home economics training to serve in the Peace Corps.

Teacher and student exchange programs have given many people here and abroad a better understanding of how to get along as world neighbors. In the last twenty-five years youths from over half the countries in the world have visited the United States under these programs. Each year more than 40,000 exchange students come to this country.

If you cannot visit a foreign country, perhaps you can start a correspondence with a young adult somewhere in the world and become a better neighbor. Many people in foreign countries can write English; however, those of you who are studying a foreign language can use such correspondence to help your studies. By exchanging pictures, magazines, and newspaper clippings you might make life-long friends. It is fun to be an armchair traveler and good will ambassador.

Groups "adopt" children in other countries through children's fund organizations. Your own church can give you the addresses of such organizations.

Many of you will travel abroad. When you do, learn all you can about the customs, history, government, and language of the countries in which you plan to spend any length of time.

If all who read this chapter could put into action some of the suggestions on citizenship opportunities, there is no limit to the effects that might be felt in your school, community, country, and around the world.

Words and Phrases to Know

delinquency	inflation
democracy	patriotism
excise tax	propaganda
fixed income	socialism
Great Seal	social security

ACTIVITIES

1. Discuss democracy, communism, and patriotism.

2. Give brief, individual reports, followed by discussions on:
• Our flag—its history and how to respect it.
• The Great Seal, our official stamp.
• The Liberty Bell.
• The Statue of Liberty.
• The Declaration of Independence.
• The Constitution.
• The Bill of Rights.

3. Investigate and discuss the following: your precinct, your congressional district, names and duties of persons in local offices.

4. Invite someone in public office to tell your group about local government. Find out which officials are elected, which appointed. Find out what you could do if you objected to an issue before your city council, commission, or other board.

5. Write for literature from the Democratic and Republican national committees and minor party committees to find out about party policies.

6. Look up the qualifications for voting in your state, including minimum length of United States citizenship, length of residence to vote in state, county, and district, and whether a literacy test or poll tax is required. In what states may persons 18 years old vote? Compare practices in your state with those in neighboring states.

7. Make a list of things your local taxes provide.

8. Secure copies of income tax forms and discuss each section. Practice filling in a form, setting up a "case" income.

9. Invite your city or county tax col-

lector to visit your class and tell how taxes are collected and spent.

10. Estimate what *sales, excise,* and *gasoline* taxes cost your family a year. Compare gasoline taxes by states.

11. Discuss government deficit spending and relate it to family installment plan buying. What can you and your parents do to curtail inflation?

12. The Consumer's Price Index shows only general spending. Make similar graphs for food, clothing, and housing over the same periods in different colored inks, and compare them. (This is a good bulletin board idea also.)

13. Discuss delinquency in your community—car stealing, vandalism, and other problems. Consider measures for decreasing delinquency. Find out how your local courts treat delinquents.

14. Review the Code for Teen-agers you formulated in Dating Diagrams and make corrections if necessary.

15. List streets in your neighborhood that show blight. Indicate symptoms; discuss improvements. (Study literature from ACTION, Federal Housing Administration, and other sources.)

16. Give reports on blight eradication in other cities and communities from reference sources.

17. Make a list of activities in your school and indicate those that tie in directly with community activities.

18. Report on the origin, organization, and success of international student exchange programs.

19. If there are exchange students in your area on the American Field Service Plan, invite them to tell you about customs in their countries.

20. Formulate Ten Commandments for Good Citizenship. You may want to refer to the Code of the Optimist Club.

21. Mention some American or United Nations organizations whose work helps to promote better international relations, such as CARE, and American Field Service.

22. Find out how members of our foreign service are chosen and what they do.

Correlation

ENGLISH: Write a brief article on any phase of citizenship. Choose your own topic.

BUSINESS: Invite a banker or economist to discuss inflation and its effects upon our economy.

ART AND PRINTING: Ask the art department to design two posters for a clean-up campaign—one for school and the other for the community. Have enough printed to place in classrooms, school cafeteria, and store windows in your community.

CIVIC CLUBS AND CHAMBER OF COMMERCE: Enlist the co-operation of these organizations to support a clean-up campaign.

HISTORY AND CIVICS: Invite the history or civics teacher to review the formation of our government and indicate the relationship between local and federal government.

Home Experiences

List all the different taxes your family pays.

Enlist the help of your family to improve the appearance of your home entrances or yard if they need to be improved.

Make a list of organizations in which members of your family participate.

Under the stately dome of our nation's Capitol, a funeral procession with full military honors begins its march to Arlington National Cemetery. The dome, known to all the world as a symbol of effective democracy, was completed in 1863.

304B

Hundreds of people each day view these important historical documents—Articles of Confederation, Constitution, and Bill of Rights—in the National Archives, Washington, D. C.

304C

The Supreme Court of the United States meets in this building. The classic, Greek style structure, typical of many beautiful buildings in Washington, is shown here in an unusual view from the side.

The Thomas Jefferson Memorial, when the cherry trees around it are in bloom, is a sight as fine as any city in the world can offer.

Photos by Michael Kenny

Graves of our nation's honored dead, row after row, are seen from a hillside in Arlington National Cemetery. The bridge in the background leads across the Potomac River to the Lincoln Memorial. The towering Washington Monument is also visible.

304D

This *contemporary* room has an Oriental air. Orange and blue, *complementary colors*, are effective against the neutral walls and floor. Furniture is grouped to fit attractively on the rug and to allow easy traffic flow in the room. Note the careful, colorful arrangement of books, repeating colors in the room; drawers for storing bedding under the studio couch; built-in desk below the bookcase; small serving tables, one on the sofa and one on the larger table near the studio couch; and Oriental lettering which acts as a floor accent.

A French Provincial bedroom could be attractively decorated using the *complementary colors* shown here. The flowered drapery fabric repeats the pink in the walls and the green in the rug. The bedspread and upholstery fabrics (left of the drapes) go well with the off-white furniture tone, and the flower arrangement repeats the drapery motif • A kitchen and dining alcove, with one or two walls painted turquoise and the others papered in the style shown here, would be attractive and in keeping with current styles. The table mats repeat the turquoise.

The cozy atmosphere in this cool setting, accented with red tulips, makes dining doubly enjoyable. Notice the similarity between the tablecloth and the valance at the top of the window. The mural, which repeats the design in the draperies, gives the room depth. The drapes pick up the blue in the crystal and the yellow tones in the brass lantern and candle sticks.

304F

Glowing warmth is the effect of this decorating scheme based on *analogous colors*. Subtle orange slip covers, matching draperies, and the gold love seat are shown to good advantage against the light beige walls and striped toast-and-beige carpet. The painting suits the room's colors and mood excellently, and the shelves provide space for an interesting display.

This painting could well set the color scheme for a room. Orange-yellow, blue, and red-orange are used in a *split complementary* color harmony. *Contemporary* styling is consistent in the painting and the Danish Modern chair.

Wood-paneled walls may call for rich fabrics with a print that repeats tones in the wood. Contrast, provided by the white lamp shade and white background in the draperies, gives a dramatic effect. Strong, masculine accessories often look best in a room of this kind. The green fabric behind the drapes would be an excellent choice for upholstery.

Traditional decor is the keynote here, originating in the drapery fabric. *Analogous colors,* like the green, green-blue, and blue used here, can make an attractive room. A smart decorator might include chairs of green upholstery fabric (shown against the drapes) and a neutral sofa with green and figured pillows on top of the cushions. White accessories would complete the room with beauty.

304H

Chapter 15

Keys to Home Beauty

It is not difficult to proceed with confidence as a decorator if you understand:

• What you and your family like, need, and can afford.

• How to judge furniture and home furnishings.

• How to combine colors and how colors change under artificial light.

• How to place furniture to provide function, space, and good design.

• How to choose lighting for its part in decoration as well as for study and work.

• How to choose and use accessories.

Magazines and literature from manufacturers of home furnishings provide a wealth of ideas on decorating. No matter what you are planning to decorate, keep a clipping file or scrapbook of ideas. The more familiar you become with color schemes, furniture styles and arrangement, fabrics, floor coverings and other details, the easier it will be to apply the information in this chapter.

MEETING THE FAMILY'S LIKES, NEEDS, AND BUDGET

A successful professional decorator must first of all know something about the family that will live in the house—what they like and need; how much they can afford to spend. This is where the husband and wife with a background in design and buying home furnishings, may have an advantage over the professional. No matter how attractive a room may be, it is a complete failure if the family is not happy about the finished product and the cost.

Some families like the space and uncluttered appearance *contemporary* furnishings provide; some like the formality and dignity of *traditional* furnishings; others like the charm and simplicity of *Colonial* or *Early American* furnishings; still others like the casual effect achieved by a combination of styles and backgrounds.

Whatever the style preference, chairs and sofas must be comfortable,

305

Contemporary furnishings make a room look spacious yet trim. Notice the amount of floor space in the attractive bedroom (above). The contemporary living room (right) is balanced, though it is not symmetrically arranged.

Biggs Antique Company

Dignity and formality are characteristics of traditional furnishings. In the bedroom (left) are a Hepplewhite bed with tester (canopy), a Queen Anne highboy, a Sheraton commode (chest of drawers), and a Brewster chair. The living room (below) has a combination of traditional furnishings —Sheraton sofa, Chippendale wing chair, Queen Anne drop-leaf table, and Martha Washington mirror.

Biggs Antique Company

Early American furnishings have warmth and charm. In the bedroom (above) are a low poster bed, a Duxbury armchair, a barrel chair (right) and a oval rag rug. The living-dining room (left) has a Welch breakfront (shelves and cabinet), a drop-leaf dining table, a wing sofa, and a wing chair.

Ethan Allen Early American Furniture—Baumritter

Young ladies, particularly those between ten and twenty, would enjoy the room at right. Notice the ample drawers, shelves, and counter space. The bedroom below might appeal as much to a young man in college as to a grade school boy. As in the girl's room, the storage units are movable and can be combined in various ways.

The Merchandise Mart

307

This studio apartment with sleeping alcove gains in privacy and appearance through the use of wooden folding doors.

well made and, of course, in harmony with other furnishings. The persons who use a room the most should be consulted in selecting the chairs for that room.

Family members are happier if they have the space to do the things that interest them. This may not always be possible. Few moderately priced homes provide a workshop for tinkering, a place to play records and dance, an area for developing photographs, and a room for sewing, or storing garden tools. However, these may be important factors in overall family living, so arrange space and facilities to suit all needs.

If you are helping your family to decorate your own room, or if you redecorate or furnish your first apartment, cost will be a big factor. You will find it wise to economize on some items but not on others. For instance:

• You can buy inexpensive scatter rugs if you expect to replace them later. If you are buying a living room rug or carpeting that you want to last, postpone it until you can afford good quality; then choose a color which will let you change wall, drapery, and furniture colors later.

• Economize on furniture that you may replace later, but buy a good set of bed springs, and a mattress with a long guarantee. Place these on legs at first; buy a headboard later.

• Buy *end tables* with drawers, cabinet space, or shelves rather than surface space only. End and console tables with drop leaves can provide extra space for books, magazines, or cups and saucers when you entertain. Many large, square, modern corner tables only take up floor space. A *long coffee table* is better than a small one, if you have the space. Buy tables in relation to height of the bed, sofa, or chairs beside which they will be used. Buy table lamps high enough to give a good light.

• Choose a desk with drawers at side as well as at top for extra storage. It will take up no more floor space.

• Go slow on cheap accessories that clutter up a room. Concentrate on really lovely things that you know you will enjoy for many years—lamp bases, bowls, vases, small table boxes, pictures, shelves, carvings, china, or pottery. If you start off with inferior accessories, replace one at a time with really good pieces.

• Buy well-designed and well-built upholstered furniture that will clean easily.

• If one room must serve many purposes, you can transform it into a dining room by placing a round, foldaway top on a card table, to seat six people. You can have a "bedroom" by making a single bed from a studio couch, or using a bed sofa.

FLOOR COVERINGS

Carpeting is becoming more and more popular for every room in the house, including kitchens and bathrooms. However, the amount of use kitchens and bathrooms receive will determine the advantages of using carpet, even though it may be easily cleaned. Where there are children and when a great deal of cooking is done in the kitchen a hard surface floor is more sanitary and more easily kept clean.

Carpeting and Rugs

Improvements in man-made fibers for carpeting have made wall-to-wall carpet less expensive and easier to maintain. It may be less costly to use wall-to-wall carpet than to lay new wood floors. Even in new homes some people prefer to lay wall-to-wall carpet over double plywood or concrete floors because of its acoustic properties and cost savings. It is easier to vacuum clean a room entirely carpeted than to have to use a dust mop and vacuum cleaner. Wall-to-wall carpet also makes a room appear larger.

When hardwood or parquet floors are in good condition, many people prefer to use room size or scatter rugs. Rugs have some advantages over wall-to-wall carpeting because they can be sent out to be cleaned; they can be turned around so that traffic lanes do not develop; and they cost less than wall-to-wall carpet.

Rugs come in *room-size, area,* and *scatter* types. A *room-size* rug should always come to within 12 inches of the wall or preferably closer all around. *Area* rugs are often used to divide a large room into different units for conversation, reading and study, dining, or card games. *Scatter* rugs may be placed almost anywhere for function or decoration.

Broadloom refers to any seamless carpet made on looms 6, 9, 12, or 18 feet wide. This wide range makes almost any rug size possible and any width wall-to-wall carpet possible by seaming in one direction.

Buying Carpet

When you buy carpeting or rugs there are a number of things to consider: fiber, weave, color and pattern, and backing. Rooms that receive heavy traffic will require highly twisted and more durable yarns and a closer weave than less frequently used rooms.

FIBER: *Wool* has been the traditional rug fiber. It is resilient, durable, dyes well, and cleans easily. But if the fiber in a carpet has not been treated to resist moths, it should be treated on the floor with a special spray or cleaned with a rug cleaner containing a moth retardant. Wool is not desirable on concrete floors below grade or in warm moist climates.

Nylon has become more important as a carpet fiber. It is abrasion resistant, moth and mildew proof, and easily cleaned. It tends to generate static electricity but sprays are available to reduce static. Nylon carpet comes in many qualities—pile and weave vary greatly in relation to cost.

Acrylic fibers give carpet a wool-like appearance. They resist mildew and moths, produce bulk, are non-absorbent, clean easily, and come in a wide color range. Acrylic fibers are less abrasive resistant than wool or nylon and less resilient, so acrylic carpets crush faster than wool or nylon.

Olefin rug fiber resists moths and mildew. It comes in continuous filament or staple yarns (short yarns with little luster). Non-absorbent, resilient, and resistant to spots and abrasions, olefin also generates less static electricity than nylon.

Cotton and *rayon* carpets are not recommended for wall-to-wall carpeting because they do not clean well on the floor and tend to crush (grease is difficult to remove). Room size rugs may be used in bedrooms. You will find that cotton or rayon scatter rugs for bathrooms are attractive and economical.

WEAVE: The weave, or method by which yarns are put together to form carpet, influences appearance and wear. For many years rug weaves were limited to *Wilton, Axminster, velvet,* and *chenille.* Now the bulk of carpeting is produced by tufting because this is the least expensive production method.

In tufting the pile yarns are looped through a jute or canvas base by a multiple needle machine. Either a coating of latex is sprayed on the back or a jute fabric is bonded to the back to keep the tufts intact. Tufted carpet may be uncut to give a looped effect, cut to form a pile, or part may be cut and part left uncut to produce a sculptured effect.

A *velvet* weave is used on solid color carpeting to produce a soft texture resembling velvet. Straight yarns produce highlights and shadows; twisted yarns look textured or dull.

True *chenille* carpeting is expensive because the tufts are tied by hand to give a luxurious deep pile. Designs and colors are unlimited. Chenille imitations do not wear especially well.

Wilton rugs are made on a Jacquard loom to produce intricate patterns. Colors are usually delicate. As the yarns are carried in the pattern they are looped and buried between the pile and the backing which is bonded to the woven rug. Wilton rugs wear well. *Brussels* carpet is woven in the same manner but the pile, unlike Wilton pile, is left uncut.

Axminster rugs are inexpensive reproductions of Orientals. The yarns are not buried as in Wiltons. One characteristic of an Axminster rug is that it can be rolled only in one direction.

COLOR: Color is important in the choice of a rug. Greens, gold, and beige are consistently popular, with reds or pink tans gaining favor from time to time.

TEXTURE AND PATTERN: Different surface effects are produced by using continuous filament or staple yarns; cutting the pile around uncut areas for a pattern effect; combining two types of yarns and cross dyeing for a tweed effect, and using slub yarns for a coarse, "shantung" effect. There is no end to the variations that can be produced by varying or combining yarns, dyeing, cutting the pile or leaving it in loops. The general idea or decor of the room will determine the choice of pattern, color, and texture.

310

Backing and   The backing on car-
Rug Cushions   pet helps to prolong
               wear. Jute and foam
rubber are commonly used backing
materials. Commercial carpet, such as
is used in institutions and hotels, often
has a foam rubber backing so it needs
no under cushion. The pile is usually
tightly twisted and uncut because
this wears best. Damaged areas can
be cut out and replaced, if the carpet
has not faded nor the pattern been
discontinued.

Most residential carpet has a jute
back and a coarse, medium, or fine
weave. Such rugs or carpets need
under cushions to absorb shocks and
extend wear.

Rug cushions come in all-hair, hair-
and-jute, or rubber in several thicknesses. A 40-ounce waffle weave hair
cushion is a good selection. Jute de-
tracts from the resilience of the cushion. Rubber rug cushions are not recommended for scatter or room-size
rugs because traffic causes the rug to
move off the cushion. If a carpet has
a rubber cushion it should be shampooed with a foaming water-soluble
substance. Dry cleaning fluids will
make the rubber deteriorate.

Composition Floor These include
     Coverings   hard surface cov-
                   erings such as
linoleum, asphalt tile, vinyl tile or
sheet, rubber tile, and *cork.*

Linoleum comes in sheet and tile
forms. It has good acoustic qualities,
repels grease, resists dents, and comes
in a wide range of designs and colors.
Inlaid linoleum has a design that
goes through the linoleum and never
wears off, whereas printed linoleum
has only a surface design. Linoleum

is not recommended for *below grade*
(underground) floors.

Asphalt tile is the least expensive
floor covering (except for printed
linoleum), the least resistant to
grease, but it dents easily. However,
asphalt tile is the best covering for
below grade floors where temperature
changes may cause some tile to crack.

Vinyl floor coverings in *tile* and
sheet form are durable, attractive,
dirt and grease resistant, easy to keep
clean, and they are available in a
wide assortment of colors and patterns. Vinyls come in several thicknesses. *Vinyl asbestos* floor coverings
are less expensive and less durable
than pure vinyl but they wear well
with proper care. A mild detergent is
the best cleaner. Vinyl asbestos may
be used *below grade.*

Abrasive powders and steel wool
never are used on any kind of composition floor covering.

Rubber tile is more expensive but
resists dents, absorbs shock and noise
better than other composition coverings. It is difficult to care for. It is not
recommended where there is a great
deal of traffic.

Cork in sheet or tile form reduces
noise and resists shock but it absorbs
grease and dirt.

WALL FINISHES

The most popular wall finishes are
paint, wood paneling, and wallpaper.
Newly plastered walls take from two
to four weeks to dry depending upon
the weather. They should not be
painted untill they are thoroughly
dry. Professional painters use a plaster meter for testing wall moisture.
Anyone can test various wall areas in

a room by running a sharp fingernail over the surface. If a mark shows, the wall is probably too damp to paint. In many new, moderately priced homes *dry walls*, or *plasterboard walls*, are used. These may be painted immediately. New plaster needs a primer coat to make the paint adhere.

A semigloss oil-base paint is recommended for kitchen and bathroom walls and all woodwork because it may be wiped off without leaving a mark. Flat paint is recommended for walls in all other rooms. NOTE: It must be washed with care to avoid streaking. Water soluble paints are easy to apply, less expensive than those requiring a chemical paint thinner, but they do not wash well. A wallpaper cleaner should be used.

Wallpaper has charm and warmth. Also the choice of colors, textures, and patterns is very wide. Often one or two walls of a room are papered and the others painted. NOTE: Regardless of wall treatment, usually paint the ceiling.

Before painting or papering any surface, all cracks should be repaired with a filler, sanded, and primed. Most wallpaper cleans well with a wallpaper cleaner. Many wallpapers can be washed, if careful. Cloth wallpapers and others with a special coating can be washed freely. Also, at an additional cost, you can order wallpaper that has been given a plastic coating at the factory to make it washable. It is also possible to give wallpaper a coat of special protective varnish on the wall without causing noticeable discoloration. NOTE: Of course any varnish or paint over wallpaper makes removal difficult. A dry (rather than steam) process will re-move coated wallpapers. It is not always satisfactory to choose wallpapers from catalogue-size swatches. Before buying wallpaper, obtain a piece to try out by holding it up in the area where it will be used.

Precut wood paneling comes either prefinished in many natural wood finishes or ready for painting. Sheets are usually 4 × 8 feet but 10-foot lengths are available if required. Panels may be interlocked so that nail heads do not show. Wood paneling is attractive on one or more walls of a room. If walls are in bad condition it may be cheaper to use wood paneling than to remove old plaster and replace it.

FURNITURE

Furniture woods include pecan, mahogany, walnut, cherry, Choosing maple, birch, oak, pine, Furniture and gum. Gumwood is less expensive. It is often stained to resemble other woods or covered with a fine layer of other woods, a process known as *veneering*.

Mahogany and walnut are found in most *traditional or eighteenth century* adaptations of Chippendale, Hepplewhite, Sheraton, Adam, and Duncan Phyfe styles. Maple, cherry, and other fruit woods are warm, informal types often used in *Provincial* and *Early American* furniture. *Modern* furniture is made of oak, birch, and light woods as well as mahogany and walnut.

To cut costs, large pieces of furniture such as chests and dressers are often a combination of gumwood and more expensive woods. Gumwood is used where it does not show. Such pieces cannot be advertised as solid wood.

It is better to buy furniture with smooth surfaces and simple lines than with decoration, unless you are a good judge of carving, veneers, or inlays. As stated earlier, a veneer finish is a thin layer of attractively grained wood glued to the surface in one piece, or in a number of pieces to form a pattern. Veneering is applied to inexpensive as well as expensive furniture. Do not let veneered furniture get wet; the thin layer will warp.

The manner in which furniture is *constructed* determines how long it will last. Double dowel or mortise-and-tenon joints make durable joints in chairs and tables. If you cannot see these joints, ask what kind a piece of furniture has. Drawers with dovetail joints are preferable to those with plain joints glued and nailed together. Chairs and small tables with stretchers or cross bars are more durable than those without them.

Springs may be flat or coiled. Coiled springs should be close together and tied in eight directions from the center. *Hair* and *Dacron fiber* are used as padding in more costly furniture; *Spanish moss* may be used in cheaper pieces. *Foam rubber* is used frequently in place of springs or to supplement them in the cushions and backs of sofas and chairs. It is usually more expensive than simple spring construction, and covers on foam rubber cushions tend to slip.

Furniture Arrangement If you can develop a sense of design and an awareness of function you will have little difficulty expressing harmony and efficiency in furniture arrangement. Furniture arrangement must conform to certain rules of design: *proportion, balance, rhythm, emphasis,* and *unity.*

Proportion or scale applies to choosing furniture that fits the room and "goes together." For example, tables used near chairs should be in good proportion to each other; bowls on a table must be scaled to the table; lamps scaled to lamp bases; and pictures must either suit a smaller area or a large wall space.

Balance need not always be even or symmetrical but it is usually best to have one wall of a room evenly balanced. Even balance on every wall results in monotony. Uneven or asymmetrical balance is hard to use, but effective when used well.

Rhythm can be obtained by: repetition—repeating lines, colors, or shapes in a room; opposition—using a horizontal cornice over draperies or vertical pictures over a sofa; *gradation*—arranging pictures in a staggered grouping or placing objects of different sizes on a mantle or chest; *radiation*—the effect obtained when curtains are tied back or small objects are arranged around a large object on a wall; *transition*—grouping wall accessories and furniture to carry the eye from one to the other without interruption.

Every room should have a *center of interest* for *emphasis;* a window arrangement, fireplace, painting, or unusual piece of furniture may be the focal point.

Unity refers to overall appearance. When everything in a room has harmony of colors, textures, lines, forms, and ideas, all contributing to a satisfactory whole, then the room has unity. Besides being esthetically correct (pleasing to the eye) a room

The furniture shows even balance while objects on the buffet are unevenly balanced.

should be functional and psychologically satisfying. To achieve these effects when arranging furniture:

Avoid using too many heavy, upholstered pieces in the living room. Secure a good balance between wood and upholstered furniture.

Avoid repeating architectural lines in furniture arrangement. For instance, a high piece of furniture should break a long wall rather than stand between two windows or along a narrow wall.

Avoid using chairs with high backs if ceilings are low, and vice versa.

Avoid using too many colors, textures, ideas, or shapes in the same room, especially if it is a small room.

Furniture should be arranged so that chairs will not have to be moved every time a few people want to carry on a conversation. Main traffic lanes should be free of furniture.

BUYING HOUSEHOLD TEXTILES

Household textiles for decorative purposes include fabrics for curtains, draperies, bedspreads, slip covers, and upholstery fabrics.

Damask, brocade, tapestry, frieze, velvet, and sometimes chintz and cretonne are used for upholstering *traditional* furniture; rep, sailcloth, gabardine, and geometric patterns in damask for *contemporary* furniture; cretonne, chintz, and printed linen for *Early American* and *provincial*.

Upholstery on chairs and sofas should be firmly woven. Wool, polyester, and nylon fabrics clean well, but all kinds of fabrics can be given a finish to make them resistant to soil, liquids, and grease.

Slip covers should be made of firmly woven, pre-shrunk material. Spots and stains will show less on textured and patterned fabrics than on solid colors.

Most *curtain fabrics* now require little care. Even sheer cottons are treated to resist dirt, and require a minimum of ironing. Curtain fabrics should be opaque enough for privacy and beauty, but should not shut out light. If there are no window shades, draw draperies should be sufficiently opaque to insure privacy.

Polyester and *fiber glass* fabrics resist fading and sunlight, but care must be taken in laundering. These fabrics should not be wrung because the yarns will slip. Polyester fabrics should be pressed with a warm iron (a hot iron will shrink and melt the fibers). Fiber glass fabrics need no ironing but they are sensitive to friction. *Nylon* is durable but it tends to attract soil and darken after use. *Rayon* fabrics wash and press easily and drape nicely, but they can be damaged by sunlight or a hot iron. Many *acetate* fabrics are popular for curtains because they hang nicely and require only touch-up pressing.

Drapery fabrics help to establish a color scheme if they are figured. When draperies are figured most other fabrics should be of solid color. However, the drapery pattern may be repeated on a chair or sofa in the same room. Avoid using figured draperies and wallpaper in the same room unless they match.

USING COLOR

Knowing how to use color successfully is like performing magic. *Wrong* colors can make handsome furniture look ordinary; *right* colors can make the commonplace very interesting.

Color works on your emotions. Pinks and yellows may make you feel cheerful; drab green, dull blues, and tans may depress you. Color can make rooms appear larger or smaller, higher or lower, longer or shorter.

Color Harmonies — There are actually few colors that clash with one another if you understand value and intensity. The term *value* refers to how light or dark a color is—sky blue, for instance, has a lighter value than navy blue. The term *intensity* refers to how bright or how dull a color is—Kelly green is bright and hunter's green dull.

Almost any colors can be used together provided they are used in the right value and intensity. Try to visualize orange and purple together. The two colors are not very companionable either in dress or in the home. Lighten the orange until it is a warm beige and use purple for accent, or lighten the purple to a cool, gray tone and add apricot for accent.

You may choose your own color schemes from a *fabric, wallpaper, floor covering, or an important accessory*, or you may use standard color harmonies. Remember, colors do not look the same indoors, under artificial light, as they do in sunlight.

How Artificial Light Affects Color — Cocoa, browns, faun, and rose beige are usually more pleasing by incandescent light than in daylight or under fluorescent light.

Mauve, lilac, and violet are lovely by daylight but drab by artificial light, especially fluorescent light. Terra cotta, rose, reds, and pinks become more orange under artificial light.

Blue-greens appear greener under artificial light and bluer by daylight. Artificial light makes yellow more creamy, but gold takes on a mustard color.

Traditional Color Harmonies — To achieve pleasing color schemes you may use similar or contrasting harmonies:

SIMILAR HARMONIES ARE:

Analogous or adjoining colors on the color chart.

It is usually desirable to use draw draperies at corner windows in a color that matches the walls.

Better Homes and Gardens

315

- Monochromatic or several values of the same color.

  CONTRASTING HARMONIES ARE:
- Complementary, or opposite colors on the color chart.
- Accented neutral, or a neutral color plus accent color.
- A triad, or three colors forming a triangle on the color chart.
- Split complementary, or a color used with the colors on each side of the one opposite it on the chart.

DECORATING WITH ACCESSORIES

Accessories are a barometer of your taste. Well chosen accessories can give a room a great deal of character. Some people cannot resist buying knickknacks. Before long, tables, shelves, and walls become so cluttered that a room begins to look like a gift shop, not a home.

A few well chosen accessories, interestingly displayed or grouped, not only express good taste but give a room character. Pictures, mirrors, and lamps are important, but other accessories may be used to the exclusion of all of these for excellent effects—

It takes careful planning for a couple to choose home decor which they will continue to enjoy for many years.

H. Armstrong Roberts

clocks, shelves, barometers, vases, ash trays, wall brackets, candlesticks, and sconces.

Accessories should have some relation to the room in idea, scale, and color. A boy's room, a den, or a library requires sturdy, manly accessories, whereas a girl's room will need delicate, feminine styles. As a rule, a living room and guest room should have impersonal accessories, unless the family has some unusual hobby to emphasize.

Picture Suggestions Since pictures are among the most frequently used accessories, you need to think about their selection, framing, and hanging. The following suggestions will be helpful:
- Avoid extremely popular reproductions because they soon become commonplace.
- Relate your pictures to the general feeling of the room. If the room has a light and airy feeling do not hang dark pictures with heavy frames.
- Avoid hanging family pictures in the living room. A few well chosen photographs look fine on a table or shelf but an array of family pictures should be in a more personal room.
- Choose still life and bird pictures only after long thought. They do not fit into many settings but they can be effective in a particular setting.
- Combine water colors, etchings, lithographs, and delicate oils. Use large heavy oils alone or in a room with strong photographs. Group photographs and block prints separately— i.e. not on the same wall with other pictures.
- Frame most oil paintings in heavy, rather deep frames. Use a mat, as a

316

rule, to frame water colors, pen and ink sketches, and block prints.
• Hang large pictures so that the center of the picture is level with the eye of the average person.
• Keep a pleasing proportion or space below a picture and any piece of furniture below it.
• Use multiple grouping of pictures with discretion. This can be interesting if done well but it takes skill.

LAMPS AND LIGHTING

Lighting needs vary with activity, size and shape of the room, colors used in the room, amount of outdoor light, and personal tastes. Lighting should be both functional and decorative. Cove, bookcase, and cornice lighting are mainly decorative. Candlelight, if well planned, gives a feeling of romance. Bright lights create an atmospheric gaiety and cheerfulness. Lamplight in the living room creates highlights and shadows, and makes the room more interesting than ceiling lighting. Lighting over work centers should be primarily functional. As a rule you should choose lamps with shades all the same color for a small room or room of average size. Lamps with colored shades, unless they are carefully chosen, can make a room look spotty. Occasionally a colored shade is needed to carry out a color scheme. If lamps are used for reading, make sure that the angle of light will fall on the reading material without having to move the lamp or tilt the shade.

This gives only a brief summary on decorating, but it should help you with most problems that you will meet. Illustrations from current magazines can supplement this chapter.

Better Homes and Gardens

Group wall accessories if they have something in common—character, frames, color.

You can save money and have a lot of fun by doing many decorating jobs yourself—you can learn to make slip covers; paint walls; apply wallpaper; and lay floor tile if you follow the step by step directions and study the illustrations.

Words and Phrases to Know

acrylic	olefin
analogous colors	polyester
asymmetric	proportion
Axminster	provincial
balance	rhythm
chenille	split
complementary	complementary
colors	traditional
contemporary	transition
Early American	tufted
fluorescent light	unity
function	velvet
incandescent light	veneering
monochromatic	Wilton

317

YARDAGE CHART FOR SLIPCOVERS*

	Cushions	48″ Wide		36″ Wide		Welting or Trimming
		Plain	Figured or Striped	Plain	Figured or Striped	
Sofa	3	14 yds.	15½ yds.	21 yds.	23 yds.	36 yds.
	1 long cushion	13½	15	20½	22½	33
	0	10	11	15	17	21
Love Seat	2	10	11	15	16½	24
	1	10	11	15	16½	23
	0	8½	9¼	12¾	14¼	14
Arm Chair	1	7½	8¼	11¼	12¼	18
	0	6	6¾	8⅓	9½	13
Boudoir Chair	1	5	5¾	7¾	8¾	15
	0	4½	5¼	6½	7½	12
Wing Chair	1	8	9	12	13½	18
	0	6½	7¼	9¾	10¾	13
Cogswell Chair	1	7	8	10½	12	16
	0	5½	6	8¼	9	11
Daybed and Mattress	3	14½	16	21¾	23¾	42
	0	11	12	17½	19½	27
Daybed	3	11	12	16½	18	29
	0	7½	8¼	11	12¼	14
Ottoman	0	2	2½	3	3½	6
Chaise Lounge	1	10	11	15	16½	23
	0	8	9	12	13¼	16
Dining Room Chair	0	1½	1¾	1⅚	2⅙	5½
Extra Cushion	1	1¼	1¾	1⅚	2⅙	5

*Approximate—consult salesgirl for large repeat-pattern yardage.

HOW TO MAKE A SLIP COVER

Consult the chart for proper yardage. Read the directions carefully, noting how to center designs, how to fit and pin, and how to sew. The step-by-step directions are easy to follow.

Important Things to Remember: Fit and cut slipcovers on the right side. *If* you fit them on the wrong side, the arms will be reversed. Chairs are rarely exactly even, so you may have trouble.

Always pin and cut goods on the straight of the thread, up and down from the floor, no matter whether a panel slants or not. Be sure to allow enough material for 5-inch tuck-in across back of seat, on each side of seat and where arm joins back.

It is very important to use sharp scissors and cut one-inch seam allowances straight and even. This cut edge is the guide for sewing and putting in welting or trim.

To Cut Center Figure Design Fabric: Use previous steps with fabric open—not folded. Cutting routine can vary to save fabric. Pin each piece to chair as it is cut.

Center figure in front back of chair, measuring with chair cushion in place. Center figure for outside back of chair.

Try to match inside arms, with boldest part of pattern toward top of arm. Match front panels, too. Outside arms need not match since you never see both sides of chair at once.

If center panel is used on bottom front of chair, center pattern. And center pattern on both sides of cushion so that it can reverse.

Instructions for Fitting and Pinning: Open material out and smooth each piece into place, right side up, pinning here and there to hold it on straight of goods. Never stretch, jerk or pull material.

Use your fingers for eyes, holding to two pieces of fabric together between thumb and finger of one hand, letting your fingers feel along natural line of chair. With other hand, put pins in straight line about 1 inch apart. If you follow lines of chair with fingers of one hand and pin with the other, you are sure to get a beautiful fit. (You can see that your slipcover fits before you cut it, and merely by changing your pins correct any error.)

Trim fabric to a 1-inch seam allowance with straight, even edges.

Instructions for sewing: Leave all seam pins in place. Take out pins holding fabric to upholstery of chair. Unpin one back seam of chair where back and front meet. Zipper goes here beginning 2 inches from top and extending to floor. Lift slipcover off chair. Do not loosen pins.

When sewing, follow same order as you did in pinning. First unpin the seam joining back and inside back (Sketch 4). Turn fabric wrong side out as you would a pillowcase.

Pin or baste welting or trim on right side of fabric, 1 inch from cut edge with finished edge of trimming down. Stitch length of seam. Bring up corresponding piece of fabric (two right sides together) and pin in place.

Place fabric on sewing machine with stitched side up and sew along line of stitching (Sketch 11). This gives a straight seam and trim line, adds strength to your slipcover and avoids puckering or wavy seams. Don't sew trim into both sides of fabric at once. Follow above procedure for all seams except tuck-ins at back, sides, and curve inside back of chair.

Where side tuck-ins meet back tuck-in, there will be a little fullness. Lay extra fabric in small folds at corner and stitch side seat tuck-ins to inside arm tuck-ins, being careful to first follow directions for spring edge.

To attach skirt, stitch trimming or welting along 8-inch chalk line marked on bottom of slipcover, with finished edge of trimming up. Pin right side of skirt to right side of slipcover and stitch according to directions above.

STEP 1: *Inside Back*—With fabric folded in half lengthwise, start 2 inches below back edge of chair (a). Bring fabric forward to (b), fold in 2 inches for welting seam. Continue down to (c), fold in 10 inches to allow for 5-inch tuck-in at back of seat. Continue across seat and down to

319

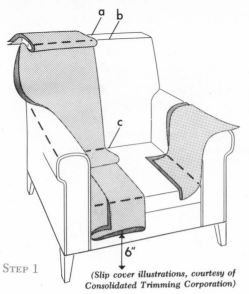

STEP 1

(Slip cover illustrations, courtesy of Consolidated Trimming Corporation)

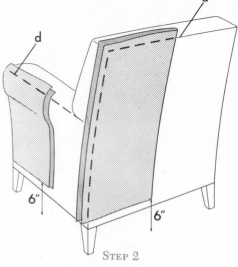

STEP 2

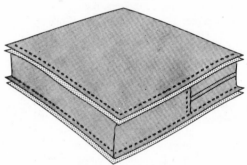

STEP 3 (part 1)

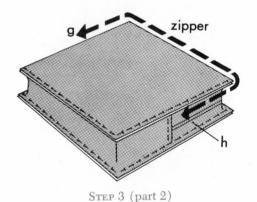

STEP 3 (part 2)

6 inches above floor, cut straight across fabric.

Inside Arms—With fabric folded in half lengthwise, begin 2 inches beyond (d) where chair arm starts to turn down. Smooth fabric over arm and down to (c) and allow 5 inches for tuck-in. Cut straight across fabric. Repeat for other arm.

STEP 2: *Outside Back*—With fabric folded in half lengthwise, begin 2 inches above top back of chair (a) and continue down back of chair to 6 inches from floor. Cut straight across fabric. Skirt is cut later.

Outside Arms—With fabric folded in half lengthwise, begin 2 inches above (d) where arm starts to turn down. Smooth fabric, hold it close under curve of arm and against side of chair to 6 inches from floor. Cut straight across fabric. Repeat for other arm. Front and side arm panels are cut later while you are pinning.

STEP 3: *Cushion*—Lay cushion on top of folded fabric. Pat into shape and draw outline with chalk. Allow 1-inch seam all around and cut. Cushion may be uneven so measure width of cushion band at widest and narrowest points. Divide total in half for average width of band. Allowing 2-inch seams, cut one band of right width from (g) around front to (h), adding 4 inches to finish ends. Cut 2 more bands same

width and length to go around cushion back.

Sewing—Fold two bands lengthwise and pin each along fold. Sew one band to

320

cushion top at (g) and around back to (h) with folded edge down. Sew other band to bottom of cushion with folded edge up. Insert zipper between folded edges. (On T cushion, back bands extend to beginning of T on one side.) Turn under ends of front band 1 inch and attach to top and bottom of cushion front from (g) to (h)—ends overlap for smooth finish.

STEP 4: Pin 1-inch seam at (b) for welting. Cut through fold of fabric. Pin front back and outside back together at (a). Fold 5-inch tuck-in at (c). Smooth fabric over chair seat and front. Fold back excess fabric (e) and, allowing 5 inches for inside arm tuck-ins, cut to back of chair. (If T-front, do not cut front piece but only fabric inside arm. Extra will go around T to meet panel or outside arm.)

STEP 5: Be sure outside arm piece is smoothed close under curve of arm. Pin to chair under curve at front and back to hold firm. Pin inside and outside arm pieces together. Begin at front where arm begins to slope down (d) and continue in straight line along arm to back of chair. Pin outside arm and back together. With fabric on straight of goods, pin in and cut front panel. Repeat for other side.

STEP 6: Smooth inside arm into crease where arm meets back. Chalk fabric along

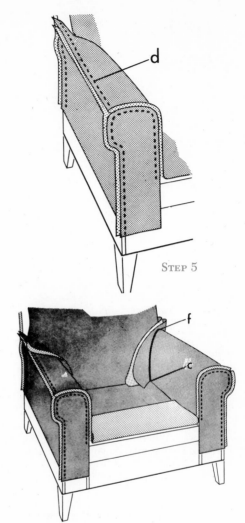

STEP 5

STEP 6

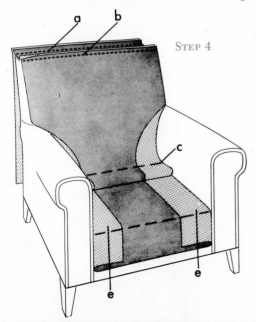

STEP 4

crease from (c) where back, arm, and seat meet to (f) where arm and back meet. Cut excess fabric, beginning 2 inches far side of (f) and taper to 5 inches from chalk at (c). Repeat on other side. Smooth inside back into crease and follow above instructions for both sides, being sure to cut on near side of chalk mark.

STEP 7: Now stand facing chair with scissors pointed toward back of chair. Clip fabric about four times 2 inches apart with alternate left and right slants, until it lays smoothly around curve where back and arm join. Be very careful not to clip too close to seam. Three or four clips should be

321

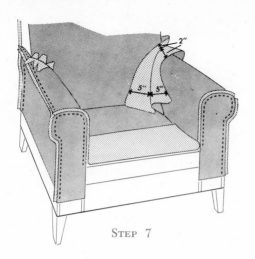

STEP 7

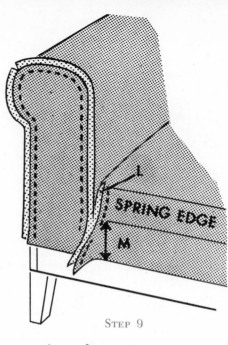

STEP 9

enough. Repeat for other inside back and both arm pieces.

STEP 8: Carry remaining piece of inside arm back and pin to outside back. Pin inside arm and inside back together (See Sketch 6) from (c) to (f) to form tuck-in that will go into chair crease. Repeat on other side. With fabric on straight of goods, cut, fit and pin side panels (k). Bottom edge of panels is pinned to inside arm piece.

STEP 9: Where chair has spring edge that bounces up and down at front edge of chair, to avoid pull on arm fabric:

STEP 8

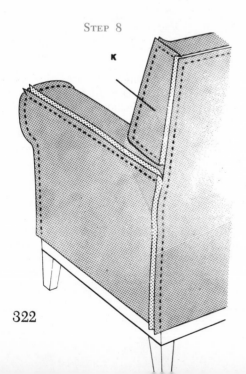

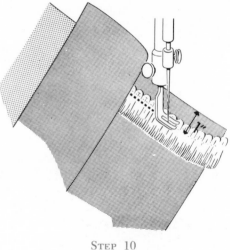

STEP 10

STEP 11

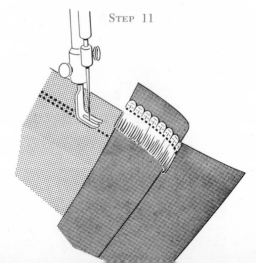

322

The finished product.

• Push seat tuck-in down between spring edge and arm. Miter corner with dart (l) and cut away excess fabric.
• Push inside arm tuck-in down between spring edge and arm and pin to front arm panel.
• Pin front of chair and arm panel together from bottom of spring edge to bottom of fabric (m).

STEP 10: Sew as shown.

STEP 11: Sew as shown.

HOW TO PAINT WALLS, WOODWORK, AND CEILING.

Always wash the surface before painting. Ready mixed paints are available in many colors, so you can avoid the problems of mixing your own. The use of quality paint and other supplies will result in savings through the years. Pastel shades generally continue to give a pleasing effect longer than darker colors. If you have trouble choosing a color, ask your dealer for small samples of the colors which interest you. Apply the sample to an inconspicuous part of the actual surface to be painted, and let it dry. You can judge the new color better if you hold a white paper over the old color next to it.

STEP 1: Repair cracks in plaster with spackling compound or patching plaster. Let repaired areas dry; sand them smooth. To permit easier, faster painting later, remove light switch plates, wall brackets, and

STEP 1

light fixtures. Use masking tape at windows and baseboard edges.

STEP 2: Dip the brush into paint, about half the length of the bristles. When removing the brush, wipe it lightly against the inside of the container to get rid of excess paint.

STEP 2
STEP 3

323

STEP 4

*Painting illustrations
courtesy of Pittsburgh
Plate Glass Company*

STEP 7

STEP 3: Start with the ceiling and paint across the narrow dimension. Use short, slightly curved strokes. Lift the brush gradually at end of the stroke.

STEP 4: On a wall, paint in narrow strips so you are always working with a wet edge. This avoids noticeable overlapping.

STEP 5: Use a roller for large areas. Start with several crisscross strokes.

STEP 5

STEP 6: On a door, coat recessed panels first. Then make the covering smooth with light, upward strokes with a nearly dry brush. Use the same procedure to coat the rest of the door. Do not brush vigorously; let enamel flow on.

STEP 7: To paint a cabinet, remove doors if possible. Then remove hinges or other hardware.

STEP 8: Paint radiators, registers, and vents the same color as the walls.

STEP 6

STEP 8

324

STEP 1

STEP 3

HOW TO APPLY WALLPAPER

Before you order wallpaper, measure your room. Here is a general rule for determining how much paper you will need for the walls of any room: multiply the total distance around the room (in feet) by the height of the room; deduct 20 square feet for each ordinary size opening. For example, a room 10 feet wide, 14 feet long, and 8 feet high, with two doors and two windows, will require 304 square feet of paper for the walls.

Wallpaper usually comes in single (6-yard) and double (12-yard) rolls. A single roll has 36 square feet, but with allowance for trimming and matching, ordinarily it will cover only 32 feet. Thus, the room described above would take ten single rolls. If the pattern is large, you may need more for matching. Unused rolls are returnable.

The amount of paper needed for ceilings of ordinary size may be found on the accompanying chart.

Carefully follow directions for mixing and applying paste. Use good brushes and a long, flat table. Keep your hands clean.

STEP 1: *Getting the Walls Ready*—If the walls are papered, remove the paper and sand the walls lightly. If they are painted

and the surface is greasy, wash them with a detergent. If the walls are painted and glossy, sand them lightly to dull the surface. If they are new plaster, brush on a sizing solution. In each case, fill cracks with patching plaster and sand them smooth.

STEP 2: *Getting the First Strip Straight*— This is very important because it determines the straightness of all other strips. Start in the least conspicuous corner. Make a mark on the wall, 23½ inches from this corner, just below the ceiling. This allows ½-inch to go around the corner to be overlapped by the final strip. Tie a weight (shears will do) to a string, and tack the string to the mark on the wall. Make sure the string and weight hang freely. Carefully press the string to the wall and make a chalk line along it from ceiling to baseboard. This plumb line starts your first strip straight.

STEP 3: *Matching and Cutting the Strips* —Match and cut several strips at a time. Unroll enough wallpaper to cut a strip 3 or 4 inches longer than the distance from the ceiling to the baseboard. Cut straight across the top at the point where you want the pattern to start. Lay this strip, pattern up, on the floor; unroll another strip beside

STEP 2

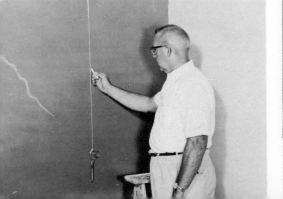

STEP 4

325

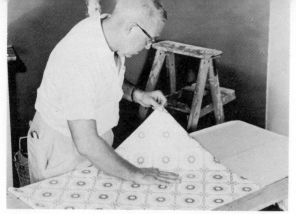

STEP 5   *Wallpaper illustrations
courtesy of Wall-Tex Company*

STEP 7

it. Adjust until pattern matches and cut the second strip same length as the first.

STEP 4: *Putting on the Paste*—Any good commercial paste may be used. Read the mixing instructions on the box carefully before you start. The paste should have the consistency of light cream. Place the pattern side down on the table and apply the paste with a wide brush. Work the paste evenly and thoroughly into the lower two thirds of the strip. *Don't overpaste.*

STEP 5: *Folding the Strip*—With the lower two thirds of the strip pasted (see step 4) fold (do not crease) the already pasted part back on itself so that the pasted surfaces stick together. Then apply paste to the top third of the strip. Folding makes strips easier to handle. *Make sure edges are well covered with paste so seams will stick tight.*

STEP 6: *Hanging the First Strip*—After the first strip is pasted and folded, pick it up by the top corners and line up the edge with the plumb line you've drawn on the wall. Now press the top of the strip into place at the ceiling and brush the top third of the strip into place with a downward

and outward motion. Then unfold the bottom two thirds, making sure it's lined up with the plumb line, and brush the rest of the strip into place. Start each succeeding strip in this same manner, lining it up at the ceiling joint so that trimming is necessary only along the baseboard.

STEP 7: *Trimming the Strips*—Brush the wallpaper firmly into the baseboard, molding, around windows or doors. Then crease along the edge with the blunt edge of your scissors. This leaves a plainly visible line on the wallpaper. Pull away the wallpaper far enough to cut along the crease with the scissors, and brush the strip back against the wall. After each strip is hung and trimmed, go over it with the smoothing brush to get out air bubbles.

STEP 8: *Matching the Strips*—Care in matching the pattern will make a big difference in the beauty of the room. Match the pattern by placing the top third of each strip on the wall next to the edge of the preceding strip, and guiding it accurately into place. Fit seams tightly against each other, without overlapping. As seams are fitted together, brush them into place, then wipe them with a damp cloth.

STEP 6

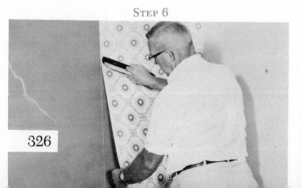

STEP 8

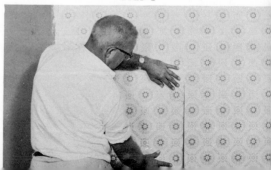

HOW TO LAY FLOOR TILE

Vinyl, linoleum, rubber, and cork tile may be cut with heavy shears without heating, but asphalt tile must be heated before cutting. Where wood subfloor is only a single layer, or when double layer floor boards are not perfectly smooth, the floor must be covered with plywood or a composition underlay especially made for this purpose. Rough concrete floors must be smoothed over.

Before selecting a tile for your home, consider these facts:

Asphalt: This is the least expensive floor tile. It is not resilient, dents are permanent, and its acoustic qualities are poor. However, it is the best type of tile for basements or covering any concrete surface below ground level. Asphalt tile will become brittle and chip under sudden temperature changes. Ordinarily it is not recommended for kitchens because it will absorb grease, but there is a *grease-proof* variety suitable for kitchens.

Cork: Cork tile is recommended for the den, library, or living room because it has good acoustic qualities. It will not wear well under heavy traffic, so it should not be used in entrance areas, halls, or recreation rooms. It will absorb grease and dirt. Cork comes in several tones and thicknesses. It must be laid above ground level because dampness causes it to crumble. *Vinyl cork* (cork

covered with a plastic) resists grease and dirt, and will take heavier traffic.

Linotile: Like linoleum by the yard, linotile is resilient, easy to maintain, grease repellent and good acoustically. It comes in a wide range of colors and designs. It is inexpensive and easy to maintain. Linotile is not recommended below ground level.

Rubber: This tile has good acoustic qualities and resists dents. It is fairly easy to maintain, if care is consistent. Buffing with steel wool will keep the gloss. It is moderate to high in cost, and may be used anywhere.

Vinyl: This is the most versatile of all tiles because it is durable, resists dirt and grease, and is fairly easy to maintain. It comes in a wide range of colors and designs. If vinyl tile is used below ground level, it should have an alkali-resistant backing.

Vinyl Asbestos: This is more resilient and more lustrous than asphalt but dents a little more easily than pure vinyl, rubber, linoleum, or cork. It resists acid and grease, and may be laid below ground level. Its cost is low to moderate.

STEP 1: Find the center point of each of the two end walls. Connect these two points with a chalk line.

STEP 2: Locate the center of this line. Using a carpenter's square, draw a per-

STEP 5

STEP 8

STEP 6

STEP 5: Measure the distance between the wall and the last tile. If the distance is less than 2″ or more than 8″, move the center line parallel to that wall 4½″ closer to the wall.

STEP 6: Spread a coat of tile cement over one quarter of the room, working from the walls out to the chalk lines. Do not cover chalk lines.

STEP 7: Allow the cement to dry about 15 minutes. Then test the cement for proper tackiness by touching lightly with the thumb. It should feel tacky, but should not stick to the thumb. If it sticks to the thumb, allow more drying time.

STEP 8: Starting at the center, place tiles in the cement, making sure that the first tiles are flush with the chalk lines and each tile is butted against adjoining tiles. Do not slide tiles into place.

pendicular line. If square is not available, place a tile with one edge on the center of the line to establish the perpendicular.

STEP 3: Along this perpendicular line, strike another chalk line extending to both of the side walls.

STEP 4: Along the chalk lines, lay one test row of uncemented tile from the center point to one side wall and to one end wall.

STEP 9: To fit border tiles, place a loose tile "A" exactly over the last tile in the row. Then take another tile "B" and place it on top of tile "A". Butt tile "B" against the wall and mark tile "A" with a pencil along the edge of "B".

STEP 7

STEP 9

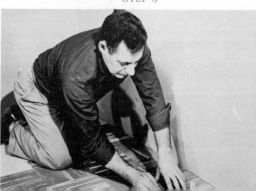

STEP 10

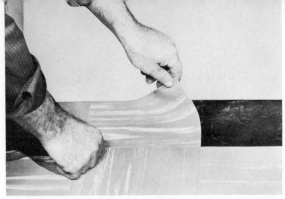

STEP 11

STEP 10: With household shears, cut tile "A" along the pencil mark. Some types of tile can be cut readily if room temperature of at least 70° is maintained.

STEP 11: The cut portion of tile "A" will fit exactly into the border space. Repeat this procedure until the border area is completely covered. Each quarter of the room should be rolled with a linoleum roller or rolling pin as it is completed.

STEP 12: To fit around pipes or other obstructions in a room, first make a paper pattern to fit the space exactly. Then trace the outline onto the tile and cut with scissors.

STEP 12

ACTIVITIES

1. Make a decorating scrapbook. You may choose your own topic: bedroom, living room, first apartment, color harmonies, built-ins, double duty furniture, furniture you can make.

2. **Bulletin Board:** Mount a group of room pictures in color. Indicate the kind of color harmony.

3. Give a "chalk talk" or show illustrations indicating four ways to secure decorative rhythm.

4. **Bulletin Board:** Show a wall composition with (a) good proportion or scale; (b) even balance; (c) uneven balance; (d) unity.

5. Select a floor plan of a living room and bedroom; make a drawing using one-fourth inch to the foot. Cut out furniture templates from construction paper and arrange furniture for good floor composition.

6. Use a scale one half inch to the foot and tape off a living room on flannel board. Use templates in the same scale and give a class demonstration of good and poor floor composition.

7. Assemble fabrics in the colors mentioned on page 315 and demonstrate the effect of daylight, fluorescent and incandescent light.

8. **Bulletin Board:** Display pictures of eighteenth-century, contemporary,

Early American, Provincial, and casual pieces of furniture. Discuss your preferences of styles and woods.

9. Invite a local rug dealer to give a demonstrated talk on different kinds of rugs.

10. Ask a decorator from a store to bring fabric swatches to class and discuss combining textures and fabrics.

11. Assemble a class file of fabrics and furniture woods for demonstrations of color schemes.

12. Experiment with redecorating or rearranging furniture in the homemaking department.

13. Divide the class into groups of three to price sofas, mattresses, end tables, lamps, and chests of drawers. Visit inexpensive as well as higher priced stores. Discuss the manufacturer's reputation, kind of wood (or construction of a mattress), types of joints, price, and guarantee. Note all labels.

14. Discuss how a hobby might be displayed in decorating a home. Assemble illustrations showing clever use of hobbies in decorating.

15. Look at unpainted furniture and discuss ways of finishing it in relation to time and cost.

16. Measure your own living room. Select carpeting and a rug cushion. Compare the cost of wall-to-wall carpeting with other kinds. (Include cushion.) Name the fiber you select and its position in the price range.

17. Visit a furniture department and have a salesman demonstrate important points on furniture—spring construction, joints, wood and wood finishes, upholstery.

Correlation

ART: Have the art teacher explain different ways to display pictures showing how important it is to select pictures in keeping with the theme or period of a room.

ART OR PHYSICS: Investigate the theory of color. Why do some color combinations blend attractively, while others clash? Find other examples of analogous, complementary, and split complementary colors, besides those illustrated in this chapter's color pictures.

WOODWORKING: Have the woodworking teacher demonstrate furniture joints, drawer construction, and other points of furniture construction.

Home Experiences

Study the arrangement of rooms at home with your parents, and experiment with different furniture arrangements where possible.

If you plan to buy any new furniture at home, have your parents read this chapter; help them with plans.

Make a list of the different kinds of floor coverings, furniture woods, upholstery and drapery fabrics you have in your home.

Can you rearrange pictures for a more pleasing effect, or use the hobby of a family member interestingly?

Chapter 16

Keys to Home Management

Home management can be a challenge or a chore. It is a challenge when a person sets goals within reach and tries to attain them efficiently and graciously. It is a chore when a person sets goals too difficult to achieve or when he is not willing to learn good management skills. No one enjoys living either in a home that must always look like model rooms in a department store or one where confusion prevails. A happy medium is best.

Are you doing your part toward good home management? Everything you put into practice now will bring returns when you establish a home of your own, or share living quarters with someone when you start to work.

You would be surprised at all the changes you could make to save time and energy if, for one day only, you could act as an *efficiency expert*. Let's begin with a study area.

ARRANGE AN EFFICIENT STUDY AREA

The following conditions are conducive to good study habits:

• A quiet spot you always associate with studying—no television or family noise to interfere. Some people can study to soft music. If there are noises in adjoining rooms, records or radio music can muffle them.

• A room with plain, light walls. Wallpaper patterns may distract you.

• A light-colored surface on the desk or table to avoid sharp contrast between the surface and paper.

• A straight chair, with a distance of 10 to 12 inches between chair seat and desk top.

• A partitioned drawer or box with sections for pencils, pens, clips, erasers, and so on, plus a place for different kinds of paper.

• A wall or floor lamp, if the desk surface area is limited, or a table lamp placed where it will not cast shadows across your work.

• Good posture. The distance between a person's eye and his work should be about 14 inches. A card table is about 2 inches too low for the average chair but it can be raised on blocks with depressions for the legs to rest in.

331

Better Light Better Sight Bureau

Check your study area. Provide good lighting, a comfortable chair, and a light-colored background for reading.

CHECK OTHER AREAS FOR EFFICIENCY

Here are a few additional ideas for efficient management of any household:

• Set the breakfast table the night before; be sure the proper provisions are on hand for breakfast.

• After meals, scrape up dishes and stack them for washing; wipe off tables and counter surfaces. Even if the dishes are not washed right away, the chore is much easier later.

• Keep excess dirt out of the house by using rugs at entrances and keeping steps and porches swept.

• Use a service cart or large tray to serve and remove dishes at mealtimes.

• Fold and put away clothes that need no ironing as soon as they are dry.

• Pick up newspapers, magazines, clothing; empty the cigarette trays before going to bed.

• Take time in the morning to make beds. When beds are made, dishes stacked, and things are put away, a house is more nearly a home. A little dust is not as objectionable as a house where clothes, toys, and papers are scattered around.

• When there are children, provide play areas or activity centers so that one room may be kept orderly if someone wants a little respite from general family activities.

• Check lamps and table heights; be sure family members are comfortable and have adequate light when studying or doing other work. You can change light bulbs and shades, use risers to give height to lamps, and rearrange tables and chairs to give better lighting.

• If you must stand long in one place for such work as ironing or washing dishes, a soft rubber mat will help avoid fatigue.

• If you find yourself stretching to reach shelves, arrange the things you use frequently within easy reach.

• If you find yourself bumping into furniture in your bedroom or living room, experiment with an arrangement to clear traffic lanes.

• Provide a panel, tool box, or drawer on the main floor for ordinary repairs. Arrange and keep in order.

• Sort and label single and double bed sheets. One homemaker stitches a blue tab on all double bed sheets.

• Hang up clothes, put household items back in place, and close drawers and closet doors before going on to other activities.

• Keep utensils washed, rinsed, and turned upside down on a rack as you prepare a meal. This may mean allowing a few minutes more for a given task, but it saves much time in cleaning up afterward.

Can you think of any other habits that might help you? It is as easy to establish good habits as bad ones.

BETTER KITCHEN PLANNING

A homemaker spends more working hours in the kitchen than in all other rooms put together. The kitchen is the hub of the house. Many activities are controlled from this area. The kitchen should be attractive, well lighted, and conveniently arranged. You can do a great deal to improve any kitchen by storing small equipment and supplies near the points where they are in use most frequently.

You are probably familiar with the three kitchen plans considered most convenient by kitchen engineers—the U-shape, L-shape, and 2-wall. A large family, or one that does a great deal of entertaining, will need a large kitchen with lots of counter space;

otherwise, you can get along with much less. Sometimes you can make more kitchen space by changing the way a door opens. The *men in the family* are often good at spotting changes for greater efficiency.

Kitchen Specifications   Comprehensive kitchen studies have been conducted by housing specialists at the U. S. De-

A portable appliance center. Electrical appliances for serving food or drinks may be stored conveniently in a portable cabinet, which you can move easily to any part of the house. You can get a cabinet wired so you can plug it into a 220-volt wall outlet. The appliances may then be plugged into outlets in the cabinet itself. (Adapted from a sketch in *Good Housekeeping*.)

Observe these dimensions if you build storage units.

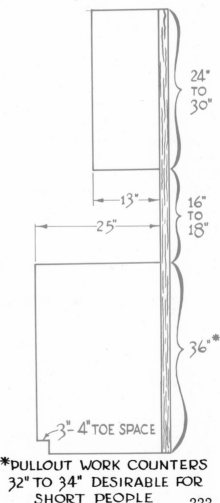

24" TO 30"

13"

25"

16" TO 18"

36"*

3"- 4" TOE SPACE

*PULLOUT WORK COUNTERS 32" TO 34" DESIRABLE FOR SHORT PEOPLE

SINK CENTER

Storage: Dishwashing supplies, towels, strainers, brushes, knives, disposal for food waste.

MIXING CENTER

Storage: Mixer, mixing bowls and spoons, measuring cups and spoons, sifter, beater, rolling pin, baking pans, casseroles, foods used in mixing (sugar, flour, shortening, seasonings, flavorings, spices).

partment of Agriculture, the Small Homes Council of the University of Illinois, the Agricultural Experiment Station of Cornell University, and other centers to determine efficient kitchen arrangements. The three

Storage: Pots and pans, lids, skillets, stirring spoons, coffee, tea, rice, macaroni.

RANGE OR SURFACE COOKING CENTER

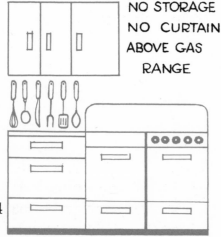

NO STORAGE
NO CURTAIN
ABOVE GAS
RANGE

kitchens illustrated on this page have been most popular. The results of the above studies are summarized.

• The *L-shape kitchen* was found to be the most efficient in the Cornell kitchen study. There is space on two

Storage: Serving cart, trays, serving dishes, dinnerware, toaster, waffle iron, ready-to-eat foods.

SERVE CENTER
(NEAR DINING AREA)

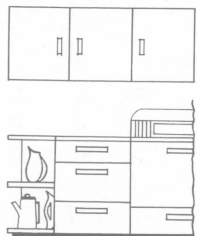

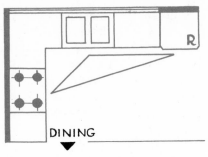

L-SHAPE (7½'×12)

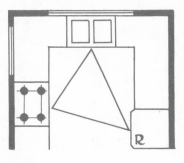

◀ DINING

U-SHAPE (10×11)

ISLANDS AND PENINSULAS
MAY BE WORKED INTO
ANY BASIC PLAN FOR
EATING OR LAUNDRY
ACTIVITIES.

Basic kitchen plans and space requirements.

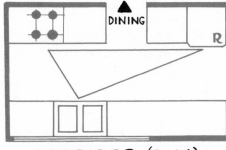

CORRIDOR (8×14)

Place major kitchen units so that work triangle is within limits indicated.

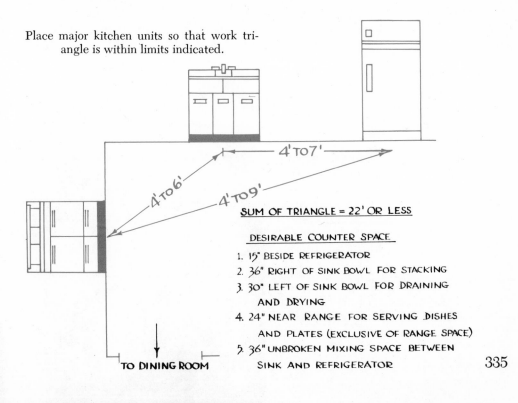

4' TO 7'

4' TO 6'

4' TO 9'

TO DINING ROOM

SUM OF TRIANGLE = 22' OR LESS

DESIRABLE COUNTER SPACE

1. 15" BESIDE REFRIGERATOR
2. 36" RIGHT OF SINK BOWL FOR STACKING
3. 30" LEFT OF SINK BOWL FOR DRAINING
   AND DRYING
4. 24" NEAR RANGE FOR SERVING DISHES
   AND PLATES (EXCLUSIVE OF RANGE SPACE)
5. 36" UNBROKEN MIXING SPACE BETWEEN
   SINK AND REFRIGERATOR

335

The open counter area in a corridor kitchen makes serving easier. No counter or storage space is lost. The laundry makes a T-arrangement at the end of the kitchen.

walls for doors that may lead to the dining room, laundry, basement, or outdoors; there is no cross traffic to interrupt work; and the cleaning closet may be located conveniently.
• The *U-shape kitchen* is the most compact for flow of activities. A laundry wall or counter for eating may be backed against either side of the U. The two corners limit the type of undercounter storage space for kitchen equipment and cleaning supplies. A *peninsula* kitchen is an adaptation of the U-shape.
• The *corridor kitchen* gives the maximum counter and storage space and opens up the service area into the dining area. There is more space for wall oven or refrigerator. A laundry unit may be worked into the counter area or planned at an angle at one end.
• An *island kitchen* provides extra work space and flexibility in a large kitchen but when an island is used, work space is interrupted. A portable island is helpful in a large kitchen. In older homes, it may house a portable dishwasher.

The following information may be applied to all type kitchens. Studies have shown that between 43 and 48 per cent of kitchen work is carried on near the sink; 20 to 30 per cent at the mixing-refrigerator center; 14 to 18 per cent at the range and the balance at the serving-dining-china center. On this basis, the following recommendations have been set up:
• Place sink between range and refrigerator, or if this is not possible, place the range near the sink with work space between.
• Plan to have 30 inches on one side of sink (average sink length 42 inches) and 36 inches on the other—more space on the side where dirty dishes are stacked. Less space is required if there is a dishwasher.
• At one side of range (average range length 36 inches) a minimum of 24 inches counter space is required. If there is a separate oven, the cooking surface is considered the range.
• At one side of the refrigerator (average refrigerator width 31 inches) there should be a counter space of 15 inches.

A lightweight, portable cleaner does many jobs such as cleaning upholstered furniture, draperies, and stair carpet.

• A desirable distance between center of sink and center of refrigerator is from 4 to 7 feet; between center of sink and center of range, 4 to 6 feet; from range to refrigerator, 4 to 9 feet. For efficiency, the floor triangle connecting these three centers should not exceed 22 feet.

• A kitchen should be wide enough to have 4 feet between counters if the arrangement is a U-shape or a corridor, in order to provide space for two people to work. A minimum width of 8 feet is recommended between walls.

• The window area should equal 10-15 per cent of the floor space. A window over the sink or food preparation area is desirable.

• Included in the Beltsville kitchen (U. S. Dept. of Agriculture) is a play area with storage space for toys. When children are older, the area may be used for storing and consulting cookbooks and recipes, and for making out shopping lists.

STORAGE NEEDS

Do you have an untidy, cluttered closet? Nearly every home has one—things come tumbling out when the door is opened. In many homes people have to store things behind doors and under beds. Few homes have adequate storage space.

Often you will find you can increase or make better use of storage space without too much expense or effort. The illustrations in this chapter will give you some help. For more detailed information write to Small Homes Council, University of Illinois, Urbana 61801, and Douglas Fir Ply-

The Hoover Company

With a shampoo cleaner it takes minimum effort to polish floors and shampoo rugs and carpet.

wood Association, Tacoma, Washington 98402.

SHORT-CUTS IN CLEANING

Cleaning schedules are like budgets. They must be tailor-made. Even though you make out a foolproof cleaning schedule, you can be thrown completely off track if there are interruptions such as phone calls, visitors, sickness, committee meetings, or merely a temptation on a beautiful day to enjoy the out-of-doors.

If you heed the suggestions in the early part of the chapter you need not be tied down constantly with housework. You should be able to make housekeeping schedules fit your own needs.

CASE STUDY: Mrs. Arthur Jennings, a young mother, liked to write children's stories. She found she could write best while the baby was taking a morning nap, then tend to the washing, ironing, and cleaning in the after-

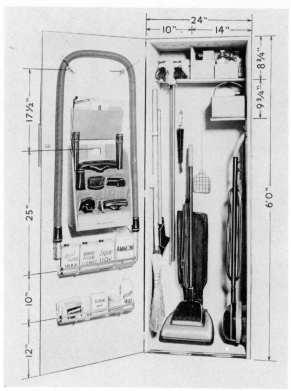

Cleaning and sweeping equipment should be stored together in an orderly way.

noon, watching the baby in the play pen inside or out. Neighbors who saw her working late in the afternoon thought she was lazy and a poor manager until they found out all she was accomplishing. Some people gear their work to fixed schedules, such as Mrs. Jennings, and others to their efficiency curve. The latter are people who do certain jobs better early in the morning—others later in the day.

As a rule, each homemaker soon falls into a daily routine to fit her own needs. It may be more important to attend a school, church, or community function on Monday morning than to do the washing. A good manager need not be a slave to her home and family.

Every homemaker should try to keep her home as orderly as possible and serve meals at regular hours, but homemaking ceases to be fun if the clock must be watched all the time.

Certain things must be done daily, others weekly, and still others occasionally. Do you agree with the following list? Can you add other activities?

DAILY: Cooking, serving, dish washing, tidying up, some dusting; caring for small children.

ONCE OR TWICE A WEEK: Laundry, shopping, mending, more thorough cleaning.

OCCASIONALLY: Window cleaning, floor waxing, cleaning silver, piano keys, light fixtures, blinds, shades and radiators, shelves, closets, turning mattresses, and relocating furniture to prevent worn spots and traffic lanes.

SEASONALLY: Thorough rug cleaning; cleaning walls; household repairs, restoring outdoor furniture, preserving, freezing, and canning foods.

When you help with cleaning at home, learn to use your vacuum cleaner and attachments properly. (Men seldom object to housework that can be done with labor saving equipment.)

NOTE: Keep a list of all the odd jobs to be done around the house, just as you would keep a shopping list, so it will be easy to fit in special jobs with regular cleaning. Suggest to family members how they can help.

The following Cleaning Round-up indicates the kind of care you should give your floors, floor coverings, walls, and furniture. This is when the man in the house can be helpful.

338

Wood Floors Hardwood floors, such as oak, are easier to maintain than softwood floors, such as pine. If you are planning to finish or refinish any wood floor, write for U.S. Department of Agriculture Circular Number 489 — *Selection, Installation, Finish and Maintenance of Wood Floors for Dwellings,* U. S. Government Printing Office, Washington, D.C.

Wash wood floors with soap and water only occasionally, if the floor is very dirty. Constant washing is harmful to wood. Most of the new waxes clean as they wax. You can add a wax remover (available at hardware stores) to the water to remove old wax. Remove shoe marks with a commercial cleaning fluid.

To wax floors, pour on a little puddle of wax, beginning at the corner farthest from the door. With a hand mop, a machine with pad attached, or a large, soft cloth, "pull" the wax lightly over the floor with the grain of the wood. Some people are satisfied with the luster of a self-polishing wax after it dries. Others prefer to go over the floor with a polishing brush or cloth tied to a floor mop.

Rugs Vacuum rugs daily if there is a great deal of traffic. A semi-weekly vacuum job is adequate in most homes and, in some, where there is very little traffic, a weekly cleaning is sufficient. If dust and grit remain in wool long, the fibers tend to disintegrate under heavy use.

A rug should be turned around once or twice a year and sent to a rug cleaner once a year or every other year. You can do a good job yourself with commercial preparations and rug shampoo appliance or attachment on a vacuum cleaner, or you can rent equipment from a paint store. Clean rugs on a day when there is plenty of heat and air circulation. *Open windows and doors* if you are using an inflammable cleaner.

If you have wall-to-wall wool carpeting, at least four times a year move all furniture, and run the vacuum cleaner over every inch of the carpet. Use a moth spray around the edges, under doors and large pieces of furniture. Since this kind of carpeting cannot be turned, some people place scatter rugs over areas where there is much walking.

In using any commercial rug cleaner, it is extremely important to follow directions. Read several times and consider the fiber in your rug, and the backing, in relation to the cleaning preparation. For instance, benzene-type cleaners will make rubber rug backing gummy.

Painted Walls Use a wallpaper cleaner if the paint has a water base. Some people prefer wallpaper cleaner on all flat paint. If you

Closets with folding doors may provide hanger as well as drawer space.

Pella Wood Folding Doors

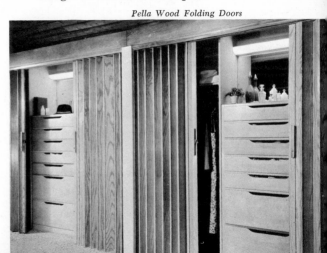

want to prevent streaking, wash walls before they begin to look very dirty. Outside walls tend to soil faster than inside walls and may need to be washed twice as often. In the long run, more frequent washings mean less work and the paint will look fresh longer. Use a wall cleaning solvent according to directions. You may have to experiment, because in different places water varies in softness. A water softener may help. If plaster walls are just tinted, not painted, washing will remove the color.

Wallpaper Use wallpaper cleaner according to directions on the container. If there are grease marks, remove them by packing soft chalk or a commercial preparation on the surface. Some wallpapers may be washed with suds or a detergent. A special dull-finish varnish may be applied to wallpaper when it is new to give it a more durable surface. It will not change the color. Plastic-coated and oilcloth-type wallpapers can be scrubbed.

Furniture A cream furniture polish will give a satinlike "hand-rubbed" luster and clean as it waxes. Be sure to follow directions on the label. Avoid using soap and water on furniture unless the surface has a special protective finish.

• It frequently happens that vases, glasses, and damp clothes leave marks on wood furniture. To remove marks, place a blotter over the surface and hold a warm iron so that it barely touches the blotter. Lift frequently. *Be cautious.*

• Alcohol and perfume will also mark wood. Blot up quickly *without rubbing* and wipe a little silver polish over the area. Polish immediately with a liquid cream polish.

• Hot dishes and coffeepots often leave marks. If the damage is only slight, stroke lightly with a soft, lintless cloth barely moistened with camphorated oil. A refinish job may be necessary, if damage is severe.

• Scratches may be concealed by using one of the furniture pastes of a matching color. These are available at any paint store.

• Vacuum clean upholstered furniture regularly. Make pads of the upholstery or slip-cover fabric to place over arms and backs of upholstered furniture, to prolong the new appearance. Many nylon surfaces and all coated fabrics may be shampooed, if care is taken. See the stain removal chart on page 149 for removing stains from upholstery materials.

Good furniture is valuable and beautiful. With proper care, it can be a source of pride to the owner for many years.

SAVING TIME AND MONEY

Efficiency Tips for the Kitchen Canned, packaged, frozen, and fully prepared foods of all types have cut hours of work from

Removable windows are easy to clean.

340

Better Living, Du Pont

Convenience foods, made possible by new packaging developments, are a major timesaver for housewives. These pictures show the difference in time and effort required by a pre-cooked, pre-packaged goulash dinner and one fixed entirely in the kitchen. Lights attached to the cook's wrists show how many more movements she had to make in the 90 minutes it took her the long way, compared with the pre-cooked way which took only 12 minutes.

the homemaker's day. Few of you have any idea how much time used to be spent cleaning vegetables, canning, and baking. As you know, you can actually get a pretty good meal on the table in a matter of minutes.

It is good to know how to use the "convenience" foods, but one can very easily get into a rut and lose interest in food preparation if frozen dinners and similar items make up most of the daily menu. Put a little imagination on at least one dish, and supplement it with prepared or semi-prepared foods if you are on a busy schedule. Strained baby foods have been one of the greatest timesavers to the busy young mother.

If you own an electric frying pan, a mixer, a pressure cooker, or a range with automatic burners and oven, learn to use them properly by studying the guides that come with this equipment. Keep frozen, canned, or cured meats and cheese on hand for a main dish in an emergency; lettuce and canned fruits for a salad; ice

cream and frozen cookies for dessert.

When you make meat sauce for spaghetti, certain soups and molded salads that freeze well, waffles, and some casserole recipes, make enough for two meals and freeze half. In warm weather, keep such foods as cottage cheese, fresh apple sauce, or fresh pickled beets in covered dishes in the refrigerator, and cheese, cold meats, tomatoes, and fresh fruit also on hand. On busy days or when guests arrive unexpectedly, an appetizing meal can be prepared in a hurry.

CASE STUDY: Mrs. Albert Joyce, with a teaching job and three children in school, loves to cook but has little time during the week. On Sunday she prepares half a ham, a leg of lamb, a small turkey, or a beef roast. Monday there will be cold slices, and Tuesday hash or a baked casserole. She also makes several pie shells at one time to store or fill with fruit and freeze. She may make three cakes one to ice, one to have later with a custard sauce, and another to serve with ice cream and fruit at the end of the week.

Simple Home Repairs This is directed mainly to the males.

If you are in earnest about wanting to save money on simple home repairs, provide a tool panel and keep it in a convenient place. It is easier to keep track of tools this way than in drawers, or shelves, and in boxes. Here are a few repairs that are not difficult.

A DRIPPING FAUCET: Turn off the water at the valve under the sink or wherever it may be. Pad the cap nut with a soft cloth to prevent damage. Remove the cap nut with a wrench. Turn handle and lift out inside mechanism. Locate screw head that holds the washer secure. Remove screw and washer. Replace washer and reassemble.

A NOISY FLUSH TANK: Make sure the float is resting on top of the water. If it is submerged, it has a leak, must be unscrewed and replaced with a new one. If the water level in the tank is too low or too high, this may be causing the trouble. If too low, bend the rod up; if too high, bend the rod down. If trouble continues, turn off the water at the water valve and flush the tank to empty it. Raise the lift wire carefully without bending and replace the tank ball.

A TIGHT OR SAGGING DOOR: Tighten all screws first; then replace loose ones, driving a used wooden match stem into the hole to help fill it up. (Plastic wood may be used.) Rub wax or soap along the edge of a door. (This helps with a window that sticks also.) If the door persists in sticking, find the tight spot, and sand it.

If the door sags badly, mark place to be planed, remove the pins that hold the hinges in place, and lift the door off. Plane the edge very carefully and replace the pins.

LOOSE DOOR KNOB: Loosen set screw, turn knob till play is gone. Tighten set screw.

WORN WINDOW SHADES: Reverse and double the wear. Stretch the shade on a large table and clean it with wallpaper cleaner, if it is not washable—a good detergent or suds, if it is washable. Rinse and dry well. Remove tacks on roller. Hem top of shade on the sewing machine, using a *long* stitch. It will help to have another person hold the shade. Trim off worn hem and tack it in place. Tighten the spring at one end of the roller by slipping the tines of an old fork over the end and rolling.

Less Work in Laundering Many young couples use laundromats. It is convenient to take the laundry on a trip to the market. After young people are settled in one location and have children, they usually find it more convenient to have laundry facilities at home.

Where to place the home laundry, what soaps and detergents to use, and how to launder the new fabrics have been important topics for many years.

Where to place laundry equipment will be determined by the kind of home in which you live. Most homemakers like to work in or near the kitchen to be close to everything. This is especially important when there are small children and no outside help.

Some people object to the laundry noises, odors, and excess heat from the dryer, and prefer a basement laundry. A few home planners put a washer-dryer in or near the bathroom or in a hall closet. Before you settle for this, ask families who have such laundries how well they like the arrangement. People with grown children often do not care for bathroom laundries.

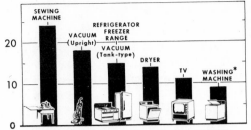

EXPECTED YEARS OF USE BY ONE OWNER
NEW APPLIANCES ONLY • ELECTRIC OR GAS RANGES,
OTHER ITEMS ELECTRIC ONLY.
* AUTOMATIC OR OTHER.

Drip-dry clothes present an increasing laundry problem. They have to be dried above surfaces that will not be harmed by moisture. For this reason many equipment manufacturers are adapting their washers and dryers for the *easy-care* garments and household textiles. Some homemakers install a rod for hanging clothes over a trough with a drain, or over the bath tub.

If you do not have a dryer or a basement, and the weather will not permit outdoor drying, pat most of the water off garments with a bath towel and hang drip-dry garments over the bathtub. Use unpainted wood or plastic hangers to avoid rust or stain from varnish. Do not use pants hangers with felt lining because the felt dyes bleed. Always save labels. *Read the washing directions.*

A washer-dryer combination is good if you are in no hurry about having your clothes. The washing-drying process may take longer than separate washing and drying, but there is less handling. Homemakers with large families find that it saves time to use a washer and dryer *and* sometimes their old fashioned electric wringer washer if space is no problem. They can dovetail all the washing operations this way and finish up faster.

Other homemakers prefer to keep a semi-automatic washer and buy an automatic dryer rather than trade in the semi-automatic washer on an automatic model. They feel that if they can afford only one piece of equipment, it is less work to wash and rinse clothes and dry them automatically than it is to wash them automatically and hang them up. Weather is never a problem with a dryer.

In planning laundry activities, follow a production line procedure. If you hang clothes on a clothesline, carry your wet clothes along in a high, folding cart with waterproof basket. If you need the bending and stretching to keep your figure trim, forget about the push cart!

CARE IS PART OF MANAGEMENT

Unless you give all equipment the proper care, you will not get full benefit from it. It will wear out faster and increase your home maintenance budget in repair or replacement bills.

Every appliance requires some special care. Be certain to follow the manufacturer's instructions. Post or file them for easy reference. Enamel surfaces of appliances should be cleaned with a soft cloth or sponge and mild detergent.

This specific advice applies to many makes and models of appliances.

RANGE: Avoid wiping enamel and glass surfaces when they are hot. Avoid using large pots that extend far over the burners because heat from them can crack the enamel surface of the range. Keep trays under broiler and burners clean with impregnated steel wool pads. Remove spilled food from electric burners by turning to HIGH; after cooling, brush off residue. Gas burners may be soaked in a solution of ammonia, then dried well and replaced.

RANGE HOOD: Keep enamel surfaces clean and free of grease. Clean and remove filters according to directions.

DISHWASHER: Scrape and hand rinse all dishes, pots, and pans. Load according to directions. Adjust controls to desired settings. Do not force a dial—some turn in only one direction. Keep drain free of food deposits. Release handle of washer door after cycle to prolong life of gasket. (The gasket is the rubber tubing around the door opening which seals tight when shut.)

REFRIGERATOR: Follow manufacturer's instructions about defrosting. Never use an ice pick or other sharp object to scrape ice from a freezer unit; this will leave scratches and may puncture the compartment lining. When defrosting freezer, wrap frozen foods in towels and store in cold unit of refrigerator. Defrosting time can be shortened by placing pans of hot water in freezer unit. Pans must be refilled when water cools. When frost is gone, clean inside freezer compartment with detergent or solution of 1 quart water and 1 teaspoon soda.

Rinse and dry inside. Be sure to dry gasket. Replace food in freezer as soon as defrosting is finished and unit is turned on again. Wipe out cold compartment with soda solution. Keep the gasket clean and dry for maximum sealing and wear.

DISPOSAL: Do not put heavy bones, seafood shells, glass, or metal in unit. Lift stopper and scrape food into drain. Fill but do not pack. On some models, stopper should be placed in cradle position. Turn on switch; use cold water to solidify grease. Let run for 30 seconds after grinding stops to flush drain. Turn off switch and water.

IRON: Avoid overheating. Avoid ironing heavily starched clothes. Keep ironing surface smooth by rubbing with beeswax occasionally. Keep steam iron free of sediment and at maximum efficiency by flushing out with a liquid made for the purpose.

MIXER: Use machine oil to lubricate bearings in motor and at base of turntable. Check directions for position of bearings and amount of oil. Avoid using high speed with heavy loads.

WASHER: Make certain that controls are properly set for the types of garments you are washing. Do not place sharp objects, pins, or buckles in washer. Be certain that washer is electrically grounded. This is especially important for appliances using water.

DRYER: Set for proper temperature and time. Keep lint container clear for maximum results. Remove clothes immediately after drying to eliminate excess wrinkling.

ACTIVITIES

1. Discuss home management on the basis of your present habits, and recommendations in the text. Name some ways you are helping to make things run more smoothly at home. In what other ways can you contribute toward better home management?

2. Pick someone to lead a discussion on using the suggestions on page 332. You may transpose the suggestions into a questionnaire and tabulate results in class.

3. **Bulletin Board:** Arrange a display of attractive and well planned kitchens and laundries.

4. Secure copies of the bulletins mentioned from the University of Illinois Small Homes Council, and Cornell University Agricultural Experiment Station, and give brief reports.

5. **Bulletin Board:** Mount clippings showing: (a) good home storage areas, (b) remodeling to provide better storage. Find out carpenter rates in your area and discuss what you save if you can do your own work on several storage projects.

6. Discuss the statement, "A very definite cleaning schedule should be followed regardless of interruptions."

7. Demonstrate the following operations (practice in advance in order to make best use of class time):
• Shampoo a small rug or sample with a commercial cleaning substance. Comment on cleaning wool, nylon, rayon, cotton, and other rug fibers.
• Clean washable and non-washable wall paper.
• Remove various kinds of spots from a table top.
• Clean a piece of upholstered furniture. Mention special care for cotton, wool, rayon, nylon, or other fibers.

8. Bring clothing labels to class. Discuss directions for care, including various methods of cleaning "wash and wear" garments.

9. Visit local appliance stores to study vacuum cleaners, washers, and dryers. Bring folders to class and compare features.

10. Have several members of the class demonstrate how to use and care for the following:

toaster	mixer
vacuum cleaner	sewing machine
steam iron	coffee pot
washer	dryer

11. Show films or film strips related to this chapter; discuss them in class.

12. Measure distance between your kitchen work centers and compare with recommendations shown on page 335.

13. Study the cost of home laundering (considering the cost of equipment); taking laundry to a laundromat; paying a laundress; and using a commercial laundry. Any compromise plan?

Correlation

INDUSTRIAL ARTS: Arrange with the teacher of industrial arts to demonstrate how to repair:

dripping faucet	loose door knob
noisy flush tank	loose window pane
sagging door	other common jobs

Home Experiences

As you make your bed, wash dishes, iron, cut the grass, or wash a car, conduct a "time-motion" study to see how you can do the job more easily.

Make one or more repairs at home and report to class.

Check areas of your home including basement, kitchen, and closets, to see if they could be used more efficiently.

Chapter 17

Keys to Money Management

If you should win $25,000 in a national big-money contest, how would you spend it? You might think first of personal pleasures. Or you might want to buy a new home for your family, or invest in a business and become financially independent.

Long before the big contest "giveaways" of today, Granddad dreamed about the things he would do "when his ship came in." It doesn't cost to dream and we always will, but to make your dreams come true, you cannot wait for good things to happen to you. Your chances are much better if you set your goals and learn how to earn and spend money wisely as you go along.

Frequently, young couples fail to look far enough ahead in order to measure present wants against future goals. For example, the Grays were happy with their second-hand car and black-and-white television until their neighbors bought a new car and color TV. Arlene Gray was no longer happy with her ordinary television set or John with his three-year-old car. In order to keep up with their neighbors, they withdrew all of their savings, meant for a down payment on a home, and began installment payments on a new television and car. They wanted a better home, but were not willing to give up anything for it.

While still in school you may want things now that will make it impossible to have more important things later. If you feel that you are not getting a large enough share of the family income to keep up with your friends, and cannot buy everything you want, pause to see if your demands are reasonable, or fair to other family members. Do you expect them to make sacrifices for you?

Most parents make financial sacrifices beyond reason for their children. Perhaps yours are trying to divide income carefully in order to pay off a mortgage, save for your education, or take out more insurance. Keeping up with your friends may not be as important as you think, when you understand your family's finances. Even if your family can afford to give you a

346

large allowance, you are wise to limit your spending. The confidence you gain from this self-control is priceless. If you are earning part of your spending money, you certainly should learn to distinguish between wise and foolish spending.

As a child, you probably spent most of your money on things of no permanent value—bubble gum or a flimsy toy. Now you are entering adulthood. You need the respect of your fellow adults.

HOW MUCH SPENDING MONEY DO YOU NEED?

This is a question that cannot be answered quickly because too many factors are involved—family income, the type of community and section of the country in which you live, whether you take a bus or walk to school, carry or buy lunch, how often you date. The chart on page 348 will be helpful in estimating the amount of money *you* will need each week. Make a copy of it and enter your own figures to cover the school year.

When you have worked out your spending plan, you will know how much you will need to lay aside each week for seasonal clothing and graduation activities. Every budget should include savings. The habits you form now of saving for things you know you will need in the near future, or for unexpected emergencies, will be of value to you all your life.

CASE STUDY: Dick Thomas estimated that he would need $18.60 a week for his senior year expenses, half of which he could earn himself.

Everything went along fine until a week before school closed. Dick de-

cided to have a new bathing suit, slacks, sports shirt, socks, and belt for the class cook-out. One evening Dick and two friends took their dates to an amusement park, where he spent $10.00. It was a mid-week date that he hadn't figured in his plans. These expenses threw his calculations off nearly $30.00 for May.

Dick found he had no money for the balance owed on his yearbook, renting a tuxedo for the senior prom, corsage for his girl, or activities after the prom. Dick was embarrassed, but decided to talk things over with his father.

"Well, Son," said his father, "we can't always anticipate every expense nine months ahead. Let's have a look at your record book. What about the $239.56 savings I see here?"

"Well, I can't touch that. With whatever I save this summer, it will take care of my spending money next year at college."

"I see. Let's go on then. How about these items—bathing suit, slacks, sport shirt, socks, belt?"

Dick explained that he needed the outfit for senior cook-out. Also, he would wear the sport clothes all summer, and next summer, too. So he had set aside enough for them.

Parents and children benefit from sharing simple money management decisions.

H. Armstrong Roberts

"Which would you rather give up, the prom or the senior cook-out?" said Father.

It sounded silly, comparing them that way. The prom seemed more important. Yet his old sport clothes were in bad shape, and the cook-out was a mark of prestige for seniors.

BUDGET ITEMS FOR ONE SCHOOL YEAR

	On the Basis of	School Year	Weekly Totals
School lunches.	.... a day		
Games and movies.	.... a week		
Dates.	.... a week		
Snacks and soft drinks.	.... a week		
Bus fare.	.... a day		
Contributions: Church. Other.	.... a week		
*Clothing and cleaning.	.... a year		
School supplies.	.... a week		
Records, reading material, hobbies.	.... a week		
Club and class dues.	.... a year		
Car and gas.	.... a week		
Hair cuts and grooming.	.... every other week		
Special lessons.	.... a week		
*Gifts.	.... a year		
*Graduation: Cap and gown. Pictures. Year book. Ring.	.... a year		
Savings and miscellaneous.	.... a month		
Margin for error.	....		

*A weekly amount may be set aside to meet these expenses when they arise.

Dick thought everything out. "I guess I'd rather have all the fun I can now," he decided. "Next year I'll be just a freshman again. I won't have a chance to enjoy a senior's privileges again for a long time. This year I'm going to live it up."

He used part of his college savings to "balance his books." Do you think he acted correctly? Remember, if you *really save*, you will have money for such emergencies. If you don't save, you always have to beg from someone—perhaps from Dad today, and from a loan agency tomorrow!

SUPPLEMENTING AN ALLOWANCE

Businesses, clubs, city, county, state, and national governments make out tentative budgets, based on all income they think they will have. Frequently they run into the same snags you do — not enough money.

There are three ways out for big business and government. (1) Examine their needs, and eliminate anything they can do without. (2) Learn more about buying, so they can spend more wisely. (3) If they still cannot get along, find out how they can raise more money. To raise more money, businesses increase prices; governments increase taxes. You can perhaps borrow but more likely must earn extra money.

At 18, about half the young men and one-third of the young women have part-time jobs. Here are typical jobs available after school and over weekends: clerking in stores (especially good for girls), washing cars, cutting lawns or shoveling snow, working in filling stations, car hop-

H. Armstrong Roberts

An evening at home is often fun, and it helps the budget.

ping, caddying, driving delivery trucks, and baby sitting.

A few talented persons play in orchestras, retouch photographs, make and sell Christmas cards and gifts. What jobs have you held? Are you sure a job during the school year is worth the sacrifice you might have to make for it? Remember what was said about work in Chapter 1.

DO YOU WASTE MONEY?

You will probably say "not much" until you give this question serious thought. Here are some ways students —and their parents—have discovered they were wasting money.

• Jean Ashley, on her first summer job in a department store, was able to buy at an employee's discount. She spent almost her entire salary on jewelry and summer clothes. She bought with no plan in mind for fall clothing or complete outfits.

• Jack Friedman had a difficult time living within his college allowance his first year until he began to record his expenses. His cigarette bill alone was shocking. He did not hang up his clothes, and as a result spent too much

349

SEASONAL SALES CALENDAR

January	July
Sheets, pillowcases, linens, soaps, toiletries, winter apparel, furs, Christmas cards and decorations.	Summer apparel, rugs, appliances, air conditioners, fans, dehumidifiers.
February	**August**
Winter apparel, housewares, furniture.	Furniture, furs, sheets, pillow cases, linens, winter coats.
March	**September**
Air conditioners, books, luggage, spring apparel.	Silverware, glassware, dishes, cosmetics, hosiery, beef.
April	**October**
Spring apparel, shoes, millinery, handbags, accessories, baby goods.	Men's winter coats, autos, veal, lamb.
May	**November**
Sheets, pillowcases, linens, mattresses, box springs, toiletries, stationery, notions, lawn and garden equipment.	Luggage, autos.
June	**December**
Summer apparel, accessories, men's sportswear, air conditioners, fans, dehumidifiers.	Glassware, lamps, home accessories.

Even a routine activity, such as a trip to a department store, can be a pleasant family experience. This family is properly dressed, which adds to the occasion.

H. Armstrong Roberts

on cleaning. He missed a dozen lunches a month at the dorm, and substituted snacks at his own expense.
• The Green family for over twelve years had a habit of letting all their bills run until the discount period had expired. They figured this alone had cost them about $76 a year, a total sum of over $900—exactly the balance on their car payments.

How are you and your family wasting money? Do you sit down together and analyze it?

Economists claim that careful planning and spending, geared to seasonal price mark-downs, can save ten per cent on personal needs.

You might show the accompanying chart to your parents.

350

COST OF BUYING AND OPERATING A CAR

Your first car will probably be a *used car*. If you do buy a used car, here are some things to think about:
• Buy from a reliable dealer—one who has been in business long enough to have established a good reputation.
• Don't be pressured into buying. Take time to look around and compare prices, performance, and appearance.
• Beware of dealers who ask for little or no down payment. The down payment (including value of your trade-in) is usually about a fourth of the cost.
• An older car that has had good care often is a better buy than a newer one which has been abused. The dealers' *Blue Book* lists standard prices for used cars, but the condition of the car often will make it worth more or less than what is listed.
• Sign nothing until you are sure you are getting the best car for your price. There will always be another "bargain."
• Decide how much you can pay down, and how much monthly.
• List all extra costs such as registration, insurance, and repairs. Collision, fire, and theft insurance are compulsory until the car is paid for.
• Compare the total cost of borrowing money from a bank or savings and loan association at prevailing interest rates, paying cash for the car, or financing it through a finance company.
• Shop around and compare models considering (1) how many owners have used the car, (2) how many miles it has been driven (mileage meters may be altered), (3) whether it has ever been in a wreck, (4) the condition of the interior, tires, chrome, and

paint, and (5) special features and accessories included in the price.
• Unless you have had experience with cars, ask a mechanic to listen to the motor and drive the car around. Find out first what he charges for his advice.
• Be just as thorough when you are trading a car on a new one.

Figures show that sixty per cent of car buyers deal through finance companies. You probably will buy your first car this way. The Federal Trade Commission protects you by declaring that you must be given an itemized statement of all costs involved. When you or your parents buy a car, read your statement carefully before signing on the dotted line.

The following chart is typical of the statement you sign.

ITEMIZED STATEMENT IN USED CAR SALE

Total selling price...............		$1,200.00
Deductions		
Trade-in allowance...........	$300.00	
Cash down payment..........	200.00	500.00
Unpaid balance...................		$700.00
Insurance (See that each kind is listed.)		
Personal liability.............	$ 83.00	
Property damage.............	24.00	
Collision ($50 deductible).....	100.00	
Credit life insurance.........	12.00	$219.00
Balance plus insurance..........		$919.00
Total finance charges (6 per cent of total owed for *18 monthly payments*)*...............		$82.71
Total amount owed to finance company...................		1,001.71
Monthly payments.............		$55.65

*Six per cent of $919 is $55.14. This is the interest for one year. Interest for the extra half year is found by adding on another half of this annual interest figure, or $27.57, for a total of $82.71.

If you borrow $600 to buy a car, and agree to repay $636 in a year, you may think you are paying 6 per cent interest. But if you make 12 monthly payments of $53 each, you will pay a much higher rate. With each payment you reduce what you owe, but you continue to pay interest on the full amount you borrowed.

From each payment, $50 goes toward the $600 you borrowed, and $3 toward interest. After six months you owe just $300, but you still pay $3 interest, which now amounts to one per cent a *month* and more than ten per cent a *year*.

In a long-term loan, this will add up rapidly. If you must borrow, try to arrange a loan in which the interest is figured on the *unpaid balance*. When this is impossible, it will be to your advantage to pay off the loan quickly.

Next to a home, a car represents the biggest cash outlay for many people. *Depreciation* (decline in value) is the largest part of this expense. The day after an owner drives his new car home it is a used car, worth less than on the day before.

Depreciation is greatest in the first year. For example, in 1968 an average-priced car cost about $3,000. Its value would decline by about $850 in the first year, and another $600 in the next year. The following charts, based on 1967-68 statistics, will give you

VARIABLE COSTS IN CAR OWNERSHIP

	Average per Mile
Gasoline and oil	2.65 cents
Maintenance	.68
Tires	.47
	3.80 cents

FIXED COSTS IN CAR OWNERSHIP

	Annual
Fire and theft insurance	$ 39.00
Property damage and liability insurance	148.00
$100-deductible collision insurance	85.00
License and registration	26.00
Depreciation (average)	684.00
Total yearly fixed costs	$982.00

a basis for determining the costs of owning and using a car.

To find the total cost per mile, add all costs and divide by the number of miles driven. For example, if the car were driven 10,000 miles, the variable cost would be 3.8 cents times 10,000 or $380. Adding this to the $982 fixed costs gives a total of $1,362. Dividing by 10,000 you learn that the cost per mile was 13.6 cents.

If the same car were driven 20,000 miles, the total cost would be greater ($1,742) but the cost per mile would be less (8.7 cents).

Most cars are expected to last ten years. After that there is little or no depreciation. Therefore if a car is used longer than ten years, the cost per mile of driving it is reduced, but maintenance costs rise rapidly with the car's age.

COSTS OF FURTHER EDUCATION

The following chart will help you determine the cost of education beyond high school. After consulting *The College Handbook* or catalogs of educational institutions, estimate your expenses at institutions where costs are low, average, and high. Compare and examine the estimates to see what you can afford.

COST OF GOING TO COLLEGE

College Costs	Low	Average	High
	Don't	write in this	book.
Tuition............			
Other fees.........			
Room.............			
Board.............			
Laundry...........			
Books and supplies..			
Transportation.....			
Clothing...........			
Spending money....			
TOTAL			

LIVING COSTS OF AN INDIVIDUAL WORKING AWAY FROM HOME

When you are on the pay-as-you-go basis, using your own hard-earned cash, you will give more thought to some problems your parents have been having for many years. To begin with, you will have a shock when your check comes through minus income tax, social security, and perhaps group hospitalization and retirement deductions.

Uncle Sam can take his share at the source. If you are an office worker earning $3,600 and have no dependents, off goes $468 for federal income tax, about $173 for Social Security and $100 or more for group hospitalization.

With the deductions above and possibly other minor ones, a $3,600 gross income is reduced to approximately $2,900 usable or net income. A $4,000 salary minus deductions leaves about $3,150 spendable income. In typical metropolitan areas this might provide for a furnished room in a home or a very modest unfurnished apartment. The same salary might go further in parts of the South and Midwest and in almost any small town.

The following chart shows how a typical beginning office worker might spend $2,900 annual net income.

BUDGET FOR BEGINNING OFFICE WORKER (BASIC SALARY, $3,600— AFTER DEDUCTIONS, $2,900)

Items	Amount per Year	Amount per Month
Food..............	$1,050	
Housing (furnished room)............	670	
Clothing............	240	
Personal............	140	
Recreation and advancement........	150	
Transportation......	180	
Church and charity...	70	
Savings, life insurance, etc..........	400	
Total...........	$2,900	

The amounts in the chart can be rearranged in many ways. For instance, it might prove less expensive to rent a small apartment. The apartment itself would cost more, but there would be considerable saving on food if cooking were done at home.

It would take good health and careful management to keep going on this income. Savings could be quickly wiped out by an emergency.

Figure this budget on a weekly basis. How would you suggest cutting corners to provide for such items as a car or a television set?

353

OUR CHANGING STANDARDS
OF LIVING

Not long ago we could define five or six standards of living, but no longer can we divide our society very clearly into even three distinct classes. The pyramid graph of income, with a large number of persons at the bottom layer, a sizable number in the middle, and a small number at the top has changed. The figure is now diamond-shaped, with only a small percentage in the lower and upper areas. In the future, it is possible that the pyramid may turn upside down, with the bulk of families at the higher income level.

Some sociologists have suggested individual pyramids to represent business, science, labor, the military, entertainment, sports, and other areas. Even within each of these pyramids, differences are less marked as families strive to improve their living conditions and achieve a higher cultural, economic, and social status. No longer is a boy willing to "keep his place" just because his father accepted a low position. Skilled workers are at a premium and demand higher standing. Education raises status.

Nowhere else in the world do people have as much money to spend on luxuries as in the United States. For instance, Americans spend more than $26 billion a year on recreation. Such spending is possible because of high income levels. In one recent year fewer than 15 per cent of our nation's families were considered poor, according to standards set up by the Social Security Administration. Therefore you can see that the diamond-shaped income chart mentioned earlier is becoming top-heavy.

Social Changes Jobs with little prestige and relatively low pay have commonly been referred to as "blue-collar jobs." Now this situation is changing. Even the term is going out of fashion. Not many years ago blue-collar workers wore work clothes to factories, rode trollies and buses, and carried lunch boxes. Now many of them wear suits to work and change to work clothes which they keep in lockers at the plant, drive their own late-model cars to work, and eat hot meals in company cafeterias. They live in suburbs, in homes ranging from $18,000 to $30,000, and enjoy a standard of living only families in the high income bracket could have enjoyed just a generation ago.

To lend prestige to many jobs, and to give workers a feeling of personal importance, ordinary jobs are frequently given impressive names. For instance, *engineer* is sometimes applied to janitorial work—custodial engineer — the same as it is to highly trained electronics and missile experts. Banks and businesses are giving more staff members titles—directors, managers, assistant vice presidents, executives. Colleges have more department heads, vice chancellors, and deans.

Some students of our culture believe that these titles satisfy a basic human need for recognition, and that they are important to help people retain dignity in this era when machines are doing many jobs faster and better than humans can do them. Others say that this search for prestige and "status" is unhealthy and false— just another form of "keeping up with the Joneses" or making all of us think and act alike.

Strong forces are at work in our culture, changing it in ways that are sometimes vast and easy to observe, sometimes gradual and hard to detect. We seem aware that we must not let our nation be divided because of political, religious, or ancestral differences. Not only our national leaders, but ordinary people as well seem willing to discuss these matters more calmly than was possible in the early part of the century.

In religion, mergers have brought together several Protestant bodies, and even larger moves of this kind are under discussion. The Roman Catholic Church also is increasing its efforts to close the gaps which separate Christians. Leaders of many faiths have said that better religious understanding is very likely to result from these steps toward unity, called the ecumenical movement. Fellowships of Jews and Christians, working together in worthy, charitable causes, are not uncommon.

Politically as well, some of the die-hard spirit seems to be fading. Healthy differences of opinion still exist among politicians, but they seem based on genuine issues, not on traditional party membership. It is no longer enough to know what party a man belongs to if you want to learn his political ideas. Many elected officials have spoken and voted against their own party when they agreed with the opposition's views.

About 95 per cent of the people now living in this country were born here. Strong feelings against nationality groups have lessened as people have realized it is more important to be good Americans than to worry about where our grandparents were born. Even in relations between the races,

where bitterness has been common, there is evidence that understanding and acceptance are growing gradually. Naturally, the troubled areas have attracted most attention, and will continue to do so, but while some cities have had difficulties, others only a few miles away have undergone similar social changes quietly and without publicity.

Another powerful influence on our society is the population growth. In 1967 the number of United States citizens passed the 200 million mark, up from roughly 150 million just 17 years earlier. At present more than half of our population is under 25. Sociologists say we have become a youth-oriented society. However, a different pattern may lie ahead because the birth rate, surprisingly, has been falling steadily since the mid-1950's. Population growth affects our nation's economy in many ways. For instance, the buying power of young people creates a constant demand for new products.

Still another change in our society has been the movement of people from farms to cities and now to suburbs. An earlier chapter discussed how this affected family life. It has also influenced the financial life of our nation. For instance, vast amounts of farm land have been converted to residential areas. Central areas of many cities have declined as wealthier people have decided to live, shop, and build offices elsewhere.

Economic Influences The preceding paragraphs discussed changes in society which have influenced our nation's economy. The process works both ways—economic forces affect society. Some economic reasons for our changed way of life are:

• Graduated income tax, taking as much as 90 per cent of earnings in the higher brackets, has leveled income possibilities.

• Social security and pension plans have relieved many of the financial problems of old age.

• Health insurance in some form, including Medicare, has been made available to most families.

• Perhaps most important of all, increased family incomes and widespread use of credit have changed American buying habits. The importance of these two economic influences is discussed in the following paragraphs.

Increased Income and Credit Despite inflation Americans have more money to spend than ever before. Because of higher salaries and more families with two or more wage earners, family income has risen faster than the cost of living. Median family income rose from $4,200 in 1950 to $6,897 in 1967. The estimate for 1970 is $8,465. (The median is the mid-point, with as many families above as below.) Although taxes were 140 per cent higher in the 1960's than in the 1950's, the average family had 22 per cent more buying power.

After paying for necessities, many families have money left. This is called *discretionary income*, meaning that the family can spend this money as it pleases. People's spending habits have changed over the years. For instance, automation at work and labor-saving appliances at home have given

people more free time; this in turn largely explains the tremendous outlay of money for recreation (mentioned earlier in this chapter). Also, because of advertising and a higher educational level, people now have tastes and interests far different from those of their grandparents.

Spending has become increasingly easy, with inducements to buy now and pay later. Credit cards and installment credit are available to most people simply for the asking. The emphasis is no longer upon thrift or "saving for a rainy day" because retirement plans, social security, group hospitalization, and mortgage payments on a home represent savings. During the first quarter of the century most people bought only very expensive items on credit. They saved until they had the money to pay cash for their purchases. Now many items are worn out before the last payment is made. (Specific forms of credit are discussed later in this chapter.)

COST OF ESTABLISHING A HOME

In 1967 the U.S. Department of Labor published its latest survey of living costs for a typical family. It was based on a nationwide study of families in large and small cities, but not in rural areas.

The survey, called *The City Worker's Family Budget*, shows costs for a family of four—father, mother who is not a wage earner, 13-year-old boy, and 8-year-old girl. They live in a five-room dwelling in a pleasant location, with modern plumbing, furnace heat, refrigerator, television, and an automatic washer. They have a second-hand car and life insurance, take a modest two-week vacation, and make ordinary contributions and gifts. This is considered moderate living.

When the first survey was taken, in 1946-47, it was found that the family needed $3,251 per year. By 1959-60 this had nearly doubled, rising to $6,147. In the 1967 survey the family's expenses were $9,191. The two earlier studies were based on lower standards (termed *adequate*). The change to moderate standards in the latest survey reflects the tendency of working-class families to raise their living standards. (Still, note the continuing difference between *median* and *moderate* incomes.)

For instance, earlier surveys assumed that the family rented its dwelling. In the latest study, costs of renting and buying are compared. It costs about $800 a year less to rent, the study shows, but the family that buys its home is building an equity or savings with mortgage payments.

The chart below is based on the most recent survey. It compares the costs of living in three types of communities. The first column of figures shows how much money the family would need, and how its expenses might be divided, in a community where living costs were average. The last two columns show comparable figures for a community where costs are highest (a metropolitan area) and one where they are lowest (a small town). Notice that the family could maintain the same living standards on

MODERATE BUDGET FOR A CITY WORKER'S FAMILY

	National Average for all Communities	Percent of Budget (col. 1)	Large Cities	Small Towns
Food	$2,143	23.2%	$2,173	$2,005
Housing	2,214	24.1	2,286	1,894
Transportation	815	8.9	815	813
Clothing and Upkeep	756	8.2	767	709
Personal Care	214	2.3	218	194
Medical Care (including insurance)	468	5.1	481	411
Recreation	306	3.3	310	291
Reading and Education	120	1.3	130	76
Gifts and Contributions	253	2.8	259	231
Occupational Expenses	80	0.9	80	80
Life Insurance	160	1.8	160	160
Miscellaneous Expenses	293	3.2	294	287
Total Spendable Income	$7,822	85.1%	$7,973	$7,151
Personal Tax	$1,080	11.8%	$1,112	$ 935
Social Security	289	3.1	291	280
Total Income	$9,191	100.0%	$9,376	$8,366

roughly a thousand dollars less in the small town.

The second column shows the percentage of the family's income that would be spent for certain items. (This is based on the average community and would be somewhat different in areas where costs are unusually high or low.) Families with below average incomes often find that a higher percentage of their money is spent for food and housing, and a lower percentage for clothing, recreation, and education. You might want to keep this list of percentages and refer to it when the day comes that you are responsible for setting up a family budget.

Among the expenses that have increased most over the years since the first survey are income tax, health insurance, transportation, and services of all kinds. The latest survey was the first one in which housing costs exceeded food costs. (Housing includes rent or mortgage payments, utilities, maintenance, repairs, and home furnishings.)

It was assumed that the average family would spend $1,824 on food prepared at home and $319 on meals away from home. Total food cost could be reduced if more meals were eaten at home.

Remember, this study was based on a family of four. It is estimated that a husband and wife alone can live on 66 per cent of the income needed by a family of four. A couple with one child can live comfortably on 87 per cent, and a family of five will need 120 per cent of the adequate income for the typical family.

The figures in the Labor Department survey apply only to families that manage their finances well and have no extraordinary expenses such as large medical bills. Emergencies often cannot be avoided, but wasting money can. The following paragraphs will offer guidance in setting up a budget or spending plan to assure proper management of money.

A FAMILY SPENDING PLAN OR BUDGET

To set up and live within a family budget or spending plan requires will power and habit more than brains, yet many people throw up their hands in despair at the mention of budget. A *family spending plan* sounds less formidable.

Whatever we call it, no business could exist without a budget, and a home is a business on a small scale. Budgets are merely spending plans projected into the future. Spending plans should serve as a guide and not a law. They should be adjustable and adaptable.

It would be as impossible to set up a budget to fit all families as it would be to make a suit of clothes to fit all men. If a family must spend more than 30 cents of every dollar for food, there will be less for other things. As a rule, the percentage for food decreases as income increases. As income increases, the percentages for shelter, savings, and advancement increase.

Perhaps you can work out a plan with your family. Never discuss financial matters outside the home. Your parents naturally would not want you telling your friends how much money your father earns, what you are buying on installments, how much you pay for furniture, and other matters that concern only yourselves.

358

Sources of Income Before setting up a spending plan you must know how much money there is to spend. This means analyzing all of the family's sources of income.

The biggest source of income is from salaries or wages based on a definite work period—day, week, month, or year.

Other sources of income are:
• *Rents* from houses, business buildings, farmland.
• *Profits* from individual enterprises or partnerships (restaurants, nursing homes, motels, and others).
• *Interest* on savings, as in a bank, savings and loan association, or credit union.
• *Commissions* or *bonuses* from sales or work production.
• *Fees* for professional services.
• *Royalties* from books or patents.
• *Dividends* from stocks and bonds.
• *Gift* and *inheritance* benefits.

Spending Plan Procedure There are six simple steps in making a family spending plan:

STEP 1. Buy a simple account book.

STEP 2. Itemize all sources of income. (See list above.) Deduct all taxes and expenses connected with property income, for example, taxes, repairs, and insurance on rented houses. Record your usable income.

STEP 3. From previous records, indicate fixed and fluctuating expense in your account book or on a chart similar to the chart that follows.

STEP 4. List your proposed expenses—immediate and long-time purchases—against your *known income*. Make necessary adjustments so the budget will work.

STEP 5. Decide who will be treasurer.

STEP 6. Treasurer's duties: Keep a separate file or drawer for all bills, receipts, canceled checks, guarantees, and special safeguards for using new equipment. These will be helpful from year to year.

THE INCREASING COSTS OF PARENTHOOD

When America was predominantly a rural society, children were a financial asset to their parents. At an early age they were put to work on the farm or possibly in the family business.

Today the typical young person helps his parents in many ways, but rarely does he contribute much to the family's financial status. As a result, children today are more of an expense than a financial asset.

The federal government recognizes this by allowing a $600 deduction from taxable income for each dependent. However, a child usually costs his parents considerably more than that in the course of a year. One approach to finding the cost of parenthood is shown in the chart on page 360. However, the figures given there are based on past and present costs. With inflation continuing, costs for a child born today will probably be sharply higher.

USE OF CREDIT

Earlier in this chapter it was mentioned that many people enjoy a higher standard of living because of credit. To use credit wisely, you must understand it. Following is a discussion of the major sources of credit.

359

Birth	Through 8th Grade	High School	College	Marriage
$500-$1,000	$14,000	$7,000	$10,000	$1,000-$1,500

The high cost of parenthood. Many middle-class American families spend $30,000 or more on each child. Boys are slightly more expensive than girls. By age 18 a typical boy has eaten about $7,500 worth of food, compared with $7,000 worth for a girl. In the same period, though, parents spend $2,900 on clothes for a typical girl, $400 more than for a boy. Parents' expenses for an average child from birth through marriage are shown in this drawing. Besides food and clothing, major expenditures are for housing, transportation, insurance, recreation, and medical care, among others. The drawing does not show those educational expenses which are paid indirectly through taxes. If these were added, the total would be sharply higher.

STORE CHARGE ACCOUNT: The well-known monthly payment plan has been modified in recent years to meet the varying needs of families. Two common types are the *optional account* and the *revolving account.*

Under the optional account the purchaser usually makes a down payment, then has two choices or options: (1) He may pay off the balance in a fairly short time, perhaps 30 or 90 days, with no interest charge. (2) He may stretch the payments out over a longer time, but pay interest. The interest is sometimes called a finance or service charge.

A revolving account is something like a budget. A customer is allowed to make purchases without down payment. However, the amount he owes must stay under a certain maximum which will depend upon his credit rating. Each month he is expected to pay off a certain amount of his debt. For instance, a customer might be allowed a maximum debt of $500. (This amount would be called his *line of credit.*) If he bought a refrigerator worth $400, he would still be allowed purchases worth another $100. However, if he bought nothing else and paid back $50 a month (plus interest) for 5 months, he would owe the store only $150. He would then be able to make new purchases worth $350. Stores offer other credit plans, but these two are the most popular.

BANK CHARGE ACCOUNT: This is a form of credit that is becoming increasingly popular. Banks issue a list of participating merchants, and the customer may charge anything (up to a figure set by the bank) at any member store. All bills are paid out of the

360

customer's account by the bank. Stores are charged a fee by banks for handling these accounts.

CREDIT CARDS: With a credit card you can make a purchase without paying any cash. Some can be used to purchase the goods and services of only one company; others are accepted by many businesses—restaurants, hotels and motels, automobile service stations, even airlines. Of course, all such purchases have to be paid for eventually. Once a month the credit card user receives a bill.

In 1968 there were an estimated 200 million credit cards in circulation. Each year about 1½ million are lost or stolen, resulting in financial loss of between $50 million and $100 million. A family should keep a list of all its credit cards, including numbers. If you carry a card, be as careful with it as you would be with money. If you lose one, immediately notify the agency which issued it, so that you won't have to pay for future purchases by the person who found or stole the card.

When you use any form of credit, find out what you are really paying in interest. The well-known phrases "low down payment" and "small monthly payments" are often misleading. Keep these general rules in mind: (1) A small down payment means a relatively large balance. Since you pay interest on the balance, a small down payment means larger interest charges. (2) The more months you take to pay for your purchases, the longer you keep on paying interest. Therefore short-term credit arrangements with substantial down payments usually cost less than so-called "easy terms."

HOW CAN YOU AVOID BEING TRAPPED IN A MONEY DEAL?

With pressure to buy from every angle—from magazine and newspaper advertisements, radio, television, and even door-to-door salesmen, few families escape being trapped in a bad deal once in a while.

Inferior Bargains   Bargain hunting is a mania with some people and makes us all gullible and a little greedy. As consumers we are not experts in every field, but we can guard against obvious frauds.

CASE STUDY: Mary and Joe Benson, newlyweds, anxious to stretch each dollar, decided to buy a porch lounge advertised as guaranteed. Before they left the store, the salesman pointed out a bedroom furniture group with dresser covers, sheets, pillow cases, spread, and lamps, for a ridiculously low price.

Mary and Joe, like many young married adults, were inexperienced. They arranged to buy the lounge *and* furniture on time payments running over a year. When it arrived, the furniture was not exactly as they had judged it in the store. It looked cheap; the upholstery was poor; woodwork and springs were inferior. But they felt it would do.

The porch lounge failed first. When Mary and Joe found their "bargain" lounge wearing badly after just one summer of use (but after the last payment) they took the guarantee back to the store. There they were given the line: "Sorry, but the guarantee only covers faulty parts, not deterioration. It looks like you must have given the lounge unusually rough treatment. Now, we might be able to give you a generous trade-in on a new lounge."

What would you do—buy the new lounge, or write your loss off as experience, and resolve not to be fooled again. Many people, strangely enough, take the salesman's offer a second or third time!

Policy: Buy standard brands from stores with good reputations, where your guarantee is clearly stated to give you real protection.

"Fire Sales" These parade under other names: *bankrupt, factory close-out, going out of business,* and other eye-catching terms, and apply to all kinds of merchandise. Often the manager buys cheap goods, stores it conveniently, and feeds it onto the market as long as the crowds keep coming.

Policy: Unless you are an expert judge of values or can afford to be cheated, stay away from such sales. Avoid "marked-down" merchandise except when you know the original price.

Home-work Racket Have you ever seen a newspaper ad such as the following?

Wanted: Women (or men) to work at home. $25-30 a week for spare time. Send $1 for information.

Occasionally such an ad is honest, but as a rule, the pay is low (if it exists), the work is complicated, there is no market for the completed projects, and most people lose interest even though left with expensive supplies. Some racketeers simply pocket the $1, send useless "information," and move on to another address.

Several million people each year be-come involved in this $500-million "home-work" swindle.

Policy: If you must "bite," don't send any money before checking with your Better Business Bureau, banker, or other adviser.

"Heart and Beauty" Mail Traps The personal mail frauds are the worst of all rackets. They work on two deeply felt human needs—the need for companionship and the desire to be healthy and attractive.

Every year, hundreds of widows are left penniless after investing in some unknown companion. Thousands of young people send away for pills to care for pimples or sluggishness, or to reduce weight, and either receive nothing or a useless product.

Policy: Don't fall for such advertisements. If you hear of anyone who has been misled, report to the Post Office Department, Chamber of Commerce, or Better Business Bureau.

Other rackets include stock, land, or home-improvement frauds. Do you know anyone who has had experience with a fraud? Have *you?*

HOW MUCH DEBT CAN A FAMILY AFFORD?

Not many years ago, people considered it almost a disgrace to be in debt except for a mortgage on a home. Now, far over half the families in the United States use installment credit, not only for cars, clothing, and household equipment, but for a new baby, a trip, or a college education.

There are no set rules on how much debt a family should incur, but there are a few general guides.

• The cost of a home should not ex-

362

ceed 2 to 2½ times your assured yearly income. Usually, wives' salaries are unpredictable and not included.

• No more than 20 to 25 per cent of the monthly salary after taxes should go into total payments on a home: principal, interest, taxes, insurance, utilities, and upkeep.

• A month's rent should never exceed a week's *take-home* pay.

• Total installment debt—besides for the home—at any one time should never exceed eight weeks' income.

• Monthly installment payments—besides for the home—should never amount to more than 13 per cent of income for the month.

• Total charge accounts, unpaid, should never exceed two weeks' income.

The more you can buy without paying carrying charges, the more you will be able to save. With carrying charges of 10 per cent and more, you can spend a lot of money and get nothing from it.

GOING BROKE IN TEN GIANT STEPS

In a recent national magazine, the R_____ family of the Bay Area in California told about their plight when they undertook too many installment payments. Their experiences are duplicated every day. Briefly, this is what happened:

1. A *house*, for $11,500 was the first purchase. The down payment of $500 and deal-closing costs of $250 were available by "scraping the barrel." The monthly payments with taxes and insurance came to .... $ 78.00

2. *Furniture* came next—$100 down and a monthly payment of   40.49

3. *Landscaping* to improve property followed — $100 borrowed, with monthly payments of 14.00

4. *Home insulation* to save fuel costs—$200 to be paid back monthly at 12.00

5. A *water softener* came next at $300, with monthly payments of 14.00

6. About this time Mrs. R_____ got a job and the future looked bright so a *television* was added—$200, or monthly 15.00

7. A *food freezer* to save shopping time and take advantage of special food sales was the next purchase — $500, at a monthly rate of 40.00

8. The old jalopy was costing more than it was worth so the *new car* bug bit, with a monthly installment of 100.00

9. The monthly installment payments *took almost all* of Mr. ——— R_____'s salary $313.49

10. Then came the shock! Mrs. R_____ lost her job and they were ....BROKE

First the car was repossessed; then, one by one, the other purchases were reclaimed until finally the home was lost. The family had to move to inadequate living quarters and ration food carefully while a reputable pro-rating firm took Mr. R_____'s small monthly pay check and spread it thin among creditors, eventually paying off debts. These people had to start all over. They had learned a lesson the hard way.

WHERE CAN A FAMILY BORROW?

When a family needs to borrow money, the following sources are available:

Life Insurance Company If a life insurance policy has a cash-surrender value, the insured may borrow up to that value. Should he die before the loan is paid back, the amount owed is deducted from the face value of the policy. Although people dislike to disturb this type of family security, such a loan has many advantages: (1) The policy holder has little difficulty securing the loan. (2) The interest rate is reasonable. (3) The borrower enjoys privacy without having another lending service investigate his credit.

Banks Banks are eager to lend money—especially for buying a home, if a good credit rating can be established. Bank deposits are federally insured. Interest rates are reasonable. For smaller loans, a life insurance policy is good bank collateral, and cuts down extra fees. Stocks, bonds, and real estate are also good collateral.

As long as a person can secure a bank loan, he is usually in good financial standing. In other words, he has "established credit."

Savings and Loan Associations Interest rates are about the same as bank rates. These agencies are, as a rule, federally insured and conveniently located.

Credit Unions Loans are limited to members only. Such unions are on the increase. Credit unions may make loans to members up to $400 or more without security. Interest rates are relatively low. The unions are established more as a service to members than for profit.

Credit unions often offer the *lowest interest rate*, consumer finance companies the highest, and banks a medium rate.

Finance Companies Most finance companies are reliable and offer reasonable interest rates. However, there are some with questionable ethics. Be sure the company is state licensed. If a borrower is in doubt, he may consult the Better Business Bureau or Chamber of Commerce. He should make sure of interest rates, which may be based on the total, rather than on a decreasing principal.

Check Credit Account This is a new type of personal loan, extended by many banks. It is a revolving loan account with checking privileges. When you open an account, you and the bank determine how much credit is to be set aside for your use. As a rule the maximum credit is determined by multiplying the amount you can pay each month by twenty-four. For instance, if you can afford $35 a month, you can check out up to $840 over a stated period any way you wish. A life insurance policy accompanies the loan to guarantee payment. Interest does not begin until after the first check has been written.

Family or Friends Parents often help a young couple by lending money toward a car or a home. Borrowing from friends is not as popular as it was thirty or forty years ago. Most people prefer to borrow commercially rather than impose on a friend.

ADJUSTING FROM TWO INCOMES TO ONE

From Husband's Income

Necessities
Food
Housing
Ordinary household bills
Medical bills
Family transportation
  (except for wife to work)
Normal insurances
Routine installments

From Wife's Income

Luxuries
Extra transportation
  (wife to work; children to nursery school)
Clothing for work outside home
Investments
Extra annuities
Travel above normal
Baby sitters
Labor saving equipment
Extra home payments

From Both Incomes

Costs which may be *reduced* without sacrifice
Entertainment
Personal
Cash savings
Vacations
Gifts

MANAGING SAFELY ON TWO INCOMES

It is a temptation for a wife to work after she is married, at least until the arrival of the first child. In fact, married women outnumber unmarried women who work by about seven to five. The wife is working in one of every three families. The highest proportion of working wives is in families whose combined income ranges from $7,500 to $12,000. Half of the wives in this income group have jobs.

There is always the question of how much a wife actually earns after deductions for taxes, transportation,

When the wife works, extra living costs should be considered.

365

extra clothes, part-time help, less economical food shopping, and higher lunch costs.

The wife's contribution to income is sometimes ignored by money lenders in taking a mortgage on a home.

Two incomes help if a family is paying for a home, saving for an education, planning a trip, or otherwise aiming over and beyond regular budget items. But when a family gears living to two incomes and suddenly finds one cut off, there is trouble.

Words and Phrases to Know

average	escalator clause
budget	fluctuating
commission	installment
Consumer's Price	median
Index	policy
credit	pro-rating
discretionary income	repossessed
dividend	royalty
economist	

ACTIVITIES

1. Discuss the following:
• Occasions during the past week when you had discussions with your family over money. Were your requests reasonable?
• Interpret the expression, "Money doesn't mean much to them," two ways.
• Your own experiences based upon, "What the eye does not see, the heart does not desire."

2. Marriage counselors feel that arguments over money are a big factor in marriage failures. Suggest ways to lessen such friction.

3. Make up your own spending plan from now until the close of school. Will your allowance or income be sufficient? If not, what can you do?

4. Discuss ways you may be wasting money. How much would such waste amount to in a year?

5. Make a class by class survey to determine what allowance students need during each year. Base your study on the chart on page 348. Include questions on employment, number of hours, and pay.

6. Discuss goods or services toward which your family is saving. Is it easier for your family to save for a large purchase or to buy on the installment plan?

7. Form a panel to discuss:
• Should you be paid for helping at home?
• If you are earning money should you share it with the family?
• Where is the best place to save your money for a future education or car?

8. Show films or film strips on spending; discuss.

9. In groups of two or three, price a secondhand car in a price range between $800 and $1500. Find out (a) amount of the down payment; (b) amount of monthly payments and the number to be made; (c) total finance charges; (d) amount you will actually be paying for the car including down payment plus the total monthly payments. How much more will this be than the advertised price?

Remember that state sales tax, insurance, license, and other items often are not included in the advertised price. These are necessary no matter what type of financing is arranged.

Find out what your local bank or savings and loan association would charge to finance the same car at the prevailing interest rate (frequently 6 per cent). Which method of financing is cheaper? How much can you save by paying cash? Are there any disadvantages in paying cash?

NOTE: With the information in the Mathematics Correlation (page 368) you can figure *equivalent interest*.

10. Using the charts on car expenses, figure what it costs to own and drive your family car. Substitute your own figures for those in the chart and you will have no difficulty. Compare the cost per mile to drive a car 5,000, 10,000, and 15,000 miles a year.

11. Compare the costs of attending the following types of colleges: (a) a state teachers college; (b) your state university; (c) private college in or near your home town; (d) "big name" private college away from home. Include transportation for vacations.

12. Secure some Federal Income Tax forms; compare the differences in various income brackets, and for different-sized families.

13. Work out the spending plan for the Office Worker's Budget which appears on page 353 on a monthly and weekly basis.

14. Figure out what it would cost a young couple to marry and live in your community. (Include housing and car expenses.)
• Itemize expenses connected with the kind of wedding you would like to have. (Refer to Chapter 9.)
• Estimate the cost of furniture for a bedroom, living room, bathroom, and kitchen.
• Determine weekly food costs by talking with young married couples.
• Figure how and when you would prefer to pay the following: income and property taxes; auto, life, and fire insurance, other bills. Try to stagger these bills through the year.

15. Find out the average family income in the United States after taxes and distribute the income according to the chart on page 357. Make comparisons on the chalkboard.

16. Discuss defective merchandise you or your family has bought.

17. Stroll through the downtown streets of a city and make a list of "fire" or similar sales. Examine merchandise, listen to sales talks, and report back to class.

18. Tell about your own experiences answering advertisements for products or services in newspapers and magazines.

19. According to the text, a total installment debt should never exceed 8 weeks' net income. Find out what that would be on a yearly net income of $2,900, $5,000, and $9,500. Use 13 per cent of the yearly net salary and compare results.

20. Estimate the size of a monthly charge account a person might carry safely on the incomes listed in the previous activity.

21. List some items and services that many people buy on the installment plan.

22. Study the percentages on page 362. Assume Mr. R_____'s take-home pay is $380 a month. Use the percentage limits for buying a house and other items. How much could he safely pay for a home and credit installments?

23. Compare the costs of the following on a cash as well as 12- and 18-month installment basis: refrigerator, washer, television, typewriter.

Correlation

ENGLISH: Write a 400 to 500 word composition on one of the following topics: *If I Had $25,000 to Spend* or *The Things Money Can't Buy.*

MATHEMATICS: Have the mathematics teacher:
• Demonstrate how equivalent interest rates are calculated. Apply this information to buying a car or any other item on the installment plan.

If this is not possible, one of the math students in class can use the following formula for arriving at equivalent interest:

$$R = \frac{2pc}{A(n+1)}$$

R—Equivalent interest rate

$$R = \frac{2(12 \times 235.70)}{2,854.70\ (18+1)}$$

p—Number of payments in one year (12 monthly or 52 weekly)

$$R = \frac{5,656.80}{54,239.30}$$

c—Total finance charges

$$R = 10.4\%$$

A—Total due finance company

n—Total number of payments

• Using *The City Worker's Family Budget* (Serial No. R.1909, U.S. Government Printing Office, Washington 25, D. C.—20 cents) apply the Consumer's Price Index to adjust budget items to present living costs. Have someone volunteer to summarize briefly what moderate living standards means. Discuss the "escalator clause" which is part of some wage contracts.

JOURNALISM: Summarize your findings in regard to money needs for high school students and publish them in the school or local paper.

Report on "fire" and other sales in school paper.

ART: Make posters showing how people waste money.

Home Experiences

Study the chart on page 350, Seasonal Sales Calendar, with your parents and try to gear family spending accordingly.

Form a family council to set up a spending plan for the family and yourself. Discuss car expenses, and the amount of interest on installment payments.

One-story homes are designed in many styles, including those shown here.

Contemporary.

Bill Hedrich, Hedrich-Blessing

Traditional.

Better Homes and Gardens

Chapter 18

Finding the Right Home

A house represents the biggest single investment of a lifetime. Despite the high costs, six out of every ten families in the United States either own or are buying homes. Nearly nine out of ten home buyers finance their homes on a mortgage plan—usually a twenty to twenty-five year mortgage.

RENTING VERSUS BUYING

Interest in owning a home increases when children arrive. This is the period in the family cycle when home ownership reaches a peak. There are, however, arguments for and against home ownership.

Arguments for buying a home are:
· Mortgage payments represent a certain amount of forced savings.
· A home, if well built and well located, is an investment which can increase in value, protecting the owner against inflation.
· In a neighborhood of owner-occupied homes, property values often are stable and homes well kept.
· Interest paid on a home loan can be deducted from federal income tax.

· Home ownership brings a sense of security, independence, and satisfaction.
· Inflation makes long-term loans desirable; that is, the price and monthly payments agreed on now may seem cheap in a few years.

Points against home buying are:
· In the early years of most home loans, payments go chiefly for interest, so equity (savings) is very small.
· An aging home or one in a poor location is likely to drop in value.
· A family whose head is subject to transfer may have to sell the home in a hurry, and this can lead to financial loss.
· In addition to mortgage payments there are costs for lawn care, water and sewer, heating, plumbing, carpentry, electrical repairs, painting, and other maintenance and improvements.

APARTMENTS—A WAY OF LIFE

As a result of the population increase, it has become harder to find conveniently located homes. This has been a problem especially for young people in large cities. Even for those who can afford to build a new home, the available sites are often many miles from the offices where they work. Rather than buy or rent an older house, many people choose an apartment.

With good new construction sites so limited, many builders started making buildings higher in order to accommodate a large number of people. Therefore the high-rise apartment is a sign of our crowded times. This type of apartment has been defined as a unit in a building which has more than three stories and an elevator. In large cities it is not uncommon to find high-rise apartments of 30 or more stories. Another popular type of dwelling is the garden apartment, in a building of three stories or less, with no more than twelve units.

The change to apartment living is taking place rapidly. For instance, in 1956 less than ten per cent of the new dwellings constructed were apartments; in 1968 this number was more than 43 per cent. Some authorities predict that in the near future a typical American will reside in an apartment for about two-thirds of his life. It is interesting to note that apartment dwelling has been an accepted way of life for generations in many other countries. This is true, for example, of large European and Latin American cities, where living space has long been a problem.

Studies show that the typical urban family can expect to move every five years, and individuals even more often. For many couples the first home is a small apartment in a remodeled house or other older building. The next move is likely to be to a better apartment, perhaps a high-rise or garden apartment. As children arrive, a move to a modest home in the suburbs, and later to a more expensive suburban home, is a common pattern. After the children have left home many couples again prefer a conveniently located apartment.

Though this pattern may be most common among middle-income families in metropolitan areas, it is not confined to any geographical area or income group. The increase in apartment construction mentioned above has taken place not only in large cities but in smaller ones as well, although perhaps on a smaller scale. Also, as tenements are torn down through urban renewal, they are often replaced by modern apartments for occupants with limited incomes.

Since our current way of life involves frequent changes of residence, it is important to know the most efficient and least expensive ways of moving. This topic is discussed near the end of this chapter. Perhaps even more important are the effects that moving has on family life. You may want to review what was said about this subject on pages 75, 76, and 200.

Renting an Apartment   Often a first apartment seems far from satisfactory. Inconveniences such as inadequate hot water and heat, too little storage space, and cooking on a gas or electric plate contrast sadly with a bride's dream of a story-book cottage with an up-to-date kitchen and outdoor patio. But when two young adults are unselfishly in love, and interested in a common goal, even a makeshift home can be a "bit of heaven on earth." On the other hand, if jealousy and selfishness replace love, the finest home can be no more than a shell for shelter.

A first home is often temporary, so it may not be wise to invest in a lot of furniture. Moving is not only expensive but sometimes hard on furniture. Renting a furnished apartment may cost less than renting a cheaper place and furnishing it. Otherwise, used or borrowed furniture will suffice for a while, especially if supplemented with a few new pieces. Choose new items that are likely to go with future as well as present decor. The purchase of expensive pieces should usually be postponed until a couple is fairly permanently settled; tastes are likely to change in a few years, causing dissatisfaction with early purchases.

Here is a good list of things to check when choosing an apartment:
- Is the neighborhood desirable?
- Is the location convenient to public transportation, work, shopping, church, and recreation? (Later you will be concerned about schools.)
- Will you have adequate storage space?
- Who will redecorate and how often?
- Who will pay for water, light, and heat?
- What provisions will you make for mail, milk, newspaper, and laundry deliveries?
- Will you be allowed to do laundry on premises?
- Who will supply the range and refrigerator?
- What provision is made for cleaning hallways and windows, removing garbage and trash?
- Are the rooms and windows of fairly standard proportions, so curtains or rugs you may buy will fit rooms in your next home?
- Are present tenants satisfied with the hot water, water pressure, drains, and toilet?
- Are there enough electrical outlets for your appliances and lamps?
- Have the former tenants had sufficient heat on cold days?
- Will you be able to stay on "when baby makes three"?
- Will you have to put up with loud noises or unpleasant odors?
- What are your obligations to the landlord? What are the terms of lease? Are improvements needed?
- When and to whom is the rent paid?
- Are fire exits well placed and in good condition?
- Is there a place to park your car overnight?
- Do other tenants like the landlord or maintenance person?

It is good business and common sense to have the terms in writing before you pay rent or sign a lease.

FEATURES HOMEMAKERS WANT IN A HOME

Homemakers with children are polled frequently by federal, local and independent agencies, magazines, and realtors to determine what they want in a home. Here are some combined findings of recent surveys:
- Over 1,250 square feet of living space (patio excluded).
- At least three bedrooms and often an extra room that may serve as a study or temporary bedroom.
- At least one full bathroom and a half bath (preferably two full and one half). It is especially good if the half bath is part of or close to a "mud space," near the back door so chil-

371

dren can clean up before tracking through the house.

• Family room near the kitchen when children are small—a room that can be used later as a dining area if there is no separate dining room.

• A recreation room for teen-agers in an area of the house where noises will not carry into bedrooms.

• A kitchen large enough to serve family meals when necessary. *Counters and snack bars were not popular.*

• A sizable living room—at least 12 by 19 or 20 feet.

• Laundry and utility room, preferably on same level as kitchen but acceptable on lower level.

• Space near back door for children to hang play clothes.

• Closets with a minimum width of 22 inches. (A 24-inch minimum is preferable.)

• Large closet near front door.

• Ample kitchen storage, food disposal, and built-in dishwasher.

• A garage with storage space for garden equipment, bicycles, and similar items.

• Zoned living—that is, one area of the house for sleeping and privacy, another for recreation, another for meal preparation and service. The concept of *family togetherness,* so much discussed a few years ago, has been replaced by greater emphasis upon privacy.

Do not be discouraged if your first home has few of the features listed above. Remember, the list shows what most people *want,* not what they *have.* This information can help you in two ways: First, it lets you share the experience of others who have learned (often the hard way) what is important in a house. Second, it

gives you a basis for thinking about which features you want most, and which you would be willing to sacrifice.

Some features that other families were willing to do without were breezeways, porches, garages (if carports could be substituted), elaborate kitchen equipment (although functional equipment and arrangements were stressed), and highly decorated bathrooms.

TYPES OF HOMES

When people decide to buy a place to live they can usually eliminate many homes immediately on the basis of cost, location, and size in relation to family needs. Still, a considerable range of choice remains.

Following is a discussion of several types of homes available on today's market:

Developer-built houses are in a new development area, sometimes with their own recreational facilities and shopping center. They account for most of the new houses. There are two main *advantages* in buying a builder's house: (1) It is easier to judge a finished house than to visualize a house from the blueprint. (2) Such a house is usually cheaper than a custom-built house. The chief *disadvantages* are lack of originality and flexibility for individual families. To offset these disadvantages builders often display sample houses and agree to make minor changes. Of course, a family must wait from three to six months to have the house built.

• *Prefabricated homes* are produced in component parts. Walls, floors, window frames, and the entire mechanical core including plumbing, heating, and wiring, are built at the factory and assembled on the lot. When they first became popular, "prefabs" were commonly thought of as strictly low priced, and somewhat inferior. Today, however, a considerable number of expensive prefabricated homes are being built. This construction method is also used for some apartments. There are many sizes and styles from which to choose.

• *Mobile homes* are not as small or mobile as they used to be. They have become more spacious and they are often fairly permanently located in specially landscaped areas. As prefabricated homes have taken a larger share of the expensive home market, mobile homes have become more popular among retired people and others with low income. In a recent year one plant alone turned out nearly 200,000 mobile units or about one-third of all homes selling under $10,000 that year. A mobile home has a number of advantages: It is less restricted by local building codes than are ordinary homes; financing is easy and the trade-in market is good; and, if necessary, such a home can be moved. The total cost usually includes all built-ins, floor coverings, and furnishings.

• *Condominium homes* are units in a duplex or apartment building, often surrounded by landscaped grounds and including recreational facilities. These units may be bought in much the same way as any other type of home, by getting a loan from a federal or independent lending agency. The owner pays his own share of the building's taxes, insurance, heat, cooling, and repair costs. An additional fee is charged for maintenance of

Mobile Home Manufacturers Association

Mobile homes are increasingly popular with young couples and retired people.

grounds and exterior of the building, and for use of recreational facilities.

• *Cooperative apartments* within a large apartment building are another possible choice. The owner, instead of holding the title to the property, buys shares in the cooperative agency. He is responsible for his own apartment and pays a fee for custodial service in corridors, lobby, and laundry area. Heat may be a part of the extra cost.

• A *previously occupied house,* purchased from the owner directly or through a real estate agent, may seem cheaper than a new house. However, a buyer should consider the cost of alterations, if needed. Unless a person is experienced in remodeling a house, the final cost may be very high, and a large part of this expense is often lost if the house is resold later. As a rule, cost of remodeling should not be more than half the appraised value of the house. Another good rule is not to improve a home far beyond the value of other homes in the neighborhood.

Even seemingly minor projects, such as painting a room, may cost more than you expect. Check costs

Two views of the same home—before remodeling (right) and afterwards (left). Notice how greatly the appearance is improved by the new siding, altered front door and porch, and landscaping. None of these changes involved the basic structure of the house. Even the beams are merely fastened to the exterior. What other changes do you notice?

carefully before starting any project. This is especially important for major work, such as remodeling a kitchen. When hiring, compare bids from several contractors.

Aside from the cost of home improvement, there are *building codes* that must be observed. For instance, one home owner neglected to apply for an electrical permit at a cost of only $3.00 when he installed some additional wiring. Some time later a fire started in the walls and burned his $27,000 home. He was not able to collect a penny of fire insurance because his wiring had not been inspected.

Custom-built houses are built by a contractor to a buyer's specifications. They cost more but are more likely to meet individual needs. Looking at display houses and homes of friends will be helpful in planning a custom-built house. Changes during construction can send costs zooming.

In order to cut costs, people sometimes accept minimum quality requirements. This is not always a good idea; paying a little more when building a house can mean saving many thousands of dollars over the years in repair and maintenance costs. For instance, an extra two thousand dollars or less can provide more durable flooring, roofing, and siding; better and more attractive kitchen cabinets, hardware, and bathroom equipment; more adequate wiring, heating, plumbing, and noise control.

Architects can give you a rough idea of costs, according to the number of square feet in the house and building materials used. *The following practices will help to hold costs down.*

• Use standard-size windows, doors, and lumber dimensions; pre-assembled walls and roof trusses; pre-finished wood paneling; "packaged" fireplaces.

• Use local building materials—wood, stone, or brick vary in cost according to how far they must be transported. The least expensive construction is concrete block. Clapboard, shingles, stucco, and brick veneer are next in cost.

• A two-story square or oblong house requires *less excavating* and *less roof area* than a ranch-type. It may be built on a smaller lot. However, if the lot is large and no excavating is necessary, a ranch house may cost very little more than a two-story house. A ranch house is usually built on a slab or over a crawl-space foundation.

• A flat roof costs less, but a sloping roof may look better and make heating and cooling easier.

• Concentrating the plumbing saves extra pipes and labor. Place kitchen and bathroom plumbing against the same divider wall, or kitchen plumbing directly under the bathroom in a two-story house.

• Plaster board is cheaper than plaster and may be painted immediately. Plaster should "season" well before you paint it.

• Short sidewalks and driveways save money.

• One chimney for all flues is cheaper than two or three.

SELECTING A LOT

The price of a ready-to-build-upon lot, including utilities and street improvements, may represent between 10 and 20 per cent of the estimated house-and-lot price. Home style should fit the slope and size of the lot, allowing space for additional rooms.

Since excavating and filling are expensive, they should be kept to a minimum. Good drainage is necessary, and for lawns and other landscaping, good top soil is an asset. Trees and shrubs can add beauty to a lawn. Trees should be planted at least fifteen feet from the house, and shrubs no closer than three feet.

Be sure you have in writing what you must or must not pay for—street paving, sewage, water extension lines, power lines, sidewalks. Will present taxes be raised considerably to cover police and fire protection? Will public transportation be available?

If your family would like to know about grass for different soils and climates, write for the booklet, *Better Lawns, Home and Garden Bulletin No. 51*, Government Printing Office, Washington, D.C.

PLANNING LIVABLE ROOMS

The Federal Housing Administration, Small Homes Council of the University of Illinois, and the mortgage department of the Metropolitan Life Insurance Company have all made studies to determine the best size rooms for livability.

The following dimensions are based upon Metropolitan Life Insurance requirements for home loans.°

Master bedroom	171 Sq. Ft.
Second bedroom	110
Third bedroom	110
(minimum bedroom width 9½′)	
Bath	40
Living room	196
Family room	220
Kitchen	112
(take off 16′ if no separate oven and no dishwasher)	
Entry (4′ x 16′)	64
Bedroom hall (3′4″ x 16′)	52
Laundry and heater . .	50
Storage	130
Subtotal	1295 Sq. Ft.
Plus partitions	70
TOTAL	1365 Sq. Ft.

To obtain an FHA loan, the master bedroom needs to have only 120 square feet—other bedrooms 80 square feet. No bedroom should be narrower than 9½ feet. A kitchen should be at

EVALUATING AN AGING HOUSE

(1) *Roof:* Check for loose shingles, leaks around chimney flashing and downspouts.

(2) *Windows:* Look for level windows, well preserved finish on frames, fitted screens, and storm windows.

(3) *Siding:* Examine for warp, peeling paint, cracks, rot, or loose calking in brick.

(4) *Gutters and Downspouts:* Check for stoppage, rust, or loose spots.

(5) *Attic (if any):* Inquire about insulation; check cross ventilation, signs of roof leakage.

(6) *Stairway:* Check height of risers (7 to 8 inches) and width of treads (8 to 10 inches). Look for handrail and light switch at top *and* bottom of stairs.

(7) *Floors:* Walk over all floors. If they squeak, framework may be sagging. Use a marble to detect extreme slope.

(8) *Basement:* Look for storage space, good drainage. Signs of moisture may mean trouble. Sawdust near wood supports may indicate termites.

(9) *Foundation:* Unevenness will show up in cracks in outside corners of rooms.

(10) *Plumbing:* Turn on faucets and flush toilets to check water pressure. Look for place near present plumbing for a second bathroom possibility. Look for shut-off valve near each outlet. Inquire about kind of pipes. Brass and copper are best.

(11) *Wiring:* Check wiring for major equipment. Note number and placement of outlets in relation to placement of furniture and use of kitchen appliances.

(12) *Heating:* Inquire about age of equipment, cost of operation; adaptability to air conditioning.

(13) *Kitchen:* Convenient outlets, adequate light, easy care surfaces, and storage space are important.

(14) *Inside Walls:* Check for cracks in plaster, bulging places that may indicate loose plaster. Be sure walls are spaced right and ceilings high enough for your furniture.

(15) *Storage:* Bedroom storage for clothing, bathroom for linens; near entrance for wraps; outdoors for tools and wheel toys; kitchen for cooking supplies and equipment; dining room for table linens and dishes.

least 8 feet wide for a corridor or L-shape arrangement—wider for a U-shape.

How to Judge a Floor Plan Few houses have all the features a family desires, so, as a rule, you must be able to balance good against bad features and be willing to compromise. A floor plan is important in house selection. Select one you like, and judge it on the following points.

• Is the space adequate for your family?

• Is the porch or terrace protected from the afternoon sun? The west side is hot in summer.

• Will traffic flow smoothly from one room to another?

• Are bed rooms away from street noises and children's play areas?

• Is there room for a workshop and for storing bulky items, perhaps in the basement, garage, or a special room?

• Is there adequate storage space near entrance, in bedrooms, in or near bathrooms, in kitchen and laundry centers, elsewhere?

• Can furniture be arranged in the living room to provide for good traffic lanes?

• Can you pass from kitchen to bedroom without going through the living room?

• Is the kitchen arrangement convenient?

• Can you watch children at play outside while you work in the kitchen?

• Can you easily dovetail laundry and kitchen activities?

• Will you have adequate outlets for lamps and kitchen appliances?

• Is there a rear entrance for deliveries and for days when shoes are muddy?

• Is there space for family meals in the kitchen, dining room, or family room (not living room)?

• Is there cross-ventilation in the bedrooms?

• Is there wall space for twin beds in one bedroom or a double bed in other bedrooms?

• Is the bathroom accessible to everyone, if there is only one bath?

• Is the bathroom out of view of the front door?

• Are doors of standard size for ease in moving furniture?

• Are there enough windows, properly located, for good light? Are windows of standard size?

HEATING AND COOLING A HOUSE

How to Save on Heat Bills Many things influence the cost of heating a home. A builder will know the best heating system for any

Size and shape of the lot, contour of the land, and exposure to the sun should influence style of the house. Good drainage is necessary.

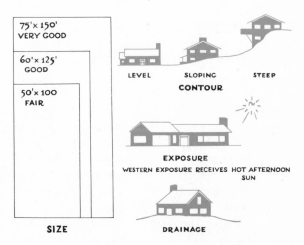

75' x 150' VERY GOOD
60' x 125' GOOD
50' x 100 FAIR

SIZE

LEVEL   SLOPING   STEEP
CONTOUR

EXPOSURE
WESTERN EXPOSURE RECEIVES HOT AFTERNOON SUN

DRAINAGE

These features are important in selecting a home.

house in relation to climate, style of house, and kind of fuel available. For instance, *gravity warm air* is recommended for small houses in moderate climates, but this system requires a basement, whereas *forced warm air*, more expensive, does not require a basement and it is suitable for larger houses. A *one-pipe steam system* is less expensive than a *two-pipe steam system*, but room temperatures are more difficult to control. A *gravity hot water* system, although economical to install, requires a basement, whereas a *forced hot water* system makes temperature control more uniform and does not require a basement. *Radiant heating* in floors, ceilings, or in wall panels eliminates radiators and vents, but is more costly and less adaptable to changing or cold climates.

The cost of fuel will depend upon availability. *Electricity* generally is expensive, unless the house is located near a large hydroelectric project or in a part of the country where the climate does not vary greatly. However, electric heating is gaining in popu-

larity. *Gas* provides clean heat but is fairly expensive. *Oil* is "less clean" than gas and in many areas less expensive. *Hard coal* is much cleaner than *soft coal*. In choosing fuel, one must weigh convenience against cost.

If a house is allowed to become very cold at night, it takes more heat to bring the temperature up the next day, and costs more. The difference between day and night temperature should not be more than five to ten degrees — with radiant heating, no more than four degrees. Close off the bedrooms at night and place a rug at base of each door to prevent cool bedroom air from going through the house.

Wall, roof, floor, and window *insulation* helps cut fuel bills. Be sure that walls which are most exposed to winter winds are especially well insulated.

Storm windows act as insulation, and *lowering the window shades* on very cold days will keep heat from escaping.

A regular fall furnace inspection, including the cleaning and repairing of chimneys, radiators, or ventilators, will improve heating and reduce costs.

How to Keep a House Cool The secret of keeping a house cool is keeping heat out. The largest amount of heat comes through the roof. That is why attics are hotter than second floors and second floors hotter than first floors. A flat roof is hotter than a sloping roof. Heat from the sun stores up in the roof all day and acts like radiant heat at night.

Here are some suggestions for keeping a house comfortable in hot weather:

· A *shade tree* or vines, arbor or trellis, especially on the west side of the house, helps to block out the strong, setting sun.

• In Mexico and Spain, the west wall is usually made of *thick masonry;* few windows are placed there. The masonry keeps out both heat and moisture. A picture window in the west wall is not recommended because it can act like a sun glass. Spacious windows should face north or south. Heat-resistant glass is available.

• *Insulation* will reduce both heating and cooling costs. Attic insulation is the most effective, although the attic requires the thickest insulation—about 4 inches. Next comes wall insulation—in the west wall for cooler temperatures in summer and in the wall exposed to cold winds for warmth in winter.

• If floors are cold in a house with no basement, *insulation under the floor* will help. Insulation comes in "blanket" or "quilt" form; fiber that may be blown between two areas; reflective metal foil sheets; and insulation boards. Insulated areas should have a vapor barrier to prevent accumulation of moisture.

• *Shutters* that may be closed outside the house keep out twice as much heat (and cold) as either *Venetian blinds* or window *shades*. Keep shades or shutters closed during the hottest time of the day in very warm weather.

• *Vents* are used in the tropics on one side just under the roof, and lower on the opposite side. Placing vents in this way—especially if they are in line with prevailing breezes—keeps a "carpet" of cool air over room ceilings. Vents are often necessary on a pitched roof.

• *Attic fans* make an inexpensive and fairly simple means of keeping heat from accumulating during the day, and allowing radiation all night. The fan may be installed in the center of the attic, between vents, *or* in one vent opposite a second vent. If there is a basement, open the windows and doors in the very early morning and let the attic fan draw the cool morning air through the house. Close windows early and block out the sun. *Kitchen fans* will remove cooking heat.

• An *overhang* from east to west keeps the north and south sides of the house cool. Where you live will determine the width of the overhang for maximum shade and protection.

• *Tall fences, walls,* or *louvered screens* may act as sun shades on the west of the house, if there are no shade trees.

• *White or light* roofs reflect heat; dark roofs absorb it. The same principle applies to window shades. With a dark roof and dark shades, a house will tend to store up heat.

• Some people *spray* the west side of their houses in the early evening to cut down temperature indoors.

• *Air conditioning* is available in room-size units, or for the entire home. Complete home air conditioning is more expensive, but has many advantages in addition to controlling temperature and humidity. It helps people with some types of nasal allergies, it saves money and time for cleaning, and it is usually quieter than room-size units.

Cooling a house costs about as much as heating it. Expenses can be reduced if windows and doors are kept shut when it is warmer outside than in; if the west wall is thick and has few windows, if the house is well insulated, and if trees shade the house.

The average built-in air conditioner is designed to maintain a summer heat of 80 degrees with 50 per cent humidity. However, a person may be as comfortable at 82 degrees if the humidity is only 40 per cent, or need 72 degrees if the humidity is 60 per cent.

For new houses in *warm* climates, provision should at least be made for future installation of an air conditioning unit when the heating system is installed. This will increase the resale value of the house. Air conditioning *as part of the heating system* may be placed in the basement, utility room, or in a large closet area.

CONTROLLING NOISE

With increased use of electrical and motor-driven equipment, the typical home has steadily become a noisier place. Competing with radio and television are the buzzes and thumps of dishwashers, laundry equipment, and garbage disposal units. All of this may be drowned out at times by noises from outdoors—airplanes, trucks, power mowers.

Noise is not a minor matter. Studies indicate that people are less efficient, more irritable, and even more likely to develop nervous disorders, when subjected to too much noise. Recognizing this as a national problem, the Federal Housing Administration may add noise-control restrictions to building codes.

What can be done to control noise? When a house is being built, certain construction methods can be used, such as making the walls extra thick and insulating them heavily. Such methods add to the cost, but are well worth considering. In a house that is already built, noise can be reduced by installing acoustic tile or plaster, draperies, and wall-to-wall carpet. When buying equipment, choose types that can be operated quietly; for instance, some models of power mowers and air conditioners run much more quietly than others. Finally, a most important step that everyone can take is to be considerate in the use of radio, television, and phonograph, and in the tone of voice used around the home.

FINANCING A HOME

Determining Cost of Home Here are two rules of thumb in estimating how much you should spend for a house:

• Invest no more than 2½ times your yearly income—excluding wife's income during child-bearing age.
• Pay no more each *month* on principal, interest, and taxes than 20-25 per cent of take-home pay. Some people, to be on the safe side, include heating and utilities in this figure.

You can expect to use 1 per cent of the cost of the house each year for upkeep on a new house or 2 per cent on an older house.

Many things will alter these rules, such as amount of down payment, how much you can borrow and at what interest, size of the house you need, temporary earning of other family members, age of breadwinner in relation to his future anticipated income, and willingness of family members to make sacrifices.

You might think that $100 a month ($1,200 a year) for 20 years will pay for a $24,000 house, but it won't. On a typical 20-year mortgage almost three-fourths of every dollar for many months goes toward repaying just the interest on what you borrow. For nearly half the life of the mortgage, 50 per cent of what you pay goes toward interest.

Types of Mortgages Two common ways to finance a home are: (1) *conventional mortgage;* (2)*FHA-insured mortgage.* Nearly all mortgages are amortized, which means you pay a certain sum monthly, including interest and principal, the interest decreasing with each payment. In many cases the insurance premium, taxes, and special assessments are included in the monthly payment. A borrower should make sure the loan may be paid off at any time (to save interest) and also that the mortgage may be refinanced for special improvements. This is called an open-end mortgage. Investigate thoroughly to find out where you can borrow at the best rate. A difference of just one per cent interest amounts to hundreds of dollars in 15 or 20 years.

The Down Payment The terms of your contract may leave you a choice between making a large down payment or a small one. Your own financial situation and your expectations will guide your decision. If you are able to make a large down payment, you will avoid some of the interest charges, and you may be able to arrange smaller monthly payments. However, if a growing family or an uncertain job situation makes it likely that you will move in a few years, you may want to keep the down payment small. That way you will not

H. Armstrong Roberts

Wise parents give children a role in planning a new home. This strengthens feelings of family unity and eases the emotional strain of moving.

have as much money tied up in the house if you have to sell at a loss.

On a *conventional mortgage,* the down payment is usually between a fifth and a third of the total cost. This is the easiest type of mortgage to secure if you have the down payment. There is no penalty for paying off the mortgage at any time. A large down payment reduces the amount on which you must pay interest. This can save you hundreds of dollars over the life of the mortgage.

Rules concerning approved mortgages under the Federal Housing Administration and the Veterans Administration change from time to time. As of late 1968 the following regulations applied to many FHA loans:

The *mortgage limit* is $30,000. The mortgage must be paid off in 30 years, with 35 years being granted in exceptional cases. Most mortgages are paid off in 15 to 30 years.

The *down payment* varies with the cost of the house. For example, the down payment is 3 per cent of the first $15,000 or less; 10 per cent of the

381

next $5,000; and 20 per cent of any amount over $20,000.

On a $26,000 house the down payment is figured thus:

3 per cent of	$15,000	$ 450
10 per cent of	5,000	500
20 per cent of	6,000	1,200
Total down payment		$2,150

Veterans can secure VA or FHA insured loans up to $15,000 with no down payment.

The Contract Your real estate agent, contractor (if any), and lawyer will help you arrange the contract. This can be complicated, so you can see that it is important to deal with honest, competent people. Suppose you have found an occupied house you want. First you may sign a binder—a statement of your intention to buy. You will probably be asked for a deposit, called *hand money* or *earnest money,* to back up your statement of intention. It is a good idea to make certain that the binder will not force you to go ahead with the purchase, in case you have a good reason for wanting to cancel.

A contract should be made out in the names of husband and wife. This provides for ownership of the property by the surviving spouse.

The contract should itemize all alterations on a house, all extras and how they are to be paid. Don't let extras such as refrigerators, wall to wall carpeting, dishwashers, Venetian blinds, or children's playground equipment be bargaining points. In one instance, a couple became so intrigued with a child's playhouse they forgot to look for the real values in the house. They found out too late that they could have built several playhouses with the extra money that had to go into new plumbing, wiring, and flooring.

Be sure you understand *easement* rights that go to gas, electric, and water companies, and other builders. You don't want wires or pipes run diagonally through your property or heavy equipment tearing up a new lawn.

The closing date (when the house becomes yours) and date of possession (when you can move in) should be put in writing. Awkward situations can arise if all parties are not certain of these dates. You should also make it clear that you can be released from your contract if you cannot have full possession at the agreed time. Be sure that the seller assumes all risks of fire and other damage until you have full property rights and possession. Otherwise, if the house burns down before the seller moves out, you may be the loser.

Closing Costs Besides down payment, certain other costs must be met before arrangements for a home loan are complete. Many people overlook these *closing costs* until the last minute; however, the transaction can be cancelled if the buyer cannot pay these expenses. Closing costs include:

• Fees for appraising the house.

• Fire and extended coverage insurance. (Increasingly popular are life insurance policies which pay off the mortgage if the wage-earner dies, so that his family keeps the home, debt free. This usually is optional, not a required part of closing costs.)

• Title clearance and insurance. Your

lending agency probably will have its lawyer or title clearance office check deeds, wills, mortgages, and contracts involving your property. If not, you should hire someone competent to do this for you. This protects you against losing your property because of some error that might have been made in previous transactions. It also guards against fraudulent attempts to deprive you of your property. Few, if any, lending agencies will grant a loan unless such a check has been made. Insurance is available to cover you in case you lose your property because of some legal matter.

• Survey of the plot to confirm boundary lines. Find out if you have underground rights.

• Special assessment (if any) for sidewalks, sewage disposal, utilities, street improvement. All extra assessments should be understood and stated in writing.

• Fees to lawyer and architect.

Deed and Abstract   The deed is evidence of ownership. In some states the owner holds the deed; in others a third party holds it until the loan is repaid. The deed should be recorded in the county register of deeds. If the owner does not hold the deed, he should at least have a copy. The *abstract* is the legal description of the property—its history and previous ownership. The abstract should have the deed and mortgage recorded on it.

SPECIAL FINANCING ARRANGEMENTS

It is becoming more and more common for home builders to sell houses with no down payment and no appar-

ent closing costs. These expenses are included in the monthly payments for the first few years. If you buy a house on this plan, be sure you deal with a well established builder.

This kind of financing appeals to the person who wants to buy a home but has not saved enough money for a down payment. The buyer will actually pay more because of higher interest charges. Without a down payment, the buyer must pay interest on a larger principal. Under this plan, of every $10 paid in the first year, $8 goes toward interest and taxes, only $2 toward the price of the home. (The amount of interest and taxes is deductible from income tax.) Each month less of the payment goes toward interest, more toward the home itself. When an amount equal to the normal down payment and closing cost has been paid over the first few years, the financing often is converted to a common kind of mortgage.

Be sure you understand your contract and obligations when you agree to any financing arrangements, especially if there is anything unusual about it.

WHEN YOU MOVE

If you are planning to move, you should contact a mover four to six

Contact movers four to six weeks in advance to facilitate moving.

Aero Mayflower Transit Company, Inc.

weeks in advance. Here are some things you will want to consider:

• Estimated weight and cost of items to be moved.

• Pick-up and delivery time and date.

• Who will pack what, and how. (Valuables and money should be packed separately because movers are not responsible for these items.)

• When charges are to be paid, and whether in cash or by check.

• Place and cost of storage, if necessary.

• Bill of lading in relation to declared value of possessions. You should take inventory of your possessions to make the evaluation easier.

Many moving companies will provide families with labels and furniture tags to indicate where furniture is to be placed, cards indicating change of address, and other valuable helps. If a floor plan of the new house is available and furniture arrangement is indicated, the moving company will even place furniture, should the new occupants not be there to direct the work. However, movers are not permitted to attach appliances.

Before you leave a residence, stop deliveries by the milkman, newspaper boy, and others who service your home. Have utility companies discontinue service where you are and begin it where you expect to be. See that all bills are paid if you are moving to another area; close your checking account, and arrange to open a new one where you will be located. You will also want to notify the post office, local credit concerns, magazine business offices, and insurance companies of change of address. Your car registration card and driver's license will have to be changed. It is good practice to notify your church, doctor, lawyer, dentist, and broker.

It will be useful to take a local telephone directory and special address lists (such as club rosters) with you for addresses you may need.

Words and Phrases to Know

abstract	interest
amortized	lien
appraisal	louvered (screen)
assessment	mortgage
contract	open-end mortgage
crawl space	overhang
deed	principal
earnest money	slab foundation
easement	title
humidity	utilities
insulation	vent
insured	zoned living

ACTIVITIES

1. Find out how much houses and apartments are renting for in your community. What rent would a young couple expect to pay for an apartment—furnished and unfurnished? If rent represents 18 per cent of income, what salary would be needed?

2. Price several kinds of houses for sale in your community. If a home should represent roughly two and a half times annual income after taxes, what income would each kind of home represent?

3. Find out what it would cost to build a home that fulfills the recommendations made by the Women's Housing Conference.

4. About what income might a typi-

cal young couple in your community expect to make? Are these people renting apartments or houses; building or buying homes?

5. List a variety of places in your community where you can borrow money; find out the interest rates.

6. Offer the apartment check list on page 371 to a young couple looking for a place to live. Find out how helpful it was and how the landlord reacted to questioning.

7. If there is a model home open, visit it and rate it according to the check list for judging a floor plan.

8. Find out how much families have paid for older homes; what they had to remodel; how much the remodeling cost.

9. Using the prices of new homes in your community, demonstrate on the chalk board how to finance a home by (a) conventional mortgage over 15 years at 5 per cent interest; (b) the same house over 20 years at 6 per cent interest.

10. Investigate the price of lots. If the lot represents 15 per cent of the total home cost, how much would house and lot cost at various sites?

11. Compare the costs of building an average priced home in your community with these materials—brick veneer, solid brick, stone, clapboard, and aluminum.

12. Trace the origin and development of Federal Housing Administration loans. Can anyone obtain such a loan?

13. Bring to class as many legal papers listed in this chapter as you can find—abstract, contract, deed, etc. Discuss.

14. Invite a real estate dealer, home builder, architect, or someone connected with a lending institution to talk about the services these firms provide.

15. **Bulletin Board:** Mount pictures of different-styled homes. Include floor plans. Discuss your favorites.

Correlation

MATHEMATICS: Invite the mathematics teacher to explain ways that interest may be compounded and give any other information he may consider useful in relation to home financing.

ENGLISH: Assign a research paper on one of the following topics: Prefabricated homes; Federal Housing Administration; Home Improvements and Their Cost; New England's Outstanding Homes; Ante-bellum Homes; Early Homes in America; Homes Designed by Frank Lloyd Wright.

SOCIOLOGY: Invite the sociology teacher to give an illustrated talk on dwellings in relation to different cultures and available building materials.

Home Experiences

1. If your family is thinking of moving, write to several transfer companies for cost estimates. Study the literature from these companies and report in class.

2. Check your floor plan at home according to the check list on page 377.

3. Follow the suggestions for keeping a house cool and saving on heat bills.

4. Measure the rooms of your home and compare sizes with the chart on page 375.

Chapter 19

Adult Investment and Security

It may seem strange to discuss future financial matters requiring a lot of money when right now you may be wondering how you can pay for a date to the Senior Prom. On the other hand, you may never take time to study important financial matters again. Here, in the order of their importance, are some family security goals:

FIRST: *Life insurance,* especially for a young married man with a beginning family; nothing else offers as much protection, should the father die and leave a young family.

SECOND: *Health insurance* to help provide for hospitalization, medical, and doctor bills.

THIRD: A *home,* or its equivalent in *securities,* as an investment as well as loan value.

FOURTH: *Savings* or *liquid assets* in available cash, sufficient to meet living expenses for six months. This is money that may be had without borrowing from outside sources—savings in a bank or savings and loan association, bonds that may be cashed, and money that may be borrowed against the cash surrender value of a life insurance policy or equity value in a home.

FIFTH: Purchase of *mutual funds* or *common stock.* Stocks are a suitable form of savings but should not be considered until after the above goals have been met and a home at least 50 per cent paid for. Stocks may not be counted as fixed assets because selling prices may vary. If a person must sell stock at a time when its value is down, he has to take a loss.

SIXTH: Investments in *real estate, preferred stocks,* and *bonds.*

LIFE INSURANCE

Some form of life insurance is a necessity for everyone, but especially for families with young children. The amount of this protection that is needed will also vary with the wage

386

earner's age, income, marital status, character of savings and investments, social security status, pensions, and other assets.

The following case studies indicate the need for life insurance:

CASE STUDIES: Jim Allison, twenty-two and out of military service, is the adventuresome type. He has no plans for marriage and his parents are not dependent upon him, so Jim says he has no one but himself to protect with life insurance. His main concern at present is to have enough money for final expenses (medical and nursing care, unpaid bills, taxes, lawyer's fees, and burial) so Jim decides to buy a $5,000 term life insurance policy and use his other savings for speculation or perhaps a small business.

Tom Burns, also twenty-two, just married and out of college, has his military training ahead of him. He feels the need for a life insurance policy not only to cover final expenses, but to provide for his widow, if he should die unexpectedly. Tom decides to start with a $10,000 life insurance policy and build it up to a more adequate amount as soon as possible.

Bob Simons, eighteen and the only son of a widowed mother, expects to go into heavy construction work after apprenticeship training, and wait until he is drafted to serve his military obligation. His mother offered to pay the annual premium on a $10,000 paid-up-at-sixty-five policy until Bob can earn enough to handle his own premiums. Bob made his mother beneficiary, with the privilege of making his wife beneficiary if he marries. In having this life insurance policy bought for him while young, Bob benefits three ways:
• He is in good health and insurable.

If he waited until he could afford it better, he might not be insurable.
• He will have lower yearly premiums to pay.
• His policy will build up a more substantial loan value for later emergencies or opportunities because of his early start.

Jean and Art Jenkins have three young children. Art feels that life insurance is of prime importance for family protection until their children are of age. Art decides to buy a policy which will guarantee a monthly income for his family in case he dies during a stated period — say twenty years. At the end of the period, his wife, as beneficiary, will receive the face amount of the policy, which may be paid in cash or as continued income.

You can see from these case studies why life insurance is important, as well as why each person or family may need a different plan.

Life Insurance Terminology You will understand life insurance better if you understand the terms used to describe it.

POLICY: This is the certificate or contract issued by the insurance company to the purchaser.

FACE VALUE: The full amount of insurance bought. If the policyholder dies after making only a few payments, the beneficiary will receive the full or face value.

CASH VALUE: In some kinds of insurance you are given credit for the amount you have paid. This is called the cash value. You can borrow up to that amount on your policy. Be sure you understand that not all kinds of insurance have a cash value. This is

387

explained further in the following paragraphs on permanent and term insurance.

TERM INSURANCE: Briefly, these are the characteristics of term insurance: it is purchased for a specified time, perhaps five years; there is no cash value; payment is made only if the insured dies; it costs less than any other kind of life insurance. *Other aspects of term insurance will be discussed later in this chapter.*

PERMANENT INSURANCE: Any type of life insurance that contains an increasing reserve or cash value (not term insurance). Straight life, limited payment life, and endowment policies are permanent insurance. They are more fully discussed later in this chapter.

PREMIUM: The amount of money paid at a time—annually, semiannually, quarterly, or monthly.

BENEFITS: Payments made by the life insurance company to the beneficiary at death of the insured *or* to the insured as "living" benefits in the form of endowments, annuity payments, cash loans, or cash surrender value.

BENEFICIARY: The person or persons designated by the insured to receive the benefits of the policy upon his death. Benefits may be paid out in one lump sum, as income over a stated period, or in other ways according to individual needs.

ANNUITY: The amount of money paid the insured person at stated periods (usually monthly) upon retirement. This sum can supplement Social Security benefits and provide a more secure income.

SURRENDER OR LOAN VALUE: You can borrow against your policy, up to the amount you have paid on it. The loan is repaid at interest, and the face value of the insurance remains in force. Of course, if the insured dies, the unpaid amount of the loan is deducted from what the beneficiary receives. It is also possible to surrender the policy for the amount you have paid on it, but this usually is done only in an emergency.

DIVIDENDS: These are not dividends in the sense of earnings on shares of stock, but are a return to the policyholder of unused portions of the premium. They may be taken in cash, applied against future premiums, used to purchase additional insurance, or allowed to accumulate as interest.

DOUBLE INDEMNITY: This may be part of the policy or a "rider" clause, assuring payment to the beneficiary equal to twice the value of the policy should the policyholder die by certain accidental means.

WAIVER OF PREMIUM: This is an extra benefit clause providing that the insurance will remain in force without any further premium payments should the policyholder become totally and permanently disabled. Usually a certain waiting period is required before the benefit begins.

DISABILITY INCOME: This is another extra benefit, specifying that the company will pay the policyholder a monthly income for life if he is totally and permanently disabled. A waiting period is required to establish that disability is permanent and total.

Life Insurance—Ordinary and Others There are four basic kinds of *ordinary life insurance,* and several other kinds. Many types of insurance are available on both individual and group basis.

Basic Ordinary Policies

Straight Life (Ordinary Life)
Limited Payment Life
Endowment
Term

Other Policies

Family Income
Retirement Income
Family Policy
Credit Life
Travel
Education

STRAIGHT LIFE INSURANCE: Straight Life or Ordinary Life insurance is the most widely used. Lowest in cost for lifetime family protection, it builds up a substantial cash or loan value for later years.

Although the contract calls for payments of a premium as long as one lives, it is possible to discontinue payments at any time, and as soon as a cash value has been established, choose one of the following options: (1) surrender the policy for its cash value; (2) exchange the policy for a reduced amount of paid-up life insurance; (3) take term insurance equal to the original amount of the policy's face value for as long as the cash value will permit.

LIMITED PAYMENT LIFE INSURANCE: This kind of policy also provides lifetime protection, but premiums are paid over a limited time—10, 20, or 30 years, or to age 60 or 65. The payments are relatively higher. There are two advantages to this type of insurance: premiums are usually paid up before retirement, and cash value builds more quickly than in a straight life policy.

ENDOWMENT INSURANCE: This policy is comparable to a savings account, with one big addition—if the insured dies before the endowment period ends, the beneficiary receives the face value of the policy. Premiums are paid regularly over a definite period of time. If the insured lives until the end of the period, he is paid the full face value. Endowment insurance assures having money at a certain date for such objectives as an education or retirement funds. Premiums are high, so few families buy endowment insurance policies unless basic insurance needs have been met. Yet an endowment insurance policy builds up a high cash value quickly.

TERM INSURANCE: This provides protection for a limited time—until a house is paid for or children are educated. Usually it provides no savings or cash value. Payment is made only if the insured dies. Premiums are lowest of all life insurance, because the risk is for a shorter time, and no cash value or savings are involved. Term insurance should allow the insured to:

—*renew* the contract without a medical examination, although at a higher rate determined by his age when he renews; or
—*convert* the policy to permanent insurance without a medical examination.

You will notice in the table on page 390 that the new policy premium increases each year in relation to age. You will notice also that the *Twenty Year Endowment* is the most expensive because premiums are paid over a short period to accumulate a definite sum of money in twenty years.

APPROXIMATE ANNUAL PREMIUM RATES PER
$1,000 OF FOUR TYPES OF LIFE INSURANCE*

Issued at age	Straight Life (Ordinary Life)	Limited Payment Life (Paid up at age 65)	Five Year Term (Renewable and Convertible)	Twenty Year Endowment
15	$15.22	$16.73	$ 6.42	$48.63
16	15.58	17.15	6.48	48.69
17	15.95	17.60	6.56	48.75
18	16.34	18.07	6.64	48.81
19	16.74	18.57	6.73	48.88
20	17.16	19.08	6.82	48.96
25	19.56	22.07	7.45	49.45
30	22.52	25.95	8.40	50.21
40	30.95	38.12	12.10	53.18
50	44.84	65.04	20.71	60.22

*Participating (dividend paying) rates of a large life insurance company in New York state. Rates shown are for policies ranging in amounts from $5,000 to $9,999. Rates for policies with face amounts of $10,000 or more are somewhat lower.

The next most expensive is *Life Paidup at 65*. At the average retirement age the policyholder can stop making payments on policies of this type. In *Straight Life* the premiums are a little lower but are paid yearly until death. *The Five Year Term* insurance is the least expensive. Premiums are paid over a short period for protection should the insured die within the five year term. If the policyholder lives beyond the term, the protection ceases and there is no cash surrender value.

In the first three types of life insurance listed on page 389, the cash surrender value or the amount against which one can borrow increases each year. Term insurance is temporary insurance, and unless there is a renewable or convertible clause the protection ends at the end of the term and there is no policy value.

Other types of life insurance include:

FAMILY INCOME POLICY: This plan is usually a combination of permanent insurance and decreasing term insurance; it may have a lower premium than for the two kinds bought separately: If the insured dies during the family income period (usually 10, 15, or 20 years, while children are dependent), the family receives a monthly income for the balance of the family income period. At the end of this period, the face value of the policy is paid.

This type of insurance has the advantage of providing a regular income to a widow during the period when children are dependent.

FAMILY POLICY: In this more recently developed type of policy, every member of the family has life insurance protection. For example:

Benjamin Andrews pays a premium of about $152 a year, which includes a $5,000 straight life policy on himself, a $1,500 term policy on his wife, and $1,000 for each child—John, 14; Edna, 12; and Alice, 9. As each child reaches 18 (the age may go up to 25, depending upon the company), the insurance coverage may be dropped or the child may convert his policy to as much as $5,000 of straight life, limited pay life, or endowment insurance, regardless of health or occupation.

Some financial advisors favor placing a large amount of insurance on the father and none on the children. However, if a child develops a serious health problem he may not be insurable later on. A family policy avoids this difficulty by the conversion privilege explained above.

RETIREMENT INCOME: In this type policy, the insured is guaranteed a retirement income for life at a specified age which will supplement Social Security, income from pensions, and investments.

CREDIT LIFE INSURANCE: This is a kind of term insurance designed to guarantee payment of a loan on an installment purchase. It may apply to the purchase of a car, household equipment, or other purchases on the installment basis.

TRAVEL INSURANCE: Most of these policies provide two major types of protection. If the insured dies as a result of an auto or plane crash or a similar accident, the beneficiary is paid a certain sum, often rather large. If the insured loses a limb, sight, or hearing in such an accident, he is paid a smaller sum. In airports you can usually buy a policy to cover all flights on a trip you are making. Other policies may cover all travel for an extended period, perhaps a year, for one person or an entire family. When buying this type of insurance be sure you know whether some travel accidents are excluded from coverage. For instance, some policies do not cover accidents on non-scheduled flights (as in private planes), or overseas flights.

EDUCATION INSURANCE: This type of insurance provides for a college education for the children in a family, in case the family head dies before college costs are paid. It is a kind of term insurance. Also, some banks and other lending agencies have education loan programs which include decreasing term insurance. Under these plans a parent can borrow money for his children's education, and the insurance pays off the loan if the parent dies before repaying it.

Where to Buy Life Insurance Nine-tenths of all life insurance is sold by "legal reserve" life insurance companies. Of the ten per cent remaining, about three-fourths is veterans' insurance, issued by the government. Other agencies offering life insurance are fraternal lodges or societies, savings banks, and mutual aid groups.

When you are ready to buy life insurance, the person best qualified to help you is a life insurance agent. He can help you decide:

· How much insurance to buy.
· The type best suited to your needs and how to plan payments.
· What extras you want in your policy —waiver of premium, disability income, double indemnity, and so on.
· How to convert your policy to another type if ever necessary.
· What settlement options are advisable for your family, if you die while your children are dependent.

As mentioned earlier, life insurance is sold on a *group* basis, as well as to individuals. Group insurance costs less. It is available in businesses, educational institutions, and other organizations in which employees have a common employer. As a rule no medical examination is required.

Most group life insurance is in the form of *yearly-renewable term insurance*, giving protection only if the insured dies, but some group plans provide for a continuation of part of the protection after an employee retires, on a paid-up basis. They have no savings or cash-in value. When an employee leaves a company with which he has had group insurance he should inquire about ways of converting it to ordinary life insurance unless he is to be insured under another group plan.

HEALTH INSURANCE

Sudden and prolonged illness can upset a budget drastically. Health insurance is as necessary as life insurance to meet sickness and accident emergencies.

A college student may often obtain low-cost group health insurance at his college. If you buy such insurance, find out if it covers summer vacations and how it applies off campus.

You may have health insurance under a family plan until a certain number of days after you reach age 17 or even 21. (Occasionally, coverage is in force until age 25, if the dependent is a full-time college student.) If possible, continue this health insurance on an individual basis until you are eligible for insurance with a group. For example, Ed Donnelley had been covered by his family health insurance policy until 30 days after his 19th birthday. There was a lapse of 10 days between coverage by his family pol-

icy and coverage by his college policy. During this period Ed became ill and had to spend a week in the hospital. His expenses amounted to nearly $300, all of which his family had to pay.

Health insurance may be obtained from general insurance companies, from companies that specialize in health insurance, and from independent organizations such as fraternal orders, industrial community plans, private group plans, and labor unions. *Individual* health insurance is available mainly from general insurance companies.

If your health insurance is with a general insurance company, you will be able to obtain *loss-of-income coverage* as well as hospital, surgical, and general medical benefits. General insurance companies usually make their payments to the policyholder who then pays his own bills. Some specialized companies give the money directly to the doctor and hospital, rather than to the policyholder. It will be helpful for you to find out which hospitals in your community honor your type of health insurance, so there will be no misunderstanding when bills are presented. As a rule, you will be asked at the admittance desk what health insurance you have.

Varieties of Health Insurance Some types of health insurance are Hospital Expense Insurance, Surgical Expense Insurance, General Medical Expense Insurance, and Major Medical Expense Insurance (to help pay medical and hospital costs resulting from illness or accident); and Loss of Income Insurance (to provide income during illness or disability).

HOSPITAL EXPENSE INSURANCE: This provides a benefit for all or part of the room and board costs in a hospital, depending upon the accommodations. In some cases, operating room, medications, and X-rays may be covered. The cost of adequate coverage varies in different parts of the country according to living and service standards. This is the most widely used of all health insurances.

SURGICAL EXPENSE INSURANCE: The benefits under this plan are usually paid according to the severity of the operation and prevailing surgical costs in the community. For instance, a tonsillectomy may be $100, removal of a gall bladder $200, and a brain operation much more. This plan is nearly as common as hospital coverage.

GENERAL MEDICAL EXPENSE INSURANCE: This insurance helps to pay for the doctor's services in the hospital, at home, or in the doctor's office. The maximum number of calls for each illness or injury is specified. You may want to "shop" for the policy that best meets medical charges in your area.

MAJOR MEDICAL INSURANCE: This kind of coverage is designed to prevent a serious accident or prolonged illness from draining all of a family's financial resources. It is sold on *individual* or *group* plans. The group plan is much cheaper. If you are eligible for this kind of group insurance, you can hardly afford to be without it.

Major medical insurance often provides coverage up to $5,000, and sometimes to $10,000 or more. Included are doctor and nurse fees, hospital bills, laboratory fees, drugs, X-rays, and other costs of treatment in a hospital, nursing home, or one's own home.

Two features of this insurance are a deductible clause, comparable to automobile collision insurance, and a *co-insurance clause*. Co-insurance means that the insured person must pay part of the costs, perhaps 25 per cent, while the insurance company covers the remaining 75 per cent. Benefits may apply to one person or to a whole family, although there is often a limitation on the number of claims a policyholder may file—perhaps one every 90 days. Provisions vary with each insurance company.

CASE STUDY: John Williams participated in a group major medical expense insurance policy where he worked. A monthly payment of $3 was deducted from his pay check. His wife and child were also protected by his policy.

John had $100-deductible insurance, meaning he had to pay the first $100. He also had 25 per cent co-insurance, which means he had to pay one-fourth of any medical expense above the deductible.

When John was stricken with a serious illness his bills were paid as shown in the chart on page 394. Major medical insurance combined with basic hospitalization and surgical plans can cover a large part of most major medical expenses.

For many years health insurance benefits stopped when a person reached 65 or 70. Then some insurance companies began to extend coverage to any person who applied, regardless of his age or state of health. This insurance became popular with older people.

In 1966 Medicare, a tax-supported health insurance for the elderly, was put into effect. As a result, insurance

Better Living, Du Pont

If you have adequate health insurance, you can leave the hospital relieved of financial worry.

companies have begun to offer policies which pay some of the expenses not covered by Medicare.

Here are some factors to consider when you buy health insurance:
· What protection you will have for illness and injury; extent of protection.
· Conditions, if any, under which a health insurance company may cancel your policy.
· Whether you may be paid for emer-

gency treatment; operation in a doctor's office; out-patient services from a hospital.
· How you may continue your insurance if you are insured with a group which you must leave.

You may want to have your family read this section of your text and examine their health protection.

SOCIAL SECURITY BENEFITS

More than nine out of ten working people are covered under the Social Security program. If you have ever held a job you probably had to get a Social Security card, and tax was deducted from your pay to finance this program.

Employers pay half of this tax. In other words, if a worker's pay check shows a $5 deduction, his employer is taxed another $5. Self-employed persons pay more than regular employees. Although the worker pays only half of this tax *directly*, he helps pay

	Total Charges	Paid by Basic Hospitalization and Surgical Plans	Expenses Not Covered by Basic Plan
Hospital room and board (30 days at $35 a day)....	$1,050	$1,050	$ —
Other hospital charges........................	600	400	200
Drugs........................	100	—	100
Physician and surgeon fees....................	800	600	200
	$2,550	$2,050	$ 500
Minus a "deductible" of $100................			100
Balance subject to "co-insurance"................			$ 400
Minus co-insurance of 20 per cent (paid by John Williams)................			$ 80
Paid to him by the insurance company (major medical)................			$ 320
Total paid by insurance (major medical plus basic)................			$2,370
Total paid by John Williams................			$ 180

the other half *indirectly,* since the products he buys are priced to include the employer's share of the tax.

A family whose chief wage earner has died can usually receive Social Security payments. So can older people who are retired. A single person who retires at age 65 receives a minimum of $55 a month. Medicare, discussed earlier in this chapter, is another part of this rather complicated program. You can check with the nearest Social Security Administration office to see how this program affects you and your family.

Since its beginning in 1935 the program has been changed several times to keep up with changing social conditions. The trend has been toward larger payments for more people, and higher taxes. Based on 1969 figures a wage earner pays a yearly maximum of about $375 toward Social Security. Higher taxes are scheduled for the near future.

OTHER TYPES OF INSURANCE

COMPREHENSIVE PERSONAL LIABILITY POLICY: This protects the insured against claims made by persons who have been injured, made ill, or accidentally killed on the owner's property. It may protect any member of the household *away* from home who accidentally injures someone. Payment is made for injury, death, and legal costs, up to a certain figure.

For instance, claims may be paid if: a dog bites a neighbor's child, requiring medical care; the mailman trips on a child's wagon and breaks an ankle; a worker in the house falls down the steps or off a ladder; a person is accidentally struck by a child riding a bicycle on the street, or injured when a child raises an umbrella or bats a ball. Baby sitters and delivery people are especially subject to accidents on the property of others. This kind of insurance is not expensive; any homeowner or tenant without it is taking a dangerous risk. Lawsuits from a serious injury may cost an uninsured family its life income.

FIRE, THEFT, AND EXTENDED COVERAGE POLICY: Insurance may cover a house and/or possessions in case of theft, fire, windstorm, explosion, aircraft and surface vehicle damage, and vandalism, as well as additional living expenses caused by dwelling damage. Extended coverage may include damage from falling objects, landslide, and structural collapse.

HOME OWNER'S POLICY: This policy combines comprehensive personal liability, fire, theft, and extended coverage, with an option of additional clauses at a lower cost than that of separate policies. Under any home insurance policy the home should not be insured for more than 80 per cent of its appraised value.

When you begin to accumulate possessions, whether furniture, jewelry, or heirlooms, you should investigate the cost of insurance. As improvements are made on a home, policies should be changed.

AUTOMOBILE INSURANCE

The automobile is our No. 1 killer! The driver is more to blame than road conditions, weather, or car failure. When a person ignores traffic laws; drives while he is intoxicated, sleepy, emotionally upset—angry, jealous, or depressed—or takes chances deliberately, he makes protection necessary for everyone.

FIRE	WINDSTORM AND HAIL	SMOKE DAMAGE	GLASS BREAKAGE
DAMAGE BY VEHICLES	EXPLOSION	VANDALISM	BROKEN PIPES
FROZEN PLUMBING	FALLING TREES	FALLING AIRCRAFT	FUR LOSS, DAMAGE
THEFT PERSONAL ITEMS	HOUSEHOLD GOODS	LOSS WHILE TRAVELING	INJURIES YOU INFLICT
ACCIDENTS TO TRADESMEN	BOATING LIABILITY	INJURIES CAUSED BY CHILDREN	COURT COSTS
ADDITIONAL LIVING EXPENSES	DAMAGE TO OUT-BUILDINGS	LOSS TO CLOTHES AT SCHOOL	GOLFING ACCIDENTS

Hardware Mutuals

Some kinds of insurance coverage you may want.

Kinds of Coverage Car insurance may provide the following coverage: *protection* in case of a lawsuit, bodily injury, or property damage; *medical coverage* (medical, surgical, ambulance, nursing care) for all family members involved in an automobile accident or struck by an automobile; *comprehensive coverage* for fire, theft, flood, windstorm, vandalism, and glass breakage, plus insurance up to $100 on personal belongings in the car; *collision* coverage with a deductible clause of $50 or $100 if your car is damaged and not covered by the other person's property insurance; *towing*, and *servicing* up to certain amount.

When you buy car insurance, price different coverages and buy the insurance that best meets your needs.

Reasons for Rising Rates Recently, *Traffic Safety* magazine revealed many of the dishonest practices that have caused car insurance rates to soar. By driving safely, by learning about corrupt practices and avoiding them, you can help to reduce rates substantially. For instance, Butte, Montana, had the highest rate in the country, $117, and reduced it to one of the lowest rates, $35. A traffic safety council broke up crooked, petty rackets, fined drunken and reckless drivers heavily, and jailed second offenders.

When a person is involved in an accident, he is usually too upset to think clearly. Beware of the following malpractices:

• Ambulance chasers, who drive around in cars equipped with short wave radio and race ambulances to the scene of the accident. They may take colored pictures of all the gory details, get signatures of witnesses, and even try to get semi-conscious persons to sign statements. Later these crooks sell such "evidence" to lawyers.

• Garage owners who pad repair costs and offer a kickback to owners as part of the deductible insurance payment.

• Lawyers who use unethical tactics to get unreasonably high settlements in damage cases. In one extreme case, a pregnant woman who merely witnessed a bad accident later had a miscarriage. A lawsuit brought her an award of $90,000, although two obstetricians felt the accident had nothing to do with the miscarriage.

Most lawyers and garage owners are honest. It is always best to deal with people whose good reputation is well established. Not only is it dishon-

est to try to pull a "shady" deal, but you may find the unethical agent cheating you as well. There is much truth to the old saying. "It's hard to cheat an honest man."

How You Can Reduce Rates As in the case of citizen action in Butte, Montana, observing good driving codes and putting an end to swindling and dishonest claims can reduce costs greatly. Over a period of ten years such savings might cover the down payment on a new car. Other ways you can reduce your annual car insurance premiums are:

• Find out if rates are reduced for an applicant who has had an accredited driver training course; if they are, take it. The savings on annual premi-

Automobile insurance protects a family against expensive lawsuits.

Liberty Mutual Insurance Company

ums from age 16 to 25 can amount to a great deal.

• Find out what companies offer lower rates to persons who have not been involved in an automobile accident for a defined period.

• Determine the use of your car. Cars used only for pleasure have the lowest rates; next in line are cars driven to work, and next, cars used for business.

• If you buy $100 deductible collision insurance instead of $50, you save considerably on premiums. Also, you can make an income tax deduction on auto repair expenses not covered by your insurance.

• Insuring two cars under one policy (if used in the same family) will save substantially on premiums.

NOTE: Ordinarily you may find it advantageous to have both husband and wife listed as joint owners of your car. However, if you lose an expensive damage suit as the result of an accident with the car, the salaries of both owners may be taken over legally to enforce payment.

SAVINGS FOR READY CASH

Every individual and family should have some cash savings. It is easier to save for a definite purpose, such as home or car ownership, a college education, or a vacation. Medical emergencies and retirement are other reasons for saving, although Social Security, insurance, and company retirement programs help meet financial needs at these times.

Some methods of saving involve almost no risk that you will lose your money. Your money will be safe and earn interest in a bank, savings and loan association, credit union, or invested in government bonds.

Commercial and Mutual Savings Banks Commercial banks provide facilities for checking and savings accounts. Such banks are located in almost all communities. Mutual savings banks, formed primarily for saving accounts, are located only in some sections. These usually pay a higher rate of interest than commercial banks.

Savings and Loan Associations These are not banks, but *credit* businesses. They offer no checking services. Their main function is to lend money to customers who need it. Also they pay attractive rates of interest or dividends on savings accounts—usually higher rates than banks pay. For instance, in early 1968 banks were legally permitted to pay no more than 5 per cent interest, while savings and loan associations could pay 5¼ per cent. These rates are regulated by the government and are changed from time to time.

Banks and savings and loan associations offer various savings plans. To obtain the maximum interest you may have to leave your money in the account for a year or longer. Other plans may pay somewhat lower interest but give you more freedom to withdraw. To learn what type of account is best for you, *investigate before you invest*. Besides finding out about interest rates, you will want to know when dividends are paid, how many days notice you must give before withdrawing part or all of your money, and how often dividends are computed. The way you manage your savings account can make quite a difference.

CASE STUDY: Mr. and Mrs. H. W. Cline had been saving for a family trip to Europe. Their final payment of $3,000 for a package tour was due June 15th. Mrs. Cline suddenly realized that if she left the $3,000 in her savings and loan account until June 30, it would earn a six-month dividend, or half of what the $3,000 would earn in one year at 4 per cent. This would amount to $60. She found that she would be ahead by borrowing the money from the savings and loan association for 15 days at 5 per cent interest ($6.25), a saving of $53.75!

Here are some terms commonly used in connection with savings accounts in banks and savings and loan associations:

ORDINARY SAVINGS ACCOUNT: This is the account which uses the passbook to record deposits and interest. Money can be withdrawn at any time with no previous notice.

TIME DEPOSIT ACCOUNT: In this type of saving, money is placed in an account for a fixed period of time—30 days or more. It cannot be withdrawn without a notice in writing 30 days before withdrawal. Interest is a little higher than in the ordinary savings account.

SAVINGS CERTIFICATE: This is a fixed contract between the bank or savings and loan association and the individual. There is a minimum deposit amount and a relatively long period of time before the certificate matures and accumulates interest. Interest rates are higher than in the above accounts.

BANK SAVINGS "BONDS": These represent another form of time deposits. They may retire in a year or five years with an interest rate of 5 per cent or more.

INSURED ACCOUNTS: During the Depression many people lost their life's savings when banks failed. Such failures are extremely rare now, but even when they do occur investors are usually protected. Nearly all savings accounts in bank and savings and loan associations are insured to $15,000 by an agency of the state or federal government. When opening an account, make certain that you will have this protection.

United States Savings Bonds United States Savings Bonds, Series E and H, are good investments for many reasons.

• Since they are backed by the U.S. Treasury, they are considered among the safest investments.

• They pay competitive rates of interest—up to 4.5 per cent.

• They provide a tax benefit. Interest on them need not be reported for income tax purposes until the bonds are cashed. If a person holds the bonds until he retires, he can usually cash them without having to pay much tax, since he will then be in a low income bracket.

• They are an investment in your country, helping to finance the activities of your government.

Series E Bonds come in denominations of $25, $50, $100, $200, $500, $1,000, and $10,000 (maturity value) and mature in seven years. Series H Bonds come in denominations of $500, $1,000, $5,000, and $10,000 (maturity value) and mature in ten years. Many financial advisors say that these bonds should be part of any well-rounded savings program.

Among other federal bonds, also backed by the U.S. Treasury, are securities of the Federal National Mortgage Association, the Home Loan Bank, and the Land Bank. Some pay nearly 5 per cent interest.

Credit Unions Any group with common interests—teachers, factory or office workers, a fraternal organization, a lodge—may form a credit union and be chartered by the state or federal government. Members contribute regularly as they would to a savings account. Some credit unions operate with assets of only a few thousand dollars and one manager, the secretary, while others operate with millions of dollars and a full business staff. A committee or board studies ways to invest members' dues in order to increase the assets. A member has the privilege of borrowing without having his credit investigated and at a fairly low interest rate.

PURCHASING STOCKS AND BONDS

As mentioned earlier, there is not much risk of *losing* money that is invested in insured accounts or government bonds. However, such investments carry a different sort of risk. They pay a fixed rate of interest, and this may not be enough to keep up with inflation. In other words, if your money earns 4 per cent a year but the cost of living rises 3 per cent, you have gained very little. If living costs rise more sharply, your investment can actually decrease in real value, even though it earns more dollars for you.

Trying to avoid this risk, many people put some money into investments which are not limited to a fixed rate

of interest. They may buy a piece of land which they expect to grow in value; or they may buy an apartment building, knowing that they can raise rents to keep pace with their own rising expenses. However, these are expensive investments, usually requiring a large down payment. The usual way for small investors to try to beat inflation is by purchasing common stocks representing ownership of corporations.

Common stocks of good quality companies can, and often do, grow rapidly in value. Also, company management is free to increase the dividends paid to stockholders. For these reasons common stocks *can be* more profitable than a fixed-interest investments. On the other hand, there is considerable risk involved in buying stocks. For instance, if business conditions are poor or if a company is not well managed, its stock will probably decline and dividends may be omitted.

Many Americans have decided that the advantages of stock ownership are greater than the risks. Statistics from the New York Stock Exchange show that 24 million people owned corporation stocks in early 1968. For several previous years this number had grown more than a million a year, six times faster than the national population was growing.

Stocks may be bought through local brokers. They handle all the business from the time you indicate what stock you want to buy until you receive your stock certificate, which is your final proof of ownership. Stocks are usually traded in round lots—that is, in lots of 100 shares. However, beginning investors often buy as few as five

HOW TO FIGURE A FAMILY'S NET WORTH

Assets	Liabilities
House (market price)........$..............	Mortgage and interest due..........$..............
Other real estate (market price).	Unpaid notes, bills and charge accounts ....
Furniture, appliances (between used value and original cost, depending on age and condition.)..................	Insurance payments due........... ....
	Car loan and interest due........... ....
	Other loans and interest due........ ....
Jewelry, silverware, etc. (used price)...................	Taxes, other than withholding....... ....
Cash, bonds, savings, stocks (market price)............	Pledged but unpaid contributions..... ....
	Others............................ ....
Car (used car price).........	TOTAL LIABILITIES.............$..............
Tax refund due (if any)	
Money owed you (collectible)..	
Collections—stamps, coins, records, books, (market price)..	
Life insurance (cash value).....	
Others	
TOTAL ASSETS ....$..............	

NET WORTH (Assets Less Liabilities)................................$..............

or ten shares at a time. Purchases of fewer than 100 shares are called *odd lots;* they involve relatively high broker's commissions, up to 6 per cent, compared with the usual 1 per cent for round lots.

Before purchasing stock, determine your financial position by listing your assets and liabilities. Although common stock has paid well in recent years, no one should purchase stock in great quantity until other security goals have been met. Financial advisers say it is unwise to borrow on life insurance or mortgage a home to buy stock.

Origin of the Stock Market Soon after our country was established, businesses and industries needed capital with which to expand. They raised much of this money by selling stocks and bonds. As business and industry became more complex, a central place was needed for selling these securities or auctioning off shares of stock. Hence the New York Stock Exchange came into being. This is the largest stock exchange in the country, with the American Stock Exchange second in size. Each has member firms in cities all over the United States. In addition, a number of large cities have their own exchanges, dealing in local stocks as well as those listed on the two large exchange boards.

Stock exchanges do not buy or sell; they only provide a place similar to an auction market for trading shares of stock. Brokers at the exchanges in New York and elsewhere receive thousands of orders daily to buy and sell stock. If you place an order with your local broker, he relays it to a broker at an exchange who makes the transaction.

If there is a large demand for a certain stock, the price per share will go up. If demand falls, so will the price of the stock. The same situation occurs in your own food market—when eggs are scarce, prices go up—when they are plentiful, prices go down.

You can follow stock market trends on the financial pages of many daily newspapers.

There is no foolproof formula for success in the stock market, or everyone dealing in the market would be rich. Even experienced economists cannot always predict what will happen to a certain stock. For example, you may get a tip on a good pharmaceutical stock and hurry out to invest all of your savings, almost certain to

make a "killing." But another pharmaceutical company may come out with a new line of drugs that sends its stock zooming, and causes the stock you bought to drop. On the other hand, you may be lucky. For instance, a man who put $1,000 into Xerox stock at just the right time in the late 1950's could have sold it for roughly $80,000 ten years later. Such success, of course, is very rare.

STOCK MARKET TERMS

Common Stock As explained earlier, common stock represents ownership in business and industry. It is the type of stock most new investors buy. Some stocks sell for just a few dollars a share, others for $200 and more. Investors with rather limited funds often prefer low-priced stocks because they can buy more shares; however, the price of a stock does not indicate whether or not it is a good investment. It is more important to know about a company's operations, earnings, dividends, and similar information. A broker can provide these facts.

When stocks grow in value they often *split* two or three for one. For instance, suppose you owned ten shares of a stock at $100 a share and the stock split two for one. You would then own twenty shares at $50 a share. One advantage of a split is psychological. The lower price attracts more interest.

Dealers who may or may not be members of a regular stock exchange sell stock in some companies *over-the-counter*. Some of these companies do not want to make public their financial plans; others have insufficient shares available to justify listing on one of the major stock exchanges. U. S. Government and municipal bonds, bank and insurance stocks are frequently sold in this manner. Any broker can find out for you how over-the-counter securities are trading.

Buying on margin means making a partial payment on stock just as you would make a down payment on a house; however, a down payment on stock must be equal to a high per cent of the current value, including fees. The Federal Reserve Board changes this figure according to market trends, and rates have ranged from 40 to 100 per cent. The broker holds your note for the difference, plus interest. Before the market crash in 1929, a stock customer could make a down payment as low as 20 per cent of the stock's trading value, hoping to pay the rest by selling at a profit as stock prices rose. After the crash, losses prevented them from completing purchases, so they lost everything.

Yield is the earning or profit on a share of stock in terms of dividends. It may be determined thus: *cash dividend divided by list price equals yield*. If a stock sells for $60 a share and pays a $3 dividend for the year, its yield is 5 per cent. You may not always want to buy the stock with the highest yield. Retired persons who want immediate income usually prefer stock with a yield of 5 per cent or more. Some people prefer low-yield stocks that show promise of growth.

Par value is the dollar value assigned to each share of stock on a company's books. It seldom, if ever, has anything to do with *market value* (the daily listed price of the stock). Par value is of little or no importance to the typical investor.

Blue chip is a loosely used term, generally applied to stocks of companies with sound financial positions, long records of profitable operation, and a history of regular dividends.

A *bull market* is a time of rising stock prices, while a time of decline is called a *bear market*.

The *Dow-Jones industrial average* is another term vaguely understood. The Dow-Jones theory is a market

---

Stocks classified. *Safety* or high quality stocks may not appreciate (grow in value) rapidly, but they should form part of a well organized investment program. *Appreciation stocks* are for people who hope to make a profit in a short time. More risk is involved than in safety stocks. *Growth* stocks, which have small immediate return but good chance for large profit in the future, are for young people who can afford to set some money aside for a long period. *Income* stock is for people interested in immediate returns rather than future growth. Older people often buy these stocks. *Speculative* stocks involve the most risk. They are only for the person who can afford considerable loss.

STOCKS CLASSIFIED

SAFETY	APPRECIATION	GROWTH	INCOME	SPECULATIVE
Quality Grade or Blue Chip	likely to increase in market value over next 12 mo.	High potential for future growth 3 to 10 years	high dividend rate 3.5%–5.5% and up	stock in which risk is great

analysis determined by averaging the prices of thirty selected industrial stocks out of more than 1,000 on the New York Stock Exchange and recording their trends by a graph.

Growth stocks may have a low annual yield because profits are being "plowed back" for research and expansion. It is estimated that our economy is expanding at the rate of about 3 per cent a year. Growth stocks may expand at an even higher rate. Many people prefer growth stocks as a hedge against inflation.

Preferred Stocks and Bonds Besides common stock some companies issue another type called *preferred*. If a company can afford to pay a dividend to only some shareholders, it must pay the owners of preferred stock first. Also, if a company goes out of business, preferred shareholders have first claim on any remaining assets. However, these stocks usually do not grow in value as fast as good common stocks, and their dividends do not increase. Therefore most preferred stocks are relatively safe but do not protect the owner against inflation.

Bonds differ from stocks. When you buy stocks, you share in the ownership of a business. When you buy bonds, it is as if you lend someone your money and they must pay it back with interest. Besides the familiar U.S. Savings Bonds, you can also buy bonds issued by corporations, state and local governments, and public agencies such as park and school boards.

Some bonds are not subject to federal income tax. For a person with high taxes, a tax-free 3 per cent bond may be better than a taxable one paying 6 per cent. Like other fixed-rate investments, most bonds do not grow in value as living costs rise.

Some corporations issue preferred stocks and bonds which can eventually be exchanged for common stock. Some investors believe that these *convertible* securities have the long-range growth possibilities of common stocks and also the relative safety and high yields of bonds and preferred stocks.

A balanced investment portfolio should contain common and preferred stock, U. S. Government, and other bonds. A broker can advise you about the distribution.

Mutual Funds When you buy shares of a mutual fund you are actually hiring someone to do your investing. These funds are managed by people who study the stock market and other investment possibilities. They take the money you pay for your shares and invest it. If they invest well, the fund will grow and your shares will increase in value.

Mutual funds offer certain advantages. Fund managers know more about investing than the average person does. This is especially true of the new investor and of the busy person

Stock certificate (part ownership in a business, sharing profit and loss).

404

who does not have time to follow the stock market. Also, fund shares represent investments in dozens of leading corporations. This is safer than owning just one or two stocks.

There are tax advantages in using mutual funds to set up college savings programs for minors and retirement funds for self-employed people. Employees in some firms are allowed to invest in mutual funds through payroll deductions. Fund shares are sold not only to individuals but also to pension and profit sharing organizations, universities, churches, and other institutions with large sums to invest.

In 1965 alone, investments in mutual funds rose $6 billion to a total of $35 billion. Because of this immense popularity, insurance firms and banks are moving into the mutual fund business.

Some mutual funds take a percentage of your money, usually about 8 or 9 per cent, at the time you invest. This commission is used to pay managers' salaries, brokers' fees, and other expenses. Such funds are said to have a *front-end load*. There are also *no-load* (no-sales-charge) funds which collect management fees in various ways such as deducting a certain percentage of the fund's total value from time to time. In newspaper listings, the *asked* price of a mutual fund is what it would cost to buy one share; the *bid* price is what you would receive if you redeemed (sold) a share. For no-load funds the bid and asked prices are the same. Usually you pay no commission when you redeem mutual fund shares.

Mutual funds should be chosen to suit individual needs. These are some common types:

Registered bond (a debt the company owes the holder, repaid with interest). The value of stock rises or falls with business trends; the value of a bond does not change.

• *Unrestricted common stock* funds represent both growth and high-yield or high-dividend stocks. These are good for the average, cautious investor. They will rise in value with inflation.

• *Balanced* funds spread investments over stocks and bonds, shifting according to market changes. These funds are recommended for regular savings toward college expenses, payment on a home, or retirement.

• *Growth* funds — concerned more with long-time capital gains than current high dividends. Good for young people planning far into the future for retirement.

• *Income* funds—These stocks yield high current income; recommended for retired people.

• *Speculative* funds are invested in stocks having high risks. Money may be made or lost rapidly. These are a gamble, recommended only if you can afford to take chances.

• *Specialized* mutual funds limit investments to stock in a special field such as utilities, chemical, paper, electronics, and so forth. General funds may be better than specialized funds for the beginning investor.

405

How Can You Invest Safely? Do not attempt any major program of investing for the future until you have taken care of the present. U. S. Government bonds are safe, and small investments through a club may provide worthwhile experience as well as fun. But moderate investments of this sort should be all you attempt until you have adequate insurance, cash reserve, and no pressure from debts or other obligations.

Investment Clubs have provided a popular way of learning about the market without becoming heavily involved financially. Any number of members may form a club — usually eight to twenty. As a rule, a rotating committee investigates the market, studies reports, and talks with a broker about good investments. Members may contribute from $10 up toward a "kitty" or operating fund. Each month a certain amount of stock is bought in the name of the club.

If someone moves away or for any reason wants to drop out of the club, he may sell his holding at the current market price, plus his part of the brokers' fees, to other members or to a new member.

The Monthly Investment Plan was introduced in 1954 for people in low and medium income brackets who wanted to buy stocks regularly but could not afford more than a small sum monthly. For as little as $40 (6% fees) either monthly or quarterly payments may be made on listed stocks. Investors pay the same fee as for odd lots.

The plan works on the investment principle of "dollar cost averaging." This is comparable to buying several dollars worth of gasoline instead of several gallons. When monthly or quarterly payments are totaled, the average cost per share can be figured and compared with current market quotations.

Here are some pitfalls to avoid:

• Don't invest too much money at one time. For instance, if a man inherited $4,000 and immediately put it all in stocks, he could lose heavily if the market dropped suddenly. However, if he invested just $1,000 at first, a falling market would give him an opportunity to buy more shares of the stocks he liked at lower prices.

• Don't put all your money into one company. Spread your investment among several industries such as utilities, electronics, foods, and automobiles.

• Keep posted on market quotations. Some people sell their least profitable stock each year and buy something else that has a better record of income and management.

• Don't buy stocks with the idea of selling them quickly for a big profit. Even the experts often guess wrong about what a stock will do over a short period. Also, frequent buying and selling means paying many commissions and high taxes on your gains.

• Don't buy stocks from door-to-door salesmen or unknown telephone callers.

• Never buy stocks on "hot tips" or rumors.

• Understand your own needs. The needs of a young couple are not the same as those of a single man in his thirties.

• Don't buy stock *just* because you can get it for a low price. A low price is often a danger signal.

• Avoid amateur "investment advisors." You can get names of reliable stock brokers from your banker.

• *Do* ask a broker to show you the rating sheets on stocks that interest you. *Study* past performance, years the company *has been in business,* type of *management* it has had, and what its *earnings* have been.

• If you buy shares of a mutual fund be sure it has investment goals similar to your own and a record of good management. Brokers rarely handle no-load funds, but you can learn about them in public libraries or by writing the Investment Company Institute, 63 Broadway, New York, N.Y. 10006.

WILLS AND ESTATE PLANNING

At your age, the idea of making a will or planning for the distribution of your estate may not seem very important. Perhaps your own parents do not have a will. Some problems that can arise when a person dies *intestate* —that is, without a will—are illustrated in the following cases:

CASE STUDY: Andrew Boone, the father of three small children, was only in his late thirties when he died of an unexpected heart attack. He left his home, a new car, securities, and other property worth all together about $60,000. He could have made a will that would have left his wife free to use the money for the whole family. He did not do this, however, so the money was divided equally four ways among the wife and children. The children's shares were put in trust funds. Mrs. Boone's money lasted only a few years, and every time she needed more she had to hire a lawyer and pay court fees. By the time her children were of age, Mrs. Boone had

spent nearly $10,000 just to get legal permission to use her children's trust funds. It would have cost her husband about $25 to make a will which would have saved her $10,000.

CASE STUDY: James Allen, a widower with no children, lived with his sister who had never married. Mr. Allen owned the home, and supported his sister in return for her housekeeping. He wanted her to have the house and his other assets after he died, but he had no will when he was killed in an automobile accident. The house and other possessions were sold, and the sister had to divide the money with three other brothers who all had their own homes and families. She had to find a cheap apartment and do part time work to meet her expenses.

Need for | Anyone who has an estate
a Will | of any size should consider making a will. A couple should make a will soon after marriage. An estate may mean only several hundred dollars in a bank and a car, or it may involve a home, farm, business, and thousands of dollars worth of assets and possessions. The distribution of them, in the event of death, too often leads to unfortunate conflicts. In one case, a family split up for years over a watch. By making a will, a person may determine the exact manner in which he wishes his estate to be distributed upon his death, the persons to whom it shall pass, and the manner in which they shall receive it; but if there is no will, the distribution of the estate is determined by state law, with no regard for the wishes of the owner, or for the financial needs of those to whom the law gives the estate.

a couple may have everything in both names, the unpredictable can happen.

CASE STUDY: Ted Collins, with a wife and two children, was left a valuable piece of property and immediately he had it put in his wife's name and his own. Ted died and the property went to his wife, Ruth. She remarried and had one more child. She made her second husbsand joint owner of the property. Soon afterward Ruth and her second husband were injured in an airplane accident. Ruth died immediately; a week later her husband died. The property did not go to the children of Ted and Ruth but to the child of Ruth and her second husband because that child was next of kin.

Procedure in Making a Will   Although many people write their own wills, this should be avoided. In many states, a holographic will—that is, one entirely in the hand-writing of the person making the will—is not recognized. The states have their own rules as to the formalities that must be observed. Before making a will, plan as follows.

• Husband and wife should discuss the way in which they wish to have their estate distributed in case one or both should die.

• They should keep a complete and up-to-date inventory of all of their important possessions.

• Husband and wife, either together or separately, should consult a lawyer about preparing their wills and have available for him the following information:

> Names of all dependents and near relatives, with ages, place of residence, and marital status.

Names of other relatives or friends whom they may wish to remember in their will.

Names of churches, charitable organizations, or funds to which they might wish to make a bequest.

A list of the assets comprising their estates, including checking or savings accounts, stocks, bonds, real estate, life insurance policies, and any others.

The name of the person or trust company to be named as executor to administer and settle the estate. The selection of such an executor should be discussed with the lawyer.

The name of a guardian for minor children.

A will can and should be revised from time to time as the family's size, needs, and financial situation change. When a new will is made, the old one should be destroyed. Do not try to change a will yourself. You may make the whole thing worthless.

STORING IMPORTANT PAPERS AND RECORDS

Many families are careless about keeping valuable papers. Records kept at home in metal boxes are not as safe as they may seem. The contents of a typical metal box may be damaged or destroyed in as little as ten minutes if the home catches fire. The most important documents, especially those that would be difficult or costly to replace, should be stored in a safe deposit box in a bank. These include:

• Notes of promise on loans.

• Mortgage on property (or duplicate).

• Deed to property. (Be sure this is

recorded in the county courthouse.)
* Certificate of title to property.
* Abstract (legal description) and survey of property.
* Most insurance papers, particularly fire insurance adjusted as improvements are added to property.
* Bond and stock certificates.
* Military discharge papers.
* Birth, marriage, adoption, naturalization, and death certificates.
* Installment sales contracts.
* Automobile titles.
* Duplicate of will. (Lawyer should keep original.)

A key to the bank safe deposit box should be kept in a metal box at home. Other items you may want to store in this way include:
* Receipts and canceled checks, especially those for large amounts and those that relate to income tax deductions.
* Guarantees on appliances, machinery, and other merchandise.
* Credentials for auto and boat ownership (other than auto titles).
* Pedigrees and licenses for pets.
* Hunting and fishing licenses.
* Social Security, educational, and medical immunization records.

* Copies of tax returns.
* Bank statements.
* Life and health insurance credentials. (You may want to keep all policies in the bank and have a list at home showing policy numbers, premiums, and chief provisions.)
* Saving and checking account books.
* Credit card list, including numbers.
* List of all important records, stocks, bonds, mortgages, deeds, and similar papers, and where they are filed.

Words and Phrases to Know

LIFE AND HEALTH INSURANCE

annuity	endowment
beneficiary	loan value
co-insurance	option
convertible	policy
deductible clause	premium
dependent	surrender
disability	survivor
dividend	waiver
double indemnity	

SAVINGS, STOCKS, AND BONDS

bear market	inflation
"blue chip" stock	margin
broker	maturity
bull market	securities
commission	speculation
dividend	yield

ACTIVITIES

1. Discuss reasons for buying life insurance, in relation to other savings, retirement funds, and other investments.

2. Take a poll of the class to find out how many have health insurance and what kind.

3. Discuss needs for term insurance. Compare term insurance and credit life insurance.

4. Compare the family income policy with the family policy.

5. Compare retirement insurance with an endowment policy.

6. Compare a family policy with a "jumping juvenile policy."

7. List the advantages and disadvantages of group life insurance.

8. Show one or two films on life

409

insurance; discuss factors to consider in buying life insurance.

9. Why does the cost of health insurance vary in different parts of the country? Find out what benefits are allowed in your local hospitals for the following operations—tonsillectomy, appendectomy, brain surgery—and for accommodations — ward, semi-private, and private room.

10. Discuss reasons for having or not having major medical insurance.

11. Visit or write to the nearest Social Security Administration office. Find out how Social Security affects you now. How will your parents benefit from it? After you are married, what will be your obligations under Social Security? Your potential benefits?

12. Find out what fire, theft, and extended coverage, plus personal liability insurance would cost on variously priced homes in your area. If you lived in an apartment house, what coverage would you need?

13. Invite insurance representatives to come to class and discuss each kind of insurance.

14. Investigate and compare the interest or dividend rates paid by banks and by savings and loan associations in your community. When are dividends paid? Compare these rates with income from government bonds.

15. Investigate the interest rates charged by lending organizations in your community.

16. Investigate the operation of a credit union. Find out how it differs from other savings and lending organizations.

17. Show and discuss films on the operation of the stock exchange.

18. Invite a broker to discuss invest-ments in common stock, mutual funds, and the monthly investment plan.

19. List some *growth, income,* and *speculative* stocks; also, some *utility, pharmaceutical, electronic, railroad, industrial, textile, oil,* and other specialized stocks.

20. Consult a banker or broker, or obtain literature from the New York Stock Exchange, for information about mutual funds. What are their advantages and disadvantages? Name some mutual funds which specialize in growth stocks.

21. Discuss the different kinds of mutual funds in relation to investment needs.

22. Make believe you have $2,000 to $4,000 to invest. Study the stock market reports in the daily paper and decide how you would invest the money. Every day or two for a month, record the price at which your stocks are selling. Include broker's commission.

23. Discuss wills in relation to various needs. Find out the cost of making a will.

24. Invite a broker or other qualified person to discuss inflation and deflation, and how they affect investments. Ask him also to compare income from various investments.

Home Experiences

Have your parents read this chapter and discuss your family's protection under each kind of insurance.

Find out where your family keeps important papers; discuss keeping records, and filing them safely.

Find out if your family is getting the best interest rate on savings and, if not, where to place money for safety and better income.

ADDITIONAL READING LIST*

Better Homes and Gardens, *First Aid for Your Family*, Meredith Publishing Co., Des Moines, Iowa, 1960

Bigelow, Howard F., *Family Finance*, J.B. Lippincott Co., Philadelphia, 1960

Brisbane, Holly E., and Riker, Audrey P., *The Developing Child*, Chas. A. Bennett Co., Inc., Peoria, Ill., 1965

Carnegie, Dale, *How to Win Friends and Influence People*, Simon and Schuster, Inc., New York, 1956

Clemensen, Jessie Williams, and others, *Your Health and Safety*, Harcourt, Brace, and World, Inc., New York, 1963

College Entrance Examination Board, *The College Handbook*, Educational Testing Service, Princeton, N. J.

Cooper, Lenna F., and others, *Nutrition in Health and Disease*, J.B. Lippincott Co., Philadelphia, 1963

Craig, Hazel T., and Rush, Ola Day, *Homes with Character*, D.C. Heath and Co., Boston, 1966

Craig, Hazel T., *Clothing: A Comprehensive Study*, J.B. Lippincott Co., Philadelphia, 1968

Cronan, Marion L., and Atwood, June C., *Foods in Homemaking*, Chas. A. Bennett Co., Inc., Peoria, Ill., 1965

Depew, Arthur M., *The Cokesbury Party Book*, Abingdon Press, Nashville, Tenn., 1959

Duvall, Evelyn Millis, *Family Development*, J.B. Lippincott Co., Philadelphia, 1960

Fine, Benjamin, *How to Be Accepted by the College of Your Choice*, Channel Press, Great Neck, N.Y., 1966

Fleck, Henrietta; Fernandez, Louise; and Munves, Elizabeth, *Exploring Home and Family Living*, Prentice-Hall Inc., Englewood Cliffs, N.J., 1964

Gawne, Eleanor J., and Oerke, Bess V., *Dress*, Chas. A. Bennett Co., Inc., 1969

Gesell, Arnold L., and Ilg, Frances L., *Child Development*, Harper and Row, New York, 1956

Gesell, Arnold L., and others, *Youth, the Years from Ten to Sixteen*, Harper and Row, New York, 1956

Hughes, Ray O., and Pullen, O. H. W.,

Building Citizenship, Allyn and Bacon, Inc., Boston, 1966

Lovejoy, Clarence E., *Lovejoy's College Guide*, Simon and Schuster, Inc., New York

Mahoney, Harold J., and Engle, T. L., *Points for Decision*, Harcourt, Brace, and World, Inc., New York, 1961

McDermott, Irene E., and Nicholas, Florence W., *Homemaking for Teenagers, Book 2*, Chas. A. Bennett Co., Inc., Peoria, Ill., 1962

McDermott, Irene E., and Norris, Jeanne L., *Opportunities in Clothing*, Chas. A. Bennett Co., Inc., Peoria, Ill., 1968

Menninger, William C., and others, *How to Be a Successful Teen-ager*, Sterling Publishing Co., New York, 1966

Meredith, Florence L., Irwin, Leslie W.; and Staton, Wesley M., *Health and Fitness*, D.C. Heath and Co., Boston, 1966

Miller, Daniel R., and Swanson, Guy E., *The Changing American Parent*, John Wiley and Sons, Inc., New York, 1958

Potter, Maurice David, and Corbman, Bernard P., *Fiber to Fabric*, Gregg Publishing Division, McGraw-Hill Book Co., New York, 1959

Raines, Margaret, *Managing Livingtime*, Chas. A. Bennett Co., Inc., Peoria, Ill., 1966

Riehl, C. Luise, *Family Nursing and Child Care*, Chas. A. Bennett Co., Inc., Peoria, 1966

Sartain, Aaron Quinn, and North, Alvin J., *Psychology: Understanding Human Behavior*, McGraw-Hill Book Co., New York, 1962

Shank, Dorothy E., Fitch, Natalie K., and Chapman, Pauline A., *Guide to Modern Meals*, Webster Division, McGraw-Hill Book Company, St. Louis, 1964

Sorenson, Herbert, and Malm, Marguerite, *Psychology for Living*, McGraw-Hill Book Co., New York, 1964

Spock, Benjamin, *The Common Sense Book of Baby and Child Care*, Duell, Sloan and Pearce, Inc., New York, 1958

Starr, Mary Catherine, *Management for Better Living*, D.C. Heath and Co., Boston, 1968

Vanderbilt, Amy, *Amy Vanderbilt's New Complete Book of Etiquette*, Doubleday and Co., Inc., New York, 1963

---

*A more complete listing of references and source materials appears in the Teacher's Guide.

Index

414